LEGISLATING MEDICAL ETHICS

Philosophy and Medicine

VOLUME 48

The titles published in this series are listed at the end of this volume.

LEGISLATING MEDICAL ETHICS

A Study of the New York State Do-Not-Resuscitate Law

Edited by

ROBERT BAKER

Dept. of Philosophy, Union College, Schenectady, NY, USA

and

MARTIN A. STROSBERG

Graduate Management Institute, Union College, Schenectady, NY, USA

with the assistance of

JONATHAN BYNUM

Dept. of Philosophy, Rutgers University, New Brunswick, NJ, USA

KLUWER ACADEMIC PUBLISHERS

DORDRECHT / BOSTON / LONDON

Library of Congress Cataloging-in-Publication Data

Legislating medical ethics : a study of the New York State do-not-resuscitate law / edited by Robert Baker and Martin A. Strosberg with the assistance of Jonathan Bynum.
p. cm. -- (Philosophy and medicine ; v. 48)
Includes index.
ISBN 0-7923-2995-3 (acid-free paper)
1. Do-not-resuscitate orders--Law and legislation--New York (State) 2. Do-not-resuscitate orders--Moral and ethical aspects. 3. Medical ethics. 4. Do-not-resuscitate orders--New York (State)--Case studies. I. Baker, Robert, 1937- II. Strosberg, Martin A. III. Bynum, Jonathan. IV. Series.
KFN5619.5.D62L44 1994
174'.2--dc20 94-19575

ISBN 0-7923-2995-3

Published by Kluwer Academic Publishers,
P.O. Box 17, 3300 AA Dordrecht, The Netherlands.

Kluwer Academic Publishers incorporates
the publishing programmes of
D. Reidel, Martinus Nijhoff, Dr. W. Junk and MTP Press.

Sold and distributed in the U.S.A. and Canada
by Kluwer Academic Publishers,
101 Philip Drive, Norwell, MA 02061, U.S.A.

In all other countries, sold and distributed
by Kluwer Academic Publishers Group,
P.O. Box 322, 3300 AH Dordrecht, The Netherlands.

printed on acid-free paper

Printed in The Netherlands

In Memory of

Freda Baker
and
Irving Strosberg MD

TABLE OF CONTENTS

PREFACE xi

ROBERT BAKER AND MARTIN A. STROSBERG / Introduction xv

PART I / THE TASK FORCE AND THE LAW

NEW YORK STATE TASK FORCE ON LIFE AND THE LAW / Executive Summary 3

MARTIN A. STROSBERG / The New York State Do-Not-Resuscitate Law: A Study of Public Policy-Making 9

ROBERT BAKER / The Legitimation and Regulation of DNR Orders 33

PART II / THE DNR CONTROVERSY IN NEW YORK STATE

TRACY E. MILLER / Taking Stock of Policies for Do-Not-Resuscitate Orders: Perception and Practice 105

JANE GREENLAW / Where Are We Going with Do-Not-Resuscitate Policies? 133

DAVID AXELROD / New York State's Do-Not-Resuscitate Law 137

GEORGE ANNAS / New York's Do-Not-Resuscitate Law: Bad Law, Bad Medicine, and Bad Ethics 141

UNION COLLEGE CONFERENCE / Edited Transcript of Question & Answer Sessions at Union College Conference 157

PART III / CASE STUDIES

CAROLYN SHEARER ANTONELLI / Implementation of the New York Do-Not-Resuscitate Law at a Teaching Hospital 163

DEBORAH DAMM O'BRIEN / One Family's Experience with the New York DNR Law 169

TIMOTHY E. QUILL / When the Ambulance Goes Home: A Tragic Flaw in the New York State Do-Not-Resuscitate Law 173
CAROL CLAY / Implementation of the New York State DNR Law at a Community Hospital 181
LAWRENCE R. FAULKNER / The New York DNR Law and the Disabled: The Experience of the New York State Office of Mental Retardation and Developmental Disabilities 187
DAVID FINLEY / Striking a Balance 205

PART IV / RESEARCH

ROBERT ZUSSMAN / The Do-Not-Resuscitate Order as Ritual 215
RUSSELL S. KAMER AND JOHN A. McCLUNG / New York's Do-Not-Resuscitate Law: Burden or Benefit? 227
JUDITH C. AHRONHEIM, SATHYA MAHESWARAN AND CARL ROSENBERG / Does the New York State DNR Law Prevent Medically Inappropriate DNR? 235
TIMOTHY E. QUILL AND NANCY M. BENNETT / The Effects of a Hospital Policy and State Legislation on Resuscitation Orders for Geriatric Patients 241
NORTON SPRITZ / The New York State DNR Law: Views of the Members of the New York Chapter of the American College of Physicians 251
ROBERT BAKER, MARTIN A. STROSBERG, JOSEF SCHMEE, I. ALAN FEIN, VIRGINIA JONAS DERSCH, JONATHAN BYNUM AND PHILIP OATES / The 1988 DNR Reforms: A Comparative Study of the Impact of the New York DNR Law and the JCAHO Accreditation Requirements 263
VIRGINIA JONAS DERSCH / Differences in Clinicians' Reactions to the New York State DNR Law 303

PART V / RETROSPECTION AND REFLECTION

TRACY E. MILLER / An Assessment of the Union College Study and a Response to Robert Baker's Analysis of the DNR Law 325
ROBERT BAKER / A Review of the Empirical Studies of the DNR Law and a Rejoinder to Tracy E. Miller 333

APPENDICES
THE GENEALOGY OF NEW YORK STATE'S DO-NOT-RESUSCITATE LAW

Article 29 (1987) – New York State Legislature – New York Public Health Law 349
Guidelines for Hospitals and Physicians on "Do-Not-Resuscitate" (1982) – Medical Society of the State of New York 369
Deciding to Forego Life-Sustaining Treatment (1983, Excerpted) – President's Commission for the Study of Ethical Problems in Medicine and Biomedical and Behavioral Research 371
Do-Not-Resuscitate Orders: The Proposed Legislation and Report of the New York State Task Force on Life and the Law (1986, 1988, 2nd Edition Condensed) – New York State Task Force on Life and the Law 381
Do-Not-Resuscitate Orders: Questions and Answers for Health Care Professionals (1988) – Medical Society of the State of New York, New York State Department of Health, Hospital Association of New York State 415
Letter to New York State Assembly Minority Counsel Larry Digiulio (1991) – Robert Baker and Martin A. Strosberg 439
Amendments to the New York Public Health Law 29-B (1991) – New York State Legislature 445

NOTES ON EDITORS AND CONTRIBUTORS 455

INDEX 459

PREFACE

The present volume would never have come into being had not the editors of the Philosophy and Medicine series, H. Tristram Engelhardt, Jr. and Stuart F. Spicker, enthusiastically endorsed our vision of taking the disparate papers on the New York DNR law and transforming them into a comprehensive case study. Nor would there have been a volume had not the contributors willingly come to Union College to share their research, and graciously consented to revise their findings to fit into the case study format we envisioned. Working side-by-side with us to assist with the transformation process has been our former student, Jonathan Bynum, whose editorial and philosophical insights proved so invaluable over the course of the year that we felt that he had earned the right to be recognized as associate editor.

The success of the conference itself must be credited to the organizational skills of Marianne Snowden, who – with the assistance of Deborah Atwood, Elizabeth Cole, Sean Hornbeck, Philip Oates, Rhonda Sheehan and Eugene Spanguolo – kept everything and everyone wonderfully on track.

We would also like to express our gratitude to the Union College administration and staff, particularly former President John Morris and Deans James Underwood and Terry Weiner, for their generous support of the conference. The conference was also supported by the Critical Care Education Foundation of the Albany Medical College, the Dana Foundation, and the Union College Humanities Faculty Development and College Research Funds.

We owe a particular debt of gratitude to Dr. David Axelrod, former Commissioner of Health of the State of New York and Chairman of the New York State Task Force on Life and the Law. Dr. Axelrod welcomed public debate of the DNR law and contributed greatly, not only to shaping the Task Force and the DNR law, but also to the DNR assessment conference upon which this volume is based. Tragically, during the time the volume was being prepared, Dr. Axelrod fell victim to a stroke. Peter Millock of the Department of Health was kind enough to act as Dr. Axelrod's surrogate, for purposes of this volume, and to

R. Baker & M.A. Strosberg (eds.), Legislating Medical Ethics: A Study of the New York Do-Not-Resuscitate Law, xi–xiii.

review the transcript of Dr. Axelrod's remarks at the conference in his stead.

In closing we again extend our gratitude for the generous cooperation of everyone who made this study of DNR policy and the New York DNR law possible – editors, contributors, the Department of Health, the Task Force, and our colleagues and associates at Union College – most of all, we thank everyone who worked with us on the manuscript, Rita Badami, Dominick Bizzarro, and, once again, Marianne Snowden.

Schenectady, New York
January, 1995

Robert Baker
Martin Strosberg

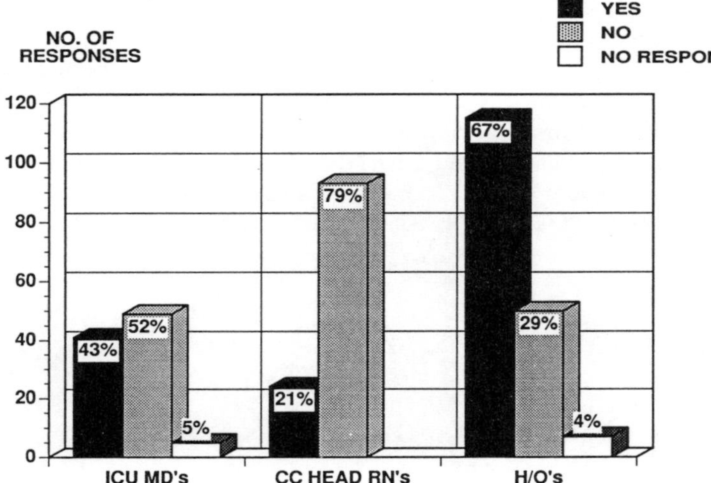

Would clinicians be better off had the NYS Legislature not passed the DNR Law?

Fig. 1.

INTRODUCTION

From the moment the New York Task Force on Life and the Law published its proposals for a law regulating Do-Not-Resuscitate orders in May 1986, the proposals excited public and scholarly interest. Not unexpectedly, when Governor Mario Cuomo signed the statute into law, on August 7, 1987, several research teams began to initiate studies of the law's impact. As members (with our colleague I. Alan Fein, Chief of the Surgical ICU of Albany Medical Center) of a long-standing research team which focused on critical care medicine, we too were curious about the impact of the new law. With the assistance of the Task Force counsel, Robert Swidler, we assessed the nature of the other research projects under way: the empirical studies of the impact of the law on the writing of DNR orders being conducted by Kamer and McClung; the study of the law's impact on the demographics of the populations for whom DNR orders are written by Ahronheim, Maheswaran, and Rosenberg; and the extensive survey of physicians' attitudes towards the law conducted by the American College of Physicians.

We decided to study the law's impact on the less readily detectable aspects of clinical practice: slow and show-coding; undocumented DNR orders; and, most importantly, clinician-patient discussion of the CPR/DNR decision. To measure these elusive effects, we knew we needed a non-conventional tool, and so we turned to an expert in moral psychology, Lawrence Ponemon. Together we developed a questionnaire which allowed us to compare clinicians' estimates of the likelihood that certain practices (ranging from discussions with patients, to slow/show coding) would occur on their ICU prior to, and after, the passage of the DNR law. The questionnaire was also adaptable for use outside of New York State, allowing us to compare the 1988 New York DNR reforms with comparable reforms implemented in the same year at hospitals in the rest of the nation as a response to changes in the Joint Commission on the Accreditation of Health Care Organizations (JCAHO) accreditation requirements.

On completing our study, we – along with other research teams – began to disseminate our findings at meetings, in publications, and to the Task

R. Baker & M.A. Strosberg (eds.), Legislating Medical Ethics: A Study of the New York Do-Not-Resuscitate Law, xv–xviii.

Force. Normally, the research cycle ends with the publication of articles. In this particular instance, however, the various research teams felt that more was needed. A complete assessment of the impact of New York's DNR law would require a comprehensive analysis of the various studies. So the different research teams agreed to meet with the Task Force and with other interested parties (administrators, doctors, lawyers, legislators, nurses) on September 10 and 11, 1990, for an assessment conference at Union College (which lies in the state's Capital District and is strategically located equidistant from the state's major population centers). The papers presented at that conference not only led to a revision of New York's DNR law, they also constitute a detailed case study of the effects of legislating medical ethics. In this volume we attempt to present to readers, not only most of the papers delivered at the conference, but a documentary history of the DNR debate, so that they can view New York's experiment with a DNR law as the outcome of decades of debate and policy initiatives aimed at the bioethical reform of CPR/DNR practices.

Section One provides the reader with the background to the law and introduces the reader to the controversies surrounding it. Prefacing the section is executive summary of the law, as it was proposed by the Taskforce (but most of the documents referred to in this section will be found in the appendix, including the New York Medical Society policy on DNR, and the President's Commission's findings on DNR). Martin Strosberg then reviews the process by which the Taskforce's proposed statute was altered first by the legislature, and then through implementation process, and ultimately by amendment. Robert Baker follows with a paper that reviews the evolution of DNR orders themselves from their initial incarnation as slow codes on the clinic floor – in effect, a form of clinician civil disobedience – to their institutional legitimation as "no code" policy statements, to their endorsement by the American Medical Association and other professional organizations, to the legitimation of those DNR orders which were based on patient or surrogate consent – but not those based solely on the futility of CPR – by such bioethical bodies as the President's Commission on Ethical Problems in Medicine and Biomedical and Behavioral Research and the Hastings Center. Baker also reviews the New York Courts' unique (some might even suggest, recondite) rulings on surrogacy and explains why they led New York to become the first and one of only a few States to pass a statute regulating DNR orders. He then summarizes the controversies the law generated, reviews the empirical studies of its impact, and reflects on the lessons to be learned from New York's bold experiment with legislating medical ethics – its implications for bioethical policy-making in general and for DNR orders in particular.

Section Two is designed to represent the controversy provoked by the DNR law. It opens with a paper by Tracy Miller, Executive Director of the Taskforce, who challenges Baker's interpretation of the law and its impact. We have also reprinted one of Jane Greenlaw's early critiques of the law, as well as critique by another lawyer, George Annas. Their position is responded to by Taskforce Chairman David Axelrod's who rejects their assessment as premature and suggests that the methods used in New York to deal with the DNR issue have "really set the standard for dealing with some of those major...ethical issues within the entire U.S."

Yet, it is evident from the case studies in Section Three, that a variety of problems marred the implementation of the law. Hospital attorneys, like Carolyn Antonelli, had to devise forms to implement the complexities of the documentation requirements. Moreover, as is clear from the tragic events related by Deborah O'Brien and Timothy Quill, there were initially gaps in the law's coverage. Perhaps most awkward of all, as Carol Clay points out, was the writing of DNR order for developmentally disabled patients (which is also discussed by Lawrence Faulkner). Yet for many physicians, represented here by David Finley, the law had an immediate and positive effect on medical practice.

Section Four contains consists of five empirical studies of DNR in New York, prior to and after the implementation of the law. It opens with Robert Zussman's compelling and detailed study of written DNR orders, which emphasizes the symbolic character of the DNR order. The next two studies, by Russell Kamer and John McClung, and by Judith Ahronheim and her associates, analyze the impact of the law on hospital practice. Timothy Quill provides us with a comparative analysis of the impact of the law at a hospital which had voluntarily opted to comply with a consent-based DNR policy prior to the law's implementation. Norton Spritz's study for the American College of Physicians, and the study we ourselves conducted with Virginia Dersch, I. Alan Fein, *et al.* explores clinicians' assessments of the law's impact. Spritz's study surveys *internists'* attitudes towards the law, ours analyzes *critical care directors'* estimates of the likelihood of discussion, documentation and consent to DNR before and after mandatory bioethical reform both in New York and nationally.

In Section Five, *Retrospection and Reflection*, there is a spirited exhange between Tracy Miller, Executive Director of the Task Force on Life and the Law, and co-editor Robert Baker. Miller again challenges Baker's interpretation of the impact of the DNR law and the methodology used in the Union College Study; Baker replies, analyzing all five empirical studies and offering a comprehensive interpretation of the impact of the New York DNR law.

The editors are grateful to everyone who contributed to this volume and to the conference on which it is based, including the staff of the Task Force, who, at every level, from Commissioner David Axelrod, to various Task Force members, to Director Tracy Miller, to Counsel Robert Swidler, were open to discussion, willing to engage in debate, and eager to suggest interpretations.

Robert Baker
Martin A. Strosberg
Union College

PART I

THE TASK FORCE AND THE LAW

DO NOT RESUSCITATE ORDERS: THE PROPOSED LEGISLATION AND REPORT OF THE NEW YORK STATE TASK FORCE ON LIFE AND THE LAW

A Do Not Resuscitate (DNR) order is an order placed in the patient's medical chart to withhold cardiopulmonary resuscitation (CPR) in the event of cardiopulmonary arrest. Although DNR orders are appropriate under certain circumstances, increasing reliance on the orders has not resolved many of the difficult medical, legal and ethical dilemmas associated with their issuance.

The Task Force on Life and the Law has concluded that legislation is essential to establish and clarify the rights, authority and protections afforded patients, family members and health care professionals in issuance of the orders. The Task Force has developed proposed legislation which addresses this critical issue.

* * *

A summary of the major provisions of the legislation is provided below. The *Report* describes the interests and concerns that had to be balanced in devising the legislation. The summary should therefore be read in light of the reasoning and elaboration set forth in the *Report*.

The major policies embodied in the proposed legislation are as follows:

- The legislation applies to decisions about the provision and withholding of CPR for hospital and nursing home patients throughout the State.
- The legislation explicitly affirms the presumption under existing law that all patients in the event of cardiac or respiratory arrest consent to the provision of CPR. In accordance with this presumption, the legislative proposal requires the attending physician to obtain the consent of a patient with decisional capacity prior to issuing a DNR order subject to a narrow therapeutic exception.
- The proposed legislation provides a means for an adult with capacity to express a decision to reject CPR. That decision may be expressed orally if the person is a patient in a hospital or in writing prior to or during hospitalization.
- The attending physician must obtain the contemporaneous consent of

R. Baker & M.A. Strosberg (eds.), Legislating Medical Ethics: A Study of the New York Do-Not-Resuscitate Law, 3–7.

a patient with decisional capacity prior to issuing a DNR order. If the patient lacks capacity at the time the DNR order is to be issued, but previously had stated his or her wishes to forego CPR in a writing which complies with the statutory requirements, the writing will constitute consent to issuance of the order.

- In the rare circumstances when the patient with capacity might suffer severe and immediate injury from a discussion about resuscitation, a narrow therapeutic exception applies and the physician is permitted to obtain consent to a DNR order from another person on behalf of the patient. A DNR order may only be issued in such cases if the patient is terminally ill or resuscitation would probably be unsuccessful and would only serve to prolong the dying process.
- The proposed legislation establishes a presumption that every adult has the capacity to make a decision about resuscitation unless it is determined that the adult lacks capacity pursuant to the standards and procedures set forth in the legislation or by court order.
- The proposed legislation includes a standard to determine whether patients have the ability to decide about resuscitation for themselves. Unlike the traditional notion of "competence," which ordinarily relates to a person's ability to make all decisions, the proposed legislation includes a standard of capacity which relates solely to an assessment of the person's ability to make a decision about resuscitation.
- For a patient without capacity, the proposed legislation requires the attending physician to obtain the consent of a substitute decision maker where such a person is available, willing and competent to speak for the patient. The legislation provides a means for patients with capacity to designate a person to act on their behalf if they lack capacity at the time the decision must be made.
- A surrogate may consent to issuance of a DNR order for a patient without capacity only after obtaining a written determination by a physician that one of three medical conditions exists: (i) the patient is terminally ill; (ii) the patient is irreversibly comatose; or (iii) resuscitation would probably be unsuccessful and would only serve to prolong the dying process.
- The surrogate is directed to make a decision on the basis of the patient's known wishes or, if the patient's wishes are unknown and cannot be ascertained, on the basis of the patient's best interests.
- A DNR order for patients who lack capacity and have no surrogate available to decide on their behalf can only be issued if: (i) two

physicians determine that resuscitation would be medically futile; or (ii) a court approves issuance of a DNR order based on clear and convincing evidence of the patient's known wishes, or, in the absence of such evidence, a finding of the patient's best interests.

- The proposed legislation requires the attending physician to obtain the consent of a minor's parent or legal guardian before issuing a DNR order for the minor. If the minor has decisional capacity, as determined by the attending physician in consultation with the minor's parents, the physician must obtain the minor's assent to issuance of the order.
- The proposed legislation requires hospitals and nursing homes to establish a dispute mediation system to address disagreements which may arise between patients, physicians, family members and others involved in the resuscitation decision. Any party to the dispute may submit the matter to the mediation system and all parties retain the right to seek judicial relief if the matter is not resolved. When a dispute is referred to the mediation system, issuance of a DNR order is automatically stayed for 72 hours or until the end of the mediation process, whichever occurs first.
- The proposed legislation grants civil and criminal immunity to physicians and other health care professionals who carry out a DNR order in good faith or who resuscitate a patient for whom an order has been issued because they were unaware of the order or believed in good faith that the order had been revoked. Persons designated to act for the patient who consent or decline to consent to issuance of a DNR order in good faith are also protected from liability.
- As mandated in the proposed legislation, no life insurance policy shall be impaired or invalidated in any manner by issuance of a DNR order nor can any person require or prohibit issuance of a DNR order as a condition for being insured or receiving health care services.

One member of the Task Force, J. David Bleich, dissents from several of the legislative provisions. Two other Task Force members, Charles Tobin, Jr. and Richard Concannon, support the legislative proposal except for the provision concerning the therapeutic exception. The remaining twenty-two members of the Task Force support the legislative proposal in its entirety.

MEMBERSHIP, APRIL 1986

David Axelrod, M.D., Chairman
Commissioner of Health, State of New York

Rev. Msgr. John A. Alesandro
Chancellor, Roman Catholic Diocese of Rockville Centre

Mario L. Baeza, Esq.
Member, Debevoise & Plimpton; Lecturer, Harvard Law School

The Right Rev. David Ball
Bishop, Episcopal Diocese of Albany

Rabbi J. David Bleich
Professor of Talmud, Yeshiva University; Professor of Jewish Law and Ethics, Benjamin Cardozo School of Law

Evan Calkins, M.D.
Head, Division of Geriatrics SUNY at Buffalo

Daniel Callahan, Ph.D.
Director, The Hastings Center

Richard J. Concannon, Esq.
Kelley Drye & Warren

Myron W. Conovitz, M.D.
Attending Physician, North Shore Univ. Hospital Clinical Assoc. Prof. of Med., Cornell Univ. Med. College

Saul J. Farber, M.D.
Chairman, Department of Medicine New York University School of Medicine

Alan R. Fleischman, M.D.
Director, Division of Neonatology Albert Einstein College of Medicine, Montefiore Medical Center

Beatrix A. Hamburg, M.D.
Professor of Psychiatry and Pediatrics, Mount Sinai School of Medicine

Helene L. Kaplan, Esq.
Webster & Sheffield
Chairman, Board of Trustees, The Carnegie Corporation

Rev. Msgr. Henry J. Mansell
Vice-Chancellor for Priest Personnel, Archdiocese of New York

Rev. Donald W. McKinney
First Unitarian Church, Brooklyn
President, Concern for Dying

Georgia L. McMurray, C.S.W.
Deputy General Director Community Service Society of New York

M. Janice Nelson, Ed.D., R.N.
Dean, College of Nursing Health Sciences Center, SUNY at Syracuse
Maria I. New, M.D.
Chief, Department of Pediatrics New York Hospital, Cornell Medical Center
Ruth A. O'Brien, Ph.D., R.N.
Associate Professor of Nursing, University of Rochester
John J. Regan, J.S.D.
Professor of Law, Hofstra University School of Law
Rabbi A. James Rudin
National Director of Interreligious Affairs, The American Jewish Committee
Rev. Betty Bone Schiess
Episcopal Diocese of Central New York
Barbara Shack
The New York Civil Liberties Union
Rev. Robert S. Smith
Director, Chaplaincy Services, Health Sciences Center, SUNY at Stony Brook
Elizabeth W. Stack
President, Syracuse Developmental Center Board of Visitors
Charles J. Tobin, Jr., Esq.
Tobin & Dempf

STAFF

Tracy E. Miller, J.D., *Executive Director*
Robert N. Swidler, M.A., J.D.
Maura A. O'Brien, Ph.D.
Leslie E. Schneier, M.P.P.M., M.P.H.
Elizabeth Peppe

MARTIN A. STROSBERG

THE NEW YORK STATE DO-NOT-RESUSCITATE LAW: A STUDY OF PUBLIC POLICY-MAKING

Policy analysts frequently describe the public policy-making process as a sequential pattern of activity. In this essay, we examine the history of the New York State Do-Not-Resuscitate (DNR) Law by applying a commonly-used four-stage template [39]:

1. *Agenda-setting*: Individuals and groups bringing an issue to public attention and formal consideration by public officials. (Example: The Task Force *Report*).
2. *Policy formulation and adoption*: Identifying, debating, and choosing among major policy alternatives, followed by the legitimization of one alternative as a collectively determined purposive course of action. (Example: Article 29-B, New York Public Health Law).
3. *Policy implementation*: Undertaking purposeful, organized activity to transform a policy into a program whose outputs correspond to the intended objectives. (Example: various New York State Department of Health Memoranda on the subject Do-Not-Resuscitate Orders).
4. *Policy evaluation*: Monitoring and review of programs and their incremental modification, reorientation, or termination. (Example: 1991 Amendments to the New York State Public Health Law).

Each of the stages described above will be treated as a separate section of this chapter.

I. AGENDA SETTING: THE ROLE OF THE NYS TASK FORCE ON LIFE AND THE LAW

An agenda, according to political scientist, John Kingdon, "is a list of subjects or problems to which governmental officials and people outside of government closely associated with those officials are paying some serious attention at any given time" [11]. Since the Karen Ann Quinlan case of 1977, bioethics has been on the legislative agenda of most states. Legislators, in this religiously pluralistic state, were exceptionally

R. Baker & M.A. Strosberg (eds.), Legislating Medical Ethics: A Study of the New York Do-Not-Resuscitate Law, 9–31.

reluctant to deal with these issues because of their inherent potential for stirring religious controversy. Legislative committees, always short of staff, moreover, felt ill-equipped to deal with such complex long-range questions. One symptom of paralysis in the State's bioethical policy-making was its inability to legislate a definition of death. Efforts to do so commenced in 1974, but the State had been unable to pass a brain death statute legislating the "Harvard brain death criteria," [8] because certain religious groups define death in terms of religious law. When, in 1986, brain death criteria were adopted in New York State, a different route was taken: the Department of Health passed a regulation but the legislature never dealt with the issue.

In 1985, as a way out of ongoing legislative deadlock, Governor Cuomo established The New York State Task Force on Life and the Law by executive order [23]. Its mandate was to make general policy recommendations on problems posed by medical advances. The twenty-six Task Force members chosen by the Governor reflected the religious diversity of the state. Influential professionals from the fields of medicine, nursing, law, and bioethics were also chosen. The Chairman of the Task Force was a trusted lieutenant of the Governor, the Commissioner of the Department of Health, David Axelrod. In effect, by setting up the Task Force, the Governor created a vehicle for placing bioethics on the governmental agenda.

The executive order which established the Task Force gave it a mandate to address the DNR question, which was one of the first items it considered. In April 1986, with only two dissenting minority opinions, the Task Force was able to present a consensus solution to the "DNR problem" to the Legislature. Facilitating the achievement of consensus was the fact that Task Force meetings were closed to the public, promoting frank discussion and compromise by members not rigidly wedded to their affiliations by the glare of public scrutiny. Moreover, although individual Task Force members were not, in any sense, official representatives of particular constituencies, affiliated interest groups and legislators, knowing that certain persons were on the Task Force, took their cues from Task Force proposals. This was particularly true in the case of the Catholic Conference and certain Orthodox Jewish groups. The unofficial representatives of these groups on the Task Force thus had a particularly strong influence on certain legislators – agreement at the Task Force level thus tended to forestall disagreement at the legislative level.

The tangible product of the Task Force's efforts was an 89 page report of April 1986, *Do Not Resuscitate Orders: The Proposed Legislation and Report of the New York State Task Force on Life and the Law* [27]. In the report, the legislative proposal is preceded by a well-documented presentation of the background and the medical, legal, and ethical reasoning behind the recommendations. The Task Force *Report*, which includes minority reports, was widely distributed to the public. As will be shown below, the Task Force achieved what it was designed to accomplish: the facilitation of serious discussion of bioethical issue by the State's public policy-makers.

II. POLICY FORMULATION AND ADOPTION: POLITICAL FEASIBILITY

In August 1987 the Legislature passed a statute based for the most part on the Task Force proposal. The achievement of consensus by the Task Force, a microcosm of major religious and philosophical opinions, had a major impact on the legislators. It is unlikely that the DNR Law or subsequent laws, such as the Health Care Proxy Law (Article 29-C of the New York Public Health Law) could have passed without a carefully crafted Task Force proposal as a precursor, and Task Force members acting as advocates.

Because the major option seriously considered by the Legislature was formulated by the Task Force, it is important to understand the Task Force's conceptualization of the problem and the assumptions behind the proposed policy.

The Task Force sought to correct two major problems associated with DNR, one unique to New York and Missouri and the other typical of all states:

1. *Legal ambiguity*. The New York Court of Appeals, in decisions such as *Matter of Storar* [14] and *Matter of O'Connor* [13], established a strict standard of "clear and convincing evidence" of the patients' wishes as the only basis for withholding or withdrawing care life support. It affirmed patients' rights to refuse treatment, while at the same time denied third parties the right to make decisions for incapacitated patients on the basis of substituted judgment or the patient's best interests. Thus the only ground for withdrawing or withholding life support was a clear decision prior to incapacitation communicated by

the patient. New York State is one of the few states to require such a strict standard (although the U.S. Supreme Court, in *Cruzan v. Director, Missouri Department of Health* upheld the constitutionality of such state evidentiary standards [5]).

2. *Lack of Communication and Informed Consent*. The lack of patient involvement in end-of-life decisionmaking because of physician reluctance to discuss DNR with patients is typical of all states and has been amply documented in the literature [41]. In New York State, however, the absence of a clear public policy with judicial sanction has been linked to the practice of covert DNR. The problem was cast into the public spotlight by a highly publicized court case in which purple dots signifying that a patient was not to be resuscitated were placed in a patient's chart without the patient's or family's consent [37]. On the other hand, fear of legal liability has also led to inappropriate CPR (resuscitation of patients when not medically indicated).

Solutions

The path taken by the Task Force during policy formulation is described in an article written by Tracy Miller, Task Force Executive Director. The title, "Do Not Resuscitate Orders: Public Policy and Patient Autonomy" symbolizes the centrality of patient self-determination as the mechanism for accomplishing the twin policy objectives of diminishing both inappropriate resuscitation and inappropriate orders not to resuscitate, problems of "overtreatment" and "undertreatment" respectively [15].

The Task Force proposal differs from many of the model DNR polices that have been recommended by various professional groups and adopted by hospitals under Joint Commission on the Accreditation of Healthcare Organizations (JCAHO) requirements [12]. Compared to most DNR protocols, there are considerably more procedural requirements that constrain the professional determination of medical futility and the appropriateness of DNR orders. In exchange for meeting the procedural requirements of the law, including the requirements for surrogate decision making, physicians, hospitals, surrogates, and other health care professionals are protected against legal liability.

The rationale for the elaborate procedures comes in part from a desire to protect the physician and the institution from legal liability, especially with regard to surrogate decisionmaking. But there was also concern about protecting the patient from slow coding and the abuse of ignoring the patient's right to give informed consent. The need to remedy abuses in CPR practices was given particular emphasis in several *New York Times* editorials, aptly titled "Death out of the Closet," [28] "Give the Dying Their Voice," [29] and "Sensible Answers to Death and Deceit" [30].

It was clear from the early stages of Task Force deliberation that the policy adopter must be the legislature. Departmental regulation would not suffice. Thus the political climate as well as the prevailing bioethical consensus regarding patient self-determination gave the Task Force proposal a "consumer protection" overtone as it entered legislative debate. The policy formulators were interested in political feasibility; that is in crafting a proposal that could win sufficient support for passage in the legislature.

The Legislative Hearings and Debate

Public testimony on the legislation proposed by the Task Force was received before a joint meeting of the Assembly and Senate Health Committees on February 12, 1987 [18]. While all the witnesses representing the major healthcare and religious interests of the state recognized the need for legislation to remedy the legal uncertainty surrounding DNR orders due to the lack of judicial sanction, physician witnesses predicted reluctance among physicians to accept and follow the policy. The Chair of the Ad Hoc Committee on DNR of the Medical Society of the State of New York, Charles B. Rogers, MD, predicted that the cumbersome nature of the procedural mandates would make it less likely that the physician would write a DNR order [39]. Rogers also objected to the proposal's narrow basis for invoking a therapeutic exception to the requirement to discuss DNR with dying patients. In supporting the minority opinion of Concannon and Tobin for an expanded therapeutic exception [4], Rogers maintained that the requirement to discuss and obtain consent from a dying patient with decision-making capacity would be inhumane and harmful to the patient [39].

There were some groups who felt that the proposed procedures left too many loopholes. A representative of the New York State Nurses Association, in testimony during the legislative hearings for the bill, stated:

> An omission in the bill that the Association feels very strongly about is that the bill requirements for a physician's DNR order do not specify a written order. Although the bill does require written documentation in the patient's chart, the Association feels strongly that the issuance of a physician's DNR order must always be in writing. The existing regulation that a physician's verbal order must be countersigned within 24 hours is not good enough in this situation. The possibility of verbal miscommunication leaves the nurse, and obviously the patient, in a tenuous position ([9], p. 182).

With regard to the concern of the New York State Nurses Association about the law's omission, research has shown that, in spite of the omission, the law was frequently interpreted as requiring the physician to sign the DNR order in person rather than give it over the telephone. This interpretation, because it delayed the issuance of DNR orders, caused considerable problems during the implementation phase. Subsequently, New York State Department of Health guidance specifically allowed physicians to issue DNR orders over the phone.

After the Hearings, in the ensuing negotiation between the Governor's Office and the Assembly and Senate leadership, the proposal, which did not include special provisions for the facilities for the developmentally disabled and mentally ill, was broadened to include special procedural protections. The protections were added because of concern over potential abuse of these vulnerable clients. Among these added protections is the requirement of giving notice to directors of facilities for the developmentally disabled, of requiring physicians or psychologists appointed by the facilities to concur in the determination of mental capacity (so clients will be protected from potential coercion to give consent to DNR), and of giving standing to the facility director to bring unresolved issues to dispute mediation and to the courts.

In the Senate debates [24], the concern for "undertreatment" (i.e., not resuscitating patients who could be "successfully" resuscitated) of all patients was emphasized, even though the Task Force deemed the problems of undertreatment and overtreatment to be "co-equal." The Legislature, in enacting the Statue, generally strengthened the procedural requirements contained in the Task Force proposal to constrain professional discretion. Some Senators saw the need to counterbalance the Task Force proposal which they saw as primarily intended to protect physicians and hospitals from legal liability. One important effect of the legislators' concern was that it further constrained physician discretion by tightening the definition of medical futility. Under the Task Force proposal, if an adult patient lacks capacity and no surrogate is available, the attending physician could issue a DNR order on the basis of "medical futility." Presumably, this determination of medical futility would be made according to the professional standard of care without reference to an explicit definition. The Legislature, however, "deprofessionalized" the meaning of "futility" by providing an explicit definition: "CPR [is futile when it] will be unsuccessful in restoring cardiac and respiratory function or when the patient will experience repeated arrest in a short period before death occurs" ([27], p. 96). Thus, the authority for defining futility, which has traditionally rested with the medical profession, was appropriated by the Legislature.

III. IMPLEMENTATION OF THE DNR "PROGRAM": CLARIFYING THE POLICY

From the policy analyst's perspective, a program is viewed as a set of activities, routines, and resources designed to accomplish the intended objective of a policy [38]. The administrative agency in charge of implementing the DNR law was the New York State Department of Health. But at the Department, the DNR law did not fit into traditional program categories such as delivery systems, age groups, and disease groups. There was no program manager or programmatic home, and the DNR proposal didn't originate from "program people." Nevertheless, certain regularized activities had to take place in the hospitals and nursing homes of New York State in order for the objectives of the policy to be accomplished. Doctors had to talk to patients, surrogates had to be located, consent had to be documented, dispute resolution bodies had to be in place. Most importantly physicians and facilities had to change their usual practices.

Implementation at the State Level

Public policy, the law, is not automatically self-implementing. As with most laws, there was a need to extend and interpret the New York DNR Law through regulations, memoranda, educational efforts, and advisory opinions. In the case of the DNR law this role was filled largely by the counsels of the Department of Health and the Office of Mental Retardation and Developmental Disabilities (OMRDD). Where possible, the counsels looked to the Task Force staff and relevant documents to discover legislative intent. Not unexpectedly, after the law's passage, questions arose that were not anticipated by the Task Force or the legislature. For example, were patients waiting in hospitals for transfer to nursing homes, considered *nursing home* patients or *hospital* patients for purposes of the three-day review of a DNR order? It was decided by Department of Health counsel that they were hospital patients and therefore required a three-day review. Another question was whether DNR orders written for patients enrolled in hospice programs were valid. In particular, do emergency medical technicians (EMT) arriving at the home of a hospice enrollee have to honor a DNR order? In a Health Facilities Memorandum, the Department decided in the affirmative, EMT personnel must honor DNR orders [20].

Implementation "in the field"

Although the law assigned the bureaucracy the task of implementing the policy, many important aspects of policy planning have taken place "in the field" in hospitals and nursing homes. Central to implementation has been the design of the forms to document consent and the conditions for surrogate decision making. Although the statute itself is silent on the subject of forms (documentation of the DNR order in the medical chart is all that is required), it invites the Department of Health to "suggest" forms:

> The Commissioner of Health may provide suggested forms that may be used for the purpose of expressing a decision regarding cardio-pulmonary resuscitation or for the purpose of designating a surrogate pursuant to this article ([27], p. 113).

In declining this invitation, the Department insured that the facilities themselves would be the key implementors.

The forms make the DNR policy concrete to health care professionals, patients, and surrogates. They, in effect, embody the *quid pro quo* manifested in the law: the legitimation of DNR orders and the removal of legal risk in exchange for the recognition that DNR decisions are appropriately made by the patient or surrogate, not the physician.

Prior to the law's taking effect on April 1, 1988, some hospitals spent considerable time in reviewing the statute and creating forms to document the fulfillment of the requirements for writing a DNR order. Typically this task fell to senior staff or to in-house counsel (if one was available). As a service to its members, the Hospital Association of New York State held informational sessions and presented sample forms.

One hospital counsel, one of the first in the state to design forms, made an effort to make the forms as "user friendly" as possible. The counsel felt compelled to develop seven different DNR documentation forms:

> (1) *Consent for DNR order by an adult patient with capacity* (physician and witness signatures), (2) *Adult with capacity – therapeutic exception* (attending and concurring physician signatures), (3) *Determination that an adult lacks capacity* (attending physician and concurring physician signatures), (4) *Consent by surrogate for patient* (attending physician, concurring physician, surrogate, and witness signatures), (5) *Designation of surrogate by patient* (patient and two witness signatures), (6) *DNR order for patient who lacks capacity and has no surrogate available* (attending physician and concurring physician signatures), (7)*Minor patient – consent by parent/guardian* (attending physician, concurring physician, parent/guardian, and witness signatures) [1].

Procedures do not exist in isolation from their social context. Implementing the DNR law also meant developing formal and informal systems to support the use of the forms. Medical, nursing, and other health professionals had to be oriented to the intentions of the law and trained in the technicalities of obtaining consent. Certain persons or offices (for example, risk management, quality assurance, legal counsel, nursing) had to be assigned responsibility for training, providing advice and monitoring compliance. Others developed expertise over time and became informal resource persons.

Hospitals also had to develop policies that reaffirmed and augmented the DNR procedures. Policies appeared in the form of (1) written documents (actually called "policies and procedures") reviewed and approved by the appropriate committees of the hospital governance system, (2) memoranda, (3) resolutions in the minutes of committee meetings, or (4) unwritten understandings. Some of these policies are directly related to the statutory and regulatory requirements, for example, those designating the physicians eligible to be concurring physicians, those delineating the workings of the dispute mediation system, and those delineating the procedures for insuring that the DNR order is recorded in the medical chart and communicated to the appropriate persons throughout the hospital. Other policies interpret and apply the statute to the individual circumstances of the hospital, for example, policies accommodating DNR orders to the contingencies of the operating room, governing the nurses taking orders over the phone, or determining how hard to press the physicians for three-day review of the DNR order (probably unwritten). A flow chart created by one hospital to help the staff understand the special requirements for writing DNR orders for developmentally disabled patients is shown in Chart I.

Although the procedures as embedded in the forms are intended to limit discretion, and to influence behavior, there is ample opportunity for health care professionals to influence patient and surrogate decision-making. Consider the issue of the patient's awareness of the option to have a DNR order entered in the chart. All patients, upon admission to the hospital, receive a copy of the American Hospital Association's Patient's Bill of Rights. Included is the right to:

> receive all the information you need to give informed consent for an order not to resuscitate. You also have the right to designate an individual to give this consent for you if you are too ill to do so. If you would like additional information, please ask for a copy of the pamphlet "*Do Not Resuscitate Orders – A Guide for Patients and Families*" ([2], p. 1).

Some hospitals automatically pass the pamphlet out along with the Bill of Rights. Patients, upon admission, may or may not read the Bill of Rights or ask for the pamphlet. Within the hospital, some units make it a practice to inform all patients of the DNR option.

Physicians obviously have an opportunity to influence patient decision making through the communication of information about CPR (by, for example, emphasizing or de-emphasizing the brutal nature of CPR), and the timing of discussion (by, for example, opening dialogue before a crisis or delaying discussion until the patient has been determined incapacitated and enter into discussion with the family instead). In addition to physicians, there are many health-care professionals including nurses, social workers, discharge planners, and patient representatives who can

CHART I

DNR DETERMINATION WHEN INDICATED FOR A DEVELOPMENTALLY DISABLED PERSON

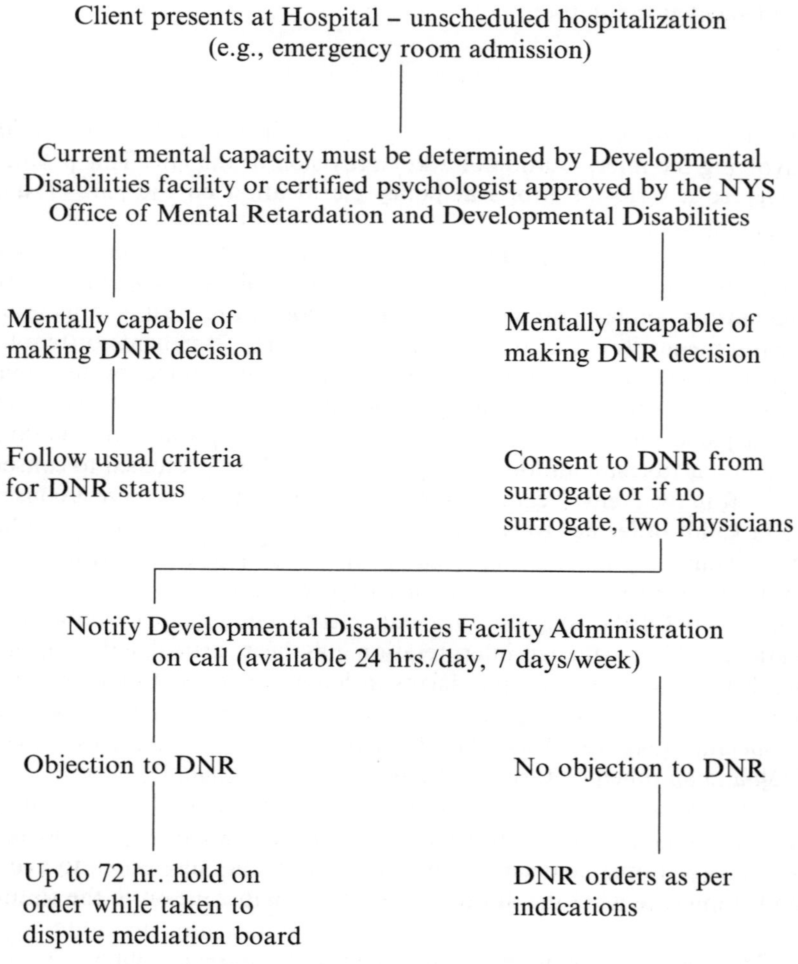

Client presents at Hospital – unscheduled hospitalization (e.g., emergency room admission)

Current mental capacity must be determined by Developmental Disabilities facility or certified psychologist approved by the NYS Office of Mental Retardation and Developmental Disabilities

Mentally capable of making DNR decision

Follow usual criteria for DNR status

Mentally incapable of making DNR decision

Consent to DNR from surrogate or if no surrogate, two physicians

Notify Developmental Disabilities Facility Administration on call (available 24 hrs./day, 7 days/week)

Objection to DNR

Up to 72 hr. hold on order while taken to dispute mediation board

No objection to DNR

DNR orders as per indications

and do play an important role in explaining to patients and families the DNR option and facilitating the exercise of that option. Once again there is opportunity to exercise discretion in timing the discussion.

In choosing not to centralize the development of forms and supporting procedures, the Department of Health, in effect, guaranteed that there would be variation in the ways in which hospitals interpreted and implemented the statute.

Policy Clarification

An important problem arose during the first few months of operation involving the interpretation of a key provision of the law. This problem triggered a series of efforts at policy clarification on the part of state policy-makers.

The crux of the problem was the interpretation of the patient's consent to DNR and two perceived negative consequences: (1) as ambivalent patients or families grapple with their decision, CPR must be attempted, even if medically futile, in the event of an arrest; (2) patients or families may request that "everything be done" which could compel professionals to attempt CPR, even though they believed it to be medically futile. These consequences arose because the statute stipulated a presumption in favor of consent to resuscitation: "Every person...shall be presumed to consent to CPR in the event of cardiac or respiratory arrest unless there is consent to [a valid] order not to resuscitate" ([27], p. 97). This presumption has been commonly read to mean that CPR is required to be performed on every patient for whom a DNR order has not been written (with forms completely filled out), even if it would clearly be futile or harmful to the patient. This particular interpretation has been articulated and well-publicized by prominent physicians in letters to the editors of the *New England Journal of Medicine* [32], *Journal of the American Medical Association* [34], *New York State Journal of Medicine* [7], *New York Times* [35], and an op-ed editorial in the *Wall Street Journal* [33].

State policymakers hold a different interpretation of the law. In an article published in the *New York State Journal of Medicine*, in February, 1989, Task Force associate counsel Robert Swidler attempted to clarify and emphasize what the drafters and the legislators meant in the statute:

> The [presumed consent to resuscitation] clause presumes that the patient who does not have a DNR order consents to CPR – that is, the

> patient would "permit" it. That presumption does not create any new obligation to provide CPR. Consent to a treatment cannot alone establish a duty to provide the treatment....In general, a physician should obtain a patient or surrogate's decision about a DNR order prior to an actual crisis. In some cases, the physician may be confronted with an arrest or an impending arrest before he or she has contemplated the DNR procedure. In some of these emergency situations, the physician's best judgment will be to withhold, or direct the withholding of, resuscitative efforts. The DNR law does not impede the exercise of judgment. ([40], p.71)

Swidler warns, however:

> Physicians who feel burdened by the requirements of the DNR law may be tempted to avoid writing appropriate DNR orders, and opt instead to await the patient's arrest or impending arrest, at which time the physician can, if available, direct the withholding of resuscitative efforts on grounds of futility. This practice would obviously thwart a key objective of the law – to place the patient, or the patient's family, at the center of DNR decisions, and to plan in advance of a crisis ([40], p.71).

It is not clear how the Department of Health, which in a memorandum warned physicians against practices along this line, could detect patterns of abuse.

The Swidler article, which also states the position of the Department of Health, makes two points: (1) In the event that a patient arrests during the process of writing a DNR order (before all the required forms have been filled out), it is permissible for the physician to withhold CPR; (2) In an arresting, non-DNR patient for whom preferences about CPR are not known, the physician is not required to administer medically futile CPR. The judgement of whether CPR is futile should follow the community standard of care (what a reasonable physician would do in such a situation).

In their essay, Baker *et al.* show that many professionals are not persuaded by the Swidler interpretation. Why isn't the Department's position (as articulated in memoranda, articles in professional medical journals, educational presentations, and formal and informal responses to individual questions) accepted? Perhaps there is a need for more extensive education. But another reason is that many hospital counsels do not accept the narrower interpretation of the presumed consent clause. Although they will acknowledge that regulatory action from the Department is unlikely, hospital counsels perceive a risk of tort liability if a DNR order is not in place prior to withholding CPR. The conservative approach taken by the hospital counsels is consistent with the desire to minimize the risk of law suits brought against the hospital. New York health care professionals, sensitive to their litigious environment, also feel vulnerable to law suits. As a practical matter, nurses are usually the first to discover that a patient has arrested. Without a proper DNR order in place, they understandably feel compelled to call a code.

What happens when a patient or surrogate demands what the physician considers to be futile CPR? According to the interpretation of Commissioner Axelrod (see Section Two, pp. 137–140), the patient is "entitled" to it. Furthermore, in assessing the realities of New York State politics, Axelrod argues that from the standpoint of political feasibility, the Task Force's legislative proposal would not have been enacted into law unless the understanding of "CPR as entitlement" were embedded in it.

IV. POLICY EVALUATION: FIXING THE PROGRAM AND RETHINKING MEDICAL FUTILITY

The law did not require and the implementation phase did not include the design of formal feedback mechanisms to monitor compliance with the procedures systematically, or to see if the objectives of the law were achieved. Presumably the Department of Health's ongoing quality assurance programs – hospital and nursing home survey inspections, individual complaint channels, and professional misconduct hotlines – monitor compliance in a general way. Informally, however, the Task Force, New York Department of Health officials, legislators and staff hear about the law's problems and achievements. Various interest groups do not hesitate to make their opinions, perceptions, and positions known. The Task Force has been actively engaged in eliciting feedback and played a major role at the Assessment Conference held at Union College at which many of the formal research studies on the law were presented.

The policy outcomes related to the implementation of the law and the achievement of the policy's objectives are summarized as follows:

1. The program procedures interpreting the law are in place and are followed, leading to appropriate consent and the accomplishment of policy objectives.
2. In addition to the accomplishment of policy objectives, there are negative consequences, anticipated and unanticipated.
3. The complexity of the procedure established to protect patients' or their surrogates' right to consent to DNR may lead to misunderstanding of the law's requirements by practitioners.
4. The program procedures interpreting the law are in place but are followed only in letter and not spirit.

With regard to the first policy outcome, the research studies presented in this volume show that there has been an increase in physician-patient/surrogate communication and in consentual and appropriately documented DNR. In their study (this volume, pp. 251–262), Baker *et al.* found that over 66% of hematologists-oncologists, and medical and nursing directors of critical care units thought that there was increased likelihood of discussing DNR with patients at risk of CPR or with families of incompetent patients. Sixty percent of critical care unit medical and nursing directors and 70% of hematologists and oncologists thought that the likelihood of giving an undocumented verbal DNR order for a terminal patient without informing either the patient or family had declined.

However, there is also evidence of negative consequences of following the procedures. For example, in the survey by Baker *et al.*, oncologists, critical care medical and nursing directors expressed the following concerns:

A. Families, as surrogates, often face guilt and anguish in signing the DNR consent form.
B. The required informed consent discussion with a dying patient is inhumane and a disruption of the traditional doctor-patient relationship.
C. As families in their ambivalence, grapple with their decision, CPR must be attempted, even if medically futile, in the event of an arrest.
D. Families may request that "everything be done" which would compel physicians to attempt what they might consider to be futile CPR.

As will be shown, some of the negative consequences stemming from following the law were rectified, for example, the requirement of a witnessed surrogate signature was eliminated. Other consequences, specifically C and D above, have proven to be more troublesome despite efforts at clarification during the implementation stage.

On the other hand, some of the negative consequences are clearly not the result of following the law but of misinterpreting the law. The complexity of the procedures that are required for the writing of a DNR order is on an unprecedented scale compared to that for any other treatment. Given the adversarial nature of the New York State regulatory environment and the litigious climate surrounding the practice of medicine, it is not surprising that physicians would tend to interpret the law's procedures as more restrictive than they really are. Many of these misinterpretations are also amenable to correction. However, it can be argued that at least some differences in interpretation will be more difficult to correct. For example, in their survey Baker *et al.* asked the question: "In situations where it is impossible to comply with all the procedural requirements of the law, is it lawful to withhold CPR on grounds of medical futility?" According to the Swidler interpretation of the law, the answer is "yes." However, 47% of the critical care unit medical directors, 60% of the nursing directors, and 57% of the hematologists and oncologists said "no."

Finally, it has been suggested that physicians, perhaps to circumvent what they perceive to be the inhumane aspects of the narrowly defined therapeutic exception, might follow the letter but not the spirit of the law. Although the implied goal of the law is the encouragement of the doctor-patient discussion, the policy's design did not include a procedural component to mandate such a discussion. To avoid engaging a patient in a discussion about DNR, the physician, sometimes with family approval, may delay discussion until the patient has been determined to be mentally incapacitated. Some studies have shown that DNR policies in general have been unsuccessful in increasing patient participation in DNR consent ([10], [36]). The improvement of physician-patient dialogue therefore depends on education and socialization in support of patient self-determination.

Changing the Law: Incremental Modification or Major Reorientation

Operational experience with a program frequently reveals deficiencies in the policy that need to be corrected. If the deficiencies are severe enough and are unacceptable to major interest groups, there may have to be a reformulation of the original policy ([38], p.151). Below are outlined vehicles for making corrections along with examples of corrective action.

1. *Problems that can be resolved through regulation and education efforts.* In September 1990, the New York State Department of Health in cooperation with the Medical Society of the State of New York and the Hospital Association of the State of New York prepared an educational booklet entitled "Do Not Resuscitate Orders: Questions and Answers for Health Care Professionals." The booklet (see Appendix, pp. 415–438), based on a shared interpretation of the law on the part of all three bodies, attempts to clarify confusion and misunderstanding about the procedural requirements of the law and to simplify its complexities. For example:

   Q: Must a DNR order be in writing?
   A: Yes. A DNR order must be in writing in the patient's chart, although the writing may be an entry indicating that a telephone order was issued by the attending physician ([22], p.5).

   Although the booklet should rectify some of the major problems resulting from the over-interpretation of the law's requirements (for example, the belief that a DNR order is not valid until signed by the physician in person, and thus the patient must be coded in the event of an arrest), there is a limit to the corrective potential of regulatory or educational efforts. For example, although the Department of Health in the pamphlet has reiterated its position that presumption to consent does not mean the duty to resuscitate, some hospital attorneys and physicians still hold a different interpretation of the law. Other efforts will be needed to convince them otherwise. Perhaps what is needed is a successful lawsuit for wrongful resuscitation, or perhaps the law must be amended.
2. *Problems that require a change in the law to resolve.* In the Spring of 1991, the Department of Health proposed amendments intended to "refine and improve the law and reduce some of the sources of tension that have been noted in practice, while retaining the central ethical premises it embraces and the protection it affords" ([21], p.6). The Legislature passed these amendments on July 4, 1991 [17]. The amendments adjusted some of the more onerous and cumbersome procedures that had been identified as leading to delay in writing DNR

orders. For example, a frequently mentioned negative consequence of the law was the guilt and anguish aroused in surrogates and parents as a result of *signing* the DNR consent form. Therefore, the amendments allowed surrogates and parents to give oral consent, changing the requirement that their consent must be in witnessed writing.

The amendments also extended the period for required hospital DNR order review from three days to seven days. It was found that the three-day review period was excessively rigid and not appropriately geared to the variability in patients' conditions.

The amendments not only modified existing procedures but expanded the legal force of the DNR orders beyond the hospital, nursing home, and developmental disabilities facility to the home. Quill and others have emphasized the problems that arise when emergency medical services personnel cannot recognize the legitimacy of the DNR order for a non-hospice patient at home (see Quill's case study in Section Three). The law now provides for non-hospital DNR orders [17].

Remaining Issues

One of the most controversial features of the law, at least from the physician's perspective, is the specter of patients or surrogates requesting medically futile CPR which must subsequently be provided by physicians [6]. For now, the Task Force and Health Department are willing to accept this negative consequence in the interests of maintaining the primacy of patient self-determination. A major assumption of the law is that the patient will choose rationally. It has been suggested that there should be a policy reformulation if this assumption doesn't hold. Tracy Miller states: "Certainly, if experience shows that patients, when fully informed, make irrational choices by insisting on futile or harmful treatment, the law should be changed to provide explicit limits on the duty to resuscitate in cases of medical futility" ([15], p.251). It is not clear what would constitute convincing evidence to law-makers that this assumption is not correct, or how the evidence would be collected. But it is clear to Commissioner Axelrod that given the Legislature's predisposition toward "consumer protection," attempts to amend the law and weaken patient self-determination will not be easily accomplished.

Furthermore, as the following statement indicates, there is little room for compromise on the major principle of patient autonomy:

> An exception to the informed consent discussion in cases of medical futility will swallow the rule at a time when physicians are still reluctant to speak with patients about resuscitation. As long as that reluctance remains prevalent, any exception on therapeutic or futility grounds is almost certain to be the escape hatch for physicians seeking to avoid conversations they have never understood as integral to the obligation to care for dying patients ([15], p.251)

Much more troublesome than the situation where patients or surrogates demand futile CPR is the situation of patient or surrogate ambivalence. In these cases, the physician is faced with the prospect of giving futile CPR while the patient or surrogate has yet to make up his/her mind. While it is certainly not the intention of the law's framers to require CPR under these conditions, there is no clear formulation of policy that unambiguously grants physicians the autonomy to write a DNR order in these cases.

The AMA, in its policy guidelines, recommends that physicians, after informing the patient or surrogate, have the right to enter a DNR order in the patient's chart in all cases where CPR would be futile, regardless of patient or surrogate disposition [3]. The compromise position Robert Baker and I suggested (see pp. 439–444) is that physicians, in cases of ambivalence, be allowed to enter an interim order which stands until the patient or surrogate makes up his/her mind.

SOME CONCLUDING REMARKS ON THE PUBLIC POLICYMAKING PROCESS

1. Agenda setting. The Task Force proved remarkably effective in bringing a complex and potentially volatile issue such as DNR before state policy-makers. This achievement is not only a tribute to the members and staff of the Task Force but to the idea of the Task Force itself, a body designed explicitly for agenda-setting.

2. Policy formulation and adoption. When a proposal enters the legislative arena as a bill, there are numerous opportunities for modification as that bill wends its way through the law-making process. With a few important exceptions, the Task Force proposal, crafted with an eye toward political feasibility, remained remarkably intact. Legislators, concerned about the problem of undertreatment, adopted an interpretation of the presumed consent clause that reinforced the linkage between patient autonomy and consumer protection.

It is interesting to speculate on what shape New York's DNR policy would have taken if it were possible to use professional self-regulation rather than legislation as the method of enactment. Based on the experience of other states, it is likely that the policy would contain fewer procedural protections for patients and more discretion for physicians.

3. Policy implementation. Most statutes require administration to put their intended policies into effect. It is not unusual for policies to undergo a complex and often frustrating period of implementation. The New York DNR Law was no exception. Furthermore, the fact that a law was chosen as the instrument of public policy meant that there would have to be some measure of accountability between physicians, hospitals, and the New York State Department of Health. Unfortunately the relationship between the Department of Health and the physicians was already severely strained.

Implementation activities often include designing the appropriate administrative arrangements – forms, guidelines, regulations, reporting and monitoring relationships. Ideally this activity should be completed in the time period between the passage of the law and its effective date (7 months for the New York DNR Law). However, the operational problems that inevitably surface after the law becomes effective extends the period of implementation. In the case of the New York DNR Law, some of these operational problems were linked to misunderstandings or disagreements in interpreting the statute. Implementation included efforts to clarify the intended policy.

One area of policy that has proved difficult to clarify was the problem of medical futility. Given the tensions between consent and futility-based approaches to DNR described in the introduction, it is unlikely that this area of disagreement can be fully resolved within the framework of the current statute.

4. Policy evaluation (resulting in incremental modification, re-orientation or termination of the policy). Based on formal and informal feedback to policy-makers, the legislature passed amendments extending and elaborating the Statute (but not with regard to medical futility) [17].

No doubt there will be continuing efforts at refining and improving the statute through education, regulation, and amendment. However, in a broader sense, efforts to "make" or "remake" policy transcend this particular statute. Other laws will influence how the policy objectives of the New York DNR Law will be achieved. For example, the New York Health Care Proxy Law has directly served to simplify the exercise of surrogate decisionmaking and expand surrogate prerogatives [25, 26]. The Federal Patient Self-Determination Act of 1990 requires that hospitals provide information to patients at the time of admission concerning advance directives [31]. Undoubtedly there will be further legislative and judicial action. Finally, above and beyond policy-making as a formal expression of government, changing social norms and attitudes will surely influence professional and public behavior either implicitly or explicitly through the influence of professional self-regulation.

BIBLIOGRAPHY

1. Albany Medical Center Hospital, Albany, N. Y., DNR Documentation Forms 1–7.
2. Albany Medical Center, Albany, N. Y.: 1988, *Your Rights as a Patient*, Albany, New York.
3. American Medical Association, Council on Ethical and Judicial Affairs: 1991, 'Guidelines for the Appropriate Use of Do-Not-Resuscitate Orders', *Journal of the American Medical Association* **265**, 1868–1871.
4. Concannon, R.J. and Tobin, C.J.: 1986, 'Minority Report', *Do Not Resuscitate Orders: The Proposed Legislation and Report of the New York State Task Force on Life and the Law*, April 1986, pp. 66–71, this volume, pp. 410–413.
5. *Cruzan, V., Director, Missouri Department of Health*, 1990 U. S. Lexis 3301 (US June 25, 1990).
6. Farber, S.: 1988, Letter, *New England Journal of Medicine*, **318**, 1757.
7. Frier, J.P.: 1989, Letter to the Editor, *New York State Journal of Medicine*, July 429.
8. Harvard Medical School: 1968, 'A definition of irreversible coma: Report of the Ad Hoc Committee of the Harvard Medical School to Examine the Definition of Brain Death', *Journal of the American Medical Association* **205**, 337–340.
9. Inuzzi, B.: 1987, 'Testimony before the New York State Assembly and Senate Health Committees: Public Hearing Regarding the Issuance of Do Not Resuscitate Orders', Feb. 12, 1987, 179–186.
10. Kamer, R. and Dieck *et al.*: 1990, 'Effect of New York State's Do-Not-Resuscitate Legislation and In-Hospital Cardiopulmonary Resuscitation Practice', *American Journal of Medicine*, **88**, 108.
11. Kingdon, J.W.: 1984, *Agendas, Alternatives, and Public Policies*, Little Brown and Co., Boston, 3.
12. Joint Commission on the Accreditation of Healthcare Organizations, *Accreditation Manual for Hospitals 1989*, MA.1.4.11, P. 82.
13. *Matter of O'Connor*, 72, N. Y. 2d 517 (1988).

14. *Matter of Storar*, 52 N. Y. 2d at 376–77 (1981).
15. Miller, T.E.: 1989, 'Do-Not-Resuscitate Orders: Public Policy and Patient Autonomy', *Law, Medicine and Health Care*, **17**, 245–254.
16. New York Public Health Law, Art 29-B (L. 1987, Ch. 818), this volume, pp. 349–367.
17. New York Public Health Law: 1991, Chapter 370, 1133, this volume, pp. 445–454.
18. New York State Assembly and Senate Health Committees: Feb. 12, 1987, Public Hearing Regarding the Issuance of Do Not Resuscitate Orders, New York.
19. New York State Department of Health, *Do Not Resuscitate Orders a Guide for Patients and Families*, 1988.
20. New York State Department of Health Memorandum, January 24, 1989, Health Facilities Series 89–5: H-2, NA-2, HRF-2, Hospice-1.
21. New York State Department of Health: 1991, Memorandum, DOH No. 23R-91, Peter J. Millock, General Counsel, 6.
22. New York State Department of Health, Medical Society of the State of New York, Hospital Association of New York State: 1990, *Do Not Resuscitate Orders: Questions and Answers for Health Care Professionals*, Albany, New York, this volume, pp. 415–438.
23. New York State, Executive Order No. 56. Dec. 20, 1984.
24. New York State Senate, July 8, 1987, Debates over Senate Bill Number 678-A, an Act to Amend the Public Health Law, in relation to orders not to attempt cardiopulmonary resuscitation.
25. New York Proxy Law, Article 29-C, New York State Public Health Law (1990).
26. New York State Task Force on Life and the Law: 'Life-sustaining Treatment: Making Decisions and Appointing a Health Care Agent', (1987).
27. New York State Task Force on Life and the Law: 1986, 1988, *Do Not Resuscitate Orders: The Proposed Legislation and Report of the New York State Task Force on Life and the Law*, New York, this volume, pp. 38–413.
28. *New York Times*: May 25, 1988, 'Death, Out of the Closet'.
29. *New York Times*: August 31, 1985, 'Give the Dying Their Voice'.
30. *New York Times*: June 12, 1987, 'Sensible Answers to Death and Deceit'.
31. Omnibus Budget Reconciliation Act of 19, Title IV, Section 4206, *Congressional Record*, Oct. 26, 1990, **136**, H12456–7.
32. Plowe, C.V.: 1988, Letter to the Editor, *New England Journal of Medicine*, **318**, 1758.
33. Praeger, K.M.: 1989, 'How CPR Can Threaten the Desperately Ill', *Wall Street Journal*, March 9.
34. Praeger, K.M.: 1990, Letter to the Editor *Journal of the American Medical Association*, **263**, 2297.
35. Praeger, K.M.: 1990, 'Letter to the Editor-You Can't Die in Peace in a New York Hospital', *New York Times*, April 6.
36. Quill, T.E. and Bennett, N.M.: 1992, 'The Effects of a Hospital Policy and State Legislation on Resuscitation Orders for Geratic Patients', *Archives of Internal Medicine*, **152**, 569-572, this volume, pp. 241–250.
37. Report of the Special January third additional 1983 Grand Jury concerning 'Do Not Resuscitate procedures at a certain hospital in Queens', (Sup. Ct. , Queens Co. , Feb. 8, 1984.

38. Rettig, R.A. and Marks, E.L.: 1981, *Implementing the End-Stage Renal Disease Program of Medicare*, U. S. Dept. of Health and Human Services, Health, Care Financing Administration, 11–14.
39. Rogers, C.B.: 1987, 'Testimony before the New York State Assembly and Senate Health Committees: Public Hearing Regarding the Issuance of Do Not Resuscitate Orders', Feb. 12, 1987, 218–244.
40. Swidler, R.: 1989, 'The Presumption of Consent in New York State's Do-Not-Resuscitate Law', *New York State Journal of Medicine*, **89**, 69–72.
41. Zimmerman, J.E., Knaus W.A., Sharpe S.M. *et al.*: 1986, 'The Use and Implications of Do Not Resuscitate Orders in Intensive Care Unit', *Journal of the American Medical Association*, **255**, 351–356.

ROBERT BAKER

THE LEGITIMATION AND REGULATION OF DNR ORDERS

In July 1987, the New York State Legislature amended the State's public health law to regulate "Do Not Resuscitate" orders, effective April 1, 1988 [23]. There immediately ensued a controversy over the limits the law placed on the physician's power to write medical orders "not to resuscitate" patients. Physicians' prerogatives in life-and-death decisions had been a subject of debate for over two decades. Bioethicists hold that there is but one legitimate answer to the question: Who shall decide whether to initiate or forego life-sustaining medical interventions? – The patient. The life in question belongs to the patient, not the physician; hence decisions concerning that life properly belong to the patient, not to the physician. To quote from the authoritative 1983 report of the President's Commission for the Study of Ethical Problems in Medicine and Biomedical and Behavioral Research:

> Respect for the self-determination of competent patients is of special importance in decisions to forego life-sustaining treatment because different people will have markedly different concerns during the final period of their lives. . . . [Therefore] the primacy of a patient's interests in self-determination and in honoring the patient's own view of well-being warrant leaving the patient with the final authority to decide ([40], p. 44).

In reality, bioethicists acknowledge that medical decision making is "a process of collaborating and sharing information and responsibility between care givers and patients" ([40], p. 44). They also acknowledge that often patients will be too incapacitated to participate in this process and will need to be represented by a surrogate – preferably a proxy designated by the patient, or, failing that, a close family member. But the foundational idea of the bioethical revolution is that it is the patient's life to live, or to die, and so the patient, not the physician, is the party who should ultimately make decisions about life and death.

In the United States, this foundational idea traces back at least as far as the *Patient's Bill of Rights* of 1973 [1]. The major impetus transforming

R. Baker & M.A. Strosberg (eds.), Legislating Medical Ethics: A Study of the New York Do-Not-Resuscitate Law, 33–101.

this idea into revolutionary force in American medicine was a 1976 case, *In re Quinlan*, in which the New Jersey Supreme Court decided that Karen Ann Quinlan's father *could* exercise her "right" to disconnect her life-support system, even though her physician objected that to do so would violate his professional ethics [29]. By favoring Karen's father over her physician, the *Quinlan* decision established a well-publicized legal precedent: patient values have priority over those of professionals in disputes over life-sustaining medical interventions; thus, in effect, providing the definitive legal precedent for the bioethical revolution.

The 1983 President's Commission report authorized the extension of bioethical reform to decisions concerning cardiopulmonary resuscitation (CPR) and Do Not Resuscitate (DNR) orders, recommending that hospitals recognize that patients have a right to decide whether or not to accept resuscitation ([40], p. 8). The Commission's recommendations became the basis for reform of CPR/DNR policies by a variety of professional organizations, including the American Medical Association (AMA) [37], and the Joint Commission for Accreditation of Health Care Organizations (JCAHO) [17]; in New York, it set the stage for the 1987 DNR law.

Neither the President's Commission's report nor the AMA and JCAHO reforms inspired by it were particularly contentious. Yet New York's DNR law was. Why? The reasons are complex, for while the arguments appear to focus on narrow procedural issues, the passions underlying these seemingly technical discussions run so deep that the controversy exploded out of the columns of medical journals [38], on to the pages of the *New York Times* [46] and the *Wall Street Journal* [39]. The debate was conducted on at least three levels: superficially it focused on the analysis of the language, intent, and impact of the DNR law on clinicians and patients. At a deeper level the debate raised questions of power and propriety in medical decision making – reopening arguments about the scope of the bioethical revolution that had appeared to have been settled by the President's Commission in 1983. Beneath these layers of erudite discussion, however, lay an emotionally charged dispute between those who saw themselves as bioethical revolutionaries intent on protecting patients against physician paternalism, and those nurses and physicians who perceived the law as an assault, not only on their professional authority and integrity, but on their fundamental obligation to serve their patients.

THE INVERTED NATURE OF "DO NOT RESUSCITATE" ORDERS

The immediate focus of the New York debate is a specific medical order, the DNR order. Medical orders are the primary means by which physicians assert their authority within the world of a hospital. Whether written or oral, their primary objective is to direct other members of the hospital staff to do something – to initiate an intervention, to change a treatment regimen. Normally, the physician orders and the staff acts – patients are not part of the chain of command.

DNR orders, however, differ from ordinary medical orders. They invert the logic of a normal order: a DNR order is issued by a physician to order the staff *not* to act. Orders directing inaction are curious and make sense only against a background in which action is likely to occur in the absence of a countermanding directive – the prevailing situation for resuscitation. Any patient suffering a cardiopulmonary arrest, or, to use hospital corridor language, anyone "coding," will automatically prompt a "code" or a "code blue," which will be "called" by *any* member of the staff who observes it, thereby mobilizing the hospital staff, or a designated resuscitation team, to administer CPR. Orders to resuscitate are thus automatic and uniquely "democratic": nurses and medical students are not only obligated to call a "code" for any patient in cardiac or pulmonary arrest, when they do so they mobilize physicians and so, in a sense, are giving orders to their superordinates in the hospital hierarchy. Physicians alone, however, retain the authority to call off a code, and only they may write an order preventing other members of the staff from calling codes for specific patients, which is to say that only a physician may write a "no-code" or "Do Not Resuscitate" order.

Just a few decades ago, the CPR order was neither automatic nor "democratic." At that time, administering CPR involved either electrical stimulation of the heart (a procedure known as defibrillation, invented by Paul Zoll in the 1950s [62]) and/or open-chest massage, a procedure in which the chest is surgically cracked open and the heart is massaged directly by hand. The nature of CPR changed after 1960, when W. B. Kouewenhoven and his associates reported the efficacy of "closed-chest" cardiac massage (a procedure involving chest compression, which we today commonly refer to as CPR) [22]. Closed-chest massage soon supplanted the older open-chest method as the resuscitation technique of choice, and hospitals established resuscitation teams to administer the procedure [10]. Speedy action proved to be crucial to successful resuscitation, so physicians ceded the prerogative of ordering resuscitation to their staff in an attempt to ensure the immediate and automatic resuscitation of any patient suffering an arrest.

Automatic CPR by trained resuscitation teams at first appeared to enjoy extraordinary success. As experience accumulated, however, the unreflective resuscitation of every patient who arrested was found to be a mixed blessing. By the late 1960s, articles began appearing in the medical literature describing the problematic effects of "successful" resuscitation. Perhaps the classic in this genre is a 1968 case reported in the *British Medical Journal* which relates the death of a sixty-eight-year-old physician with end-stage cancer.

> [After being resuscitated by the hospital team] he expressed his appreciation of the good intentions and skill of his younger colleague. At the same time he asked that if he had a further cardiovascular collapse no steps should be taken to prolong his life, for the pain of his cancer was now more than he would needlessly continue to endure. He himself wrote a note to this effect in his case records, and the staff of the hospital knew his feelings.
>
> His wish notwithstanding, when the patient collapsed again, two weeks [later] – with acute myocardial infarction and cardiac arrest – he was revived by the hospital's emergency resuscitation team. His heart stopped on four further occasions during that night and each time was restarted artificially. The body then recovered sufficiently to linger for three more weeks, but in a decerebrate state, punctuated by episodes of projectile vomiting accompanied by generalized convulsions. Intravenous nourishment was carefully combined with blood transfusion and measures necessary to maintain electrolyte and fluid balance. In addition, antibacterial and antifungal antibiotics were given as a prophylaxis against infection, particularly pneumonia, complicating the tracheotomy that had been performed to ensure a clear airway. . . .
>
> This case is submitted for publication without commentary or conclusions, which are left for those who may read it to provide for themselves [53].

The scenario presented in this case is representative of the era of unrestricted resuscitation. All that is exceptional is that the patient, as a physician, understood both the nature of the relentless resuscitation which awaited him and its ultimate futility. Understanding this, he asked the staff (orally and in writing) not to resuscitate him – in effect, requesting a DNR order. Like many requests made ahead of their time, this one would not be honored. The DNR order had yet to be invented and in the absence of an accepted institutional mechanism for preventing the resuscitation process, the resuscitation team evidently felt obligated to resuscitate. And so, the patient's "wish notwithstanding," they resuscitated him five more times.

Civil Disobedience and the Legitimation of DNR Orders

By the 1970s a consensus was formed within the medical community, that there had to be limits placed on automatic reflexive resuscitation. More often than not, the successes of CPR were transient. One could "successfully" resuscitate a patient six times within a fortnight and achieve little more than a temporary restoration of cardiopulmonary function which did not, and (as in the case considered above) could not, alter the imminent terminal outcome of a patient's illness. In such cases resuscitation merely prolonged dying. So clinicians came to regard these cases as "medically futile," not because CPR was ineffective in restoring cardiopulmonary function, but because it could not reverse the course of the illness sufficiently to allow the patient to leave either the ward or the hospital alive and conscious.

As experience with "medically futile" CPR increased, as nurses, interns, residents, and attending physicians came to understand the brutal effects of unrestricted futile CPR on their patients, it became increasingly common for those most directly involved in patient care, the nurses and interns, to refuse to call "codes" when they believed resuscitation to be medically futile. They, in effect, engaged in a passive form of "civil disobedience," putting themselves at personal risk (not only of reprimand, but of legal sanctions) by refusing to obey authority for reasons of conscience. Acts of civil disobedience with respect to futile CPR moved up the hierarchical chain of hospital command and increasingly became a collaborative effort: when codes were called for patients for whom CPR was believed to be medically futile, entire resuscitation teams responded too *slowly* to be effective; alternatively they would respond, but merely made a *show* of going through the motions of CPR, without actually attempting to resuscitate the patient. Collaborative civil disobedience in cases of medically futile CPR became so commonplace in hospitals that a new set of terms entered into everyday clinical discourse: "slow code," "show-code," and "chemical code" (a form of show-code in which drugs are administered without chest compressions, defibrillation, or other physical interventions – even though drugs alone will not suffice to resuscitate the patient).

The pervasiveness of slow and show-coding did not go unnoticed by those in positions of institutional authority. Since they were sympathetic with the moral grounds on which nurses and physicians refused to initiate medically futile CPR, their eminently reasonable response was to legitimate slow codes at the institutional level, developing procedures for formally issuing an order not to code a patient, or, as they came to be called, a "no-code" order. Standards for issuing or documenting no-code orders varied from institution to institution: at some institutions no-code orders were entirely oral, at others they were indicated in the medical record by covert devices such as purple dots, or cryptic initials (e. g., "OBP," which is said to be an acronym for "on the banana peel" which, in hospital corridor jargon, means "slipping away" or terminally ill). The most common method of writing a no-code order, however, was simply to write "DNR" or "Do Not Resuscitate," in the patient's chart. In 1974, the National Conference Steering Committee of the American Heart Association and the National Academy of Sciences issued formal guidelines through the American Medical Association stating that "CPR is not indicated in certain situations, such as in cases of terminal irreversible illness where death is not unexpected" [35]. As they came to be legitimated by pronouncements such as this, the no code orders symbolized by the initials 'DNR' evolved into formal "DNR orders"; that is, orders written in the medical chart *in advance of any arrest*, instructing the staff *not* to resuscitate patients so designated.

It is evident from the first published policies [54] that the legitimation of the slow code as a DNR order affected more than the method of recording the no-code decision. Legitimation transformed the very nature of the decision. Show and slow-codes were spontaneous staff decisions, typically made at the moment of an arrest, and executed immediately. They were either undocumented, or duplicitously documented in the medical record, and so not subject to the normal mechanisms of medical accountability. No-code orders, while often documented, were usually entered without an accompanying rationale. DNR orders, in contrast, are formal decisions, made in advance of an arrest, by physicians anticipating an emergency; they are documented in the medical record, along with their rationale, and are subject to the normal canons of accountability. Most importantly, because DNR orders are issued in advance of the event, they allow, as slow and show-codes do not, time for consultation and discussion. With the advent of the DNR order it became possible for the medical staff to discuss the DNR decision with each other formally – and it also became practical to include the patient and/or the patient's family in the discussion.

On August 12, 1976, the *New England Journal of Medicine* placed its imprimatur on formal policies regulating written DNR orders, endorsing them on its editorial pages and publishing descriptions of the DNR policies and practices at Beth Israel Hospital [44] and the Massachusetts General Hospital [27], two teaching hospitals associated with Harvard Medical School. The process of legitimating DNR orders continued during the 1980s as many state medical societies – including the New York Medical Society [32] – endorsed them; they were also validated in reports issued by such major bioethical policy-making bodies as the President's Commission [40], and the Hastings Center [15]. DNR policies ultimately came to be regarded as a moral requisite of institutional practice and so effective January 1, 1988, the JCAHO required all health care organizations to develop DNR policies as a condition of their accreditation.

THE PROBLEM OF LEGALIZING SURROGACY IN NEW YORK

In 1987, therefore, DNR orders were accepted practice in American hospitals, including those in New York State. Why, then, did the New York State Legislature pass a law regulating DNR orders? They were prompted to act by a report of the New York State Task Force on Life and the Law. To appreciate, why the Task Force itself was motivated to act consider again the case of the physician with end-stage cancer discussed above. A DNR order for such a patient could be justified on two grounds: first, the patient had requested not to be resuscitated; second, resuscitation was "medically futile."

The first ground for writing a DNR order, in effect, recognizes the patient's right to refuse treatment – a right which was upheld by the U. S. Supreme Court in *Cruzan* in 1990 [12]. Although the theoretical right to refuse CPR was considered morally and legally unproblematic in the 1980s [58], some practical difficulties reamined unresolved. The nub of the practical problem was that DNR orders tend to be considered *only* when patients are so compromised by their illness that they are unable to speak for themselves [7]. Recognizing a *patient's* right to refuse CPR, therefore, will not resolve the practical problem of actually initiating DNR orders in a medical context, because patients themselves are seldom in a condition to be consulted about their wishes concerning the use of cardiopulmonary resuscitation.

One widely accepted solution to this impasse is to deed the right to act as surrogate to a close family member – who is likely to share the patient's values and may well know the patient's wishes about cardiopulmonary resuscitation. Policies empowering family members to act as surrogates in DNR decisionmaking had been endorsed by the President's Commission [40] and by the Hastings Center [15]. Unlike most other jurisdictions, however, New York's Court of Appeals, the State's highest court, held that family members may not act as surrogates for incompetent patients unless these patients had provided "clear and convincing evidence" of their wishes ([28], [30]). The Court explained its limitation by noting that families may have values and interests which conflict with those of the incapacitated patient. The upshot was that family members could act as surrogates in decisions involving life-sustaining interventions (such as CPR) only if they were simply transmitting the known wishes of the patient – a conception of "surrogacy" so narrow that one might question whether the court really permitted families to act as surrogates. The practical import of this decision was that, since few incapacitated patients had the foresight to provide their families with the type of evidence the Court required, most New York families found themselves legally powerless to request a DNR order.

Since the requests of the family seldom provided physicians with a legally valid justification for writing a DNR order for an incapacitated patient, physicians were left with little legal choice except to forego writing DNR orders altogether – or to write DNR orders on the basis of medical futility. To make matters worse, however, the New York Medical Society had endorsed *only* consent-based DNR orders. New York's Court of Appeals, moreover, had never explicitly ruled on the legality of DNR orders written on the basis of medical futility and had explicitly opted *not* to broaden its rulings on surrogate consent, nor to comment on medically futile CPR, declaring that "unlike the legislature. . . courts are. . . not empowered to change laws" [30].

The legal situation in New York prior to the DNR law, therefore, was that physicians writing DNR orders were at risk of legal prosecution, even in contexts where CPR was medically futile, and even when they had the consent of the patient's family, unless they also had "clear and convincing evidence" (which is to say, evidence over and above the testimony of the family) that a patient refused resuscitation. Since physicians seldom had such evidence, the practical import of the legal situation was to minimize formal written DNR orders. Testimony was given to the 1983 President's Commission that "Few DNR orders are being written for incompetent patients in New York State at present, largely because district attorneys state that they consider such orders to be illegal and subject to prosecution" ([40], footnote 31, p. 239).

THE NEW YORK TASK FORCE ON LIFE AND THE LAW'S REPORT ON DNR

The Court of Appeals had as much as invited the Legislature to remedy the situation. Yet, as Martin Strosberg observes (in the previous chapter), it is one thing to have a legislative need, and quite another to place this need on the legislative agenda. Despite the practical importance of the DNR issue to nurses, physicians, and their patients, a subject so obscure and complicated is not likely to pique the interest of a legislative committee. Headlines, however, tend to catch a legislator's eye. In 1982 and 1983, media attention focused on a Queens County grand jury investigation of certain New York hospitals which surreptitiously implemented futility-based DNR orders by placing purple dots on patients' medical records [41]. The *New York Times* headlined: "Hospital Is Investigated On Life-Support Policy" [26], followed by "Hospitals Seek Rules on Withholding Support" [50]. Less circumspectly, *Newsweek* reported that writing a futility-based DNR order was a "Crime of Compassion" [16]. By spotlighting the furtive mechanisms to which New York physicians had been driven to cope with the dubious legality of writing DNR orders under New York law, these news stories presented the need for legal reform in graphic terms. In 1985, the subject of DNR orders was officially placed on the legislative agenda when Governor Mario Cuomo set up a special advisory task force, the New York State Task Force on Life and the Law, and charged it with developing legislation to resolve the problem.

The twenty-six member Task Force was chaired by a physician, David Axelrod, State Health Commissioner; its Executive Director and its Counsel were two lawyers, Tracy Miller and Robert Swidler. Miller and Swidler report that after conducting an investigation:

> The Task Force concluded that concerns about the legality of DNR orders led to dual untenable practices: (1) the issuance of DNR orders covertly, without the consent of the patient or the patient's family, and (2) the failure to issue DNR orders when medically appropriate ([33], p. 31).

Notably absent from this list of concerns is the right of physicians to issue a DNR orders on the grounds of futility.

THE DNR LAW AND THE BIOETHICAL CONSENSUS

In declining to legitimate futility-based DNR orders, the New York Task Force was voicing the consensus of the bioethical and legal communities, which had been articulated by the 1983 President's Commission ([33], p. 245) and was later echoed in the 1987 Hastings Center *Guidelines*. Thus both the statute proposed by the Task Force, and the Hastings Center *Guidelines*, concur with the following findings of the President's Commission with respect to DNR orders:

19. A presumption favoring resuscitation of hospitalized patients in the event of unexpected cardiac arrest is justified.
20. A competent and informed patient or an incompetent patient's surrogate is entitled to decide with the attending physician that an order against resuscitation should be written in the chart. When cardiac arrest is likely, a patient (or a surrogate) should usually be informed and offered the chance to decide for or against resuscitation.
21. Physicians have a duty to assess for each hospitalized patient whether resuscitation is likely, on balance, to benefit the patient. . . . When a patient will not benefit. . . a decision not to resuscitate, with the consent of the patient, is justified. When a physician's assessment conflicts with a competent patient's decision. . . the physician must follow the patient's decision or transfer responsibility for that patient to another physician ([40], p. 8–9).

Moreover, the argumentative strategies of the three documents are remarkably similar. All three assert a presumption favoring CPR (or consent to CPR) and then proceed to state the *limits* of that presumption, which is to say that they stipulate the contexts in which the presumption favoring CPR may be overridden, so that physicians may issue a DNR order. As in President's Commission Finding 20, all three documents state that the primary ground for a DNR order is the consent of the patient (DNR law, §2964, Hastings A. II.4, pp. 26–27) or, if the patient is incapacitated, consent of a surrogate (DNR law §2965, Hastings A. II.4 c p. 27). All three documents consider the possibility of disagreement between physician and patient and hold, as stated in Finding 21, that "the physician must follow the patient's decision." Thus the Hastings *Guidelines* state that the "patient is the ultimate judge of the benefits and burdens of life-sustaining treatment" and that "if [he or she] choose[s] to forego [life-sustaining] treatment. . . that choice should be honored" (A. II.4a, pp. 26–27). In all three documents patient/surrogate consent to the DNR order functions as the mechanism enforcing physician compliance with patient/surrogate choice.

It is important to appreciate, however, that there are subtle but important differences between the way bioethical and legal positions are articulated in the President's Commission's findings and in the other two documents. Finding 19 is echoed in DNR law §2962.1 and Hastings Center *Guidelines* B.II.9c – each of which state a presumption in favor of CPR. The *Guidelines*, however, state the presumption straightforwardly:

> B.II.9 (c) Presumption in favor of providing CPR. Any patient without a DNR order should receive CPR in the event of a cardiac or respiratory arrest ([15], p. 51).

The Task Force, in contrast, states a presumption, not to CPR, but to *consent* to CPR.

> §2962.1 Every person admitted to a hospital shall be presumed to consent to the administration of cardiopulmonary resuscitation in the event of cardiac or respiratory arrest.

We call the reader's attention to this seemingly slight difference to note the variation in the consensus, and because the idea of "presumption to consent" was to play a significant role in the technical debates that were to unfold in New York.

The DNR law appears to be somewhat less restrictive than the President's Commission's *Report* and the Hastings *Guidelines* because it allows a "therapeutic exception" to the consent requirement. The law states that physicians may exercise this exception in circumstances in which the attending physician determines that "discussion of CPR with a patient who has capacity" would "injure" a patient (§2964.3). Appearances are deceptive here, for as Task Force members Richard Concannon and Charles Tobin argue in their Minority Report (see Appendix), New York Public Health Law contains a very broad therapeutic exception. The wording of the DNR law, however, "virtually eliminates the therapeutic exception in the DNR context" ([55], p. 67); in fact, standards set for therapeutic privilege in the DNR law were so stringent, that as the Minority Report predicted, it became impractical for physicians to exercise this privilege in the case of DNR consent. Thus what might appear to be liberality in the DNR law, is just the opposite; it is an exercise in narrowing physicians' options in the context of DNR, which again brings the DNR law into close alignment with its sister documents, the President's Commission's *Report* and the Hastings *Guidelines*.

On the specific issue of medical futility, the DNR law parallels the President's Commission in empowering "uncontroversial" futility-based DNR orders, but only for patients lacking a surrogate, and only with the proviso that they have the written concurrence of a second attending physician. The Hastings *Guidelines* eliminate futility-based DNR orders written in advance of the event altogether, envisioning a different mechanism for handling patients lacking surrogates. They recommend the formation of a hospital surrogacy committee which will provide surrogate decisions for surrogateless patients.

In one important respect, however, the Hastings *Guidelines* are more permissive than prior bioethical policy. They permit physicians to "call off" resuscitation, if, at the time of the arrest, the physician believes that resuscitation will prove to be medically futile: "At the time of. . . an arrest, the health care professional may call off the resuscitation if the effort clearly cannot restore cardiac and respiratory function" (II.B.9 (C), p. 51). This provision, while seemingly reasonable – because it does not require physicians to resuscitate corpses when there is no valid consent to non-resuscitation – has the curious effect of reinstituting "no coding." For even if a physician knows, in advance of an arrest, that resuscitation will be futile, the physician must still maintain the charade of honoring patient autonomy until the moment of arrest – at that point, however, the physician may rescind the prior commitment. Thus, like no- and slow-coding, futility-based "calling off" CPR makes the DNR decision physician-centered and allows it to be made at the moment of crisis, rather than in advance. Even its proponents recognize its potential for abuse and so the Hastings *Guidelines* warn "Health care professionals . . . [to be] vigilant not to allow this exception to justify failure to discuss the issues with the patient or the surrogate in advance" ([15], p. 51).

These few differences having been noted, it is important to appreciate that the New York DNR law is not an isolated piece of legislation; it is the legal codification of bioethical thought on DNR orders, as reflected in the President's Commission's *Report* and the Hastings Center *Guidelines*. As two physicians, McClung and Kamer, observe in an article in the *New England Journal of Medicine*:

> From a clinical perspective there is very little difference between the procedures outlined in the New York State law and those previously described in the medical literature. Despite complaints of many New York physicians that the requirements are cumbersome, they represent little more than the legislative codification of recommended policy, past and present ([31], p. 279).

Implicit in McClung and Kamer's statement appears the presumption that since the DNR law simply codifies the bioethical and legal consensus – past and present – New York physicians have no legitimate grounds for complaint.

THE FUTILITY CONTROVERSY

If the DNR law merely codified policies endorsed by the New York State Medical Society, the President's Commission, and the Hastings Center, if it was merely "the legislative codification of recommended policy, past and present," why did New York physicians protest against it so vociferously? What was there to protest?

Consider once more the case of the physician dying of cancer in the era of unrestricted resuscitation. As we noted earlier, there are not one, but two, rationales for a DNR order in this case: A physician could issue a DNR order on the grounds that the patient requested one; alternatively, an order might be issued on the grounds that CPR was medically futile (recall that despite six "successful" resuscitations and three weeks lingering in a decerebrate state, the patient died without recovering consciousness). The President's Commission, the New York DNR Law and the Hastings Center all legitimate consent-based DNR orders, but they provide little recognition for futility-based DNR orders.

Yet many medical organizations typically treat futility-based DNR orders on a par with consent-based orders. Although in 1987, the AMA changed its position to that of the President's Commission, its 1974 [35], and 1980 [36], guidelines on CPR ruled that resuscitation is inappropriate in situations where it is medically futile. Many leading acute care hospitals, including Massachusetts General Hospital [27] and Pittsburgh Presbyterian Hospital [14], explicitly recognize medical futility as grounds for writing a DNR order. Indeed, a 1988 survey conducted for the JCAHO indicates that DNR policies recognizing medical futility as the basis for DNR orders were probably more common than policies recognizing consent as a rationale for DNR orders [25]. The survey found that while 85% of acute care hospitals had policies regulating DNR orders, only 40% of hospitals required discussion of DNR orders with patients, and only 28% required evidence of informed consent for a DNR order.

It is easy to appreciate why futility-based DNR orders should be considered legitimate. In effect, this view of DNR orders merely normalizes the CPR/DNR decision, treating it in the same manner as decisions about other medical interventions. Normally, physicians are not obligated to offer patients medically useless interventions, nor need they seek consent not to offer a useless or futile intervention. On the contrary, offering patients interventions known to be useless is typically considered inappropriate; administering interventions known to be futile is unprofessional; billing patients for interventions known to be futile is usually considered fraud. To the extent that CPR is comparable to other interventions, therefore, it would appear improper for physicians to offer medically futile CPR to patients, or to inflict it upon them – even at their request. From this point of view, it is unnecessary to seek the patient's consent to withhold medically futile CPR. Of course, in cases where CPR was potentially effective, the only grounds for writing a DNR order would be the request of the patient or the patient's surrogate. But insofar as CPR is treated on a par with other potentially life-saving medical interventions, it would seem that it could be withheld if the physician believes the intervention to be medically futile.

The apparently straightforward logic of this analysis tends to be obscured by the automatic calling of CPR codes and the concomitantly "inverted" nature of consent in DNR orders. In most cases, a physician refrains from offering a useless treatment simply by remaining silent. In the case of CPR, however, refraining from treatment is more complex; for unless a physician voices or writes an explicit order prohibiting it, CPR will be administered automatically. The only way to refrain from offering medically futile CPR is to write or voice a DNR order. And therein lies the source of moral controversy. For by issuing a DNR order, the physician *appears* to be performing the sort of action which normally requires consent. But to treat DNR orders – which are really orders *not* to intervene – as if they were orders initiating interventions is to *invert* the consent process; insofar as consent is required it ought to be required for CPR, not for DNR ([56], [4], [57]).

BIOETHICAL RATIONALES FOR DELEGITIMATING MEDICAL FUTILITY AS THE BASIS OF DNR ORDERS

The President's Commission

Arguments about the inverted nature of the DNR order and the concomitant irrelevance of consent to futility-based DNR orders were presented to the President's Commission by the attorney representing the National Institutes of Health (NIH).

> Consent of the patient [to DNR orders] is irrelevant because we are dealing with a situation in which there is no course of treatment for which to secure consent. This is different from the case in which there is a medically accepted course of treatment, but the patient does not wish to be subjected to this care ([40], p. 241).

Yet – and herein lies the crux of the conflict played out in New York – the President's Commission expressly rejected this argument.

> The Commission finds it necessary for the patient or surrogate to have given valid consent to any plan of treatment whether involving omissions or actions, and rejects this claim ([40], p. 241).

Both the NIH's argument, and the President's Commission's reply, are in a footnote to the President's Commission's report, not in the text itself. Given the prevalence of futility-based DNR orders, one might wonder why an issue of such potential consequence was disposed of with a few sentences in a footnote? Perhaps the Commission believed that, as a policy recommending body, its primary objective was only to develop the rationale underlying policies it actually proposed; perhaps they thought it impolitic to remind the medical establishment, at the NIH, at Massachusetts General, at Pittsburgh Presbyterian and other major teaching hospitals, and at the AMA that, in the Commission's view, their present DNR policies were morally deficient. Whether politics, practicality, or prudence motivated the Commission, in point of fact – with one significant exception – scant space is spent in the body of the Commission's Report reproving medical practices or arguing over rejected alternatives.

The significant exception is the entire second chapter of their report, in which they reject as useless four "traditional moral distinctions, including the distinction between "acting and omitting to act" ([40], pp. 60–90, 126–131). In arguing against the act-omission distinction, the Commission draws on an argument developed by the philosopher James Rachels [45], which purports to demonstrate that nothing of moral consequence can rest on a distinction between *actions* and *inactions*. Although, as the Commission duly notes, Rachels' argument was not (and is not) universally accepted by bioethicists or philosophers (the Commission cites Tom Beauchamp's critique [5]), incorporating this fashionable argument into the body of the text appeared harmless, since it really served to make the eminently sound point that public bioethical policy should not rest on subtle rhetorical distinctions.

Notice that the President's Commission construes Rachels' argument about the moral equivalence of *actions* and *inactions* in terms of *actions* and *omissions*. *Omissions*, however, are subtly different from *inactions*. The distinction between the two is that, unlike an *inaction*, an *omission* presupposes that something normal or appropriate has *not* been done. Consider the following trivial example. It is legitimate for us to complain of an *omission* if our waiter does not bring us cream or sugar for our coffee. But we cannot complain about an *omission* if our waiter fails to bring salt or Tabasco for our coffee (unless, of course, we deliberately requested salt or Tabasco). The difference between the cases is that cream and sugar are appropriate or normal condiments for coffee, while salt and Tabasco are not. Thus, as the example illustrates, talk of *omissions* presupposes that certain actions left undone (in this case, bringing cream and sugar with coffee) are accepted as normal or appropriate; *inactions*, in contrast, do not presuppose the appropriateness of actions not done.

In rebutting the contention that, since no treatment is contemplated, consent is not required for a DNR order, the President's Commission draws on Rachels' theory that *actions* and *inactions* are morally equivalent, replying that "valid consent to any plan of treatment [is necessary] whether involving omissions or actions." Notice again that in this reply they follow their usual practice, characterizing *not acting* as an "omission." In the context of this particular argument, however, the subtle distinction between the two terms makes an important difference. By calling a decision not to administer CPR an *omission*, the Commission presupposes that (just as cream and sugar are normally appropriate to coffee) CPR is normal and appropriate in an arrest. Yet the appropriateness of CPR in arrests – particularly in cases where it is believed to be medically futile – is precisely the question at issue. Thus by using the term 'omission' and thereby presupposing the appropriateness of CPR, the Commission presupposes the answer to the very question being debated – which, to use the language of logicians, is to say that the Commission's rebuttal is invalid because it commits the logical fallacy of begging the question.

In fairness to the Commission's intent, it is best to treat the term 'omission' as a slip of the pen (or word processor). What the Commission appears to intend in their rebuttal is an application of Rachels' theory of the moral equivalence of *actions* and *inactions* to the context of consent. Thus their point would seem to be that a patient or surrogate ought to give valid consent to any plan of treatment whether it involves an action (for example, administering CPR) or an inaction (for example, not administering CPR).

So stated, however, the theory of consent urged by the Commission in its rebuttal is quite radical because it requires that actions and inactions be treated symmetrically with respect to consent. On this view, wherever we currently require consent for an action, we should also require consent if we do *not* perform the action. Consent, it should be recalled, is a pervasive feature of our moral life: it differentiates entry from trespass, fornication from rape, and borrowing from theft. Symmetry between actions and inactions in matters of consent would thus appear to generate an ethic in which people must seek consent *not* to enter, *not* to fornicate, and *not* to borrow. To take a simple example, a theory of consent to inactions would appear to require the editors of this volume to seek consent from authors whose papers we did *not* publish. Whatever merits such a theory of consent may or may not have, the point we wish to emphasize is that it constitutes a radical departure from the view of consent we commonly use in life and in the law.

It is the latter point that we wish to underscore in telling these tangled tales of semantics and moral logic. The technical details that dog this discussion, as they do any analysis of the DNR debate, should not obscure the point that the President's Commission relegated direct discussion of its reasons for rejecting the legitimacy of the most common form of DNR order, futility-based DNR orders, to a footnote; that the grounds for rejection they gave in that note either begged the question or were based on an abstruse, philosophically controversial theory that would require a radical reconceptualization, not only of physicians' own understanding of what they were doing when they write DNR orders on grounds of futility, but of our ordinary sense of when it is morally or legally appropriate to seek consent. Thus the Commission was urging a major change in medical practice on the basis of abstruse and uncertain logic, articulated only in a footnote.

The New York State Task Force

The New York State Task Force had the opportunity to rethink the issue anew. Curiously, they followed the precedent set by the President's Commission and they too relegated discussion of futility-based DNR orders to a footnote. That footnote was attached to a text discussing the possibility of allowing a therapeutic exception. We begin our analysis by considering the text.

As we remarked earlier, New York Public Health law contains a generous therapeutic exception, permitting physicians to eschew the obligation of seeking consent directly from a patient, if they believe that the discussion would be psychologically painful to the patient. The Task Force argued – over the forceful objections of lawyers Concannon and Tobin – that in the specific case of DNR, the therapeutic exception was too broad.

> Where the decision relates to the withholding of life-saving treatment, such as CPR, the rationale for a therapeutic exception is strained; a patient is spared the harm of a discussion about CPR and is thereby denied the right to insist upon or refuse its application. * Moreover, physician reluctance to discuss resuscitation with patients heightens concern about the exception. Unless workable limits be established, the

> exception will swallow the rule and deny persons with capacity the right to decide whether or not they will be resuscitated in the event of cardiopulmonary arrest ([55], p. 26).

It is in a footnote to this discussion that the Task Force deals with both the question of futility-based DNR orders and the argument that consent for such orders is unnecessary because, as orders not to treat, there is no treatment for which consent is requisite.

> [*] Since issuance of a DNR order is a decision not to provide treatment, the notion of an exception to the consent requirement is arguably misapplied; consent is not ordinarily required for non-treatment. However, because CPR is applied in emergency circumstances and consent to treatment for emergency care is ordinarily presumed, the requirement of consent to withhold CPR is entirely consistent with medical practice and principles. See. . . . President's Commission, p. 241, n. 39 ([55], n.17, p. 62).

As the reader might suspect, the President's Commission n.39 is the very footnote analyzed earlier. Observe, however, that although the Task Force cites the Commission's arguments, they do not avail themselves of them. Instead they proffer the quite different, rather legalistic argument that since consent is *presumed* for CPR in the emergency context, requiring "consent to withhold CPR is entirely consistent with medical practice and principles." And, indeed, as we saw earlier, in §2962.1 the Task Force stipulates that "Every person. . . shall be presumed to consent to administration of cardiopulmonary resuscitation." Thus what the footnote indicates is that the Task Force regards the presumption of consent as grounds for rebutting the argument that consent for DNR is irrelevant and that it also regards it as the basis of the patient's "right to decide whether or not he or she will be resuscitated in the event of cardiopulmonary arrest" (which it asserts in the text footnoted).

How, one wonders, can a presumption of patient consent to CPR justify this rebuttal and ground a right to decide about resuscitation? Unfortunately, the Task Force itself provides no further clarification on this point – offering even less of an argument-sketch than the Commission. A similar analysis, however, emerges in a more full-blown form in the later Hastings Center *Guidelines*.

The Hastings Guidelines

The *Guidelines* treatment of futility differs from that in the President's Commission and the Task Force reports: whereas there is not even an entry under the heading "futility" in the index to the President's Commission's *Report*, and whereas there is no direct discussion of futility by the Task Force, the *Guidelines* explicitly hold that clinicians are under no obligation to administer treatments which they believe to be futile, even if expressly requested by the patient.

> II.8 (c) Futility. In the event that the patient or surrogate requests a treatment that the responsible health care professional regards as clearly futile in achieving its physiological objective and so provides no physiological benefit to the patient, the professional has no obligation to provide it. However, the health care professional's value judgment that although a treatment will produce physiological benefit, the benefit is not sufficient to warrant the treatment, should not be used as a basis for determining a treatment to be futile ([15], p. 32).

Since in II.8 the *Guidelines* expressly state that "the professional has [no] obligation to provide" treatments which are "clearly futile," even if "the patient or surrogate requests" them, one would anticipate that the *Guidelines* would legitimate futility-based DNR orders. And, indeed, they do not require the actual administration of futile CPR *at the time of an arrest* (II.B.9 C)). Yet, as we observed earlier, the *Guidelines* nonetheless require patient or surrogate consent for DNR orders written *in advance of a patient's arrest* – even in cases in which CPR is predictably futile.

The Hastings *Guidelines* thus treat the DNR order as exceptional, exempting it even from the guidelines governing (other) futile interventions: CPR, uniquely, may be required by patients and surrogates, even in those cases when physicians predict that CPR will be futile. What grounds are offered for this singular exemption of the CPR/DNR decision from the general guidelines on futile treatment? None that are explicitly stated. Yet there seems to be a coherent theory underlying the positions taken in the *Guidelines*. The position makes sense if one reads it as predicated upon a hypothetical agreement between practitioners and patients on which the former agree to provide, and the latter to receive CPR, whenever the patient is in cardiopulmonary arrest. This agreement generates a presumptive right to CPR and is thus compatible with the position taken in the *Guidelines* that: "Any patient without a DNR order should receive CPR in the event of an arrest" ([15], p. 51).

More importantly, if such an agreement is presumed, the distinction offered in the *Guidelines* between decisions not to initiate CPR *in advance of an arrest*, and decisions made *at the moment of an arrest* appears to be reasonable. What is crucial here is the patient is presumed to have a right to CPR; and such a right can only be waived with the permission of the patient, or a surrogate. Thus, any issuance of a DNR order *in advance of an arrest* would require the consent of either the patient or a surrogate. The *Guidelines* state, however, that as circumstances change, so does the validity of consent, presumed or actual: "A patient's or surrogate's consent to initial resuscitation should not be presumed to constitute consent to further resuscitations" ([15]. pp. 48–49). So the *Guidelines* assert, quite reasonably, that if changes occur, "the patient, or surrogate should have an[other] opportunity to consent to or refuse CPR" ([15], p. 51). It follows therefore that although, normally, *at the moment of arrest*, no consent would be needed to initiate CPR (since consent would be presumed to have been given), if circumstances change at the moment of the arrest – so that CPR is obviously futile – the conditions for the original consent no longer apply. But *at the moment of arrest* there is no opportunity to consult the patient, or a surrogate, and so the physician may properly do that which is in the best interests of the patient – which is not to administer futile CPR.

The theory of presumed consent sketched above provides a coherent, even an elegant explanation of the Hastings Center *Guidelines*, including the different treatment accorded futility *in advance* of an arrest and *at the time* of an arrest. But this theory is *not* explicitly stated in the *Guidelines*. Like the President's Commission and the Task Force before them, the Hastings *Guidelines* delegitimate the most prevalent form of DNR order, those based on futility, *without* a clearly stated public rationale. And – again following in the precedent set by the President's Commission – the implicit semi-articulated rationale involves abstruse, innovative theory which is *not* widely accepted by courts, nor is it endorsed by any widespread consensus among legal scholars – as is evident from the critique of the theory offered by lawyers George Annas and Jane Greenlaw (Section Two). Worse yet, the theory of presumed consent never forthrightly addresses the basic issue of "consent" to a futile intervention. Can a patient's request for a futile intervention legitimate that intervention? According to the *Guidelines*, the answer is "no" – a patient's actual request for, or actual consent to, a futile treatment does not generate a right to a futile treatment. How, then, is it possible, for the patient's *hypothetical* consent to a futile treatment to generate such a right? How can a hypothetical agreement confer more rights on a patient than it would were it an actual agreement? It cannot and does not. We suspect that had the rationale for exceptionalism been articulated, the drafters of the *Guidelines* would have appreciated and dealt with this inconsistency. Yet, like the President's Commission and the Task Force, those drafting the Hastings *Guidelines* chose not to articulate the abstruse arguments underlying their position fully – and while this may have been politic, it meant that they could not see the inconsistencies inherent in their delegitimation of futility-based DNR orders. It also meant, to reiterate our basic point, that they provided clinicians with no coherent explanation of why futility-based DNR orders were being delegitimated.

THE ARGUMENT FROM ENFORCEMENT

There may be a measure of tact and political realism in the unwillingness to articulate arguments justifying the delegitimation of DNR orders, for the most potent argument for delegitimation was initially unspoken for precisely these reasons. As the last line in the passage from the *Guidelines* makes clear, any leeway granted physicians on grounds of futility potentiates paternalistic abuse. Thus the unvoiced reason for the reluctance to legitimate futility-based DNR orders may have less to do with abstruse theories about presumed consent than with practical concerns that a futility exemption will allow physicians to circumvent the CPR/DNR discussion.

The fears were voiced publicly as the debate over the New York DNR law heated up. The Task Force Chairman, Dr. David Axelrod, stated frankly at the Union College Conference (Section Two) that the Task Force was mindful of the literature documenting the extraordinary infrequency with which physicians discuss the CPR/DNR decision with their patients [7], and its intent was to draft a law that spoke to this issue by enforcing patient-physician discussion of the DNR decision. Director Tracy Miller fills in the details of the Task Force's ratiocinations, pointing out that it feared that permitting loopholes in patient/surrogate consent requirements would undercut the reformist objective of promoting physician-patient/surrogate discussion of the CPR/DNR decision.

> An exception to informed consent discussions in cases of medical futility will swallow the rule at a time when physicians are still reluctant to speak with patients about resuscitation. As long as that reluctance remains prevalent, any exception on therapeutic or futility grounds is almost certain to be an escape hatch for physicians seeking to avoid conversations they have never understood as integral to the obligation to care for dying patients ([33], p. 251).

Consequently, the law the Task Force proposed and the Legislature enacted allowed no exemption to the requirement of patient/surrogate consent to DNR orders – except in those cases in which no surrogate was reasonably available. Whatever abstruse theories they may have proffered for declining to legitimate futility-based DNR orders, they admit that their decision was also motivated by eminently practical concerns about enforcement.

THE PROBLEM OF LEGISLATING MORALITY

In seeking to force physicians to engage in "conversations they have never understood as integral to the[ir] obligation[s]," the Task Force appears to be attempting to *legislate medical morality*. The expression "legislating morality" means something quite specific in the philosophy of law. It does not refer to the ordinary case in which pervasively shared values and norms are formally codified for purposes of adjudication and enforcement. A law is held to legislate morality only in situations in which a significant minority (or even a majority) of those affected by the law *reject* the morality of the norms (or the interpretation of the norms) formalized in the law. These laws are said to legislate morality because, to those who reject the moral norms codified, obedience to the law is not a matter of conscience, but of legal coercion. Perhaps the most notorious example of the legislation of morality is the nineteenth amendment, better known as "Prohibition." Other examples are laws prohibiting the sale of pornography, or the non-medicinal use of such psychoactive drugs as cocaine, heroin and marijuana. What intrigues scholars about the legislation of morality is the presumption that the laws in question enforce a particular vision of the good as authoritative, even though a significant portion of the public either fails to recognize this authoritative morality, or appears to lack the will to act on this recognition. (The prohibition of alcohol consumption in the 1920s, for example, presumed the moral superiority of abstinence while recognizing that substantial portions of the public either did not accept, or would not act upon, an ethic of abstinence.) What is intriguing here is that public dissent and/or disobedience is not seen as evidence against the authoritativeness of the ethic in question. The vision of the good is thus taken as unquestionably authoritative – even though the theoretical grounding for such unquestionable authority has eluded secular philosophers.

On a more practical level, the legislation of morality is intriguing because it attempts to enforce a law without the assistance of conscience (since those disobeying the law will not feel guilt for performing actions they do not regard as immoral), relying entirely on coercion to ensure compliance. Enforcement which relies entirely on coercive threats, however, becomes problematic whenever the advantages of non-compliance outweigh those of compliance, for those who do not share the moral norms underlying these laws will then have little reason to obey them. (It is worth recalling that prohibition was ultimately repealed as unenforceable and that, despite numerous Presidential declarations of war against drug use, the use of psychoactive drugs has not been eliminated.)

Many scholars believe that the answer to the problem of legislating morality lies in respecting a principle first articulated by John Stuart Mill in *On Liberty* (1880).

> The object of this Essay is to assert one very simple principle. . . That principle is that the sole end for which mankind are warranted, individually or collectively, in interfering with the liberty of action of any of their number, is self-protection. That the only purpose for which power can be rightfully exercised over any member of a civilized community, against his will, is to prevent harm to others. His own good, either physical or moral, is not sufficient warrant. He can not rightfully be held to do or forbear because it will be better for him to do so, because it will make him happier, because in the opinion of others, to do so would be wise or even right ([6], pp. 155-156).

In stating his principle, Mill ingeniously engages the consensus pervasive in society and shared (at the level of theory) by almost all philosophers that harm to others is morally unjustifiable. What this means, in practical terms, is that, even though philosophers are unable to determine authoritatively whether an ethic of abstinence is morally preferable to an ethic of indulgence, there is an overwhelming social and philosophical consensus that it is wrong to harm others. Laws drawing on that consensus – for example, laws prohibiting piloting a passenger plane or train while under the influence of drink or drugs – will thus be readily enforceable by conscience, cued and reinforced by the pervasive societal consensus supporting the wrongfulness of harming others. Laws enacted in violation of this principle, on the other hand (for example legislating abstinence when no harm to others is involved), are bereft of the support of conscience (and often of community) and so are merely coercively, that is weakly, enforceable.

ANTI-PATERNALISM AS THE BASIS OF BIOETHICS

The very idea that the DNR law, or any other legal codification of bioethical ideals, could be said to legislate morality might well seem absurd. Bioethics was born out of respect for Mill's principle. Indeed, the passage from *On Liberty* quoted above is taken from the first edition of Tom Beauchamp and James Childress's *Principles of Bioethics* (1979). One appeal of this influential book is the authors' often ingenious analysis of medical ethics in terms of the interrelationships and conflicts among four basic principles: autonomy, beneficence, justice, and nonmaleficence (or not doing harm). The passage from Mill is cited in Beauchamp and Childress's discussion of the principle of beneficence, where it is used to introduce the concepts of strong and weak paternalism. They characterize *strong paternalism* as the position that beneficence may justify interference in the decisions of autonomous persons (by, for example, prohibiting adults from consuming alcoholic beverages). *Weak paternalism*, in contrast, is the view that such interference is justified *only* for those incapable of acting autonomously (by, for example, prohibiting children from drinking alcoholic beverages). Articulating the position of mainstream bioethical thought, Beauchamp and Childress assert that "to the present writers it is difficult, perhaps impossible to justify strong paternalism, though many forms of weak paternalism may be justified" ([6], p. 160).

To an extraordinary extent, the anti-paternalist stance of the *Principles of Bioethics* structures the reports of the President's Commission, the Task Force, and the Hastings *Guidelines*. All three documents analyze the CPR/DNR decision in terms of a conflict between physicians acting on a principle of *beneficence* and patients seeking *self-determination* ([40], pp. 240-244; [55], pp. 9-12; [15], pp. 6-9; 18-20). All three documents reject strong physician paternalism, and the "primacy of a patient's interests in self-determination. . . warrant leaving with the patient the final authority to decide" ([40], p. 44). Perhaps the most graphic illustration of this construction of the issues is in two tables in the Commission's *Report*, which compare "Physician's Assessment" of the "benefits" of CPR with patient/surrogate "preferences" – visually presenting the issue in terms of a conflict between physician beneficence and patient preferences. Since physicians may believe that CPR may be either beneficial, non-beneficial, or of uncertain benefit, and since patients might favor, or oppose, or have no preference about CPR, this construction of the issue generates a decision matrix of nine different outcomes ([40], p. 244, p. 247). Consistent with Mill's principle, the Commission recommends that wherever the patient or surrogate has a clear preference (for or against CPR), that preference should override the physician's perception of benefit. Where patients and/or their surrogates have no clear preference, however, Mill's principle is inapplicable and so presumably the physician could decide on the basis of what is beneficial to the patient.

Table 1. Resuscitation (CPR) of Competent Patients – Physician's Assessment in Relation to Patient's Preference

Physician's Assessment	Patient Favors CPR*	No Preference	Patient Opposes CPR*
CPR Would Benefit Pat't	Try CPR	Try CPR	Do not try CPR; review decision**
Benefit of CPR Unclear	Try CPR	Try CPR	Do not try CPR
CPR Would Not Benefit Pat't	Try CPR; review decision**	Do not try CPR	Do not try CPR

* Based on an adequate understanding of the relevant information.

** Such a conflict calls for careful reexamination by both patient and physician. If neither the physician's assessment nor the patient's preference changes, then the competent patient's decision should be honored.

Table 2. Resuscitation (CPR) of Incompetent Patients – Physician's Assessment in Relation to Surrogate's Preference

Physician's Assessment	Surrogate Favors CPR*	No Preference	Surrogate Opposes CPR*
CPR Would Benefit Pat't	Try CPR	Try CPR	Try CPR until review of decision**
Benefit of CPR Unclear	Try CPR	Try CPR	Try CPR until review of decision**
CPR Would Not Benefit Pat't	Try CPR until review of decision**	Try CPR until review of decision**	Do not try CPR

* Based on an adequate understanding of the relevant information.
** Such a conflict calls for careful reexamination by both physician and surrogate.

The Commission's nine square decision matrix reverberates through the Task Force's *Report*, the Hastings *Guidelines*, and most importantly, in the structure of the New York DNR law. Thus, to return to the point being emphasized, questions concerning the appropriateness of DNR orders are consistently construed in terms of a conflict between physician beneficence and patient autonomy. As adherents to Mill's principle, bioethicists consistently resolve the conflict by favoring patient autonomy.

PATIENT PREFERENCE VERSUS PHYSIOLOGICAL FUTILITY: A CLINICAL CONCEPTION OF DNR

The New York DNR law – precisely because it is a codification of bioethical policy, past and present – conceptualizes the issues surrounding DNR orders on the standard bioethical paradigm; that is, it construes the moral conflict over DNR as between physician beneficence and patient/surrogate preference. But what if the conflict is conceptualized as arising from a different source? What if some group affected by the DNR law perceives the CPR/DNR conflict in different terms?

The arguments originally offered by the NIH, the words which erupted at the Union College Conference on the DNR law, and the terminology ultimately used by the AMA reflect a substantially different conception of the conflict. These clinical voices articulate a conception in which problems arises not because patient preferences conflict with physician beneficence, but because patient preferences conflict with physiological futility; that is, patients, fearing death, request interventions that it is physiologically futile for physicians to confer. From this perspective, the DNR law – and the bioethical policy, past and present embedded in it – appear quite differently. It is one thing for bioethicists to pass legislation defending patients against physician paternalism, and quite another to legislate futile and irrational gestures toward immortality. As George Annas remarked when he lampooned the DNR law at the Union College Conference, according to the DNR law, "In New York, patients aren't allowed to die without giving consent."

At some level it seems absurd to grant patients the right to medically futile treatment (and the Hastings *Guidelines*, as we noted earlier, concede this point). The question is when a medical intervention should be considered futile. The concept of futility is said to trace back to the myth of the daughters of Danaus, who were condemned to Hades, and set the task of drawing water from a well with a sieve [48]. The image of water slipping through a sieve is an apt metaphor for the attempt to resuscitate the physician with end-stage cancer described earlier. He was, it will be recalled, resuscitated six times in five weeks, despite the irreversibility of his underlying disease and the inability to revive him from a coma during the final fortnight. These and similar experiences inform the clinical meaning of futility. As Diana Crane found in her 1977 study of critical care clinicians [11], as Baker *et al.* found in their 1990 study of New York critical care medical and nursing directors (in Section Four, hereafter referred to as the "Union College Study"), and as the American College of Physicians (ACP) found in their survey of New York internists (also Section Four), when clinicians speak of administering "futile" CPR, they are not merely talking about CPR which will fail to restore cardiopulmonary function. For clinicians CPR can be "futile" even if it restores cardiopulmonary function, if the functioning heart and lungs fail to provide a meaningful level of existence to the person to whom they belong, especially if they merely prolong the dying process.

In contrast, non-clinicians tend to have a narrower conception of futility. They tend to conceptualize CPR as "futile" only if it fails to restore cardiopulmonary function. Not surprisingly, therefore, since the DNR law was passed by a legislature, the narrower conception of futility is expressly stipulated in the DNR statute which defines CPR as "medically futile" only if it fails to restore cardiac or respiratory function, or if the patient will suffer repeated arrests in the *short* period of time before death (§2961. 9). Applying this conception to the physician with end-stage cancer described earlier, it would seem that, except for the last resuscitation, *none* of the first five administrations of CPR would have been regarded as futile – even though they merely prolonged the dying process, and even though, in the last two weeks, the patient was in a coma.

These incompatible conceptions of futility exacerbate differences between the bioethical conception of DNR (as codified in the law) and the clinical conception. On the bioethicists' conception, a terminal month of dying in hospital is viewed as an option, properly open to the patient, even if the final two weeks are spent in coma. Insofar as CPR keeps the option open, it is not "futile" and the claim that is "futile" is merely paternalism proffered in the guise of a medical judgment. To the clinician administering it, however, CPR in such circumstances is a medically meaningless gesture, which is properly deemed "futile" because it cannot reverse the inexorably fatal income of this particular hospitalization.

CLINICAL PERCEPTIONS THAT THE DNR LAW REQUIRES ADMINISTERING FUTILE CPR

There appear to be two reasons why bioethicists opt for their narrower conception of futility. First, their experiential world is different from that of acute care clinicians – especially clinicians who work in critical care units or with cancer patients. Bioethicists are not constantly treating terminal patients; their conceptual framework is not informed by direct experience of resuscitation and of lingering dying, so they do not have an experiential basis for the conception that, for terminal patients, the outcome of resuscitation is as inexorable as the attempt to hold water in a sieve. Their narrow construction of futility is also, no doubt, a reflection of their fear of physician paternalism – which prompts them to design public policy to protect patients from their physicians.

Yet these fears are unlikely to convince physicians of the propriety of futile CPR – given the gap between the broad experientially-based conception of futility in the clinical world and the narrow conception of futility defined in the law. The American College of Physicians survey of New York internists found that 77% of internists held that DNR orders should be issued when resuscitation is "inappropriate or futile on medical grounds. . . based on clinical judgment, without obtaining consent." Testing the conception of futility involved, the survey asked those giving assent to the propriety of futility-based DNR orders whether it was appropriate to write a futility-based DNR order for a "terminal cancer patient" if the effect of resuscitation would be to "enable him to live a few days without hope of real improvement or discharge from the hospital alive." Seventy-seven percent checked the "Yes" box.

These findings parallel those of the independent Union College survey of New York critical care directors and hematologist/oncologists in which clinicians also protested against being forced to administer "futile" CPR. The basic problem is laid out in the following comment by a critical care medical director.

> The formalization of DNR makes it physician-friendly. However the length, detail, and formality of the form is threatening to patients and surrogates. The obligatory resuscitation of patients for whom there is insufficient time to discuss [DNR] with surrogates (but in [sic] whom the prognosis is grave) subjects such patients to cruel and useless measures.

The above quotation is characteristic of the views of about half the critical care medical directors and hematologist/oncologists responding to the Union College Study – those who answered "No" to the question "Does the New York State Law provide humane DNR?" Nor, as the following comment from a nurse makes clear, is the problem resolvable by the clause in the law permitting physicians to write a DNR order on grounds of futility, when no surrogate is reasonably available (§2966), for in that case two attending physicians must sign a form concurring that the prognosis is futile.

> Patients who do not have capacity and have a known wish for DNR must be seen by a second doctor. In small community hospitals it may be hours before a second doctor is available. When patients are admitted from the emergency room the doctor will most times not take the responsibility of writing a DNR, leaving the nurse with the responsibility to code the patient. In her heart she knows this is a travesty, but feels compelled to code the patient (Critical Care Nursing Director).

Moreover, even the availability of surrogates does not resolve the problem of futile CPR since surrogates may request CPR, despite its futility, or, more commonly, they find themselves unable too conflicted to make a decision, forcing physicians to administer CPR by default – as is clear from the following comments.

> The current DNR law was a well-meaning attempt to codify the physician and patient's responsibilities on the subject of CPR. The implementation of the law has been difficult for hospitals and physicians and has increased the number of patients who are having CPR who would not otherwise have this intervention. The single most valuable aspect of the law has been to increase the dialogue between physician, patients, and family on the subject of CPR. Some of these conversations have been productive, others have been harmful. Some families have been unwilling to participate in the process and refuse to make the most hopeless patients DNR and these patients are then subjected to futile and painful attempts at CPR.
>
> Perhaps the fundamental premise of the law is invalid. Recent published trials have confirmed what many doctors have concluded from experience, that in the hospital setting, few patients over 70 benefit from CPR. As an oncologist it is difficult for me to recall a single patient in which CPR was successful and altered the outcome of the illness. I believe that the law should be rewritten to require consent to CPR not DNR (Oncologist).

DISAFFIRMING AND DISOBEDIENT CLINICIANS

Many physicians not only protest against being compelled by law to administer medically futile CPR, they also admit to defying this aspect of the law.

> [CPR for] a competent patient, in terminal phase, does not offer any potential for therapy and *I therefore write a DNR order without the New York State [consent] form.* It is often very unkind to patients to ask them to sign this form. It gives the impression that we are withholding therapy that is available. As physicians, we do not need the New York State law to permit us to offer something that is not therapy by any account!! Many doctors feel this way but practice inhumane medicine because the law requires it (Hematologist – *emphasis added*).

Civil disobedience of this type appears to be prompted, not only because the DNR law appears to some clinicians to be legislating medical morality, but because it does so without providing a clear public rationale. The philosopher, John Rawls, perhaps the most important contemporary thinker writing on the theory of justice, has observed that "citizens affirm their existing institutions in part because they reasonably believe them to satisfy their public and effective conception of justice." Public policies command public obedience because they satisfy what Rawls calls the "publicity condition," a condition in which

> everyone accepts and knows that others likewise accept [the rationale for a policy]. . . and that this knowledge in turn is publicly recognized. Also, the institutions that constitute the basic structure of our society actually satisfy these principles [or rationales], and everyone with reason [to be concerned] acknowledges this on the basis of commonly shared beliefs confirmed by the methods of inquiry and ways of reasoning agreed to be appropriate ([46], p. 537).

On Rawls' view, publicity is requisite for the "affirmation" of public policy by ordinary people in their daily lives. Conversely, when policy violates the publicity principle it is open to disaffirmation – which can manifest itself either as disobedience, or as a failure to censure those who disobey. Insofar as Rawls' analysis is correct, therefore, the DNR law, and, indeed, bioethical policies banning futility-based DNR orders, were ripe for disaffirmation. For neither the President's Commission, the Hastings Center, nor the Task Force reports satisfy Rawls' publicity condition. None of these justificatory documents clearly state their reasons for proscribing futility-based DNR orders.

This point is best appreciated by contrasting the bioethical delegitimation of futility-based DNR orders with the concurrent legitimation of consent-based DNR orders. The bioethical rationale for legitimating the patient's right to refuse treatment has not only been clearly but often eloquently articulated; it is also persuasively grounded in generally accepted ideas about autonomy. Everyone with an interest in the DNR decision could come to know this rationale and know that almost everyone likewise interested also accepts it. They could thus "affirm" and therefore enforce patient autonomy – and expect that others would likewise enforce it. Non-compliant paternalists, therefore, would – and, indeed, did – find themselves at odds, not merely with a report, or a statute, or an institutional rule, but with the people with whom they work.

At the Union College Conference, for example, one coronary care nurse related how, with the backing of other nurses, she confronted a paternalistic surgeon committed to aggressive intervention – despite the patient's patent desire to be let alone – and how, by brandishing the law, she forced the surgeon to ascertain the patient's wishes. (When asked, the patient refused CPR.) Responses to the Union College survey are replete with similar tales. Overwhelmingly, clinicians welcomed the DNR law as a mechanism for empowering patients and surrogates, giving them the right to address the DNR decision. They report that nurses did indeed resort to the law to "raise the issue [of DNR] with the physicians – who act surprised and reluctant to pursue this further." They also report that physicians often "rebel against discussing DNR when nurses ask," and attribute physician recalcitrance, not to paternalistic beneficence (the motivating factor attributed to physicians in bioethical theory), but to simple "squeamish[ness]," to a disinclination to confront an unpleasant duty, or to be bothered with the "hassle." Comments about doctors who "avoid this conversation with their patients or their families" almost always have disparaging overtones. The consensus is that "without a DNR law, the situation would present too high a risk to an individual's rights to control his own care and/or life. . . . Doctors do not have, nor should have, the responsibility or authority over an individual's fate. . . ." In this respect all three categories of respondents to the Union College survey overwhelming welcomed the DNR law because it "gives the patient and the family the decisive voice in making such a choice."

Moreover, a surprisingly high number of physicians report being forced to comply with the law by nurses and others on the hospital staff. Here is one such report.

> In real life the law has not been working well for my patients. One typical example: [A] 92-year-old nursing home resident with three advanced malignancies, cirrhosis, and almost no platelets. His wife, age 90, is mentally alert and lives in [a nearby state]. Travel is difficult and no children live [near] by. Problems encountered: (1) appropriate form difficult to find, (2) ethicist hard to find. Disturbed ethicist then accosted me for not getting the statement from the patient earlier. (3) I was unhappy discussing problems with [the patient's] wife over the telephone. The patient's expected immediate demise precluded a trip to

> the home with a hospital witness, if I would have been willing. (4) Nurse would not accept advice not to call for CPR and stated that she would report me if I pursued this. (5) Patient died within an hour, [but] had full CPR, managing to hemorrhage during the intubation (no platelets!) (Oncologist).

In this case the oncologist has cast her/himself in the classic role of paternalist, attempting to circumvent the consent requirement, and being unwilling to discuss the CPR/DNR decision with either the patient or, by self-admission, with "[the patient's] wife over the telephone." Thus the oncologist is rebuked by "the ethicist" (note, this is in all likelihood a nurse, physician, or social worker, with some bioethical inclinations or training, since few hospitals maintain specialists in clinical ethics on their staff). Finally, the oncologist attempts to give a non-documented oral no-code order, only to be rebuffed by the nurse, who threatens to report the oncologist (probably to the Department of Health), if he or she "pursued this." The DNR law is thus enforced against this attempt to circumvent patient-family discussion, even though, as predicted, CPR proves futile.

In striking contrast is the reported reluctance of nurses to enforce the law in those cases where physicians are *not* attempting to avoid discussing DNR with their patients. Nurses often tolerate deviation from the letter of the law where the issue is solely futility – uncontaminated by suspicions of avoidance. Recall that policy-makers never gave a rationale which "everyone accepts and knows that others likewise accept" for prohibiting futility-based DNR orders; nor were clinicians ever presented with a rationale, "confirmed by the methods of reasoning agreed to be appropriate," explaining the delegitimation of futility-based DNR orders. On the contrary, the methods of reasoning used to justify the prohibition of futility-based DNR orders (theories about the moral equivalence of consent to actions and inactions, and about presumed consent), insofar as they were publicly stated at all, are off-handed, recondite, and controversial. Not surprisingly, nurses and physicians unable to comprehend the reason for the prohibition did not affirm it.

> I think that the law should be improved if the area of medical futility were better developed. Currently, a DNR [order] can be written on the basis of medical futility [only] in the absence of capacity, absence of a surrogate, and [if] futility [is] documented by first and second [medical] opinions. Why should a family or a patient even be offered

> a choice of a treatment that is medically futile? (Critical Care Medical Director).

Perhaps more importantly, since they neither understood nor approved the constraints placed on futility-based DNR orders by the law, a sizeable number of physicians proclaimed that they disobeyed the law. Here is one oncologist's explanation of why, even though he believed the intent of the law to be good, he nonetheless found himself morally obligated to disobey it.

> [The] impulse behind the law is good. The fact that patient is [made] DNR should not be a secret – [there is] nothing to hide. [It is] valuable to force open the discussion with the patient and the family concerning prognosis. Unfortunately the law is unnecessarily cumbersome and adversarial. [It] starts with the presumption that resuscitation is always a good thing and places road blocks in the way of obtaining DNR (pages of forms, multiple signatures, requirement that forms be resigned by [the] patient or family at a new admission [which] is cruel). At my hospital, fortunately, the nurses don't force us to stick to the letter of the law. [There is] not always another M.D. available to co-sign forms in a pinch, etc. If they were really strict about it, we would be torturing dying people and their families all the time (Oncologist).

Mention of the need for another "M.D. . . . to co-sign forms in a pinch" indicates a significant difference between this case, where "the nurses don't force us to stick to the letter of the law," and the case discussed earlier, in which the law was enforced against a non-compliant physician. These forms are used only when a surrogate is not reasonably available; hence what appears to be in the forefront is not an attempt to circumvent discussion and consent, but to write a DNR order in a context where consent was unattainable. Nurses appear to refrain from enforcing the letter of the law in cases like this one, in which the physician's disaffirmation of the rationale for the law does not conflict with elements affirmed by nurses. Since nurses and physicians overwhelmingly affirm the ideal of patient self-determination, futility-based DNR orders that contravene the law tend to be tolerated only when the patient or surrogate is incapable of voicing a preference (either because they are uncertain about their preferences, or because, as in the case above, it is physically impossible to consult them). Where there is a possibility of consultation, however, nurses appear to enforce the law.

THE EFFECTIVENESS OF FORCING DISCUSSION

The oncologist is nonetheless uneasy about disobeying the law and closes his comment with a simple proposal that, he believes, would remedy the problem.

> Why not [a] simple statement in [the] chart that [the] patient is dying of cancer, [that] resuscitation would serve no purpose, that [the] patient is therefore DNR and that the patient/family have been informed?

Notice that the oncologist does not wish to avoid the CPR/DNR discussion since there is an express willingness to accept the requirement that the patient and/or family be *informed* of the CPR/DNR decision. What the oncologist finds problematic is not discussing the futility of CPR with the patient or the family, or documenting this discussion in the patient's medical record, but the further requirement that consent is needed before writing a futility-based DNR order. In short, the oncologist believes in informing and in documentation, but not in seeking consent.

The oncologist's proposal seems eminently reasonable. Why didn't the Task Force propose – or even consider – such a policy? The answer appears to be two-fold. As Tomlinson and Brody point out (in a series of articles which will be discussed later ([56], [57])), there is a tendency in the bioethical and legal literature to conflate the three different acts of being informed, giving consent, and documenting consent. The almost automatic association between these three different activities makes it natural to link them in policies and laws. Insofar as the Task Force contemplated the possibility of separation, however, the simple – but initially unvoiced – answer to the oncologist's question is that the Task Force feared that if physicians had the power to write futility-based DNR orders, they would abuse it, using the loophole created thereby to avoid discussing DNR with patients or their surrogates – as, in fact, the first oncologist attempted to do (until prevented by the nurse).

In point of fact, the data provided in both the American College of Physicians and the Union College surveys appear to certify the effectiveness of the Task Force's enforcement strategy. The data clearly indicate that clinicians perceive the law as increasing the likelihood of physicians discussing the DNR decision with patients. In the ACP survey, 68% of internists agreed with the statement that "the law made it more likely that I will raise the issue of DNR status with my patients"; the

Union College survey found that between 66% and 70% of each of the three clinician groups surveyed thought the law had increased the likelihood of such discussions on the critical care units on which they work. These data are entirely consistent with, and can be taken to justify, the rationale, latter voiced by Axelrod and Miller – that it was necessary to prohibit futility-based DNR orders in order to compel doctors to discuss the DNR decision with their patients.

COMPLIANCE WITH THE LAW

Yet, as we saw earlier, some physicians disaffirm and disobey the law – reacting to it as a classic case of legislating morality. What differentiates disaffirming from compliant clinicians? It is not, as we shall see, a more favorable opinion of the law. What appears to differentiate the two categories of physicians is that those who affirm the law conceptualize its flaws as "perversions" of a legitimate purpose. And so, even as they lament and lambaste the law's flaws, because they accept its basic purpose, they ultimately affirm and obey it. The New York DNR law can be said to be so preoccupied with prevention of (morally unjustifiable) *strong* paternalism on the part of physicians, that, in the process, it eliminates justifiable forms of *weak* paternalism (which protect patients against futile CPR). Compliant clinicians recognize and accept the legitimacy of prohibiting strong physician paternalism, but they resent the concomitant elimination of justifiable forms of *weak paternalism*. Thus, although their acceptance of the underlying rationale of the law (abetted, no doubt, by the coercive power of the DOH) rendered them compliant even with the original law, their perception of the perversities of implementation made them, if anything, more vituperative then disaffirming clinicians in their denunciations of the original codification of the law.

Compare the vehemence of the following reactions from *compliant* clinicians to the relatively calm denunciation of the disaffirming and non-compliant oncologist quoted earlier.

> Damn armchair quarterbacks!!
>
> This law often intrudes upon the doctor-patient relationship. Trust is often destroyed by the legalese and the requirement of signatures. Many times families will request DNR but will balk at actually signing the forms. Even worse is shoving the forms at the patient himself to sign.

> [Does the law provide Humane DNR?] No! This DNR issue is at the intimate heart of the doctor-patient relationship. This law intrudes and makes a difficult area even more difficult (Critical Care Medical Director).
>
> The law is another intrusion on the doctor, family, patient relationship. My practice has not changed with respect to DNR orders, but [the law has] only added extra paperwork and created a legal aura. Many spouses find the act of signing the form an emotional trauma almost equivalent to a death warrant. . . . Also many patients cannot bring themselves to sign their own form. I would eliminate all of the extra forms and keep [the DNR order] in the body of the medical record only (Oncologist).
>
> The emphasis is placed on obtaining signatures on multiple forms rather than the physical and emotional needs of the dying patient and his family. Without the completion of all the forms the DNR law is not valid. Humane DNR can only be accomplished by the continual interactions of the health care team with the patient and family throughout the dying process. . . . We do need a law in New York State saying that DNR orders are valid and under what circumstances. However the law as it is written is very complicated. In order to meet the letter of the law we address the need to get consent forms signed. The [educational] programs that I have attended address the consent process, not the dying process. I feel that the signing of consent forms has suddenly put new meaning to the cliche "signing your life away." The guilt feelings for some must be enormous (Critical Care Nursing Director).

Notice that these *compliant* clinicians complain only about the *mechanisms* by which the law is implemented. Thus while the medical director damns "armchair quarterbacks" who have "intruded" on "the intimate heart of the doctor patient relationship," destroying "trust," he or she never argues against the principles on which the law is predicated. Similarly, the compliant oncologist, by stating that the law has not changed her or his practice, indicates that he or she previously required consent for DNR orders and so seems to accept the propriety of the principles underlying the law. The complaint which is lodged is thus about the perversity of asking patients and families to sign a "death warrant," not about the principles underlying the law. The same complaint is made by the nursing director, who also points out that by focusing on the formalities, "the consent process" distracts from tending to the "physical and emotional needs of the dying patient and his family." All three of these clinicians regard the consent forms as a "bureaucratization of the dying process" (to use the words of another hematologist), which, by intervening in the "intimate heart" of the clinician-patient relationship, adds unnecessary "emotional trauma," detracting from clinicians' efforts to care for the dying. They do *not*, however, raise their voices to challenge the anti-paternalist principles underlying the law – and so are ultimately compliant. Affirming the law's underlying rationale, they are led to comply even though they would agree with the disaffirming hematologist that compliance often leads them to practice "inhumane medicine."

In contrast, the disaffirming physicians challenge the *rationale* for requiring consent for futile CPR. To reiterate the words of the hematologist quoted earlier, "we do not need the New York State law to permit us to offer something [CPR] that is not therapy by any account!!" The disaffirming critical care medical director makes a similar statement, "Why should a family or a patient even be offered a choice of a treatment that is medically futile?" So does the disaffirming oncologist who challenges the law's "presumption that resuscitation is always a good thing and places road blocks in the way of obtaining DNR (pages of forms, multiple signatures, requirement that forms be resigned by [the] patient or family at a new admission [which] is cruel)." Thus while both compliant and disaffirming clinicians agree on the deleterious effects of the law, only the disaffirming physicians trace these negative effects to the principles underlying the law.

PROTECTIONISM IN THE DNR LAW

The DNR law sought to protect patients against incompetent physicians as well as against paternalistic ones. Conceiving CPR as a right, it required physicians to be vigilant in protecting this right. It codified this protection by mandating that DNR orders be written only by attending physicians and be reviewed at three-day intervals. These review requirements were almost universally regarded as senseless (rather than perverse) and were widely disaffirmed. Most nursing directors and many medical directors report that the requirement of three-day review was routinely ignored on their critical care units.

The DNR law also contained an elaborate set of protections for patients under the care of the Office of Mental Retardation and Developmental Disabilities (OMRDD). As Martin Strosberg notes (this volume, pp. 9–31), these special protections for OMRDD patients were added to the Task Force proposal as a consequence of lobbying at the state legislature by advocates of the handicapped who feared that DNR orders would be used as a tool of discrimination. In practice, however, the added protections often acted to deny OMRDD patients equal access to DNR orders – causing them to suffer CPR in cases in which their non-handicapped peers would have had the relief afforded by a DNR order. A particularly visible example of the perverse effects of well-intended protectionism for the developmentally disabled is related by Carol Clay (Section Three). She tells the tale of an OMRDD patient who was denied a DNR order, against the wishes of both his physicians and his family – acting with the approval of a hospital ethics committee – because the supervisor of the OMRDD facility at which he resided was reluctant to allow the DNR order. (For a survey of OMRDD's overall handling of the DNR law, see Lawrence Faulkner's analysis, also in Section Three.)

There were, moreover, some problems with educating various medical services (in particular the Emergency Medical Services (EMS)) about the law – which often resulted in cruel problems for patients seeking to avail themselves of the new protections against CPR provided by the DNR law (as the cases related by Deborah O'Brien and Timothy Quill in Section Three illustrate). Within months of its passage it became clear to all concerned that some reinterpretation and revision of the DNR law would be required.

THE TASK FORCE AND DEPARTMENT OF HEALTH IMPLEMENTATION OF THE DNR LAW

As Martin Strosberg points out in this volume (pp. 9–31), policy analysts conceptualize the monitoring, review and revision of laws as integral to the implementation process. Unlike the report of the President's Commission and the Hastings Center *Guidelines*, the Task Force's *Report* had culminated in the passage of a particular piece of legislation, for which it became responsible. Yet, as Strosberg also observes, there are significant differences between bioethical policies implemented within the medical community itself, and those promulgated and enforced by means of a law. The most important of these is that when a policy is implemented as a law, implementation follows patterns typical of laws. As in all other public health laws, implementation of the DNR law proceeded by means of regulations issued by the DOH. These regulations were issued on February 12, 1988, and were supplemented, on March 13, 1988, by an official memo to health facilities summarizing their institutional duties under the law. Accompanying the memo was a pamphlet, designed by the Task Force, to explain the law to patients.

For the most part, the DOH regulations and the Task Force pamphlet simply restate the DNR law. Both state that patients are presumed to consent to DNR orders and that a legally valid DNR order requires the consent of either a patient or the patient's surrogate, except when neither is available. To this point, the regulations accurately reflect the law – which is what one would expect. There is, however, one significant departure. The departure occurs in the interpretation of §2962. 4, a section designed to assure nursing homes and other hospitals which did not have the trained personnel or the equipment to administer (advanced) CPR that they need not so train their staff or acquire new equipment. The section states that: "Nothing [in the law] require[s] a hospital to expand its existing equipment and facilities to provide cardiopulmonary resuscitation." The parallel section in the regulations, (c) 4, is quite close: "Nothing in this section shall require a hospital to expand its existing personnel, training, equipment and facilities to provide cardiopulmonary resuscitation."

Note carefully that the point being made in §2962. 4 and in the parallel (c) 4 is about the expansion of *equipment* or *personnel*. Yet in their accompanying *commentary* on these sections, Thomas Hartman, Director of Health Care Standards and Analysis, and Raymond Sweeney, Director of the Office of Health Systems Management, transubstantiate these stipulations about people and machines into a claim about *duties* – expressly stating that the DNR law creates no new *duty* to resuscitate.

No New Duty to Resuscitate

> Article 29-B [the DNR law] imposes no new duty on facilities *or staff* to resuscitate patients in arrest where such a duty did not exist before the law. Patients are presumed to consent to resuscitation absent a contrary order, but facilities without the capability of providing CPR are not required to develop such a capability. Also, *the authority of a physician to make a medical judgment that resuscitation measures would be futile* in

a particular case *has not changed*, but *decisions made on this basis cannot become so common as to constitute a policy of unwritten DNR orders* (*emphasis added*).

By dint of adding the two simple words "or staff" in their commentary, these DOH officials radically transform §2962. 4 and regulation (c) 4 from an exemption to an obligation to add equipment into a fundamentally new and significantly different proposition: that the DNR law "imposes no new duty on staff to resuscitate patients."

We will not speculate on the reasons why this turn of phrase was used to assuage clinician protests about being forced to perform "futile" CPR, but we do note that the language and logic adopted are strikingly similar to that in the 1987 Hastings *Guidelines*, which, while prohibiting futility-based DNR orders *in advance* of an arrest, made an exemption "at the time of. . . an arrest. . . [if] the effort clearly cannot restore cardiac and respiratory function" (II.B.9 (C), p. 51). Moreover, both contain parallel warnings about abusing this futility-at-the- time-of-an-arrest-exemption: the *Guidelines* warn against "allow[ing] this exception to justify failure to discuss the issues with the patient or the surrogate in advance," the DOH warns that "decisions made on this basis can not become so common as to constitute a policy of unwritten DNR orders." We note this last minute attempt at reinterpretation not only because it piques scholarly curiosity, but also because it turned out to be the basis on which the Task Force chose to defend the DNR law.

The Task Force's Initial Response to Clinician Criticisms of the DNR Law

The Task Force appears to have been caught off guard by the nature and focus of the clinicians' criticisms of the DNR law. Everything in the bioethical tradition suggested that its opposition would come from medical paternalists. And certainly there were a few physicians who seemed to reject the law for classic paternalist reasons. Yet the evidence of the ACP survey was that it was not the therapeutic exception that was of primary concern to New York internists, it was futility. As noted earlier, 77% of the New York internists surveyed believed that physicians should be empowered to write futility-based DNR orders. In contrast, only 9% of internists agreed with the proposition that there was no need to discuss DNR with patients because of the negative impact of the discussion; and only 47% of internists wished a "broader" therapeutic exception "than permitted under the law," while an almost equal number, 45%, "agree[d] with the position taken in the DNR law [that] with rare exceptions the possibility that those discussions will lead to an adverse effect is overcome by the importance of the patient's making an informed decision about CPR."

The open-ended responses of critical care directors and hematologist/oncologists to the Union College survey suggest that, even for apparent "paternalists," the underlying attitude is informed by a perception of the futility of administering CPR to terminal patients.

> Requesting all patients who are terminal with no chance of recovery or reversibility of their illness to consent to the concept that they will die shortly and [that] nothing can be done to alter the course places an unfair burden on the ill, dying patient and their family. Numerous terminal patients have had severe terminal depression when the concept of DNR or the terminality of their cancer was discussed. This is inhumane if the treatment offered is meaningless (Oncologist).

As is evident from the last six words – "if the treatment offered is meaningless" – what might otherwise be considered a classic paternalist response is partially a reaction to the futility of administering futile CPR to these patients – in the broad clinical sense of "futility." So, even where the underlying issue may be paternalism, it is futility, not paternalism, that is the disputed conceptual terrain – and this, in fact, is the issue on which the debate over the DNR law centered.

The first official response by the Task Force staff took the form of three 1989 articles: one co-authored by Tracy Miller and Robert Swidler in the *New York State Bar Journal* [34]; one by Miller in *Law, Medicine and Health Care* [33]; and one by Swidler in the *New York State Journal of Medicine* [52]. All three articles deal directly with the futility issue and follow the position staked out in the DOH commentary, by denying that the law requires the administration of futile CPR in the event of an arrest. Swidler adamantly asserts that:

> The view that the presumption of consent [in the DNR statute] constitutes an absolute duty to resuscitate is at odds with what the statute says, what the drafters and legislators intended, and what good medical practice requires. The Department of Health has already taken steps to correct this misinterpretation by a health facilities

> memorandum. This article suggests the proper, narrower reading of the presumption of consent [in which] the presumption does not. . . define a duty to provide resuscitation [except] based on the applicable standard of care. . . ([52], p. 69).

Swidler then articulates the Hastings *Guidelines'* distinction between giving an order *in advance* of an arrest, and not initiating treatment *at the moment* of arrest – the very distinction echoed in the commentary section of the DOH memorandum.

> It could be argued that because the law permits a DNR order to be entered on the grounds of "futility". . . where no surrogate is available and two physicians authorize the order – that it implicitly mandates CPR in all other instances of arrest, even if CPR would be futile. That inference should be rejected. The. . . statutory references to futility relate to the grounds for entering a DNR order – an instruction, in advance of a patient's arrest, not to attempt CPR. They do not relate to or logically govern the separate issue: how a physician must respond to a non-DNR patient's arrest. . . the DNR law does not define the duty of health care professionals to respond to a non-DNR patient's arrest. . . ([52], p. 70).

Swidler's analysis is puzzling on two scores. At the most basic level one wonders, if this is the position taken in the law, why does not the law explicitly state that "if, at the time of arrest the physician believes CPR to be futile, it need not be administered"? The Hastings *Guidelines* explicitly state such a futility exemption, the DOH implicitly states such an exemption (although to do so they needed to alter the wording of the law), so, if, as Swidler claims, "the drafters and legislators intended" such an exemption, and if "good medical practice requires" such an exemption, why isn't there a direct statement of this exemption in the law?

Suppose one grants, however, that the drafters and the legislators intended to permit physicians not to initiate futile CPR at the time of an arrest. As Swidler admits, the law nonetheless clearly prohibits futility-based DNR orders issued in advance of an arrest. Thus a puzzle remains: why is it permissible for physicians to make a decision at the moment of an arrest, which they could not make in advance of the event? Denying patients the knowledge of their physician's intention (of not initiating futile CPR at the moment of arrest) effectively denies patients the right to a second medical opinion. The Task Force and *Guidelines* policy reinstitutes what is, in effect, a no-code order, eschewing, thereby, the advantages of the DNR order – the advantages of a decision made reflectively, *in advance of a crisis*, in collaboration with staff members, documented in writing, and subject to the patient's right to secure a second medical opinion. Oddly enough, the defense of this distinction on offer in the Hastings *Guidelines* – and originally offered by Task Force itself in the footnote analyzed earlier – appears to be precisely the broad theory of presumed consent that Swidler is now rejecting. Thus the Task Force needed a new justification, a new explanation, for distinguishing futility-based DNR orders issued *in advance of an arrest* from those issued *at the moment of arrest*.

Fortuitously, Task Force Director Miller voices such an explanation. Miller argues that permitting DNR orders in advance of an arrest "without discussing the decision with capable patients" would create an "exception" that "will swallow the rule." Many physicians "are reluctant to speak with their patients about resuscitation" (recall the case of oncologist's treatment of the 92-year-old nursing home patient described earlier) and, Miller contends, "As long as that reluctance remains prevalent, any exception on. . . futility grounds is almost certain to be an escape hatch for physicians seeking to avoid conversations they never understood as integral to the obligation to care for dying patients" ([33], p. 251).

As Miller points out, there is no need to be "draconian" in the attempt to compel reluctant physicians to discuss DNR with their patients.

> Policies on resuscitation must also acknowledge that time and circumstances will foreclose the possibility of a dialogue between patient and physician in some cases. This will be true not only for patients brought into the emergency room, but also for patients who have no prior relationship with health professionals and who arrest shortly after being admitted to the hospital. In these cases physicians treating the patient have a duty to provide needed and beneficial treatment which may include CPR. . . . It does not, however, give rise to an obligation to provide CPR the physician believes is medically futile and of no benefit to the patient ([33], p. 251).

Problematic Aspects of the Task Force's Interpretation of the DNR Law

Despite the carefully crafted arguments urged by the Task Force, their interpretation of the law seemed to elude the grasp of clinicians and lawyers. As one medical director commented (in an open-ended answer in the Union College survey):

> Patients who are hopelessly ill are being resuscitated because doctors cannot obtain a DNR consent. Resources are being wasted. Doctors interpret the law as, "if your patient has not given written consent to not [being] resuscitated, then you must resuscitate regardless of the patient's condition or the futility of the act." [Robert Swidler's article in] the *New York State Medical Journal* stated in essence, "you must not resuscitate if the patient wishes DNR status, otherwise use your medical judgment." As this is not clear, doctors, with their knees knocking with the fear of legal action, subject terminally ill patients to resuscitation and invasive procedures (Critical Care Medical Director).

Why wasn't Swidler's distinction and the DOH reading of the law accepted by clinicians? Like other laypersons, clinicians turn to their lawyers to interpret the law. As The Union College Study shows, these lawyers are disposed towards conservative readings of the law. And, in their view, the two words inserted into the *commentary* on the law in the DOH memorandum neither count as law, nor provide a reasonable interpretation of the law. As late as September 1990, at the Union College Conference, several lawyers concurred with James Horwitz, attorney to an upstate hospital, who became livid at the cavalier treatment of the DNR law by the DOH – charging the DOH with exceeding its power by promulgating an interpretation that was not supported by the statute. He also asserted that he was not inclined to expose the hospitals he advised to legal action by accepting a loose interpretation of the statute. Other health care lawyers clearly agreed with Horwitz and, indeed, one of the lawyers interviewed as part of the Union College Study initially instructed hospital staff to show code every patient for whom a valid DNR order had not been issued. (This particular reaction could not have been too widespread, since the Ahronheim *et al.* and the Kamer and McClung studies of teaching hospitals, in Section Four, found no significant change in CPR/DNR practices consequent to the implementation of the law.) To this day, however, while most health care lawyers now understand that the risk of litigation involved in following the DOH/Task Force interpretation of the law is minimal, they still cannot reconcile it with the actual written statute and believe that, in the unlikely event it ever should reach the courts, it would not withstand judicial scrutiny.

Worse yet, even if one accepts the revised reading of the law urged by the DOH and the Task Force, the inverted nature of the DNR order still renders the revision inoperable in the acute care context – that is, in the context in which CPR is typically administered. The DOH and Swidler claim that the law prohibits futility-based DNR orders written *in advance* of an arrest but does not prevent withholding futile CPR *at the time of arrest*. Their claim is valid for a family physician working as a solo practitioner in the patient's home. Such a physician can indeed assess a patient in arrest, determine that CPR would be futile, and decide not to administer it – without *issuing* a DNR order. To reiterate, for the solo practitioner, Swidler's claim, as reinterpreted by the DOH, that "the DNR law does not define the duty of health care professionals to respond to a non-DNR patient's arrest" is entirely accurate.

The DOH-Swidler claim, however, is invalid for hospital contexts. Hospital practice is by nature collaborative, not solo. This fact is particularly important with respect to DNR orders because, as we observed earlier, the order is essentially inverted. A code will automatically be called by nurses, medical students, and other clinicians working at the patient's bedside *unless* and *until* a DNR order has been written, or actually uttered aloud by a physician; CPR will continue to be administered until a physician *utters* an order not to resuscitate – a DNR order. It is at this point that what is sometimes referred to as the "Catch-22 of the DNR law" emerges. For uttered orders not to resuscitate are precisely regulated by the DNR statute and even by the DOH regulations. These define an "order not to resuscitate" as follows:

[DNR Law] §2961. 13. *Order not to resuscitate* [or DNR order] means an order *not to attempt* cardiopulmonary resuscitation in the event a patient suffers cardiopulmonary arrest.

[DOH Regulations] (b) (13) *Order not to resuscitate* means an order *not to attempt* cardiopulmonary resuscitation in the event a patient suffers cardiac or respiratory arrest. Such an order may cover all

> cardiopulmonary measures or [only a part] depending on the scope of the consent.

The key word to observe in these definitions is "attempt"; a DNR order is an order not to *attempt* CPR. Thus any order to the effect that CPR should not be attempted – any utterance of a "no code" order – constitutes a DNR order under the statute and the regulations. Since the only condition under which a physician can issue a futility-based DNR order is with the concurrence of a second physician (provided, of course, that no surrogate is available), a physician cannot issue such an order without concurrence – and so the code must be attempted, even though it is known to be futile.

Thus, even if one accepts Swidler's very "lawyerly" distinctions, in the acute care context, all dying patients for whom a DNR order has not been written must still receive CPR (unless there is a second physician to concur that CPR is futile). Ingenious though it was to distinguish between a DNR order in advance of an arrest and not initiating CPR at the moment of the arrest, since the relevant distinction *in the law* is between *attempting* CPR and *not attempting* CPR, given the inverted nature of the DNR order, the only way to call off futile CPR in the event of an arrest is first to attempt to give it – hence the advice of lawyers to show-code all patients; hence the willingness of nurses to disaffirm the law and to permit physician non-compliance with the futility requirement.

Revising the DNR Law to Eliminate Perversely Paternalistic Protections

The Union College survey found that for clinicians, the most nettlesome aspect of the DNR law was the patient consent forms. These forms were written on the advice of health care lawyers and tend to embody their stringently protectionist interpretation of the DNR law – exacerbated by their desire to secure documentation that would be useful in the event of litigation. The most glaring example of the perversities their protectionist inclinations inflicted on the clinical context was the requirement that patients themselves *sign* consent forms. As should be evident from the few clinician comments cited earlier, this requirement was continually denounced as perverse, onerous, and inhumane. Yet, ironically, neither the DNR law (§2964. 2 (a)), nor the DOH regulations (e (2) i) require hospitalized patients to *sign* consent forms. They clearly state that while such consent must be witnessed by two persons, it "may be express[ed]...

orally" and then "recorded in the patient's medical chart." The requirement that *patients* sign their own DNR orders is entirely an artifact of legal advice: for, to repeat for clarity and emphasis, there is no such requirement in the DNR law; this inhumane requirement was inflicted upon patients and practitioners, not by the Task Force, the Legislature, or the DOH, but by lawyers.

The DNR law is not entirely blameless, however, for it engendered the atmosphere that prompted lawyers to give such advice by requiring that *surrogate* consent be witnessed and in writing. Thus DNR law §2965. 6 (a), and the DOH regulations (f (6) i) require that *surrogate* consent to a DNR order be "expressed in writing, dated, and signed in the presence of one witness. . . who shall [also] sign the decision." This initiated the idea of signed consent forms. Hospitalized patients were exempt from signing them, but symmetry, bureaucratic convenience, and the inclination towards precautionary documentation, combined to subvert this exemption. Thus the bureaucratization of the dying process which the Task Force and legislature inflicted on surrogates, was extended – in spite of the humane instincts of the Task Force and the Legislature to create an exemption – to the dying person.

On July 15, 1991 (see Appendix), the law was revised to eliminate the requirement for external documentation of surrogate decisions in the hope that hospitals would no longer feel obligated to require patients to sign their own DNR orders (Public Health Law, Chapter 370, section 8 (a), section 11 (a)). Provisions were also made to recognize the validity of DNR orders for non-institutionalized patients (for example, terminal patients receiving hospice care at home), and for legitimating the recognition of these orders by emergency medical technicians (who staff ambulances). These provisions resolved the difficulties highlighted in the case studies presented by Timothy Quill and Deborah O'Brien (Section Three). In addition, the revisions relaxed the requirements for three-day review of DNR orders (extending it to seven days for hospitalized patients), clarified the status of DNR orders in interinstitutional transfers, and (by means of an accompanying DOH memorandum) permitted second physician concurrence to DNR orders to be given by telephone.

Perhaps the most important "revision" of the law, however, was its incorporation in the Health Care Proxy law. As its title proclaims, the law formalized the process of designating a surrogate to act as the patient's proxy in health-care decisions, should the patient become incapacitated. Thus, insofar as hospitals assiduously cultivated the appointment of proxies, no patient need ever be left intestate with respect to medical decisionmaking. There would, in effect, always be someone with whom a physician could discuss CPR, and, perhaps more importantly, there would typically be a non-threatening context in which to discuss a patient's wishes with respect to the DNR decision. Ironically, routinization and bureaucratization (the reviled nemesis of the DNR law) was now seen as defusing the emotional trauma of prospective decisionmaking and was welcomed as a singular virtue of the proxy law.

Thus the proxy law, together with the broad reading of the DNR law urged by the DOH and Swidler, the enforcement rationale offered by Miller, and the specific revisions of July, 1991, made the law palatable to most clinicians. DNR orders have again become a routine and relatively non-controversial feature of acute care medicine in New York State – as have proxy consent forms and patient-physician conversations about the CPR/DNR decision.

Comparing New York's DNR Law with National DNR Reform

The hubbub over the DNR law has subsided and one can now ask: what implications does this experiment have for bioethical policymaking? The significant accomplishments of the New York DNR law were fourfold: first, establishing the legality of DNR orders in New York; second, legalizing true surrogacy in decisions to withdraw or withhold life-sustaining treatment (thus providing precedent for the health care proxy law); third, authoritatively determining that DNR orders should be consent-based; fourth, delegitimating futility-based DNR orders. Although we have focused on the controversy surrounding the implementation of the law, these should not be allowed to obscure the extent to which the law was positively received. Both the ACP and the Union College surveys indicate that by legalizing consent-based DNR orders the law effected a significant and well-received change that was actively enforced at the institutional level. In the decade and a half since the *Quinlan* case – in which, it should be recalled, physicians *repudiated* the patient's right to refuse life-sustaining treatment – this right was now almost universally affirmed and enforced in New York at the institutional level.

How much of this change can be attributed to the DNR law? Prior to the law's enactment, bioethical policy on CPR/DNR for New York hospitals had been set by the New York State Medical Society *Guidelines* of 1982 ([32]) which also endorsed consent-based DNR orders (see Appendix). There appears to have been a significant level of voluntary compliance with this policy [42]. The Union College survey found that between one quarter and two thirds of New York critical care directors report that various discussion, documentation and consent practices at their ICUs were both *unchanged* by the DNR law and *in compliance* with the Medical Society *Guidelines*. Yet the same data indicates that compliance was only partial: between 37% and 73% of New York critical care directors report that some specific CPR/DNR discussion, documentation or consent practice on their ICU was *not* in compliance with Medical Society policy and was changed by the DNR law. Where change was reported, the likelihood of *discussing* DNR with a patient or a family *doubled* consequent to the passage of the DNR law. Correlatively, the likelihood of an *undocumented*, or *unconsented* DNR order *decreased* by between 30% and 50%. It would appear, therefore, that although voluntary adherence to professional guidelines significantly affected practice, the law was undeniably more effective and eminently more successful in compelling discussion, documentation and consent to DNR orders.

Laws, however, are not the only mechanism available for formalizing and enforcing professional bioethical policy. In the nation outside of New York, the route to enforcement was through the accreditation process. All health care institutions must be accredited in order to be recognized by local, state, and federal governments, and to qualify as recipients of insurance monies (from both governmental and private insurers). Accreditation is achieved by a regular audit of hospital practices, most commonly by the JCAHO (formerly known as the Joint Commission for the Accreditation of Hospitals). Recognizing the saliency of this phenomenon to their objectives, the President's Commission saw the accreditation process as a natural mechanism for enforcing bioethical policy.

> Hospital Accreditation. Much of medical practice is governed by independent and private organizations which, like the government, bear a responsibility for encouraging sound decisions regarding resuscitation. Organizations that accredit health care institutions do not now mandate any policy or education on the subject of resuscitation beyond the requirement of the Joint Commission on the Accreditation of Hospitals that [critical] care unit staff know the

> medical procedures involved and that all orders about patient care be written ones. At the least, in order to be accredited, hospitals should be required to have a general policy regarding resuscitation – preferably one that addresses the three basic needs discussed in this chapter [that is, (i) explicit policies, which (ii) balanced protections of patients, and (iii) provide internal advice and review] ([40], p. 255).

In 1988 the JCAHO, citing the President's Commission, initiated a literature survey and a questionnaire of hospital DNR practices [25]. The survey reviewed studies by Andrew Evans and Baruch Brody [13], Stuart Youngner [59], and Susanna Bedell and Thomas Delbanco [7], which indicated uneven and haphazard compliance with professional standards for DNR discussion, documentation and consent. Longo and associates' survey of institutional practices confirmed this picture [25]. They found that although 85% of acute care hospitals had policies which dealt with DNR, in 29% of institutions these policies were only *informal*, that is, unwritten. They also found that 50% of long-term care institutions (excluding psychiatric hospitals) had no DNR policies, formal or informal, and that, (surprisingly) neither did 38% of hospices. The article ultimately concluded that:

> The response of health care providers to establishing strong formal DNR policies is disappointing. . . . It is time. . . for providers to accord these ethical issues the same priority in teaching and research as they accord to the technologies that to a large degree have raised the issues ([25], p. 73).

In 1988 the JCAHO changed its accreditation standards to require:

> hospital-wide policy on the withholding of resuscitative services from patients. . . [which] describes the mechanism(s) for reaching decisions about the withholding of resuscitative services from individual patients,. . . the mechanism(s) for resolving conflicts in decisionmaking should they arise and. . . the roles of physicians, and when applicable of nursing staff members. . . and family members in the decision to withhold resuscitative services. . . . The policy [must] include provisions designed to assure that patients' rights are respected when decisions are made to withhold resuscitative services, [and] requirements that the appropriate orders be written by the physician primarily responsible

for the patient and that documentation be made in the patient's medical record if resuscitative services are withheld ([17], p. 82.).

The JCAHO accreditation standards address the three basic needs pointed out by the President's Commission, but left the interpretation of bioethical policy to the discretion of each hospital. Questions concerning the details of patients' rights (whether, for example, a patient has a right to futile CPR unless there is consent to a DNR order) were to be settled by the nurses and physicians at the various hospitals affected. The JCAHO approach to mandatory bioethical reform of DNR practice is thus the polar opposite of that taken by the New York Task Force. Where the Task Force sought to impose an authoritative and detailed interpretation of bioethical policy through the coercive power of law, the JCAHO was content to use the power of accreditation to force institutions to adopt any hospital-wide bioethical policy as long as that policy "assur[ed] that patients' rights are respected when decisions are made to withhold resuscitative treatments." Other than requiring written documentation of decisions in the patient's medical record and the development of a dispute reconciliation mechanism, the JCAHO gave each individual hospital *latitude* to implement bioethical reform at the institutional level.

The JCAHO's *latitudinarian* approach to reform contrasts sharply with the *authoritarian* approach of the New York Task Force. Although in both cases reform is mandatory and enforced, what is enforced by the latitudinarian JCAHO approach is *having* a bioethical policy; the authoritarian Task Force approach, in contrast, requires institutions to implement a specific, highly detailed policy. The latitudinarian JCAHO strategy of reform permitted institutional variation; it empowered hospitals to revise their policies themselves, allowing them to evolve naturally in response to institutional experience and changes in the professional consensus on bioethical policy. In contrast, the Task Force's DNR law, as a law, could only be changed by DOH reinterpretation (for example, the reinterpretation which released physicians from the obligation to administer futile CPR to an arresting patient) or by legislative amendment (for example, the amendments of July 15, 1991, which, among other things, rescinded the requirement that surrogates sign DNR consent forms). The procedures for revising policy are thus relatively inelastic and not readily amenable to change in response to evolving professional experience.

Nineteen eighty-eight, therefore, turned out to be the year of an inadvertent but nonetheless intriguing natural experiment. Every hospital in the country was mandated to implement a bioethical policy with respect to DNR orders. Those outside New York had latitude to implement a bioethical policy for DNR orders which reflected the evolving professional consensus on the appropriate handling of the DNR decision. Those in New York were required to adhere to a single authoritative statement of bioethical propriety, as codified in the New York law. To analyze this natural experiment, The Union College Study surveyed a constructed sample of Non-New York critical care medical directors. The ICU directors reported that, prior to the JCAHO mandate, there was significant, albeit partial, adherence to bioethical policies endorsed by professional medical associations. Pre-reform compliance with professional standards for discussion, documentation and consent for CPR/DNR was reported by between 35% and 70% of critical care medical directors. This finding is similar to the figures reported by New Yorkers in the Union College survey (chapter 20), between 37% and 73%; it is also consistent with Longo and associates finding that prior to the mandatory bioethical reforms of 1988, only 44% of acute care hospitals required documentation of the DNR order, only 40% required discussion of the DNR order with the patient or the family, and only 28% required evidence of informed consent. Thus in the nation, as in New York, prior to the mandatory reforms of 1988, professional bioethical policy exerted a significant but uneven influence.

Hospital *policies* changed dramatically in response to the mandatory reforms of 1988 outside of New York, just as they did in New York. Longo *et al.* reported that, *prior* to the 1988 reforms, only 40% of policies required that the DNR decision be discussed with the patient or the family. The Union College Study found that, *after* the 1988 reforms, 87% of Non-New York ICU directors report that patient consent was required for a DNR order on their ICU. *Practices* changed as well: between 56% and 83% of Non-New York medical directors report an increase in discussion, documentation or consent to DNR orders after the JCAHO revised its accreditation requirements; these figures are comparable to the 58% to 92% post-law increase reported by New York medical directors. Similarly, the level of undocumented, unconsented DNR orders reported by Non-New Yorkers *fell* in the aftermath of the JCAHO reforms from a pre-reform level of between 27% and 42%, to a post-reform level of 10% to 13%. These figures are, again, comparable to New York figures which indicate a decline from a pre-law level of 35% to 37% to a post-law level of

5% to 13%. Most importantly, however, The Union College Study found no statistically significant difference between the compliance levels effected by the latitudinarian JCAHO reforms and the authoritarian New York Task Force reforms: both routes to bioethical reform appear to have been equally effective.

There are, however, some significant differences between the consequences of these two strategies of enforcing bioethical reform. The JCAHO reforms appear not to have been contentious beyond the institutional level. The fractious cacophony of dissatisfaction which surrounded the New York DNR law was nowhere in evidence in the medical literature, much less in the popular press. One suspects that there must have been some policies which had perverse effects. Yet, whatever the perversities of the implementation process, because control remained at the institutional level, these could be, and no doubt were, rectified as soon as they became recognizable. Moreover, because implementation lay in the hands of the health care professionals themselves, they could and did institutionalize bioethical policy without relying upon lawyers to serve as intermediaries. They were not prey, therefore, to the legal conservatism which led New York practitioners to such perverse practices as requiring patients to sign DNR consent forms.

The most significant difference between the two strategies of enforcing reform, however, was that JCAHO accreditation standards did not mandate the specifics of bioethical policy, and so did not – indeed could not – legislate morality. This left them open to resolve the futility issue in a number of ways. The Union College Study found that only one third of Non-New York critical care directors report that their hospitals have DNR policies which *permit* them "to write a DNR order on the grounds of medical futility *alone*, without obtaining the patient's or the surrogate's consent." Yet even the two thirds of Non-New York institutions which opted to limit or eliminate futility-based DNR orders were in a radically different situation than New York institutions. For, in the unlikely event that they adopted a DNR policy identical to that mandated in New York, their policies would still be functionally dissimilar. Outside of New York, *the staff themselves* have adopted this policy and, in enforcing it, they can affirm its underlying rationale and assert positive reasons for obedience. They are thus implementing an ethic they themselves understand and embrace, not an alien morality coercively imposed by legislation.

Consequently, even though Non-New York polices may be similar in substance to those in New York, because they have been adopted, affirmed and implemented by health care professionals themselves, they provoked none of the visible dissatisfaction that accompanied the New York DNR reforms proposed by the Task Force and enforced by the Department of Health. The figures gathered by The Union College Study are striking: 58% of New York critical care medical directors report an *increase* in the "failure to write a DNR order because of bureaucratic technicalities." By contrast, only 1% of Non-New Yorkers report such an increase. Forty-three percent of New Yorkers report an increase in the likelihood of "administering futile CPR to irreversibly terminal patients"; by contrast, only 3% of Non-New Yorkers report an increase. Thus the two major complaints New York clinicians lodge against mandatory DNR reform (the bureaucratization of the DNR order and the compulsory administration of futile CPR) are strikingly absent from the experience of Non-New Yorkers.

What makes these findings even more noteworthy is that the JCAHO reforms appear to have achieved the same level of discussion, documentation and consent as the DNR law. Thus professionals, autonomously developing and implementing bioethical policy at the institutional level as a requirement of accreditation, were able to achieve reforms as effective as those mandated by state law, and to do so without the perverse and sometimes inhumane side effects of legally mandated bioethical reform in New York State.

There are several morals to be gleaned from the 1988 natural experiment with mandatory bioethical reform. The most evident of these is that standards set by national and state medical organizations, while influential, tend to be unevenly implemented. Enforcement can be enhanced either through the accreditation or the legal process – which can achieve comparable levels of compliance. Laws, however, because they are instituted through the legislative process, because they are enforced by regulatory bureaucracies, and because they are almost unavoidably interpreted by lawyers, are potentially more problematic. The intrusion of non-clinicians, who inevitably view clinical events from a non-clinical perspective (as is evident from the non-clinical conception of 'futility' built into the New York DNR law), creates the possibility, not only of miscommunication (evident in Swidler's tangled ratiocinations which attempted, but failed, to create a rationale for issuing a no code order for arresting patients for whom CPR is futile), but also a potential for legislating morality – coercively imposing alien moral standards in the clinical context. The New York DNR law fell afoul of all these problems:

it was dogged by problems of misinterpretation, which, in turn, were exacerbated by clinician rebellion (at times to the point of civil disobedience) against what clinicians correctly perceived as an attempt to legislate medical morality.

Perhaps the most important lesson to be gleaned from the experiment is that, despite (or perhaps, because of) a deep commitment to anti-paternalism, bioethical reformers may think themselves immune from the temptation to legislate morality. In its most militant form, however, over-zealous anti-paternalism codified as law is identical in its effects to the legislation of morality and generates classic problems of disaffirmation and disobedience. The contrasting success of the latitudinarian JCAHO reforms highlights the point that extreme anti-paternalist measures are not essential to mandatory bioethical reform: for, if it demonstrated nothing else, 1988 demonstrated that a latitudinarian accreditation strategy wedding mandatory bioethical reform with a recognition of professional autonomy can enforce reform as effectively as an authoritarian state law.

A TURN IN THE DIRECTION OF THE FUTILITY DEBATE

With the onset of the 1990s, the New York Task Force's approach to DNR reform faces yet another problem. The bioethical consensus supporting the delegitimation of futility-based DNR orders is dissolving. In two articles published in 1988 and 1990 ([56], [57]), clinical ethicists Tom Tomlinson and Howard Brody (both of the Michigan State University's Center for Ethics and Humanities in the Life Sciences) developed a set of incisive, detailed, and highly persuasive arguments challenging the rationale for delegitimation offered by the President's Commission and the Hastings Center *Guidelines*. In their 1988 article, Tomlinson and Brody attempt to disentangle the hitherto automatic linkage between *informing* patients and families about a CPR/DNR decision in advance of an arrest, and seeking patient *consent* for such a decision. Patients and families, they argued, have the same right to be informed about CPR/DNR decisions that they would have for any other major alteration of a treatment plan, but they have no more right to *consent* to DNR than for any other decision to deny useless treatment.

The distinction that Tomlinson and Brody draw between informing patients and asking their consent does indeed appear to have been overlooked by bioethicists in the debate over DNR orders. Consider again Tracy Miller's argument about the relationship of consent to enforcement.

> An exception to *informed consent* discussions in cases of medical futility will swallow the rule at a time when physicians are still reluctant *to speak* with patients about resuscitation. As long as that reluctance remains prevalent, any exception on therapeutic or futility grounds is almost certain to be an escape hatch for physicians *seeking to avoid conversations* they have never understood as integral to the obligation to care for dying patients ([33], p. 241, *emphasis added*).

In this passage (which, it will be recalled, states the only clearly articulated and defensible argument for delegitimating futility-based DNR orders), Miller does indeed seem to fuse the concept of being *informed* about a DNR order with the idea of *consenting* to that order. More importantly, insofar as Miller's avowed objective is that of getting reluctant physicians "*to speak* with patients about resuscitation," it would appear that all that need be required of physicians is that they *inform* patients about the DNR decision, since informing patients requires speaking to them. Thus while Miller's argument, in this key passage, may provide a rationale for documentation of the fact that a patient has been *informed* that a DNR order is being contemplated, it is difficult to see why it also provides a rationale for the further requirement of seeking patient or surrogate *consent* to a DNR order.

In their 1990 paper, Tomlinson and Brody develop their analysis further, offering a powerful argument *against* recognizing a patient's right to *consent* to a DNR order. The focus of their second paper is "CPR exceptionalism," that is, the tendency to treat CPR as an exceptional treatment exempt from the normal canons of medical practice. Normally (for example, when considering administering antibiotics), physicians do *not* seek patient consent if they contemplate *not* initiating a non-beneficial or futile medical intervention. Those who would require consent for DNR – which is an order *not* to initiate CPR – are thus treating CPR as an exception to normal practice. Tomlinson and Brody challenge them to provide rational grounds for treating CPR as an exception: "those who oppose futility judgements about intervention must point to some relevant difference that marks a moral distinction between CPR and most other medical treatments" ([57], p. 1277). They then review the possible arguments for making an exception for CPR and find none. This leads them to conclude that there are no rational grounds for treating CPR as exceptional and so they recommend the following policy to normalize CPR/DNR decision making:

> physicians. . . should inform the patient or family of their decision that resuscitation would be futile and should not be attempted, explaining the medical facts that support the decision. . . .
>
> When a patient or family continues to insist on futile resuscitation, the physician may be justified in honoring the demand, but not out of respect for patient autonomy. Rather what their insistence reveals is the depth of their need for denial. Consideration of the patient's *welfare*, rather than his or her rights may support. . . a reluctant promise of attempted CPR. . . . The authority to make a judgment about the balance of harms and benefits of the attempted resuscitation for the patient remains with the physician ([57], p. 1279).

As these and other arguments were voiced, and as new data surfaced on the overall ineffectiveness of CPR ([4], [9], [48], [59], [60], [61]), the tide of organized medical opinion began to turn in favor of futility-based DNR orders. In 1991 the American Medical Association's Council on Ethical and Judicial Affairs revised its 1986 DNR guidelines [37] to legitimate futility-based DNR orders. The new guidelines expressly permit physicians to withhold futile CPR "*even if previously requested by the patient*" ([2], p. 1870). (The emphasis is in the original, and probably reflects the fact that this policy statement *reverses* the stand taken in the 1986 guidelines, which – influenced by the 1983 President's Commission's report – had, in turn, reversed the earlier guidelines of 1974 and 1980 ([35], [36]). The upshot is that the AMA was now returning to its original view that futility-based DNR orders are legitimate.

The new AMA policy also continues to recognize patient refusal of CPR as a second rationale for a DNR order. They also recognize a right which, hitherto, had not been mentioned in any of their policy statements: the right to be informed of a DNR order. Another intriguing development in policy is the following redefinition of 'medical futility':

> Resuscitative efforts should be considered futile if they cannot be expected to restore cardiac or respiratory function to the patient, or to achieve the express goals of the informed patient ([2], p. 1871).

In this passage, the AMA, in effect, offers *two* definitions of futility: a narrow definition in which 'futility' is characterized as the inability to restore cardio-respiratory function; and a broader goal-oriented conception of futility – the inability to achieve the express goals of the patient. The narrow definition is standard in bioethical and lay usage, but the broad notion of futility the AMA here embraces is *not* the normal clinical usage documented by Baker *et al.* and Crane *et al.* (which treats resuscitation as futile if the patient will not survive acute care hospitalization in a conscious state), it is instead a notion developed in, and hitherto unique to, the Hastings *Guidelines* – the notion that intervention is futile if it cannot achieve a *patient's* goals. By accepting the Hastings' conception of futility, the AMA cedes to the patient the power of defining the objective of medical interventions, but nonetheless insists that, where CPR cannot achieve these objectives, the physician has no obligation to administer CPR.

The AMA, therefore, would appear to be attempting to distinguish the physician's authority over medical fact (about the likely success of an intervention) from the patient's autonomy, the right to determine the values which define the purpose of treatment. The result appears to respect both medical authority over means and patient autonomy with respect to ends. Unfortunately, the subtleties of this elegant compromise tend to get lost in the AMA's actual guidelines, in which they are indicated by the italicized statement:

> The physician has an ethical obligation to honor the resuscitation preferences expressed by the patient or the patient's surrogate. *Physicians should not permit their value judgments about the quality of life to obstruct the implementation of a patient or surrogate's preferences regarding the use of CPR*. However, if, in the judgment of the treating physician, CPR would be futile, the treating physician may enter a DNR order into the patient's record. Where there is adequate time to do so, the physician must inform the patient, or the incompetent patient's surrogate, of the content of a DNR order, as well as the basis for its implementation. The physician should be prepared to discuss appropriate alternatives, such as obtaining a second opinion or arranging the transfer of care ([2], p. 1871).

At the time that this is being written, the implications of the AMA's sophisticated effort to resolve the bioethical issues of autonomy, authority and enforcement for the New York DNR law are uncertain. It seems unlikely that physicians will appreciate the subtle nuances embedded in the AMA's characterizations of 'futility'. Studies of the impact of earlier professional guidelines on CPR/DNR (Baker *et al.* and Longo *et al.*)

indicate that these guidelines tend to become stripped of their subtleties in the process of implementation. Thus physicians are likely to read only "the bottom line" which says that "if, in the judgment of the treating physician, CPR would be futile, the treating physician may enter a DNR order into the patient's record" and ignore the nuances.

The AMA's retrenchment, therefore, would appear likely to constitute a radical break with the classic bioethical positions, at least on the level of implementation. This is unfortunate because both the ACP and the Union College surveys indicate strong clinician support for the classic bioethical ideal of respecting patient autonomy – perhaps more support than is acknowledged by either the AMA guidelines or Tomlinson and Brody's recommendation. The Union College survey found that most clinicians did not actually object to the use of consent as a mechanism compelling CPR/DNR discussion with patients/surrogates; nor did they object to consent as a safeguard against strong paternalism. What most clinicians objected to was being required to administer "futile" CPR by *default*; that is, they objected to administering futile CPR in cases in which neither patient nor surrogate had expressly requested it.

One medical director's crude comments epitomize this reaction.

> The law is ass backwards. . . [we are] caught between family desires and actuality, and when [they] have doubts, [we] resuscitate. Make the law that CPR [is] instituted only at patient/family request, not its opposite.

Notice that the medical director was willing to administer "futile" CPR, provided that it was *expressly* requested by a patient or surrogate. The absurdity was administering futile CPR when no one had expressly requested it. As one nurse remarked during an interview with Baker *et al.*

> Do the people who write these laws understand the sort of brutal assault they ask us to inflict on patients – just because no one can make up their mind?

Thus the Union College Study found that, in practice, clinicians appear to be willing to administer futile CPR at the direct request of patients, or even (as in the quotation above) of their families, out of respect, it would appear, for a person's right to a symbolic gesture of defiance in the face of death. What they find objectionable is futile CPR administered by default; for when futile CPR is not administered in response to a request, it is emptied not merely of physiological efficacy, but also of symbolic content. Neither accomplishing nor representing anything, this administration of CPR is worse than useless, it is also meaningless – and clinicians naturally resent it.

A DIFFERENT STRATEGY FOR ADDRESSING THE ISSUE OF CPR/DNR

There is, in our view, no satisfactory resolution of the moral conundrum posed by DNR orders currently on offer. The absence of a satisfactory policy is not a function of any lack of reflective analysis, or good will; it is, we believe, because one piece of the policy dilemma has been ignored, or rather, masked by the clinician's broad use of the term 'futile' – the difference between the problems of inefficacious CPR, and those of efficacious but meaningless or valueless CPR. It is reasonable to characterize CPR as *inefficacious*, if, to appropriate the language of the AMA, CPR "cannot be expected to restore cardiac or respiratory function to the patient." Sometimes, however, CPR is problematic, because it is *efficacious*: it actually restores cardio-respiratory function, but either prolongs the dying process, or extends life in a state that is held to be meaningless or valueless (for example, a persistent vegetative state).

With this distinction in place it should be evident that the analysis offered by the Tomlinson and Brody and current AMA policy are entirely apt with respect to *inefficacious CPR*. Insofar as CPR will not achieve the objective of resuscitating the patient, it need not be initiated. Moreover, the determination that CPR is inefficacious (or 'futile' in the narrow sense) is entirely a matter to be left to medical expertise, although, as with all such matters, the patient/surrogate has a right to be informed of the physician's determination and to seek a second medical opinion.

There seems, moreover, to be no reason to treat the determination that CPR would be inefficacious, and the consequent writing of a DNR order as in any way exceptional. Indeed, the history of various attempts to treat inefficacious CPR as an exception simply serve to underline the reasons for *not* doing so. The conventional bioethical policy of fettering the non-administration of inefficacious CPR to the consent of the patient/surrogate effectively holds DNR hostage to patient/surrogate indecision or denial. And since these all too human reactions are understandably common, the policy inevitably results in administration of inefficacious CPR – despite advance knowledge of the futility and brutality of the intervention. The various attempts to mitigate the inane consequences of the policy (for example, giving physicians the right not to administer inefficacious CPR at the moment of arrest, as recommended by the Hastings *Guidelines* and the DOH-Swidler interpretation) merely complicate matters (by permitting physicians not to code at the moment of crisis) yet fail to resolve the underlying irrationality of the policy itself.

The analysis reverses when we turn to CPR which is problematic, not because it is inefficacious, but because the temporary extension of life it effects is not considered valuable or meaningful. In these cases the classic bioethical analysis seems entirely appropriate, while the newer rationales offered by Tomlinson and Brody and the AMA seem suspect. For when it comes to the meaning or value of life-extension, the expertise of the physician seems irrelevant, and the original rationale for requiring consent offered by President's Commission remains relevant:

> different people will have markedly different needs and concerns during the final period of their lives; living a little bit longer will be of distinctly different value to them. . . . [Therefore] the primacy of a patient's interests in self-determination and in honoring the patient's own view of well-being warrant leaving with the patient the final authority to decide ([40], p. 44).

We concur with the Commission, and question any rationale which accords to physicians the right to make decisions about the meaningfulness of a few hours, or days, or weeks, of life- extension. The valuation of the patient's state during this extension is not properly within the domain of medical expertise; only the patient is in a position to assess the value of such an extension. Hence, as the Commission properly argued, the final authority to decide should rest with the patient, or, if the patient cannot exercise this authority, with the patient's surrogate.

Thus when AMA deeds to the physician the *unrestricted* right to refuse CPR deemed medically futile "*even if previously requested by the patient*," and when Tomlinson and Brody assert that "the authority to make a judgment about the balance of harms and benefits of the attempted resuscitation for the patient remains with the physician," they mistakenly conflate two situations: those in which CPR is inefficacious, in which physicians have a legitimate right to determine the appropriateness of CPR; and those in which CPR is efficacious but the meaning and value of the effects are open to question. By (inadvertently) extending the physician's authority to questions of meaning and value, they violate the fundamental tenet of the bioethical revolution: that the right to determine the meaning and value of life properly resides with the patient. Worse yet, to allow this right, as Tomlinson and Brody propose, only as a function of the *physician's judgment* of harms and benefits is to patronize it and to deny its basic meaning. It is not up to physicians to prescribe our reactions to death, or to impose their own value judgements on the all-too-human desire to delay death. Our response to our own end should be ours to determine as a matter of right, not as a matter of medical sufferance.

Moreover, to turn Tomlinson and Brody's argument against their own analysis, when we fail to require consent for a DNR order in cases in which CPR is efficacious, but of questionable value, we treat CPR as an exception. Normal practice, since the *Quinlan* case, since the very beginning of the bioethical revolution, has been to accord to patients and/or their surrogates the right to determine the *value* of ventilators and other life-extending treatments which merely delay death. As Tomlinson and Brody argue so eloquently, there are no grounds for treating CPR as exceptional, or for judging the value of this particular mode of life-extension as entirely a matter of medical *fact*. Thus the logic of their own argument would appear to require them to deed to the patient the right to determine whether to initiate CPR even in cases when it is likely to be minimally efficacious.

The AMA's treatment of futile CPR is more sensitive than Tomlinson and Brody's. It implicitly recognizes, and urges physicians to recognize, a second, broader, sense of futility, by asking them to consider "the express goals of the informed patient" in their determinations of the futility of CPR ([2], p. 1871). Nonetheless the good intentions of the policy are blurred because it does not clearly distinguish the problems of inefficacious CPR from those of effective CPR. Worse yet, the AMA's actual policy statement is entirely physician-centered and the tone of some of its rhetoric is paternalistic.

Moreover, it seems to us that both the AMA and Tomlinson and Brody fail to give due weight to the problem of enforcing physician compliance. Every study of pre-reform physician compliance with the bioethical ideal of shared physician-patient decisionmaking about terminal care, including those cited in the AMA's own report [7], documents pervasive pre-reform resistance to this ideal. The singular achievement of the mandatory 1988 DNR reforms was that they revolutionized patient-surrogate-physician discussion/consent to CPR/DNR. Integral to that achievement was the conception of patient/surrogate consent as a precondition of non-emergency DNR orders. To exempt physicians once again from *all* consent requirements is likely to reverse the achievements of 1988. To borrow Miller's felicitous turn of phrase, the AMA's proposed revision of DNR policy is likely to create an "exception [that] will swallow the rule."

We believe DNR policy should rest on a frank and open recognition of the difference between those cases in which the problems arise because CPR is *inefficacious* at restoring cardiopulmonary function, and those where problems arise because it is *efficacious*, but the life extended is deemed to be *valueless* or *meaningless*.

When physicians determine that CPR will be inefficacious, they should inform their patient, or their patient's surrogate, of their determination that *CPR would be inefficacious* and therefore will not be administered in the event of cardiopulmonary arrest. They should document both the grounds for this determination, and the fact that the patient/surrogate has been informed of the determination, in the patient's medical record. They should also remind the patient/surrogate of their right to a second medical opinion.

When physicians believe that CPR may be *efficacious*, but that the resulting life-extension may have limited *value* or *meaning* to the patient/surrogate, they should so inform the patient/surrogate and ask them to chose between CPR or DNR. In the meantime, as the President's Commission observed in its report:

> [There should be] some operative policy while a patient is being encouraged to make a choice and patients should be informed about what that will be. Until the patient expresses a clear preference, the policy in effect should be based on the physician's assessment of benefit to the patient ([40], p. 245.).

Thus the physician should also explain to the patient or surrogate that until they chose either CPR or DNR, an *interim* policy (of either CPR or DNR) will temporarily be operative (and placed in the medical record). This policy should be based on the physician's assessment of whether or not it would be in the patient's *best interest* to receive CPR. Physicians are appropriate parties to make a *best interest* decision, not because of their medical expertise, but because of their familiarity with the effects of efficacious CPR and their moral standing as a concerned third party. If and when the patient expresses a considered desire for CPR or DNR, or if the surrogate comes to a decision about what the patient would have desired, this decision overrides the physician's assessment of the patient's best interests. Thus, if there is an express patient-surrogate decision in favor of CPR or DNR, physicians should write orders directing the staff to act accordingly.

Our proposed policy rests on an open distinction between the physician's right, as a medical expert, to determine the inefficacy of CPR to restore functionality, and the patient's right, as an autonomous agent, to determine the meaning and value of life-extension. The proposed policy is biased neither towards the futile administration of inefficacious CPR (the conventional bioethical error), nor towards unconsented termination of an extendable life (the traditional error of futility-based DNR orders, which is reintroduced in both the AMA and the Tomlinson and Brody proposals). It thus recognizes the physician's medical expertise, while still preserving the hard-fought, anti-paternalist gain of the bioethical revolution: that each of us has a right to die our death as we lived our life, according to our own choices and values, not according to those of our physicians.

BIBLIOGRAPHY

1. American Hospital Association: 1973, 'The Patient's Bill of Rights', *Hospitals* **47**, 41.
2. American Medical Association Council on Ethical and Judicial Affairs: 1991, 'Guidelines for the Appropriate Use of Do-Not Resuscitate Orders', *Journal of the American Medical Association* **265**, 1868–1871.
3. Annas, G.: 1989, *The Rights of Patients: The Basic ACLU Guide to Patient's Rights,* Southern Illinois University Press, Carbondale, Illinois.
4. Baker, R.: 1989, 'Beyond Do-Not-Resuscitate Protocols', in M.A. Strosberg, I.A. Fein and J. Carroll (eds.), *Rationing of Medical Care for the Critically Ill,* Brookings Dialogues on Public Policy, The Brookings Institution, Washington D.C., pp. 52–63.
5. Beauchamp, T.: 1978, 'A Reply to Rachels on Active and Passive Euthanasia', in T. Beauchamp and S. Perlin (eds.), *Ethical Issues in Death and Dying*, Englewood Cliffs, New Jersey, 1978, at p. 246, cited in [40], p. 64.
6. Beauchamp, T. and Childress, J.: 1979, *Principles of Biomedical Ethics*, Oxford University Press, New York.
7. Bedell, S. and Delbanco, T.: 1984, 'Choices About Cardiopulmonary Resuscitation in the Hospital – When Do Physicians Talk With Patients?', *New England Journal of Medicine* **310**, 1089–1093.

8. Bedell, S. *et al.*: 1986, 'Do-Not-Resuscitate Orders for Critically Ill Patients in the Hospital: How Are They Used and What is Their Impact?', *Journal of the American Medical Association* **256**, 233–237.
9. Brett, A. and McCullough, L.: 1986, 'When Patients Request Specific Interventions – Defining the Limits of the Physician's Obligation', *New England Journal of Medicine* **315**, 1347–1351.
10. *Circulation*: 1962, [editorial], 'The Closed-Chest Method of Cardiopulmonary Resuscitation: Benefits and Hazards', *Circulation* **26**, 324.
11. Crane, D.: 1977, *The Sanctity of Social Life*, Transaction Books, New Brunswick, New Jersey.
12. *Cruzan v Director, Missouri Dept of Health,* 1990 U.S. Lexis 3301 (US June 25, 1990).
13. Evans, A. and Brody, B.: 1985, 'The Do Not Resuscitate Order in Teaching Hospitals', *Journal of the American Medical Association* **253**, 2236–2239.
14. Grenvik, A. *et al.*: 1978, 'Cessation of Therapy in Terminal Illness and Brain Death', *Critical Care Medicine* **6**, 285.
15. Hastings Center: 1987, *Guidelines on the Termination of Life-Sustaining Treatment and the Care of the Dying*, Indiana University Press, Bloomington, Indiana.
16. Huttman, B.: 1983, 'A Crime of Compassion', *Newsweek*, August 8, 15.
17. Joint Commission on the Accreditation of Health Care Organizations: 1989, *Accreditation Manual for Hospitals,* MA.1.4.11, 82.
18. Jonsson, P., McNamee, M. and Campion, E.: 1988, 'The "Do Not Resuscitate Order": A Profile of its Changing Use', *Archives of Internal Medicine* **148**, 2373–2375.
19. Kamer, R. *et al.*: 1990, 'The Effect of New York State's Do-Not-Resuscitate Legislation on In-Hospital Cardiopulmonary Resuscitation Practice', *American Journal of Medicine* **88**, 108–111.
20. Kapp, M. and Lo, B.: 1986, 'Legal Perceptions and Medical Decision Making', *Millbank Quarterly* 64, Suppl. 2, 163–202.
21. Katz, J.: 1972, *Experimentation with Human Beings*, Russell Sage Foundation, New York.
22. Kouewenhoven, W., Jude, J. and Knickerbocker, C.: 1960, 'Closed Chest Cardiac Massage', *Journal of the American Medical Association* **173**, 1064–67.
23. Lantos, J. *et al.*: 1989, 'The Illusion of Futility in Clinical Practice', *American Journal of Medicine* **87**, 81–84.
24. Lo, B., McLeod, G. A. and Saika, G.: 1986, 'Patient Attitudes to Discussing Life-Sustaining Treatment', *Archives of Internal Medicine* **146**, 1613–1615.
25. Longo, D. *et al.*: 1988, 'Extent of DNR Policies Varies Across Health Care Settings', *Health Progress* June 1988, 66–73.
26. Margolis, D.: 1982, 'Hospital is Investigated on Life-Support Policy', *New York Times* June 20, 1982, at A34.
27. Massachusetts General Hospital – Clinical Care Committee: 1976, 'Optimum Care for Hopelessly Ill Patients', *New England Journal of Medicine* **295**, 362–364.
28. *Matter of O'Connor*, 72 N. Y. 2d 517 (1988).
29. *Matter of Quinlan,* 137 N. J. Superior (1975); *In re Quinlan*, 70 N. J. 10, 355 A. 2d 647, 429 U.S. 922 (1976).
30. *Matter of Storar*, 52 N. Y. 2d 363 (1981).
31. McClung, J. and Kamer, R.: 1990, 'Legislating Ethics: Implications of New York's Do-Not-Resuscitate Law', *New England Journal of Medicine* **232**, 279–283.

32. Medical Society of the State of New York: 1982, *Guidelines for Hospitals and Physicians on 'Do Not Resuscitate'*, Lake Success, New York, reprinted in [40], this volume, pp. 369–370.
33. Miller, T.: 1989, 'Do Not Resuscitate Orders: Public Policy and Patient Autonomy', *Law, Medicine and Health Care* **17**, 245–254.
34. Miller, T. and Swidler, R.: 1989, 'Legislative Initiatives on Life-Sustaining Treatment: The Do-Not-Resuscitate Law and the Health Care Proxy Proposal', *New York State Bar Journal* February 1989, 30–35.
35. National Conference Steering Committee on Cardiopulmonary Resuscitation and Emergency Cardiac Care: 1974, 'Standards for Cardiopulmonary Resuscitation (CPR) and Emergency Cardiac Care (ECC)', *Journal of the American Medical Association* **227**, 837–864.
36. National Conference Steering Committee on Cardiopulmonary Resuscitation and Emergency Cardiac Care: 1980, 'Standards and Guidelines for Cardiopulmonary Resuscitation (CPR) and Emergency Cardiac Care (ECC)', *Journal of the American Medical Association* **244**, 453–509.
37. National Conference Steering Committee on Cardiopulmonary Resuscitation and Emergency Cardiac Care: 1986, 'Standards and Guidelines for Cardiopulmonary Resuscitation (CPR) and Emergency Cardiac Care (ECC)', *Journal of the American Medical Association* **255**, 2905–2984.
38. Plowe, C.: 1988, correspondence, *New England Journal of Medicine* **317**, 281–85.
39. Praeger, K.: 1989, 'How CPR Can Threaten the Desperately Ill', *Wall Street Journal*, March 9, 1989, 16.
40. President's Commission for the Study of Ethical Problems in Medicine and Biomedical and Behavioral Research: 1983, *Deciding to Forego Life-Sustaining Treatment: A Report on the Ethical, Medical, and Legal Issues in Treatment Decisions*, U. S. Gov't Printing Office, Washington D. C, this volume, pp. 371–380.
41. Queens County, Superior Court: 1984, 'Report of the Special January Third Additional 1983 Grand Jury Concerning "Do Not Resuscitate" Procedures at a Certain Hospital in Queens County', February 8, 1984.
42. Quill, T., Sanakaitis, J. and Krause, C.: 1986, 'The Effect of a Community Hospital Resuscitation Policy on Elderly Patients', *New York State Medical Journal of Medicine* **86**, 622–625.
43. Quill, T. and Bennett, N.: 1992, 'The Effects of a Hospital Policy and State Legislation on Resuscitation Orders for Geriatric Patients', *Archives of Internal Medicine* **152**, 569-572, this volume, pp. 241–250.
44. Rabkin, M., Gillerman, G. and Rice, N.: 1976, 'Orders Not To Resuscitate', *New England Journal of Medicine* **295**, 364–366.
45. Rachels, J.: 1975, 'Active and Passive Euthanasia', *New England Journal of Medicine* **292**, 78, cited at [40], p. 64.
46. Rawls, J.: 1980, 'Kantian Constructivism in Moral Theory: The Dewey Lectures 1980', *The Journal of Philosophy* **77**, 515–572.
47. Rosenthal, E.: 1990, 'Rules on Reviving the Dying Bring Unendurable Suffering, Doctors Contend', *New York Times,* October 4, 1990, A1, B20.
48. Schneiderman, L., Jecker, N. and Jonsen, A.: 1990, 'Medical Futility: Its Meaning and Ethical Implications', *Annals of Internal Medicine* **112**, 12.

49. State of New York, Department of Health Memorandum, Health Facility Series 88-24; H-13, NH-8, HRF-8; 'Do Not Resuscitate Orders', March 18, 1988.
50. Sullivan, R.: 1982, 'Hospitals Seek Rules on Withholding Support', *New York Times*, November 17, 1982, B3.
51. Swendler, P.: 1989, 'Reflections on the New York Do-Not-Resuscitate Law', *New York State Journal of Medicine* **89**, 57–58.
52. Swidler, R.: 1989, 'The Presumption of Consent in New York State's Do-Not-Resuscitate Law', *New York State Journal of Medicine* **89**, 69–72.
53. Symmers, W.St.C., Sr.: 1968, 'Not Allowed to Die', *British Medical Journal* **442**, cited in [21], p. 709.
54. Tagge, G., Adler, W. and Browne, C.: 1974, 'Relationship of Therapy to Prognosis in Critically Ill Patients', *Critical Care Medicine* **2**, 61.
55. The New York State Task Force on Life and the Law: 1986, 1988, *Do Not Resuscitate Orders: The Proposed Legislation and Report of the New York State Task Force on Life and the Law,* New York State Task Force on Life and the Law, New York, this volume, pp. 381–413.
56. Tomlinson, T. and Brody, H.: 1988, 'Ethics and Communication in Do Not Resuscitate Orders', *New England Journal of Medicine* **318**, 43–46.
57. Tomlinson, T. and Brody, H.: 1990, 'Futility and the Ethics of Resuscitation', *Journal of the American Medical Association* **264**, 1276–1280.
58. Weir, R. and Gossin, L.: 1990, 'Decisions to Abate Life-Sustaining Treatment for Non-Autonomous Patients: Ethical Standards and Legal Liability for Physicians After Cruzan', *Journal of the American Medical Association* **264**, 1846–1853.
59. Yougner, S. *et al.*: 1985, 'Do Not Resuscitate Orders – Incidence and Implications in a Medical Intensive Care Unit', *Journal of the American Medical Association* **254**, 54–57.
60. Yougner, S.: 1988, 'Who Defines Futility?', *Journal of the American Medical Association* **260**, 294–295.
61. Younger, S.: 1990, 'Futility in Context', *Journal of the American Medical Association* **264**, 1295–1296.
62. Zoll, P.: 1952, 'Resuscitation of the Heart in Ventricular Standstill by External Electric Stimulation', *New England Journal of Medicine* **247**, 768

PART II

THE DNR CONTROVERSY IN NEW YORK STATE

TRACY E. MILLER

TAKING STOCK OF POLICIES FOR DO-NOT-RESUSCITATE ORDERS: PERCEPTION AND PRACTICE

In the waning hours of the 1987 legislative session, the New York State Legislature passed Article 29-B of the Public Health Law, commonly known as the do-not-resuscitate (DNR) law [25]. Based on a proposal by the New York State Task Force on Life and the Law [26], the law embodied a widely accepted consensus about policies that should guide advance decisions to withhold cardiopulmonary resuscitation (CPR). That consensus reflected a judgment that CPR offered little or no benefit for some patients and should not be provided. The consensus also recognized the participation of patients, or surrogates for incapacitated patients, as an important part of the process for deciding whether an order to withhold cardiopulmonary resuscitation should be entered for patients in a hospital or other health care facility.

By 1990, when a team of researchers from Union College conducted a study of the law [7], physicians had begun to challenge that consensus. A chorus of voices in the medical literature questioned the appropriateness of involving patients and families in all cases, asserting that in certain circumstances physicians should make a medical judgment about the potential benefits of CPR ([10], [24], [43]). Under this approach, the consent of patients and families, or as proposed by some physicians, even their awareness of the order, becomes irrelevant.

The studies of New York's DNR law, offer an opportunity to reflect on the law one year to approximately eighteen months after its implementation when the studies were conducted. The studies also yield insight into the debate about DNR policies unfolding nationally. Three of the studies are based on an examination of patients' charts, presenting data about several important factors before and after the law, including the number of orders written, the medical condition of the patients for whom the orders were written, and the extent of discussion about CPR between patients and physicians ([3], [19], [32]). Two other studies, the study by Baker *et al.* [7] and Spritz [38], present health care professionals' perceptions about the law, and its impact.

Both the documented changes in DNR practices, and the perception of those changes by health care professionals, yield important information.

R. Baker & M.A. Strosberg (eds.), Legislating Medical Ethics: A Study of the New York Do-Not-Resuscitate Law, 105–132.

The differences between these two kinds of data, however, must be recognized. One reports on fact, the other on impressions. In contrast to the studies of actual practice, studies of perception are inherently subjective. Especially when those perceptions diverge from the findings about actual practice, as occurred so dramatically with the perception data reported and relied upon by Baker *et al.*, the perceptions convey more about their source than they do about the reality of what is perceived. Indeed, the data of physician perception presented by Baker *et al.* cannot be used to gauge the actual "impact" of the DNR law. It can, however, shed light on the debate about futility nationally. Why do physicians' perceptions differ so significantly from studies of actual practice, and what does this mean for policies on medical futility?

Another characteristic of the data and attitudes presented in this volume is also crucial to analysis of both the DNR law and medical futility. Apart from one anecdotal account, the perspective of patients and family members are not presented in the studies or articles in this volume. The articles focus exclusively on the personal experience or impressions of health care professionals or on data about clinical practice. Yet, a similarity between the perspective of patients and physicians cannot be assumed. In fact, a growing body of data about patients' wishes concerning CPR and their desire to participate in the decision-making process suggests that patients and physicians often have profoundly different perceptions and attitudes about CPR decisions. This data too must be considered in assessing the DNR law.

This article evaluates the studies of the law in the context of the goals identified by the Task Force and available data about patient attitudes about the CPR decision. It also discusses the 1991 amendments to the law, as well as the Task Force's 1992 proposal for surrogate decisions. That proposal would incorporate decisions about CPR into a broad legislative framework for surrogate decisions about all treatment. I have also written a short piece responding to the article by Robert Baker, "The Legitimation and Regulation of DNR Orders" [5]. I chose to respond separately to the article, and to comment on the data upon which he relies, because he draws such sweeping conclusions from Baker *et al.*'s study of physician perceptions and because of the serious flaws in their analysis of the law. [Editors note: Miller's critique [23] and Baker's reply [6], both appear in this volume (pp. 325–332; pp. 333–346), in Part V.]

1. DEVISING POLICY – PROBLEMS AND PROPOSALS

At the request of Governor Cuomo, the issuance of DNR orders was one of the first questions the Task Force addressed. The problems associated with DNR orders in New York State captured public attention as a result of several prominent cases. One of these cases prompted a special Grand Jury investigation in 1982 [33]. Focusing on the death of an elderly woman in a Queens hospital who had not been resuscitated because of an unwritten DNR order, the Grand Jury found that the hospital had devised a system of removable purple dots administered at the nurses' station to indicate DNR status. The system had been developed in response to a decision by the hospital board that written DNR orders were "of doubtful legality" ([33], p. 18). The Grand Jury report concluded that procedural abuses and the failure to openly discuss and document CPR decisions appeared to be widespread. It attributed the abuses, in large measure, to physicians' fears about civil and criminal liability for documenting the decisions.

When the Task Force began to explore the issue in March 1985 [27], it found that problems persisted. In some cases, orders were entered without the knowledge or consent of patients or family members involved with their care. Worried about liability, yet unwilling to subject their patients to resuscitation they believed was inappropriate, other physicians relied instead on covert practices such as slow codes and show codes; the provision of CPR too slowly to be effective, or a pretense that CPR had been provided. While the visible public cases pointed to undertreatment as the primary concern, the Task Force concluded that overtreatment was also a pervasive problem, since physicians and facilities in some cases simply did not enter DNR orders even when it was medically and ethically appropriate to do so ([27], p. 7).

The Task Force also concluded that the patient's right to decide about CPR was well-established in legal principle and often overlooked in medical practice. In contrast, surrogate decisions were not recognized by legal doctrines but were often relied upon for both patients who had the capacity to decide for themselves, and for those who did not. Fears about liability seemed to attach to the order itself, independent of the source of consent.

A. *The Options for Public Policy*

Existing legal precedents delineate the alternatives for public policy, dictating whether new policies must be implemented through legislative, regulatory or educational initiatives. In New York State, decisions reached by the New York Court of Appeals in companion cases, *In re Eichner* and *In re Storar*, created the legal framework for decisions about life-sustaining treatment. Eichner [1], concerned Brother Fox, an elderly member of a religious order, who lapsed into a coma in October 1979. A fellow member of the order, Brother Eichner, sought a court order permitting the withdrawal of the respirator sustaining Brother Fox. The Court of Appeals held that the respirator could be withdrawn, based on "clear and convincing" evidence that its removal was consistent with Brother Fox's wishes ([1] at 72). In contrast to the approach taken by many courts as early as the Quinlan case, the Court expressly declined to recognize Brother Eichner's authority to decide on the patient's behalf.

In the companion case, *In re Storar*, the Court extended these principles and rejected substituted or third party consent to the withdrawal or withholding of life-sustaining measures. John Storar was a 52-year-old profoundly retarded man dying of incurable bladder cancer. The state-run facility caring for him sought a court order to permit continued blood transfusions over the objections of John Storar's mother, who had been appointed his legal guardian. The Court granted the facility's application, explaining that no one, not even a loving relative, could refuse life-sustaining or life-saving treatment for another.

In the *Storar* opinion, the Court also articulated its vision of the appropriate role of the courts and the legislature in the medical-ethical arena, a vision it would reiterate implicitly or explicitly in the cases which followed. Unlike courts in other states that had called for legislative attention to these issues but had reluctantly set forth broad rules for treatment decisions, the Court of Appeals ruled narrowly on the case before it. Alluding to the need for legislative direction, the Court stated, "Unlike the Legislature, the courts are neither equipped nor empowered to prescribe substantive or procedural rules for all, most, or even the more common contingencies."

The Task Force members recognized the difficulty of translating ethical principles into law. As observed in their report, "Legislation is not the only means, nor is it always the best means, to establish public policy – especially where those policies involve sensitive and controversial moral questions" ([27], p.18, this volume, p. 394). However, neither professional standards nor regulations would suffice in New York State. Only legislation could overcome judicial precedents established by the Court of Appeals. Without legislation, physicians would be expected to choose between social and ethical principles supporting family members as surrogates for incapable patients and conflicting New York State legal doctrines. This rift undermined the interests of patients at the same time that it left physicians in an untenable position.

The lack of legal support for surrogate decisions to decline treatment was not particular to CPR; it potentially covered all life-saving and life-sustaining measures. Recognizing that comprehensive legislation for treatment decisions would be necessary in the long-run unless judicial rulings changed, the Task Force chose to address CPR first. One of the first issues posed by medical advances, DNR orders had been considered by many segments of society. The sharply limited benefits of CPR for some patients and the highly invasive nature of the treatment contributed to a shared acceptance of the limits of this particular medical technology. This consensus, at least in New York State, did not extend to other life-sustaining measures such as antibiotics or artificial nutrition and hydration. As a result, while it certainly would have been theoretically neater and more desirable to enact legislation covering surrogate decisions for all treatments, as George Annas argues (this volume, pp. 141–155), this was not an option in New York State in 1987. Nor was reliance solely on professional guidelines an alternative; they could not establish legal authority for surrogate decisions in the face of clear judicial precedents to the contrary. In this regard, Jane Greenlaw's assertion (this volume, pp. 133–136) that legislation was unnecessary for policies on CPR or other treatments is odd. It bears no relationship to the legal realities particular to New York State.

B. *The Public Debate*

The Task Force released its report and legislative proposal in April 1986. The report discussed the social, legal and ethical issues presented by resuscitation decisions and the rationale for policy choices made by the Task Force [27]. The proposal set forth a decision-making process, with separate guidelines for patients in the following circumstances: (i) adults with decision-making capacity; (ii) adults without capacity who left a clear prior expression of their wishes about CPR; (iii) adults without capacity and no prior wishes who have family members or others to decide on their behalf: (iv) adults without capacity and without anyone available to act as a surrogate; and (v) children. The proposal identified the decision-making process in each case and standards to guide surrogate decisions. It also granted health care professionals and facilities protection from liability if they followed the law's provisions.

The Legislature held public hearings on the proposed legislation in February 1987 [42]. The public testimony revealed widespread recognition of the need for legal guidance about DNR orders. The Hospital Association of New York State, the Medical Society of New York State, the State Nurses Association, the Greater New York Hospital Association, and advocates for patients stressed the need for legislation, pointing to the fact that pervasive fears about liability had undermined the interests of patients and the decision-making process ([42], pp. 57, 83, 185). The public hearings also provided a forum for debate about particular issues raised by the bill. The most significant debate centered on the therapeutic exception; an exception which recognizes that physicians may enter a DNR order without speaking to a competent adult patient if they determine that the conversation itself would harm the patient. The New York State Medical Society characterized the decision about CPR as a burden for both patients and family and argued for a broad therapeutic exception ([42], pp. 243–244). In contrast, advocates for patients supported the opportunity to participate in the CPR decision ([42], pp. 287–288).

During two days of public hearings, the issue of medical futility, and the option for physicians to enter an order on that basis without consent, were barely mentioned, despite the fact that these questions would become the center of controversy following the law's enactment. However, the debate about the therapeutic exception, touching on the rights of patients and prerogatives of physicians, foreshadowed many of the same underlying issues and tensions.

Following public hearings in February 1987, intensive legislative negotiations about the bill took place. During that process, the balance in the bill shifted. The Task Force had crafted its proposal to address two co-equal problems – undertreatment (wrongful withholding of CPR) and overtreatment (wrongful provision of CPR because of failure to discuss the issue openly with patient or family). In the legislative process, only one problem was emphasized, the problem of undertreatment. Additional procedures were added as safeguards against the inappropriate entry of a DNR order ([27], p.22).

II. ASSESSING THE DNR LAW

The studies of the DNR law present an interesting, complex and contradictory picture. The study findings based on data of actual practices differ dramatically from the studies of perceptions by nurses and physicians. Significantly, the studies of perception and practice diverge most on the two most crucial outcomes examined: the frequency of physician consultation with patients about CPR, and the provision of CPR physicians consider "futile."

A. *Promoting Patient Autonomy*

The Task Force regarded patient autonomy and participation in decisions about CPR as a primary goal for public policy. Promoting autonomy serves both instrumental purposes and important values. Involving patients in the decision accords respect owed to them as individuals. It also enhances decision-making by incorporating their values, beliefs and preferences into the decision-making process. The Task Force embraced the notion of a partnership between patient and physician as an ideal, recognizing that patients should decide in consultation with their physician.

The studies by Kamer *et al.*, and by Quill and Bennett, examined the change in physician practices in seeking consent to DNR orders by reviewing medical records for patients who died during hospitalization ([19], [32]). Unfortunately, both studies found that there was no significant increase in patient participation under the DNR law, with families deciding about CPR on behalf of patients in most instances. Kamer *et al.* determined that patients participated in the decision to forgo CPR in only 13% to 16% of the 245 cases studied. The authors of the study observed that, "There appears to have been little change in the common practice of deferring decisions regarding CPR status until later in the hospital course, at which time the patient's deteriorating physiologic status often renders him or her incapable of making an informed judgment" ([19], p.110).

In contrast, health care professionals who participated in the Union College Study perceived a dramatic increase in patient participation in decisions about CPR ([7], 269). Critical care nurses estimated that the likelihood of physician discussion about CPR with patients increased 38.5%, from 37.5% to 75.8%, while critical care physicians estimated a 30.7% jump to 66.2% after the law's passage ([7], Table 2, p. 269). The survey of the members of the New York Chapter of the College of Physicians conducted by Spritz also showed that physicians believed that they were far more likely to discuss resuscitation with their patients [38]. Significantly, the Spritz study asked physicians about their own practices, a more reliable estimate than the impressions of a general shift in the practice of all physicians measured by the Union College Study. Sixty-eight per cent of the 743 members of the College of Physicians that responded to the survey agreed with the statement, "the DNR law has made it more likely that I will raise the issue of DNR status with my patients" ([38], p. 253).

Discussion between patient and physician protects both aspects of the right to decide about treatment: the right to refuse and the right to consent to or request treatment. Unless informed by their physician, most patients will not know that they are at risk for cardiac arrest, that CPR may be withheld, or that an important decision is pending. While much of the recent medical literature has focused on patients' desire for CPR that physicians believe is not beneficial, the right to decline CPR is often sacrificed in the silence between doctor and patient. Once informed, many patients would choose to forgo CPR that physicians would otherwise provide ([8], [9], [14]). Studies have shown that physicians' knowledge of patients' wishes errs in both directions: physicians overestimate and underestimate patients' desire for CPR ([29], [44]).

B. *Patient Autonomy – Burden or Benefit?*

The Union College Study asked physicians and nurses to estimate the likelihood or frequency of certain events linked to patient autonomy, such as discussion between patient and physician about CPR before and after the law was enacted. It also asked for more general assessments of how well the law worked. Is it "humane?" Are patients and physicians "better off?"

Whether the law is "humane" or "better" for patients or physicians can only be assessed in relation to identified, or implicit, values and goals. Is it humane to talk to patients and families about CPR? Are patients better off if families participate in decisions for incapacitated patients or if physicians decide unilaterally? Any assessment of policy inevitably begs the question of what yardstick will be used to calibrate success or failure.

In an effort to make patients and those close to them active partners in the decision about CPR, the DNR law removed physicians' option to enter a DNR order unilaterally, without talking with patients or surrogates. This practice appears to have been widespread. According to one study, prior to 1988, only 40% of hospital policies nationally required discussion of the DNR order between patient and family [22]. The evaluations of the law by health care professionals reflect, in large measure, their assessment of whether this change benefitted them and their patients.

The split between critical care nurses, critical care physicians and the hematologists/oncologists is most significant in this regard. In their written comments, the critical care nurses often characterized the law, and their own role, as important to promoting patients' rights. As explained by Virginia Dersch in her analysis of the Union College responses, the nursing directors "reveal their primary attitudinal and behavioral orientation as Patient Advocate in their support of the DNR Law," ([13] p. 319). As expressed by one nurse, "Patients and families have been able to make their wishes known and have them respected under this new law" [12]. Nurses also frequently identified physician reluctance or failure to discuss CPR with patients and enter a DNR order as a continuing problem; one-third of the nursing directors reported this problem ([13]). In response to the question about whether the law is humane, 38.9% of the critical care nursing directors responded that the law had increased the likelihood that patients would be treated humanely, 8% reported a decrease, and 53.1% stated that there had been no change ([7] Table 4, p. 282).

In contrast, many of the hematologists/oncologists who provided written comments on the law, pointed to the obligation to talk with patients as harsh and inhumane. As expressed by one physician, "It is often inappropriate and unnecessarily cruel to discuss DNR with desperately ill patients" [12]. According to the analysis of physician comments provided by Virginia Dersch, many hematologists/ oncologists objected to the law because of the stress they believe is placed on patients when they discuss decisions about resuscitation. They also objected to the "stress and guilt" placed on families by discussing the issue with them. As summarized by Dersch, "many of these hematologists-oncologists reveal in their comments that they 'oppose' the law because it, in their view, prevents them from performance of a core component of their role as Patient Guide, i.e., 'making good and appropriate decisions *for* patients'." ([13], p. 319, *emphasis added*).

This attitude was undoubtedly reflected in the subjective assessment about whether the law had increased or decreased the chance that patients would be treated humanely: 18.2% of the hematologists/oncologists noted an increase, 36.4% noted a decrease and 45.5% stated that there had been no change ([7], Table 4, p. 282). Many of the critical care physicians shared these concerns. Baker and Strosberg report that 47% of the critical care physicians believed that the therapeutic exception to discussing CPR with competent patients should be broader than permitted by the law. Dersch explains that they also strongly resented the interference with their clinical prerogatives ([13], p. 314).

A rich body of data about patient attitudes and preferences shows that the views of these critical care physicians and many of the hematologists/oncologists are at odds with the public's own wishes and attitudes about the decision-making process. Studies of patient attitudes have consistently shown that patients desire information about their medical condition and want to participate in decisions about their own treatment, including the hard choices at life's end. One study of elderly outpatients found that 87% of the patients thought that discussions about CPR should take place routinely, but only 3% had discussed the issue previously with physicians ([16], [21]). Another study of 198 competent nursing home residents showed that 92% of the residents had not been asked about CPR, with 61% reporting that they would like to be involved in the decision [45].

The attitudes of the hematologists/oncologists and critical care physicians who oppose discussing CPR with patients and families also diverge from professional standards embraced by the medical community itself. The guidelines for the appropriate use of CPR issued by the Council on Ethical and Judicial Affairs of the American Medical Association state, "Physicians should discuss with appropriate patients the possibility of cardiopulmonary arrest. Patients at risk of cardiac or respiratory failure should be encouraged to express in advance their preferences regarding the use of CPR" [11]. The Council also characterized the lack of patient participation in decisions about CPR as disturbing, noting that it may result in decisions that do not respect the patient's wishes and values.

C. *Surrogate Decision-making*

The DNR law was designed to grant family members and others the legal authority to decide about CPR on behalf of incapacitated patients, including children. By granting this authority, the legislation would bring

New York's law into line with the law in virtually every other state in the nation. Long-standing ethical premises justified and fostered this grant of legal authority in states across the country. A consensus had emerged that family members are most familiar with the patient's wishes, and most devoted to patient's well-being. They are therefore best able, or have the strongest moral claim, to make a judgment under the prevailing standards identified in the fields of law, medicine and ethics – the substituted judgment and best interests standards. In its report, the Task Force embraced these premises as the moral foundation for surrogate decisions ([27], pp. 36–40).

The DNR law clearly established the authority of family members to decide about CPR. The list of potential surrogates also included a category of "close friend," an individual with a personal relationship with the patient such that he or she is familiar with the patient's health care preferences and personal beliefs. This model has now been followed by many other states. In essence, the law granted these individuals as well as family members a specific role in the decision-making process.

The studies in this volume provide an incomplete picture of whether such participation by surrogates, a goal in and of itself, also achieved the law's underlying purposes of promoting patients' wishes and interests. However, data from other studies has shown that requiring family participation in decisions about CPR fosters decisions in accord with patient preferences about who should decide on their behalf, and whether CPR should be provided. While some patients would choose their physician to decide about life-sustaining treatment on their behalf, the overwhelming majority of individuals would select a family member to decide, in consultation with their physician ([16], [17], [18]). Studies have also shown that families are more familiar with the patients' wishes than physicians. One study matched patient wishes about CPR in four, different hypothetical cases with the predictions of spouses. Spouses' predictions were better than chance alone in three of four scenarios while physicians predictions of patient wishes were better than chance alone in only one of four [44]. In other studies, spouses and other family members have also predicted patients' wishes about treatment accurately in a significantly higher percentage of cases than physicians [29].

At the same time, studies have demonstrated that family participation is hardly as reliable as direct communication with the patient [47]. For example, Quill and Bennett found that in most cases the medical record showed that families had decided about CPR based on their own wishes, not on an assessment of the patient's wishes [32]. Available data therefore suggests that family participation falls far short of direct input from the patient, but promotes the patients' choices about CPR to a greater degree than unilateral physician decisions.

A judgment about whether participation by family members and others close to the patient serves other interests, and furthers the best interests of patients more broadly, is complex. A study by Fader *et al.* indicates that, at least for some elderly nursing home residents, family relationships are too attenuated to fulfill the surrogate function [14]. That study of CPR decisions for 233 nursing home residents found that 45% of the family members of 185 incapacitated residents failed to respond to the facility's request for a CPR decision.

The other studies of the DNR law provide no direct data about whether family participation furthered the interests of patients. The Union College Study does present, however, physicians' and nurses' estimates about increased failure to write DNR orders because of family ambivalence or hesitance and bureaucratic delays associated with the requirements for surrogate consent under the law ([7], Table 4, p. 282). Failure to write the order, without further information about the patient's wishes and medical condition, cannot be judged a good or bad outcome. However, failure to write the order is harmful to patients if correlated with the provision of CPR that is futile (CPR that achieves no physiological benefit), contravenes the patient's wishes, or imposes burdens which far exceed any potential benefit. The data on resuscitation rates under the law, and the issue of futile CPR, must therefore be examined carefully to determine whether the law increased futile or harmful CPR, and, if so, the extent to which family participation, or other factors, contributed to this result.

D. *Futile CPR*

The studies of the DNR law show a clear split between perception and practice on the issue of futile CPR. The three studies that examined actual practices before and after implementation of the DNR law found that the law did not significantly alter the number of DNR orders written or lead to an increase in the provision of CPR. In contrast, physicians perceived a clear increase in CPR they deemed "futile."

Studying practices at an acute care hospital, Kamer *et al.* concluded that the number of CPR attempts had not risen following implementation of the law, although use of explicit DNR orders increased dramatically, from 13 of 60 (22%) patients who died without CPR in 1987 to 64 of 69 (93%) in 1988 ([19], p. 109. Tables 1 and 2). Focusing on elderly patients in a community hospital with a well-established policy of explicit DNR orders before the law became effective, Quill and Bennett found an insignificant rise in the number of DNR orders written before and after the law [32]. The study did show that CPR was more likely to be performed when ordered (56% in 1984 compared to 92%) under the DNR law. Also significant is the high success rate of CPR in 1988 (39% for patients over 65), a success rate that far surpasses the rate demonstrated in other studies. The authors attribute these positive outcomes to the appropriate selection of patients for CPR, and to advance decisions to forgo CPR for patients with a poor prognosis for CPR, such as end-stage terminal illness [32].

The study by Ahronheim *et al.* [3] of three large acute care hospitals found that the DNR law did not significantly alter the number of CPR attempts, the number of patients accorded DNR status, or the medical conditions of patients for whom DNR orders were entered. Like the study by Fader *et al.* [14], the three-hospital study did show a sharp increase in documentation of the orders at two facilities, with an increase from 8.5 to 99.1% at one facility. Both before and after the law, patients placed in the category of "hopeless illness" based on their diagnosis, were far less likely than other patients to undergo CPR. The authors state that they undertook the study to "evaluate the impression on the part of some of our colleagues that the DNR law was leading to an increase in the number of medically inappropriate resuscitations" [3]. They concluded that their study failed to confirm the hypothesis.

That hypothesis corresponds to the perceptions of many health care professionals reported by the Union College study. Diverse reasons might explain why physicians and nurses perceived an increase in "futile" CPR: (i) patient or family insistence on CPR that physicians deemed futile, under a broad understanding of futility; (ii) patient or family insistence on CPR that was physiologically futile; (iii) family ambivalence; (iv) physician failure or delay in entering the order, and (v) misunderstanding of the law's policies about contemporaneous resuscitation decisions in the absence of a written DNR order (the default CPR decision).

The professional perceptions of "futile" CPR documented by the Union College Study [7] must be examined in light of the lively debate about the meaning of futility in the medical literature. That debate has highlighted the elastic nature of the term "futile" as used by physicians to describe CPR ([11], [20], [35]) Some physicians use the term to mean that treatment will provide no physiological benefit while others use the term as a placeholder for an expected, although not certain, poor outcome or for a judgment that the burdens of treatment outweigh the benefits. As explained by the American Medical Association Council on Judicial and Ethical Affairs in its recent statement of DNR policy, "Evidence suggests that terms such as futility when used by physicians to express the probability of achieving a specified outcome, have a variety of potential meanings that are understood differently by different physicians" [11].

The Union College Study never defined "futility," in the questions asked of participants. It did, however, ask the respondents to define the term themselves: 70% of hematologists/oncologists, about half of all nursing directors, and almost two-thirds of medical directors defined "futile" CPR to mean that the patient will not survive to leave the hospital or will survive but in a coma ([7], pp. 294–295). While Baker *et al.* did not provide the remaining responses, debate about futility in the medical literature suggests that many of those physicians would have defined futility more broadly.

E. *Patient and Surrogate Preferences for CPR*

Many decisions about CPR are value-laden, requiring a judgment about the benefit of continued life against the risk of significant disability or a life of short duration. The DNR law was designed to shift the locus of control from physician to patient or surrogate for these decisions, to give patients and surrogates the chance to decide whether to assume those risks. Given the broad notion of "futility" embraced by physicians in the Union College Study, estimates by physicians that the DNR law increased "futile" CPR undoubtedly reflect many instances when patients or surrogates opted for CPR that physicians believed was of marginal benefit, although it was not futile in the narrow sense of offering no physiological benefit.

In some cases, however, patients or surrogates may have insisted on CPR that was physiologically futile and offered no realistic hope of continued life. The DNR law was not intended to stretch the boundaries of patient or surrogate autonomy to encompass a right to insist on futile treatment, a right not accorded for other treatments. Implicit, although not explicit, in the legislation was the notion that physicians have no duty to provide treatment that offers the patient no physiological benefit. At the time the law was passed, the issue of futile CPR had not emerged as pressing, and this implicit assumption about medical practice was not stated explicitly. When the issue was first debated following the law's passage, the New York State Department of Health clarified that the law does not require physicians to provide CPR at the insistence of patients or surrogates, if physicians determine that CPR is futile as defined in the statute ([26], [28]). Instead, physicians must seek a second medical opinion that CPR is futile and inform patients or their surrogates before entering a DNR order on grounds of medical futility. The statute defines medical futility as instances when CPR will not restart the patient's respiration and circulation, or when the patient would be subjected to repeated resuscitation in a short-time period before death occurs ([25], section 2961).

F. *Family Ambivalence*

Nurses and physicians surveyed by the Union College study reported that the DNR law had led to a rise in the failure to write DNR orders because of family ambivalence ([7] Table 4, p. 282). Family ambivalence is certainly one cost of asking and involving families. The comparison of perceptions by physicians inside and outside New York suggested a greater increase in family ambivalence in New York than in other states. Two factors could explain this difference. Because of the absence of legal support for surrogate decisions, physicians may have been far less likely to involve families in New York before the reforms occurred, thus leading to a stronger perception of increased family ambivalence. Moreover, Baker *et al.* report that after the reforms, approximately one-third of hospital policies outside New York allowed physicians to enter orders without obtaining consent from the patient or family (and possibly without disclosing the order). Limiting family involvement would naturally decrease ambivalence ([7] Table 5, p. 283).

Specific requirements in the DNR law may have both contributed to and ameliorated the problem of family ambivalence. While the requirement of written consent to a DNR order may give some surrogates a greater sense of control or resolution, it proved onerous and unnecessary for others. Based on recommendations by the Task Force, the DNR law was amended in 1991 to allow surrogates to provide oral consent [2].

Two other provisions were designed to minimize or address family ambivalence and conflict. The law requires all facilities to establish a process to mediate disputes that arise about CPR decisions ([25], Section 2972). The flexible process was established to resolve conflicts that arise because family members have not been fully informed about the patient's condition, or because one family member may not be reconciled to the decision, even if others agree. In the event that conflict cannot be resolved, physicians may enter a DNR order based on the consent of one or more members of a surrogate class, such as one child for an elderly parent, even when other children disagree, if physicians believe in good faith that the order is consistent with the patient's wishes, or if those are not known, with the patient's best interests ([25], Section 2965).

None of the studies of the law provided information about whether health care professionals relied on these alternatives when faced with family ambivalence or conflict. Anecdotally, health care facilities and professionals have reported to the Task Force that these alternatives are rarely used for a variety of reasons: facility concern about adverse publicity, legal advice to avoid the confrontation despite the legal protection afforded by the law, and clinicians' own reluctance to override family members and enter the order. Notably, these concerns are an important part of the "futility" equation, and have little to do with legal solutions or hurdles.

G. *Delay in Entering DNR Orders*

Following the law's implementation, several procedures in the law, including the requirement of written consent by surrogates, proved problematic. Many concerns centered on the forms used by health care facilities. The forms were not mandated by the statute, but were developed by hospital counsel to obviate the need for physicians to make notes in the medical record that would demonstrate compliance with the law. A discussion of the complex role of legal counsel to health care providers and providers' fear about liability is outside the scope of this paper. Clearly, however, complications from these concerns are not unique to the DNR law, although they may be more far-reaching in New York State generally than in other states.

Based on recommendations by the Task Force, the Legislature amended the law in 1991 to eliminate or modify several procedures that had proven cumbersome or confusing, including the requirement of written surrogate consent, the procedures for re-entering an order following transfer from one facility to the next, and the requirements for physician review of the orders ([2], Ch. 370). It is important to note, however, that under both the Task Force's proposal, and the law as enacted, the process for seeking the patient's consent to a DNR order remained simple and straightforward – the law required a dialogue between patient and physician, and consent orally or in writing by the patient. Even if the law was misunderstood by some health care professionals to require written consent, the process still presented few bureaucratic hurdles.

This is especially true for hematologists and oncologists who treat patients over a long illness which affords ample opportunity to discuss CPR, and to do so within the context of a well-established patient-physician relationship. Estimates by hematologists/oncologists about the inability to write DNR orders due to bureaucratic technicalities therefore reflect far more about their own failure to talk to patients, than they do the law's requirements. If willing to talk to their patients at any time in the course of treatment, they could simply have noted patients' decisions in their medical charts and written the orders at the appropriate time.

H. *Default CPR*

Baker points to "default CPR," the provision of CPR to dying patients because a DNR order has not yet been entered, as a problematic result of the DNR law [5]. Such default CPR exacerbates, and indeed, determines the outcome for patients when an order has not been entered for a variety of reasons, including family ambivalence or physician failure to discuss the issue in advance with the patient or family.

On March 18, 1988, two weeks before the DNR law was implemented, the Department of Health issued a health facilities memorandum (Series 88–24) to all hospitals and nursing homes, providing interpretive guidance about the law. The memorandum clarified that although the law presumes that patients consent to CPR, facilities are not required to develop the capacity to provide CPR. Continuing the discussion about the duty to resuscitate, the memorandum stated, "Also, the authority of a physician to make a medical judgement that resuscitation measures would be futile in a particular case has not changed, but decisions made on this basis cannot become so common as to constitute a policy of unwritten DNR orders." An article by Robert Swidler, then staff counsel to the Task Force, that appeared in the *New York State Medical Journal* in 1989 [41], elaborated on this guidance from the Department of Health. Swidler pointed out that the presumption of consent has long been a part of medical practice; the presumption protects physicians from liability for treating without consent in an emergency. Consent alone, however, does not give rise to duty, or the obligation to resuscitate, if resuscitation offers the patient no medical benefit.

These principles would apply in the emergency room, or any situation that is akin to an emergency, when an advance decision has not been made about CPR. In such cases, the DNR law essentially leaves physicians and patients with the preexisting legal framework; an assumption that patients consent to CPR, and a duty imposed on physicians to make a judgment about appropriate treatment in accordance with prevailing medical standards of care (see [23]). Contrary to the arguments made by George Annas (this volume, pp. 141–155), the DNR law did not change the presumption of consent in an emergency in New York State nor did it render New York law distinct from the law in other states where consent is also presumed in an emergency. The law did however shift the perception of that legal principle for many clinicians from a presumption of consent to a presumption or duty to resuscitate.

This change in perception underscores the importance of professional education in the wake of significant legal developments. This is no less true for court decisions, than for legislation. Both require concerted outreach to health care professionals, and to those who provide them with legal advice. Professional organizations have an important responsibility in this educational effort, especially at a time of shrinking government resources. In 1990, the New York State Department of Health, in conjunction with the Medical Society of the State of New York and the Hospital Association of New York State, prepared a booklet on the DNR law for health care professionals [26]. The booklet was designed specifically to respond to the questions that had arisen about the law.

Based on experience with the DNR law, the Task Force and the Health Department prepared a guidebook on the health care proxy law soon after the law was enacted in 1990. In preparing and disseminating the guidebook, they sought the participation of a range of professional organizations: The Medical Society of New York State, the Hospital Association of New York State, the Greater New York Hospital Association, the New York Academy of Medicine, the New York State Nurses Association and the Association of the Bar of the City of New York.

Comparing New York and other States

A comparison between New York and other states on the question of CPR is difficult for several reasons. First, surrogate decisions were not authorized in New York before the DNR law was enacted. Second, problems before the law appeared to be more widespread in New York State. In general, concerns about liability for treatment decisions seem to be more far-reaching in New York than elsewhere.

The Union College Study of New York and non-New York critical care physicians presents particular problems, many of them stemming from the methodology of the study conducted. That methodology, especially as it relates to non-New York clinicians, is seriously flawed. First, the national or comparison sample was drawn from members of a specialty society who attended a conference. Baker *et al.* offer no reason to believe or assume that the conference participants are representative of the nation's critical care doctors. Second, only 14% of the conference participants responded to the questionnaire, a response rate well below acceptable standards for survey studies. The study essentially relies on an average of one or two critical care doctors from each state to assess the impact of the Joint Commission on Accreditation of Health Care Organizations (JCAHO) policy in all hospitals in the state and nationally. While these responses may provide anecdotal insight or opinions, they do not constitute "data." Third, like the New York study, the national sample presents information on physician perception. Unfortunately, no studies of actual practice outside New York exist to clarify the nature and extent of the disparity between perception and practice.

There were also two significant differences between the composition of the national group and the New York group that undermine the ability to draw any comparative conclusions: (i) only 56% of the national group of critical care physicians were directors of the intensive care unit, compared to 100% of the New York sample ([7]. p. 267); (ii) 82% of the national sample worked in a large hospital compared to 51% of the New York sample ([7], p. 268) As Virginia Dersch points out in her analysis of the Union College respondents, intensive care unit directors in New York State at larger hospitals were significantly less critical of the DNR law than their counterparts at smaller hospitals (85% of clinicians from university hospitals believed that the law benefitted patients and clinicians compared to only 44-48% of clinicians from community hospitals) [12]. Likewise, medical directors who spent little time on the unit, characterized as "paper directors" by Dersch, were far more likely to be critical of the reforms achieved in New York State. Baker *et al.* never account for these differences in comparing the perceptions of the national group to the New York sample. Taken together, these methodological problems render Baker *et al.* sweeping generalizations about the DNR law and JCAHO reform unsupportable. They simply have no valid data on which to base the comparison.

Finally, on the question of "futile" CPR, the national and New York samples commented on entirely distinct policies. In contrast to policies in New York, approximately 30% of the policies at facilities in other states allow entry of a DNR order without consultation with patients or surrogates, if physicians determine that CPR is "futile" [5]. This difference alone could account for the different responses by New York and non-New York physicians on the futility issue. In particular this difference, and not the distinction between self-regulation and law, may also account for the higher level of physician dissatisfaction with the policies in New York; New York's law constrains the discretion of physicians more than facility policies in other states. The critical question left unanswered is the actual impact of policies permitting physicians to enter DNR orders based on a broad or undefined notion of "futility" without speaking with patients or surrogates – how do those policies affect the rights and interests of patients and those closest to them?

III. RETURNING TO SILENCE

DNR Orders Based on Medical Futility

The debate about medical futility and the obligation to speak with patients or family members about CPR is national, not local, in scope. In 1990, articles by physicians decrying the obligation to speak with or seek consent from patients for DNR orders proliferated (e.g. [10], [24], 43]). In New York State, the debate has centered on the DNR law.

Articles appearing in the medical literature have urged several solutions. The approach advocated by many New York physicians in response to the DNR law has been a return to policies that pre-existed the law – the option for physicians to enter a DNR order for patients without speaking with patients or family members based on the physician's judgment that CPR is futile ([30], [31], [34]). Under this approach, the term futile is loosely defined to mean CPR that an individual physician believes is inappropriate.

The rationales put forward for this approach suggest its shortcomings. As stated by one New York physician, Kenneth Praeger, in an editorial in the *Wall Street Journal*, Critically ill patients often cannot cope with the stress of discussing the possibility of their imminent death and of rationally weighing the pros and cons of CPR. They often have no idea of what the procedure involves and of the possible state to which they might be restored in the event of a "successful resuscitation" [31].

This argument undercuts not just patient participation in decisions about CPR, but the entire concept of informed consent. Do patients understand a heart transplant or quadruple bypass better, or should we forgo consent for those procedures as well? Praeger's comments also beg the question of why he waits until his patients are critically ill before raising the issue of CPR, or why he fails to inform them about the procedure or the potential outcome for them.

Other physicians have echoed these concerns, stressing the therapeutic harm of the discussion more than the ignorance or inability of patients to decide. As expressed by one physician lamenting the lost ability of physicians to act without consulting patients or their family members, "The new law thus forces a competent person, perhaps moribund but still optimistic and clinging to the last vestiges of hope to confront a hopelessness that has been carefully defended against and perhaps denied. If a surrogate is appointed, it adds an onerous burden to what may already be a difficult situation" [40]. These arguments amount to a plea for a broad therapeutic exception, and corresponding physician discretion about which patients should have an option to decide about CPR, and which patients should be resuscitated. The arguments also highlight the extent to which the language of "medical futility" has subsumed long-standing paternalistic assumptions and practices previously asserted as "therapeutic privilege."

Whether cast in terms of medical futility or the therapeutic exception, policies that would permit physicians to enter DNR orders without seeking consent from or informing patients or their surrogates must be assessed in light of three trends that are overwhelmingly clear in the data available about DNR decisions: the reluctance of physicians to discuss CPR with patients, physicians' lack of familiarity with patients' wishes about CPR, and the expansive notion of futility as that term is used by physicians. The first trend suggests that any exception to the obligation to speak with patients, on grounds of futility or therapeutic harm, will serve as the escape hatch for physicians seeking to avoid a conversation they do not want to have. The second finding in the data, physicians' lack of familiarity with patients' wishes, indicates that unless they ask, physicians often do not know what patients want and will err in both directions, resuscitating some patients who would not have wanted the treatment and denying others the chance to opt for aggressive treatment. The third trend, the elastic and varied character of the futility concept when applied by physicians, underscores the potentially expansive nature of any exception based on futility.

For many physicians, the term futile CPR signifies CPR they believe should not be provided. For some physicians, the term may be triggered when the patient is diagnosed with a terminal irreversible illness, despite the fact that CPR might offer additional months of life, albeit a life burdened by disease and disability. Advanced age or residence at a long-term care facility may predispose other physicians to determine that CPR is futile. Others may draw the futility line more narrowly, concluding that CPR is futile only when the patient is imminently dying and CPR will not restore cardiac or respiratory function.

Regardless of how physicians assess or understand futility, CPR becomes futile for virtually all patients at some stage in their dying process. Hence, if physicians wait long enough to talk about CPR, they could enter the vast majority of orders on grounds of futility, without speaking with the patient or the family. Such a system would resemble the "secret" DNR orders of the 1970's, returning to the silence which once characterized these decisions.

Certainly, seeking consent to a DNR order is a difficult task. Informing patients or families that CPR is futile and will not be provided despite a request to the contrary, is even more demanding. Yet it serves important purposes ([15], [28]). The information enables patients or surrogates to seek a second opinion about futility, an important option given the uncertainties of diagnoses at life's end. It also avoids the mistrust that would be engendered if patients or families learned about the order. Finally, it provides a crucial safeguard for futility determinations, assuring that such determinations will not become the norm rather than the exception.

IV. SUMMING UP

The split in the data about the DNR law between the measurements of actual practice, and health care professionals' perceptions, makes definitive conclusions about the law hard to discern [23]. Since the studies were conducted just one year to eighteen months after the law was enacted, it is also likely that practices have shifted significantly since that time. Specifically, clinical practice may have caught up with perception in terms of physician discussion about CPR with patients. The law sought to overcome deeply-rooted clinical attitudes and practices, a change likely to occur over a longer time period than the year assessed by the studies in this volume. Hopefully too, the amendments to the law improved practice as did further understanding of the law over time.

Much of the discussion at the Union College Conference in September 1990 centered on the question of medical futility. However the only consensus reached at the conference about changing the law supported its extension to a setting not previously covered. Specifically, many of those who attended the conference urged that the law should be extended so that DNR orders could be issued and honored for patients cared for at home and in other community settings. In consultation with advocates for patients, including physicians who care for terminally ill patients, and emergency medical service providers, the Task Force developed policies for outpatient DNR orders.

Based on comments and concerns identified since 1988 when the DNR law first became effective, the Task Force also proposed other amendments to the law. By and large, those amendments simplified the procedures for entering a DNR order and made the law more compatible with New York's health care proxy law enacted in July 1990. The Task Force proposed the amendments in March 1991. Three months later, on July 4, 1991, the Legislature passed the amendments [2]. Those amendments included policies for non-hospital orders, making New York the third state in the nation to address CPR decisions in the outpatient setting. The Task Force did not propose, nor did the Legislature enact, amendments that addressed the question of futile CPR. In particular, the law was not changed to enable physicians to issue DNR orders without consulting patients or their surrogates. Instead, the Health Department recognized the need to reinforce and extend understanding of existing policies that allow physicians to enter an order on grounds of futility, but require them to inform the patient or surrogate first.

Studies about patient attitudes have consistently shown that patients want to participate in decisions about CPR. If they become unable to decide, most individuals want family members or others closest to them to decide in consultation with their physician. The current debate about futility presumes that patients and family members make poor choices, that they insist on treatment that confers no medical benefit. While this undoubtedly holds true in some cases, especially when patients or their surrogates are not well-informed about the patient's prognosis following CPR, the data on the DNR law do not support this as a general trend. The studies of actual practice after implementation of the law showed that the number of resuscitation attempts remained the same, as did the medical condition of patients for whom the orders were entered.

A consensus about the duty to talk with patients, and the limit on the right of patients to request or insist upon CPR, has not yet emerged in the national debate. Unquestionably, however, most of the problems with the DNR law identified by physicians would be addressed if they discussed CPR openly with their patients, rather than waiting until patients become too ill to decide about a DNR order. Family ambivalence would decline sharply as would the incidence of default CPR. In addition, many patients might opt to forgo CPR earlier than physicians would otherwise enter the order.

A. POSTSCRIPT

In March 1992, the Task Force recommended legislation on surrogate decisions [28]. That proposal has now been introduced into the Legislature as part of Governor Cuomo's legislative program. The proposal covers all patients incapable of deciding for themselves, including infants, children and incapacitated adults. It also encompasses all treatment decisions, including decisions about CPR. Essentially, the law would fold policies about CPR into a broader statute, eliminating a separate law on DNR orders. This is the path suggested by the Task Force when it first proposed the DNR law in 1987.

In the intervening years, the DNR law achieved several important goals: it granted surrogates the authority to decide about CPR, removed the secrecy that had surrounded DNR orders in New York State, and reinforced the notion of dialogue as central to the CPR decision. It also served as a testing ground for policies on surrogate decisions. The new legislative proposal builds on many policies in the DNR law, although it also departs from the law on certain issues. Among other differences, the new proposal does not state a presumption that patients consent to treatment in an emergency. This will not change New York law. The presumption will still be implied under common law legal principles. It is likely, however, to affect clinician perception.

The new legislative proposal also explicitly addresses the futility question. It contains the following provision, "Nothing in this article shall obligate a physician to provide a treatment, service or procedure at the request of a surrogate that the physician would have no duty to provide at the request of a patient with decision-making capacity." The provision does not define when treatment is futile – a daunting task when applied to all possible treatments and patient circumstances. Such a statutory definition is also premature given the current ongoing debate about the meaning of the term and its implications for the prerogatives of physicians and rights of patients. The statement in the proposed legislation will allow the meaning of "futility" to evolve as defined in court decisions, professional standards or other avenues. The statement does, however, recognize a limit on the right of both competent adults and surrogates to insist on CPR. Consistent with policies articulated for the DNR law, the Task Force urged that physicians should still talk with patients or their surrogates before withdrawing or withholding life-sustaining treatments they deem futile. The Task Force also restated its position that neither patients nor surrogates have any right to insist on treatment that is physiologically futile [28].

In December 1992, the Legislature held public hearings on the proposed legislation in three cities. Many individuals and organizations testified, several commenting on the problem of medical futility. No concrete proposals emerged to address the issue. In addition, representatives of the Task Force have met with health care professionals and others to discuss the problem of medical futility. No solution beyond that proposed by the Task Force has been devised, but the dialogue and debate continue.

NOTE

A response to Tracy Miller's critique of The Union College Study by one of its authors, Robert Baker, is in this volume, pp. 333–348.

REFERENCES

1. 52 N.Y.2d 363, 420 N.E.2d 63, cert. denied, 454 U.S. 858 (1981).
2. Act of July 4, 1991. ch. 370 (amending N.Y. Public Health Law, 2965, 2967), this volume, pp. 445–454.
3. Ahronheim, J., Maheswaran S., and Rosenberg, C.: 1992 'Impact of Do-Not-Resuscitate Legislation on the Use of Cardiopulmonary Resuscitation in Three Teaching Hospitals', *New York State Journal of Medicine*, 92:181–185. See also this volume, pp. 235–240.
4. Assembly Bill No. A 7166, New York State Assembly, May 1993
5. Baker, R.: 1995, 'The Legitimation and Regulation of DNR Orders', this volume, pp. 33–101.
6. Baker, R.: 1995, 'A Review of the Empirical Studies of the DNR Law and a Rejoinder to Tracy Miller', this volume, pp. 333–346.
7. Baker, R., Strosberg, M., *et al.*: 1994, 'The 1988 Do-Not-Resuscitate Reforms: A Comparative Study of the Impact of the New York DNR Law and the JCAHO Accreditation Requirements for DNR Policy', this volume, pp. 263–301.
8. Bedell, S. and Pelle, D. *et al.*: 1986, 'Do-Not-Resuscitate Orders for Critically Ill Patients in the Hospital – How Are They Used and What is Their Impact', *Journal of the American Medical Association* **256**, 233–37.
9. Bedell, S. and Delbanco, T.: 1984, 'Choices About Cardiopulmonary Resuscitation in the Hospital: When Physicians Talk with Patients', *New England Journal of Medicine* **310**, 1089–93.
10. Blackhall, L.: 1987, 'Must We Always Use CPR?', *New England Journal of Medicine* **317**, 1281–5.
11. Council on Ethical and Judicial Affairs, American Medical Association: 1991, 'Guidelines for the Appropriate Use of Do-Not-Resuscitate Orders', *Journal of the American Medical Association* **265**, 1868–71.
12. Dersch, V.: 1992, Summary of Written Responses by Critical Care Nurses, Unpublished manuscript version of the essay in this volume.
13. Dersch, V.: 1995, 'Differences in Clinician Reactions to the New York DNR', this volume, pp 303–321.
14. Fader, R., and Gambert, *et al.*: 1989, 'Implementing a Do-Not-Resuscitate (DNR) Policy in a Nursing Home', 1989, *Journal of the American Geriatrics Society* **37**, 544–48.
15. Farber, S.: 1988, [Letter] *New England Journal of Medicine* **318**, 1757–58.
16. Finucane, T., Shumway, J. *et al.*: 1988, 'Planning with Elderly Outpatients for Contingencies of Severe Illness," *Journal of General Internal Medicine* **3**, 322–25.
17. High, D.: 1988, 'All in the Family: Extended Autonomy and Expectations in Surrogate Health Care Decision-Making', *Gerontologist* **28**, Suppl.: 46–51.
18. High D., and Turner, H.: 1987, 'Surrogate Decision-Making: The Elderly's Familial Expectations', *Theoretical Medicine* **8**, 303–20.
19. Kamer, R., Dieck, E. *et al.*: 1990 'Effect of New York State's Do-Not-Resuscitate Legislation on In-Hospital Cardiopulmonary Resuscitation Practice', *American Journal of Medicine*, **88**, 108–11, reprinted in this volume, pp. 227–234.
20. Lantos, J., Singer, P. *et al.*: 1989, 'The Illusion of Futility in Clinical Practice', *American Journal of Medicine* **87**, 81–84.

21. Lo, B., McLeod, G. *et al.*: 1986, 'Patient Attitudes to Discussing Life-Sustaining Treatment', *Archives of Internal Medicine* **146**, 1613–1615.
22. Longo, E.: 1988, 'Extent of DNR Policies Varies Across Health Care Settings', *Health Progress* June, 66–73.
23. Miller, T.: 1995, 'An Assessment of the Union College Study and a Response to Robert Baker's Analysis of the DNR Law', this volume, pp. 325–332.
24. Murphy, D.: 1988, 'Do-Not-Resuscitate Orders: Time for Reappraisal in Long-term Care Institutions', *Journal of the American Medical Association* **260**, 2098–2101.
25. New York Public Health Law Art. 29-B, 2960–2978 (McKinney 1992), this volume, pp. 381–413.
26. New York State Department of Health, Medical Society of New York State, and the Hospital Association of New York State: 1990, 'Do Not Resuscitate Orders: Questions and Answers for Health Care Professionals', this volume, pp. 415–438.
27. New York State Task Force on Life and the Law.: 1986, *Do Not Resuscitate Orders: The Proposed Legislation and Report of the New York State Task Force on Life and the Law*, New York, New York. Reprinted in part in this volume, pp. 3–7, and pp. 381–413.
28. New York State Task Force on Life and the Law: 1992, *When Others Must Choose: Deciding for Patients without Capacity*, New York.
29. Ouslander, J., Tymchuk, A., and Rahbar, B.: 1989, 'Health Care Decisions Among Elderly Long-Term Care Residents and Their Potential Proxies', *Archives of Internal Medicine* **149**, 1367–72.
30. Plowe, C.: 1988, 'Letter to the Editor', *New England Journal of Medicine* **318**, 1758.
31. Praeger, K.: 1989, 'How CPR Can Threaten the Desperately Ill', *Wall Street Journal*, March 9.
32. Quill, T. and Bennett, N.: 1995, 'The Effects of a Hospital Policy and State Legislation on Resuscitation. Orders for Geriatric Patients', this volume, pp. 241–250.
33. Report of the Special January Third Additional 1983 Grand Jury concerning "Do not resuscitate procedures at a certain hospital in Queens" (Sup. Ct., Queens Co., Feb. 8, 1984).
34. Rosner, F.: 1988, 'Must We Always Offer the Option of CPR: The Law in New York', *Journal of the American Medical Association* **260**, 3129.
35. Schneiderman, L., Jecker, N., and Jonsen, A.: 1990, 'Medical Futility: Its Meaning and Ethical Implications', *Annals of Internal Medicine* **112**, 949–54.
36. Schonwether, R., Tesdale, T. *et al.*: 1991, 'Educating the Elderly Cardiopulmonary Resuscitation Decisions Before and After Intervention', *Journal of the American Geriatric Society* **39**, 372–377.
37. Shmerling, R., Bedell, S. *et al.*: 1988, 'Discussing Cardiopulmonary Resuscitation: A Study of Elderly Outpatients', *Journal of General Internal Medicine* **3**, 317–321.
38. Spritz, N.: 1994, 'The New York State DNR Law: Views of the members of the New York Chapter of the American College of Physicians', this volume, pp. 251–261.
39. Steinberg, A. Fitter, J. *et al.*: 1986, 'Patient Participation in Treatment Decision-Making in the Nursing Home: The Issue of Competence', *Gerontologist* **26**, 362–366.
40. Swender, P.: 1989, 'Reflections on the New York Do-Not-Resuscitate Law', *New York State Journal of Medicine* **89**, 57–58.
41. Swidler, R.: 1989, 'The Presumption of Consent in New York State's Do-Not-Resuscitate Law', *New York State Journal of Medicine* **89**, 69–72.

42. Testimony at Public Hearings before the New York State Senate amd Assembly Health Committees, February, 1987.
43. Tomlinson, T., and Brody, H.: 1990, 'Futility and the Ethics of Resuscitation', *Journal of the American Medical Association* **264**, 1276–80.
44. Uhlmann, R., Pearlman R. and Cain, K.: 1988, "Physicians' and Spouses' Predictions of Elderly Patients' Resuscitation Preferences," *Journal of Gerontology*, **43**, M115–21.
45. Wetle, T., Levkoff, S. *et al.*: 1988 'Nursing Home Resident Participation in Medical Decisions: Perceptions and Preferences' *Gerontologist* **28**, Suppl.: 32–38.
46. Youngner, S.: 1988, 'Who Defines Futility?', *Journal of the American Medical Association* **260**, 2094–5
47. Zweibel, N. and Cassel, C.: 1989, 'Treatment Choices at the End of Life: A Comparison of Decisions by Older Patients and Their Physician Selected Proxies', *Gerontologist* **29**, 615–621.

JANE GREENLAW

WHERE ARE WE GOING WITH DO-NOT-RESUSCITATE POLICIES?*

Whenever there are technologic advances in medicine, there are necessarily questions concerning their appropriate use. Cardiopulmonary resuscitation (CPR) is a noteworthy exception to this statement. Questions about CPR concern the appropriateness of *not* using it. Developed as a means to respond to sudden, unexpected cardiac or respiratory arrest, CPR has given rise to a technologic imperative that mandates its use and which has spawned a sizable body of medical, legal, and bioethical literature, as well as institutional policies and procedures pertaining to decisions not to use it. In New York State, the Governor's Task Force on Life and the Law has even issued a proposal for legislation governing such decisions [4].

Quill, *et al.* (this volume, pp. 241–250) describes one institution's experience with its policy regarding decisions about CPR and other resuscitation methods [5]. It provides a timely opportunity for a retrospective and prospective view of the development of "do not resuscitate" (DNR) policies.

This editorial commentary asserts that there are no new or special legal principles regarding resuscitation decisions, nor is there any need for any. It maintains that development, clarification, and refinement of medical standards regarding resuscitation decisions are properly the responsibility of the medical profession and are not appropriate matters for legislation. It examines the utility of institutional policies and procedures regarding resuscitation decisions, and points to some indications of future developments regarding resuscitation decisions.

The law has long recognized the important distinction between medical decisionmaking by physicians and personal decisionmaking by patients. In modern-day law, the informed consent doctrine embodies this distinction by delineating the physician's responsibility to disclose information and the patient's responsibility to consent to or refuse treatment [3]. Through the exercise of medical judgment, the physician

---

* This article is reprinted with the permission of the *The New York State Journal of Medicine* **86**, 618–620, December 1986.

R. Baker & M.A. Strosberg (eds.), Legislating Medical Ethics: A Study of the New York Do-Not-Resuscitate Law, 133–136.

forms a diagnosis or differential diagnosis and determines the medically appropriate course of action. After this medical decisionmaking has taken place, the physician informs the patient about diagnosis, prognosis, the recommended course of action and its risks and expected benefits, and treatment alternatives. Thus informed, the patient must either accept or reject the proposed course of action.

Under the law, resuscitation decisions are not different from other medical decisions. It is incumbent upon the physician to decide, in accordance with accepted medical standards, which resuscitation methods, if any, should be offered for each patient. Then it is incumbent upon the patient to consider the array of medically appropriate alternatives and either accept or reject them. There is no valid legal reason to presume that resuscitation is required for every patient, with the narrow exception of a bona fide medical emergency.

In its lengthy report proposing DNR legislation, the New York State Task Force on Life and the Law begins by stating that "medical choices are moral choices" [4]. This erroneous statement may reflect the thinking at the root of the confusion regarding the legality of DNR orders. Medical choices are medical choices, and existing law recognizes them as such. It may be stimulating or interesting to discuss moral questions that technology presents, but it is not useful to confuse them with established legal or medical principles. Resuscitation legislation is inappropriate because it necessarily narrows existing provider and patient rights, because it confuses physicians and the public by making some think that those rights do not exist without a statute, and because it usurps the medical profession's responsibility to establish standards for medical decisionmaking.

Establishing accepted medical standards is and always has been the responsibility of the medical profession, whether it is the accepted standard for prescribing antibiotic therapy or for instituting resuscitation efforts. The mechanisms for this process are in place: scientific and medical research, evaluation, reporting in the medical and scientific literature, and developing consensus. The process is not served by enactment of a DNR statute.

An obvious next question is whether the development of medical consensus is aided by institutional policies regarding resuscitation decisions. It is beyond the space and conceptual limitations of this essay to speculate at length on the genesis of such policies. A variety of factors culminated in the pervasive but inaccurate belief that resuscitation was legally required for every patient whose cardiac or respiratory function ceased, regardless of its clinical indication. Nonetheless, many physicians recognized this as illogical and verbally instructed staff not to initiate resuscitation for certain patients. Discomfort with this practice inevitably led to the development of institutional guidelines for determining the resuscitation status of each patient.

The first generation of these policies was based on the presumption that every patient should be resuscitated unless a written order specified otherwise. Some of these policies contained consent provisions. The major focus of these early policies was to provide for documentation and communication of each patient's resuscitation status.

A second generation of DNR policies evolved, reflecting a recognition that mere designation of "DNR" was too broad and did not allow for consistency in utilizing differing levels of resuscitation methods for different patients. The policy described by Quill, *et al.* is of this type [5]. Policies such as this evidence a clearer understanding that resuscitation is not appropriate for every patient, and that for those patients for whom intervention is appropriate, there is a need to determine what level of intervention is indicated. Nonetheless, these policies paradoxically still require that the patient consent to *not* having an intervention which is not medically appropriate, rather than recognizing the patient's right to consent to or refuse an intervention which is medically appropriate.

The potential utility of carefully written institutional policies regarding resuscitation decisions is multifold. First, such policies encourage uniformity in terminology and consistency in response by minimizing confusion about the specific interventions to be implemented. The old "Code Blue" type of designation provided no guidance as to which measures should be applied or how far resuscitation efforts should go, and left much to individual interpretation of the designation. Second, such policies can provide a clear mechanism for communication of a patient's resuscitation status. Third, these policies can enhance accountability for medical decisionmaking by providing requirements for documentation, including both a written order and an explanatory progress note. Finally, the policies can provide an opportunity for review and evaluation as a means of contributing to the ongoing process of clarifying and refining medical standards.

Indications of future directions can be seen. Two official statements were recently issued, more clearly acknowledging the distinction between medical and personal decisionmaking. The first is the American Hospital

Association's Policy and Statement, "The Patient's Choice of Treatment Options," calling for institutional methods to assure the patient's right and responsibility to select among treatment options [1]. The second is the 1986 Statement of the American Medical Association Council on Ethical and Judicial Affairs, "Withholding or Withdrawing Life-Prolonging Medical Treatment," emphasizing the patient's choice as controlling, even when this conflicts with what the physician deems medically appropriate [2]. Both of these statements point out the need for carefully drawn guidelines regarding patients lacking decisional capacity.

These indicators will be reflected in future policies. Indeed, a third generation of institutional policies is already emerging in the long term care setting. These are "patient treatment preference" policies, which focus on the patient's right to refuse treatment. Typically, they provide for a determination upon admission of the patient's express preferences regarding medical treatment, including resuscitation, and also provide guidelines for decisions about patients lacking decisional capacity.

Further refinement of existing institutional policies will likely lead to a broader emphasis on the patient's right to choose among the medically appropriate alternatives, and away from the view that special rules apply to resuscitation decisions.

BIBLIOGRAPHY

1. American Hospital Association: 1985, *The Patient's Choice of Treatment Options*, American Hospital Association, Chicago.
2. American Medical Association Council on Ethical and Judicial Affairs: 1986, *Withholding or Withdrawing Life-Prolonging Medical Treatment*, American Medical Association, Chicago.
3. New York Public Health Law, Article 29-B, Statute 413-A, Effective April 1, 1988. Reprinted in this volume, pp. 349–368.
4. New York State Task Force on Life and The Law: 1986, *Do Not Resuscitate Orders: The Proposed Legislation and Report of the New York State Task Force on Life and the Law*, New York State Government, Albany, New York. Reprinted, in part, in this volume, pp. 3–7, and pp. 381–413.
5. Quill, T.E., Stankaitis, J.A. and Krause, C.R.: 1986, 'The Effect of a Community Hospital Resuscitation Policy on Elderly Patients', *New York State Journal of Medicine* **86**, 622–625, reprinted in this volume, pp. 241–250.

†DAVID AXELROD

NEW YORK STATE'S DO-NOT-RESUSCITATE LAW

When asked about the impact of the French Revolution on the twentieth century, Arnold Toynbee said that it is too early to tell. I think that, with respect to the New York State Do-Not-Resuscitate [DNR] Law, what I hope is that it's a little too early to tell what the impact has been. We are in the process of evolution of a very major departure in the way in which government deals with moral and ethical issues. I say that not lightly, because I think that the precedents which have been established by the New York State Task Force on Life and The Law have really set a standard for dealing with some major moral and ethical issues that concern the entire U.S.

I think that this is in some ways a reflection of the excellence and diversity of the people who are members of the Task Force. The Task Force selected by the Governor reflects to a very large degree the religious pluralism that exists within the State of New York. Those of you who have watched the debates that surround the moral and ethical issues that effect health care in New York cannot be unaware of the extent to which religious opinion from the most conservative to some of the most liberal elements of our diverse society has been reflected on the floors of the legislative bodies. The Task Force *Report* is an enormous accomplishment, and the members of the Task Force deserve a great deal of credit for the extent to which consensus has been achieved despite the broad variety of views that exist. Now this is not to suggest that the DNR law, as it has been enacted, is precisely the law that was recommended by the Task Force, nor that each individual member of the Task Force feels that the compromises made with respect to the DNR law are all entirely appropriate. This does not suggest that everyone was happy with everything that was openly enshrined in the DNR law, nor that the members of the Task Force or bioethicists feel that it represents the absolute best law that we would have wanted. But I think it represents a compromise not only with respect to religious pluralism, but also between what the legislative bodies sought to achieve and what the Task Force sought to achieve.

Students of democracy will recognize that in the legislative process

R. Baker & M.A. Strosberg (eds.), Legislating Medical Ethics: A Study of the New York Do-Not-Resuscitate Law, 137–140.

there is the opportunity for every conceivable pressure group to make known its will and concerns, and to have an impact on the ultimate legislation. There is, I think, a great deal to be said for such a process, but it also results in some very strange twists. Some of those have led to the problems that the medical community has encountered in the implementation of the DNR Law, problems which have resulted from subtle changes in some of its major initiatives.

It is generally held that an area of concern and perhaps confusion was introduced by the presumption in favor of resuscitation that exists within the statute. As I mentioned, there was a need to accommodate a variety of different religious groups as well as groups concerned with patient autonomy. The presumption in favor of resuscitation is a fact of compromise; it is made in recognition of the difficulties that arise in a state that has a wide spectrum of interest groups involved in the political process. Problems are also often identified with the method of delegating surrogate authority when the patient lacks decisionmaking capacity. Inevitably, everyone finds fault with the way in which these surrogate processes take place. Some find redundancy, and all inescapably find excessive complexity. Indeed, perhaps there is room for reform here. Part of the reason for this volume is to enter into a dialogue to determine the effectiveness of the current law, whether or not there is a reason for change, and the nature of the changes that can be made. At the same time we must not lose the impact of the original legislation or sight of its goals. What must be recognized is that when legislation is amended, the consensus is once again opened for discussion. It is conceivable that some of the most beneficial elements of the statute might be removed during the course of legislative debate.

Those who have followed the debate on the DNR decision and legislation in New York know that much of the concern has centered around the proper role of the physician as opposed to the patient, in other words the extent to which paternalism should be exercised on the part of the patient. In some cases this has fostered responses, including a series of articles in the *New England Journal of Medicine* about the physician's discretion in involving the patient [2]. Dr. Saul Farber, representing the American College of Physicians and also a member of the Task Force, took the authors of an article to task for the suggestion that in cases of medical futility, the physician make the decision on DNR and then, after the fact, influence the patient to come to the same decision [1]. I do not think that was what was intended; it was always a concern of the Task

Force to respect the autonomy of the patient. It was also simultaneously the responsibility of the Task Force to protect a professional staff from the humiliation of unethical charades; to free administrators from unnecessary and groundless concern about liability (which still remains an issue); to reduce some of the irrational fears that led to unjustified and sometimes cruel decisions to subject patients to useless cardiopulmonary resuscitation [CPR]; and to standardize the general practice of DNR orders and foster their acceptance by the general public. Finally, the Task Force's aim was to establish a legal right to DNR that was clearly delineated and articulated in statute which could be referred to by everyone, in which there would be no difference with respect to applicability, and in which there would be a level of accountability for everyone when an individual served as a surrogate or when a patient lacked decisional capacity. But above all else, the focus of the *Report* was on the preservation of patient autonomy and dignity, and the mechanism by which this could be achieved.

Another widely perceived problem is that of informed consent, and what that represents with respect to DNR. I fear that the whole issue is one which is going to continue to be a thorn in our side. Is informed consent simply a ritual formula designed to meet legal requirements, or is it a process through which we communicate with and thereby manifest the autonomy of the patient? If it is not a mechanism for facilitating communication and putting the patient at the center of the decision-making process, then obtaining informed consent is simply an empty ritual. I say this while recognizing fully the concerns all of those in the medical profession have with respect to the whole issue of liability. But I think that the issues of liability and fiscal responsibility are much less significant than that of moral accountability. Information of whatever nature, whether relating to DNR or a whole host of other procedures, needs to be communicated to the patient clearly, and often more than once, in order that the provider can support the patient's right to chose among a variety of alternatives. We need to focus upon the patient's right to exercise his or her autonomy.

I think that the paternalistic mind-set of the "golden days," when the trusted physician would do the right thing on his own and the public was prepared to accept that "he" (the gender is here appropriate) would act in such a way as to promote the welfare of the patient, must be eradicated from our way of thinking. The assumption of moral virtue on the part of anyone, including the physician, in this religiously and ethnically diverse society, is not acceptable. Consequently, I think that the issues of informed consent and the primacy of the patient's autonomy are going to continue to confront us in the future.

BIBLIOGRAPHY

1. Farber, S.J.: 1988, Correspondence, *New England Journal of Medicine* **318**, 1757–1758.
2. Tomlinson, T. and Brody, H.: 1988, 'Ethics and Communication in Do-Not-Resuscitate Orders,' *New England Journal of Medicine* **318**, 43–46.

GEORGE ANNAS

NEW YORK'S DO-NOT-RESUSCITATE LAW: BAD LAW, BAD MEDICINE, AND BAD ETHICS

I can begin by telling you that I disagree with almost nothing Commissioner Axelrod states about his goals. He is absolutely correct about the need for more communication and the need for informed consent. Physicians do not have the final answers to what patients want; we must do more to treat patients properly. I am glad that I agree with Dr. Axelrod on these points because I have always admired him. I have stated publicly a number of times that he is the most effective and innovative commissioner of health in the United States.

Although Commissioner Axelrod and I agree on goals, we do have areas of disagreement, especially on whether a DNR statute of the kind in force in New York can meaningfully contribute to meeting our goals of better care and better communication between physicians and patients. I believe New York's DNR law is likely to create more problems than it solves. I do not mean to criticize the New York Task Force – I think they are doing a terrific job – but the DNR statute was the first thing the Task Force did, and one can not expect perfection on the first try.

I shall approach this issue, first by looking at the doctor-patient relationship, second, by making some general observations about the direction we are headed legally, and finally by scrutinizing New York's DNR legislation.

Informed Consent and the Doctor-Patient Relationship

Consider informed consent and communication in the doctor-patient relationship. Reasonable communication between doctors and patients is very difficult. My favorite *New Yorker* cartoon is a psychiatrist telling a patient, "I can't put it into lay language; I don't know any lay language." I think there is some truth to that. In 1977 (shortly after the *Saikewitz* opinion in Massachusetts – which led to very similar debates in that state about DNR, see [1], p.244–250), I put together a schema which I still think correctly reflects the law in the United States. Basically the schema classifies patients, as the law generally does, into competent and incompetent. For each category there are three bases on which patients or

R. Baker & M.A. Strosberg (eds.), Legislating Medical Ethics: A Study of the New York Do-Not-Resuscitate Law, 141–155.

others might make treatment decisions. They might make a decision on the basis of medical judgment, legal liability, or personal preferences. That oversimplifies a bit, but it is a useful framework for our purposes.

I think that we can all agree, certainly after *Cruzan*, that competent adult patients can refuse *any* treatment for *any* reason [2]. The most difficult cases involve incompetent patients when we are what treatment they would or would not want. Despite this uncertainty, someone must nonetheless make decisions on their behalf. We as a society, or a physician, or a family, could make treatment decisions, on any of the three bases indicated above: medical, legal, or personal. I want to look at each one of those briefly, because the history of how we have dealt with these issues helps explain why we are where we are with regard to DNR orders.

Medical decisions

By medical reasons, I mean reasons that the doctor can use to decide about treatment without consulting the patient or the family. Traditionally these have been when the patient is dead (the doctor has the legal right and obligation to declare death), or where the progression of the disease makes treatment hopeless, (a situation now commonly referred to as "medically futile"). There are also medical emergencies, in which the doctor has the privilege of treating first and asking legal questions later.

The hardest event to deal with, of course, is death (especially our own, but also someone else's), because a tremendous amount of denial that goes on. When can doctors make decisions about death on their own? The easiest case is determining when the patient is dead, although the concept of brain death has led to some confusion. One telling cartoon pictures three doctors discussing a body that has been decapitated and sliced into four parts. The caption is: "But is it dead according to the accepted definition of the term?" Brain death criteria came into use in 1968 when a Harvard *ad hoc* committee suggested a new definition for irreversible coma (although they really meant death), so that organs could be harvested while circulation and respiration were artificially maintained. The original Harvard proposal suggested, correctly, that there was no need for a brain death law because the law had always been that "you're dead when the doctor says you're dead" (as long as the doctor makes his decision on the basis of good and accepted medical criteria). That is still the law ([1], pp. 365–370).

Nevertheless, the concept of brain death has produced legal problems. In Massachusetts, for example, we had physicians literally asking courts if they could stop treating brain-dead corpses. And our Supreme Judicial Court actually had to say: "There is no legal duty to administer medical treatment after death." This may seem hard to believe, but it is true, and that's the law. In response to the questions raised by brain death, Kansas passed a brain death statute in 1970, primarily at the prompting of the American Medical Association and the Kansas Medical Association. A series of states followed suit, yet there are differences in the various statutes passed. This means that theoretically (but not really), you could put someone in an ambulance in California and drive them across to the east coast and they would be alive, alive, dead, alive, dead, dead; that is, their life or death status would change based on the state in which they were. Of course, that is silly. The definition of death must be universal – you can't be resurrected just by crossing state lines. This kind of paradox arises from the notion that we must have a new law for every new issue that confronts us.

Even though Massachusetts and New York are two of the only states in the nation that do not have brain death statutes, neither these, nor any other states, need one. Brain death has been accepted not only by the medical profession, but also by every court that has ever examined the issue. This is the law everywhere whether there is a statute or not: you are dead when you sustain either irreversible cessation of circulatory and respiratory functions, or irreversible cessation of functioning of the entire brain, including the brain stem. The determination of death must be made in accordance with accepted medical standards. Indeed, *all* medical practice must be in accordance with accepted medical standards. The point is that there are some decisions that physicians can make. Physicians don't have to consult anyone about them, including the patient and the family.

Legal Liability

Legal liability issues have a great impact on medical decisionmaking. Historically, they have been important, primarily because of fear and ignorance. Dr. Axelrod used similar language, when discussing unfounded legal fear here in New York. In fact, there is unfounded fear of legal liability across the country. That is not to say that there is nothing to fear: There is criminal liability for homicide or murder, and there is malpractice liability for negligence. But there are occasions when this fear interferes with indicated medical treatment.

This is exactly what happened in the most famous "right to die" case, the 1976 case of Karen Ann Quinlan. Her family and physician had basically agreed to take her off a ventilator because she had no chance of regaining consciousness. Her physician apparently had second thoughts, talked with a lawyer and others, and then said he would not take Karen off the ventilator unless the family got a court order granting him legal immunity for this action. And her family did in fact get a court order from the Supreme Court of New Jersey. The physician said he was worried about legal liability. He seemed to picture himself somewhat like Daniel in the lion's den, only surrounded by lawyers. To safeguard himself from the danger of a lawsuit, a request for advance legal immunity from a judge seemed reasonable to him. Whether or not going to court to seek legal immunity was reasonable fifteen years ago, the question to which we will soon return is when it is a reasonable thing for physicians to do so today ([1], pp. 261–267).

Personal preferences

The third basis on which one might make a decision are one's personal beliefs and values. Personal decisions are what the now incompetent patient would make, if the patient could make them (the so-called *substituted judgment* standard that New York does not recognize but sometimes quotes, [2], pp., 206–207). The alternate "personal" standard is an objective standard, what is in the *best interests* of the patient, or simply what is best for the patient ([2], p. 153). These are the two basic standards that the law recognizes.

The major problem that the Task Force seemed to have with DNR orders prior to the legislation is that New York physicians were making decisions themselves, on the basis of what they thought was best for the patient. There was an interesting study done at Beth Israel Hospital in Massachusetts that was published in the *New England Journal of Medicine* [5]. It concluded that physicians often fail to guess accurately the wishes of their patients with respect to resuscitation. The study included a series of patients who were resuscitated successfully, and were able to talk to researchers thereafter. Of that group of patients, 42% said they did not want to be resuscitated again, nor had they wished to be resuscitated in the first place. That was contrary to what their physicians had thought, so it seemed wrong to let physicians continue to make DNR judgments by themselves.

It is one thing to *ask* patients what they want. It is much more difficult to make "best interests" judgments. You will recall the Baby Doe days, when the Reagan administration demanded that *all* neonates get *all* available life-sustaining treatment, as long as it could keep them alive ([1], p. 132–146; [2], p 212-213. Under this standard there is no such thing as contraindicated treatment. It is assumed that every treatment that can keep a child alive is an indicated treatment, and that denying a "handicapped newborn" any medical treatment that can sustain its life is child neglect. We've backed away from that rigid rule because it made no sense. It also turned out that the major problem in the United States was not under-treatment of infants in the neonatal intensive care units, but over-treatment. It is still difficult to know how to make decisions for neonates – don't let me give you the impression that it is an easy issue – but it is not made any easier by pretending it's not a decision, and just ordering "everything" for everybody. That simply leads to abusive and futile over-treatment.

Advance directives

A consensus is forming around the strategy of trying to get as many adults as possible to write down what they want before they become incompetent. One approach is to encourage everyone to write living wills in which they state their wishes regarding treatment under various circumstances, should they become incompetent. Since it is difficult to predict for every possible circumstance, however, it is more practical to use health care proxies to designate someone else to make decisions for you, should you become incompetent [4]. I think that when it implements the health care proxy law New York will take a tremendous step towards empowering many of the State's people.

American Health Law

Before going to the specifics of the New York DNR law, consider the context of American health law. The United States health care system is moving towards cost-containment, and the doctor-patient relationship is under increasing strain. Many physicians in HMOs and other prepaid health-care settings have a financial incentive to give patients less, rather than more treatment. Karen Ann Quinlan's case may thus be an anachronism – the more typical problem may not be a patient who wants to refuse treatment, but a patient who wants access to treatment. Certainly there are those who worry that in the new era of cost-containment, doctors will discontinue treatment not because they do not think it will help the patient, but because they think it is just too expensive.

The case of Nancy Cruzan

The Nancy Cruzan case has brought the issue of patient autonomy to national prominence because the U.S. Supreme Court, for the first time in its history, has decided a "right to die" case. Perhaps the most important points of the *Cruzan* case are on the one hand that the U.S. Supreme Court assumed that the right to refuse treatment was constitutionally protected, did not require a person to be terminally ill to refuse treatment, and made no distinction between a feeding tube and other medical interventions [3]. On the other hand, it seems to have made the horrible mistake of deciding that a decision to begin treatment is different in kind from a decision to discontinue treatment. In contrast, the President's Bioethics Commission and almost every philosopher (and, indeed, most every court) who has looked at this issue has said you cannot make an ethically meaningful distinction between starting and stopping a medical intervention.

Obviously in CPR if there is anything that is clear it is that you cannot make that distinction: otherwise once you have started CPR, you would have to continue it forever, which is absurd. Similarly, no one thinks that you have to continue with nutrition forever once you've started it; it is equally preposterous. At some point it becomes evident that you should be able to terminate both procedures. Nonetheless, the U.S. Supreme Court has decided that it is not unconstitutional for Missouri to say that once a physician starts a life-sustaining treatment, the physician must continue it as long as it sustains the person's life. Missouri can claim an "unqualified interest" in a patient's life. Therefore, as long as that life can be sustained, it must be sustained, unless the physician or family can show by clear and convincing evidence that the patient has made a prior informed refusal of that particular treatment. That's a pretty horrible outcome, and is out of touch with human and medical realities.

The suicide movement

Jack Kevorkian's suicide machine has recently made headlines. As wacky as Kevorkian is, it is nonetheless important to realize that there are many of our fellow citizens who would prefer to die at their own or their doctor's hands rather than be subjected to treatment in a modern hospital. Janet Atkins, for one, flew from Oregon to Michigan to have her life ended when she was diagnosed as having Alzheimer's disease. The Hemlock Society is dedicated to changing the law so that physicians may legally assist patients in committing rational suicide. I have some sympathy for that view. I do not think the law should be changed, but one has to recognize that there is a significant number of people who would like doctors to end their lives, rather than have doctors use futile, or unnecessary, or even contra-indicated medical procedures to keep them alive. (Hospices represent a better alternative, but that's another story.)

Wherever one falls on the assisted suicide question, we must all recognize that we *are* getting near the limit of total amount of money we can spend on health care, if we're not there already. Accordingly we must no longer tolerate either useless or unwanted treatments. That certainly includes futile CPR, for example, CPR performed on those categories of patients where there are *no* documented survivors. I am very pleased at the clarification the New York State Department of Health has made to the DNR law: that futile CPR need not and should not be performed, and that the decision regarding futile CPR should be made just the way it has been made in the past – by physicians.

Medical miracles

The AIDS epidemic hangs over our entire health care system, especially in New York and Boston. There is a movement – one that is understandable but which must be resisted – to demand expensive, ineffective, experimental treatments. Many people say that AIDS patients should have the right to take any medicine they want (as long as they can pay for it), and yet at the same time argue that we need to rationalize our health care system, and contain costs by only paying for effective medical treatments. We cannot have it both ways. The dangerous message is that we should make useless treatments available to patients simply because they are dying. That's exactly what futile CPR is, and that's exactly what tube-feeding was for Nancy Cruzan.

We use the term 'medical miracle' a lot to mean a hope without very much scientific likelihood; I think this phrase shapes our thinking more than we give it credit. Former President Bush, in a speech to physicians at Johns Hopkins University talked about such miracles. He said that he believed in miracles, especially modern, medical miracles, and he encouraged the physicians to get on with their miraculous work. Well, 'miracle' is not a medical word, and when we start talking about miracles we should realize that the most important and famous miracle is the resurrection; CPR.

When CPR works it really seems miraculous. When CPR was first used it almost was a miracle; it had been unprecedented that people whose hearts stopped beating did not die, that a medical procedure could reverse the process. The first person to publish an article on CPR claimed a 70% success rate. That seems fantastic: now 20% is very high, and it's 5% in most areas. We need to *evaluate* CPR as a medical intervention, not take it on faith, like a miracle.

New York's DNR Law

New York's DNR law has several problems: it treats CPR as unique; it presumes consent to CPR; and it guarantees immunity to health care providers that follow the statute in good faith.

Is CPR unique?

CPR *is* something special. When CPR works it looks like we turn a dead person into a live one. It is dramatic; it looks like we can actually prevent death. On the other hand, CPR is a medical procedure like every other medical procedure. Other procedures prevent death and keep people alive, too. Tube feedings kept Nancy Cruzan alive, and so impressed the majority of the U.S. Supreme Court that they ruled that Missouri could require their continued use just for that purpose. But the Court did not treat tube feeding as unique, nor should CPR be so treated. The point is that medical procedures should be treated as a *whole* rather than separately. We saw this problem a bit with brain death when we implied that there are two kinds of death (and many people still think this way): there are "regular death" and "brain death." The fact is that there is *death*, one phenomenon, that can be determined two different ways.

When you pass a statute that says that the patient is entitled to some choice with respect to medical procedures, you leave people with the impression that they are actually getting a choice, that you are really giving them something. But you are not giving them anything. You are giving them the *illusion* that you are giving them a choice – in this case whether or not to have CPR. In fact, that choice is no different than the choice whether or not to have CPR for 10 minutes, 20 minutes, 30 minutes, or 40 minutes. No one wants to give people a choice like that, and for obvious reasons: it makes no medical sense, and it provides no real choice.

Some have said that it is inappropriate to "slow code," or "show code," or perform any other type of code between a full code and no code. I think that is right and speaks to what is and what is not an appropriate medical procedure. It is either appropriate to do a code or it is not. If it is appropriate to do a code, then it should be done properly. Inappropriate codes should not be done at all, whether or not the patient wants one.

The law has always been that the patient has a right to refuse treatment, but does not have a right to demand mistreatment. A patient has no legal right to be mistreated, and cannot demand contraindicated procedures. This is not a very difficult issue in general, but we have a difficult time applying it specifically to CPR. Some people think that if a patient says "I want CPR," physicians must provide it to them. Unfortunately, I think that under the New York DNR law that is true. But if that is true, then the law sometimes requires physicians to perform contraindicated CPR (CPR against the medical standards) and to inflict something that is basically torture on patients – something that we would never consciously permit. One doe not see that anywhere else in medicine.

It is like a mother bringing her son into a hospital and saying to a doctor, "I just can't hit my kid but he needs to be hit – you hit him." You might think that is good for the child. But hitting children is not a medical procedure; it may be child abuse; and physicians cannot do it just because the parent consents. Even if the child said, "Yes, doctor, hit me, I deserve it!" it would still be wrong to do. And if the mother brings her child, (or if the mother comes in herself) and says, "I want a kidney transplant," or, "I want a heart transplant," you would not do either of these procedures unless you believed they were medically indicated.

I hope that New York is not only the first state to enact a DNR statute, but also the last. It seems unlikely that any other state will follow its lead. Perhaps New York has unique problems with respect to CPR, and that is certainly possible. Since the *Cruzan* opinion, affirming Missouri's scheme, New York and Missouri are the only two states in the Union that require "clear and convincing evidence" of a person's wishes before terminating life-sustaining treatment. There is something unique about New York, and perhaps it needed the DNR law to prevent even worse abuses of patients' rights. I am not qualified to discuss the internal workings of New York State politics or medicine, but the DNR law is a strange statute, partly because it is limited to just one procedure.

The only other statutes like it that I can think of are the breast cancer consent statutes that many states have, including Massachusetts. When it was enacted, I was still on the Board of Medicine in Massachusetts, and I opposed it. I felt strange doing so because I share its goal. The breast cancer statute requires physicians to tell women who are diagnosed with breast cancer what their treatment options are. Is that wrong? Of course it's not! It is exactly what physicians should do. On the other hand, should we pass these separate statutes for breast cancer? Doesn't this imply that physicians have an obligation to tell people with breast cancer the treatment alternatives, but do not have an obligation to disclose alternative treatments for other types of cancer? Or must we pass a statute for every type of cancer, and then for every other disease that a person can have?

I am very sympathetic to the breast cancer statute. But I believe it is more important to look at the process of informed consent generically, to require all physicians to get informed consent for *all* procedures, and to tell patients what their alternatives are all the time, irrespective of their specific disease. I think the practice of passing statutes for each particular disease or procedure is a mistake. I do not think (although I may be wrong, I do not know the Task Force's views) that we will see in New York, for example, separate statutes governing tube feedings, resuscitation, kidney dialysis, kidney transplants, radiation therapy, chemotherapy, and so on. I think that the practice of enacting separate statutes for each of these treatments is counter-productive, even though every one of these procedures is life-sustaining, every one of those procedures could be terminated, and every one of those terminations could be considered a life-and-death decision in which the patient should take part.

So the first problem with the New York State DNR legislation is a conceptual one: one should not have unique statutes for specific procedures. I think that such statutes take the focus away from the patient (where you want it), and put it on the procedure. They seems to imply that the obligation to use the procedure is greater than the right of the patient to decide whether or not to undergo them.

The problem of presumed consent

The second problem, presumed consent, is more fundamental. It probably arises out of the type of political compromise that goes with the legislative process. Nonetheless, it is a fundamental flaw in the statute, and I think it is the source of most of the problems the statute has generated, including those involving medical futility. The statute explicitly *presumes* that all adults in New York State consent to CPR. The truth of the matter, of course, is that if everybody in New York actually consented to CPR, there would be no need for a DNR statute. The only question would be that of medical futility, and in such cases we would not honor the consent because the treatment would be contraindicated. The presumption of consent is a destructive legal fiction; the fact of the matter is that people have not consented to CPR. What the statute requires is giving CPR without consent.

In the past the law has dealt with this problem of administering CPR in the absence of consent without presuming consent. Consider an emergency room, where there is seldom explicit consent. What is really happening is not an "emergency consent," but rather physicians exercising their *privilege* to treat in emergencies. This is one lesson I have taught my medical students for twenty years: in an emergency, treat first, and ask legal questions later. It may not always be framed quite that clearly, but that's the law.

The problem with saying we presume everyone consents is that once we have everybody consenting (and that's the model in New York), then to deny someone something to which they have consented seems to be taking something away from them. In so doing, we seem to assume that CPR is always beneficial, always good, and by not doing it are depriving people of a benefit. The United States Supreme Court in the *Cruzan* case made a similar assumption. They assumed that tube-feeding could not hurt anybody, that it *always* helped Nancy, since there was no harm to her in being kept alive by tube-feedings, only a benefit. Justice William Brennan strongly disagreed. He argued that you could harm someone by invading their body for your own purposes.

CPR is not always beneficent. But the assumption of consent makes it look beneficent, since the law implies that the patient always wants it, unless he or she has specified otherwise. But what people really consent to is CPR *that their doctors think can be beneficial to them*. People do not implicitly consent to futile CPR, CPR that can not work, —CPR that is only going to add an extra three-to-five-thousand dollars to their medical bill.

Passing a statute saying that everybody in New York consents to CPR seems to convert what is a medical procedure into an entitlement. To put it another way, it seems to say that New York citizens have a legal right to be resuscitated, and, that if they are not, something must have gone wrong. It puts tremendous and inappropriate pressure on the loved ones and next-of-kin to agree to a resuscitation because, if not, they are taking a benefit away from their loved ones, a benefit that the state guarantees. After all, why would the state guarantee CPR unless it was something that was always good?

The immunity provision

Another part of the statute that is equally bad (although physicians probably like it) is the provision that gives physicians immunity for following the statutory scheme. Physicians have immunity anyway, as long as the statute tells physicians what to do and they follow it. But the notion which in part motivated the New York statute (just as, in New Jersey, it motivated the *Quinlan* decision) is that physicians are not writing DNR orders when it is appropriate because they are worried about legal liability. So the solution must be to give them legal immunity. But if fear of legal liability is really the problem, then this is a phony solution. The real solution should be to educate physicians, so that they are less ignorant about the laws, not to pass a statute that says "follow these rules, and you will be legally immune."

What does an immunity clause teach physicians? First, it teaches them that the law is arbitrary. It seems to suggest that physicians have been right in regarded the law as something they should fear because it is totally irrational – it can strike at any time, like an alien – and doctors have to protect themselves. How do they protect themselves? By filling out the forms – I know that communication is what the statute is supposed to promote – but what it winds up promoting is filling out more forms. If you fill out the forms, and have the family fill out the forms, you are protected. The DNR law teaches physicians that the law is just a bunch of forms.

They have already learned this said lesson with respect to informed consent. It is common to see a resident coming out of a patient's room, waiving a paper and declaring, "I've got the consent." What they mean by this is not that they have talked to the patient, not that the patient understands, but that they have the patient's signature on the consent form. The assumption is that everything is fine if you have a signed form. This, unfortunately, is where we are headed – if we are not there already. I call this process, "formal substitution," since we are substituting forms for real communication.

Surgeons are the most guilty of formal substitution, since they have always looked at informed consent as red tape – getting the signature on the consent form so that needed surgery could be done. Who can blame them? That is what the law dictates. We confuse getting a signature on a form with the informed consent process. DNR does not yet stand for "Doctors Not Responsible," but we are moving in that direction. We want to hold our physicians accountable, and yet we continue to invent mechanisms that try to assure them that they won't be accountable.

Insofar as the DNR law teaches that forms are more important than communication, the statute has a major negative consequence.

CONCLUSION

Dr. Axelrod and I agree about the direction in which we should be headed: toward better patient care and improved doctor-patient communication, so that patients play a major role in their medical treatment. But the right to consent and the right to refuse are not symmetrical. Patients have a right to refuse anything. Patients do not have a right to demand everything. The most patients can legitimately demand is indicated and appropriate medical treatment, and guaranteeing access to such treatments would be an amazing achievement, which would require some form of national health insurance. Many patients now are lucky if they even get to see a doctor, let alone the inside of a hospital. So the notion that they can demand a full range of services, whether indicated or not, is quite incredible.

The New York position that the only medical service to which citizens have a legal right is CPR should strike everyone as strange. Assume the Department of Health placed an advertisement in the *New York Times* that said citizens had a choice: the state will guarantee you that when you are in the hospital (sick or dying) you will be resuscitated, or we will resuscitate you but will instead send your family a check for a thousand dollars (or whatever one-half or one-fourth of the cost is of CPR is). My guess is that the overwhelming number of citizens would take the thousand dollars. We could also give actual patients in the hospital a choice. My guess is that most would prefer $5,000 to help pay the tuition for their grandchildren than guaranteed resuscitation. I do not believe that CPR is a high priority item for most people; indeed, for most people it promises little, if any, benefit.

I know an older physician who says that when he was in training, shortly after blood transfusion came into vogue, everybody had to get a blood transfusion before they died. Today everybody gets CPR before they die. I suspect that in ten years it will be something else. Everybody will get something before they die, a new drug or a new procedure or something, but it will not be CPR. CPR is going through a fashionable stage of the sort that almost all medical procedures go through, but the fashion for CPR is more spectacular than most. When it becomes clearer to physicians that CPR does not work as well as we seem to think it does, it will not be used the way it has been.

Let me conclude by parphrasing Alexander Solzhenitsyn, the brilliant Russian writer who came to the United States at the end of the 1970s. Shortly after he arrived, he gave his first (and last) public address, a commencement speech at Harvard. [I think they thought he would talk about what a horrible country Russia was and how happy he was to be here in the U.S. He did say a bit about that, but mostly what he talked about were the kinds of problems that he thought we had in the U.S.] The main problem he thought we had was that our adherence to law as our only moral standard. What he said was that he had lived in a society that had no legal standards, and that was a terrible, horrible society. But he also said that a society with no other scale but a legal one is not quite worthy of man, either: "A society that is based on the letter of the law and never reaches any higher is taking a small advantage of the high level of human possibilities. The letter of the law is too cold and formal to have a beneficial influence on society. Whenever the tissue of life is woven of legalistic relations, there is an atmosphere of mediocrity, paralyzing the man's noble impulses."

One could argue that mediocrity pervaded medicine long before the New York DNR statute, and that medicine is already bureaucratic and legalistic, and that physicians are not willing or able to talk to their patients about what their patients want. If that is true, we need to change it. I take issue with the opinion that medicine is just a series of laws, and that a good doctor is a doctor who stays out of jail or court. The truth is that a good doctor is a doctor who works with his patients on a partnership basis and tries to do what is best for them, consistent with good medical practice and his patients' informed consent. That is the core of medical ethics and, thankfully, that is what a good doctor needs to know about the law. To the extent that the DNR law undermines both good medical practice and the doctor-patient relationship, it will continue to create more problems than it solves.

Notes

Sources for most of the material used in this speech can be found in [1–4].

REFERENCES

1. Annas, G.J.: 1988, *Judging Medicine*, Humana Press, Clifton, New Jersey.
2. Annas, G.J.: 1989, *The Right of Patients*, Southern Illinois University Press, Carbondale, Illinois.
3. Annas, G.J.: 1990, 'Nancy Cruzan and the Right to Die', *New England Journal of Medicine* **323**, 670–673.
4. Annas, G.J.: 1991, 'The Health Care Proxy and the Living Will', *New England Journal of Medicine* **324**, 1210–1213.
5. Bedell, S. and Delbanco, T.: 1984, 'Choices About Cardiopulmonary Resuscitation in the Hospital: When Do Physicians talk With Patients?', *New England Journal of Medicine* **310**, 1089–1093.

EDITED TRANSCRIPT OF QUESTION & ANSWER SESSIONS AT UNION COLLEGE CONFERENCE

BENNETT: I am Dr. Alan Bennett from New York City. Dr. Axelrod, I guess the one question that has gone through every talk we've heard today is the question of a medically futile CPR when a patient wants it. What is the physician to do?

AXELROD: It's interesting, that has come up time and time again. I don't know that anybody has the answer. I think that if a patient wants it, then the physician is confronted with the responsibility to provide it under those circumstances. As is pointed out very clearly in the preamble to the statute (the "presumed consent" clause), there is a right to get CPR, and even though futile CPR may be requested occasionally, what is going to happen in those infrequent circumstances is that the patient is going to receive futile treatment. The difficulty is one I tried to address with respect to the question of a religious controversy in the preamble, which was meant to provide a basis for dealing with the religious issue. Without that preamble it is unlikely that we could have gotten the statute passed. As George Annas has indicated, we probably would have been better off without a statute unless New York State was unique. Well, I suggest that in many ways New York is unique, and that the need for a DNR statute was one which did exist, and which was perceived by the rather diverse group of individuals who represent society in New York State. So the answer to your question is that in any situation, whether CPR is medically futile or not, the statute turns it into an entitlement, which clearly tells us that the patient has the right to CPR under such circumstances.

BENNETT: But don't we have conflicting laws here? There has always been common law in New York that medically futile therapy has never been required.

AXELROD: Common law isn't going to help you very much when you have a specific statute enacted by the legislature which clearly says that there is an obligation. And that was not an idle comment I made concerning the preamble to the statute. Without that preamble, the statute would not have been enacted into law. I would say to you that you will not get the presumption in favor of resuscitation removed from the statute in the State of New York.

R. Baker & M.A. Strosberg (eds.), Legislating Medical Ethics: A Study of the New York Do-Not-Resuscitate Law, 157–159.

UNIDENTIFIED INTERLOCUTOR: Commissioner, you indicated that the statute has been passed in response to specific pressures. Could you tell us to which pressures you responded, or is that a secret?

AXELROD: I think one of the benefits of discussing the amendments to the Task Force proposal has been that the discussions have taken place in an open and forthright fashion. I think that it would be betraying confidence if I were to provide you with a summary of the Task Force deliberations. But I think if you look at the debate on the floor of the legislature at the time the DNR statute was passed, you can probably get a pretty good idea of the issues. And I would simply add one issue to which George Annas alluded – whether the issues of death and brain death have been clearly dealt with in New York State. They have not. There are those in the State of New York who feel that death has a religious component, that it has nothing to do with the medical definition. And the suggestion that brain death equals death is not readily accepted by significant portions of the population. That's why there is no statute in New York on brain death, not because there was no desire to clarify the situation. What we have done in New York State is to utilize a decision by the Court of Appeals as a regulatory basis for providing some clarification as to the medical (as opposed to the religious) definition of death. Believe me, the issue is far from resolved in the minds of many physicians.

JAMES HORWITZ: I would like to jump into the controversy concerning DNR orders and the issue of medical futility. Before I do I'd like to put my view of the whole situation in proper context. It's my view that every time there is a baby delivered in the hospital where I work, there is a greater risk of legal liability and regulatory sanction than there is from the procedures attached to the entire implementation of the DNR law.

Be that as it may, I was particularly interested by Professor Baker's question about situations in which it is impossible to comply with all of the procedural requirements of the law – is it then lawful to withhold CPR on grounds of medical futility? The problem with which I think hospital lawyers in general are faced is that we have a law which specifically defines medical futility. Furthermore, the law has a section which indicates exactly what a physician must do in order to issue a DNR order on the basis of medical futility. On the other hand, we have the Department of Health (DOH) memorandum, which indicates that the DNR law does not create a new duty for the physician, and that the physician can still issue a DNR order on the basis of futility where the law's requirements cannot be exactly fulfilled. Yet, undeniably, the statute alters the physician's duty.

Professor Annas asserted last night that the law creates a new entitlement to CPR. I think he is right. What hospital lawyers are confronted with are physicians who are afraid of legal liability. As hospital counsel I am bound to advise staff as to the provisions of the law. And what I feel obliged to indicate to them is that the DNR law has a specific procedure defining what physicians must do before they can issue a DNR order on the basis of medical futility. There are two specific immunities for health care professionals written into the statute; one for providers who withhold resuscitation in compliance with a fully documented DNR order, and the other for providers who resuscitate when genuinely unaware of the presence of a DNR order. There is, however, no immunity for providers who do not resuscitate where there is no advance directive. Consequently, I advise my physician-clients that there is no immunity for withholding of resuscitation on the basis of medical futility where the required procedures are not carried out. The DOH memorandum which suggests the contrary does not have the force or the effect of law; it is simply an interpretative guideline.

When I get a question from an emergency-room physician who wants to know whether his or her staff has to resuscitate in the case of an incapacitated 95-year-old patient for whom the proper DNR paperwork is not in place before cardiopulmonary arrest, my advice is that I don't think there is much risk if the staff withholds resuscitation. But if the physician wants to know what the law is, I tell him or her that it requires resuscitation in this case. Rather than claim that lawyers are giving bad legal advice, rather than claim that physicians are ignorant of the law, rather than claim that physicians are confused by the law, I suggest that the Task Force and the New York State Legislature need to expand the immunity provisions in the law such that they codify the unsupported interpretation of the law's "No duty to expand equipment" provision (§2962.4) given in the DOH memorandum.

PART III

CASE STUDIES

CAROLYN SHEARER ANTONELLI

IMPLEMENTATION OF THE NEW YORK DO-NOT-RESUSCITATE LAW AT A TEACHING HOSPITAL*

The first time I read the Task Force report on Do-Not-Resuscitate (DNR) legislation, I refused to believe that a proposal so cumbersome and complicated could ever become law. But eventually, my disbelief gave way to anxiety as we faced the challenge of implementing the law. As the day on which the law would go into effect drew near, we wondered if the Health Department was going to accept the Legislature's invitation to develop consent forms, but they declined that invitation. (To give you some idea of how much sympathy we were given from the Health Department, in December, 1987, when it published its proposed regulations implementing the DNR statute, the impact statement indicated that no appreciable increase in overall paperwork was anticipated.) Clearly, we were on our own.

Through the winter, the law was discussed many times at our Ethics Committee meetings. The task of developing strategy was delegated to three Committee members, the Medical Director, a critical care nurse and myself. Because I was the person in our small group who had the most experience reading law and convoluted statutes, the task of developing compliance policies fell to me. So I read the statute again, again, and again and I became intimate with its ten pages of dense prose. Even after many readings, I still couldn't remember which types of consent require two witnesses, which require one witness, and when one of the two witnesses has to be a physician. So I drew up a flow chart. I read through the statute to determine which categories of patient the statute identifies, then for each of those categories I determined which elements of documentation would be required. Finally, I compared those lists with our existing policy and standard of care on DNR and found that there was virtually no correspondence. Prior policy, and indeed the standard of care, requires physicians to obtain consent, to document consent, and then to write an order. But this statute requires more. As has already been pointed out (by Baker, Miller and Strosberg), forms are not required or even mentioned in the law. But I challenge anyone to put forth a feasible way to get all

* Edited Transcript of Conference Paper, Reproduced with the Consent of the Author.

R. Baker & M.A. Strosberg (eds.), Legislating Medical Ethics: A Study of the New York Do-Not-Resuscitate Law, 163–168.

the elements of documentation in the chart without using forms. Ultimately, we were forced to draft forms, not as a reflection of the legal climate, and not as a reflection of what hospital attorneys are looking for, but rather out of necessity, because that is the only way to document compliance.

We had two objectives in developing our forms: one was to make them as user-friendly and convenient as possible (so as not to discourage their use); the other was to make the forms as self-contained and self-explanatory as possible – because there is high staff turnover in hospitals, especially among nurses; but there is also turnover in physicians and a new house staff cohort is introduced every July.

In the end, we felt it necessary to develop a set of seven different forms, each dealing with a separate context of consent. The back of each form contains definitions of six key terms and a chart explaining the form to use. For example, if the patient is an adult without capacity who has a surrogate available – use forms 3 and 4.

Our intent was to make compliance palatable to the people on the hospital wards who are going to have to use the forms. So we developed documentation forms with instructions. Each form also contains the sequence of activities that have to be documented according to the law (and which, frankly, would not be documented without the law). Just one example: the law requires that when physicians seek informed consent, they must disclose to the patient or the patient's surrogate information about prognosis, the risks and benefits of cardiopulmonary resuscitation (CPR), the range of available resuscitation measures, and the consequence of the DNR order. Ordinarily, one would never see this written out in the progress notes, or in the physician's handwritten description of informed consent discussions. So, with our forms, an exquisitely personal decision and a very delicate discussion between physician and patient or physician and family has become a cookbook.

In addition to our forms, our other implementation tool was policy. Like all hospitals, we live and die by our policy book and we had to incorporate the DNR law therein. So we distilled the statute into a four-page description of what needed to be done under various circumstances. With these tools – our forms and our policy – we set about the task of educating staff. In October 1987, there was a presentation for the Medical Center's Managers meeting, a gathering of several hundred middle managers. As the day when the law went into effect approached (April 1, 1988), we sent a mass mailing to the medical staff, house staff, and all nurse managers containing policy information and information about the forms. In addition, we had special sessions for our on-call administrators. Our pledge to the medical staff and the nursing staff was that we would provide them with 24-hour access to information and answers to any questions that they might have about the DNR law. Also, in late March, we held general information sessions, open to all physicians, nurses, and house staff. These sessions were very well attended by nurses, but not by physicians. We also scheduled sessions for nursing grand rounds, made presentations to the medical board, and had an open offer to go anywhere, anytime, to talk to any group about the DNR law. Family Practice and the Department of Medicine accepted our offer. We had special presentations for social workers, and later it became an item for health staff orientation. So we did everything we could to make everyone as aware possibly.

April first finally came: Everything had been distributed, all of our on-call administrators had been briefed, we all put fresh batteries in our beepers and the most remarkable thing happened! Nothing! An ominous silence on the subject ensued, and we wondered whether the law was being embraced at all. This suggests that interested parties like those assembled at this conference tend to overestimate the impact of the DNR legislation on clinical practice.

Eventually the enquiries started to trickle in: Concern was expressed about the difficulty of obtaining surrogate consent to a DNR order when the highest person on the surrogate list did not live nearby. In response, we reminded physicians that, just as for other interventions, "faxed" consent was legally acceptable. Nonetheless, this is a problem within the statute: What if the incapacitated patient's sister in Idaho does not have easy access to a fax machine? Another frequent question had to do with the three-day review of the DNR order. This requirement is particularly confusing because the concept of periodical review of standing orders is foreign to health-care professionals. Physicians and nurses are familiar with certain types of orders needing renewal, for example controlled substances orders automatically expire after a certain length of time, and in many hospitals some antibiotic orders have to be renewed after a certain period. But the three-day review of DNR orders is different, because the statute mandates that failure to review an order in time does not render the order ineffective. Moreover, there is no clinical justification for such a review because, in practice, patients' conditions seldom change quickly and suddenly for the better, particularly in the case of DNR patients, who are likely to have very poor prognoses.

Nor is it only the unprecedented documentation requirement in the law that lacks a foundation in clinical reality. For example, where a close friend of an incapacitated individual puts him or herself forward as a surrogate, the hospital needs an affidavit from that person testifying to her or his close relationship with the patient over a substantial period of time. An affidavit by definition has to be notarized. How many notaries are working in a hospital at night or over the weekend? Another example of a legal requirement that is not clinically justified is the need for a concurring opinion on lack of capacity, no matter how obvious that lack of capacity is. Similarly, the law requires a description of the cause, nature, extent and probable duration of that lack of capacity, again no matter how obvious.

Not unexpectedly, the highest degree of noncompliance is with respect to documentation items that are mandated without clinical justification. Our Medical Records Department held an informal audit of documentation compliance, in April, 1988, in August, 1988, and in December, 1988. I should emphasize that this is not empirical research, it was just a survey. The first finding was that most DNR orders are written for patients without capacity upon consent of a surrogate. In each of three months reviewed – April, August and December – the hospital had approximately fifty deaths. The number of those patients for whom there were DNR orders was also pretty constant – around twenty five. But the number of DNR documentation mistakes in April was one, in August nine, and in December twelve. This suggests that attention to detail was actually decreasing over time. We do not know whether this was because of indifference, or because of the feeling that there would be no adverse consequences, or whether it reflected physician resentment.

On the basis of an actual log of physician enquiries, we also observed that when physician resistance was articulated, most often it focused on the issue of futility. Typically physicians' believed that the only way to withhold CPR was by following statutory recipe, otherwise resuscitation was mandated. Frankly their confusion was understandable. Prior to Robert Swidler's article in the February 1989 *New York State Journal of Medicine*, the standard of care was in a Health Facilities Memorandum of March 18, 1988, in which the Health Department said, "The authority of a physician to make a medical judgment when resuscitative measures would be futile in a particular case has not changed." The Health Facilities Memorandum is not law, it's not regulation, it's just an interpretive guideline. Even this statement is confusing, because it does not address cases in which physicians agree that CPR is not indicated, but where CPR is not futile according to the narrow definition stated in the law. I do not think it is any wonder that physicians would be confused and resentful.

Other issues that emerged in the initial months suggest that physicians were resentful about compliance issues, for the requirements of the law imply distrust of the medical profession. For example, the law requires a *personal examination* of the patient by the concurring physician in cases of incapacity. Moreover, the law leaves important questions unanswered – can this concurrence come from a resident? If not, who pays for the services of a concurring physician? Another example: If a patient is a minor a physician who has obtained DNR consent from the custodial parent is still obligated to make diligent efforts to contact the non-custodial parent before writing the order. Perhaps the non-custodial parent is very involved, or absent, or in jail, or abusive. The law does not allow physicians any leeway to exercise their judgement in promoting the best interests of their patients. Diligent efforts are required and no exceptions are permitted.

Another compliance and implementation problem arose out of the Health Department pamphlet on DNR orders. Originally the requirement was to distribute this to every patient on admission – a cheerful addition to the admissions packet – especially for obstetrics patients, patients who are otherwise well coming in for an elective procedure, or parents of a pediatric patient. The inappropriateness of this requirement has been widely recognized, and it has since been deleted from Department of Health regulations, but it's still in the law.

Ironically, one area that did not produce implementation problems was the dispute mediation system. The law outlines an elaborate mechanism for resolving decision-making conflicts between healthcare professionals, family members and other interested parties, but at my hospital, resort to this process was extremely unusual – somewhere in the region of once a year. Here, once again, those who drafted the legislation seemed have an exaggerated mistrust of the medical profession; they underestimate the ability of physicians to act in a sensible, compassionate way. The law does not seem to recognize that differences in opinion over DNR are inherently not responsive to a formal resolution process. A family grappling with the issue of a DNR order has actually begun the grieving process. Differences of opinion have been and continue to be resolved *ad hoc* with good communication, negotiation and time. The rare case in our institution that comes before the Life Support and Medical Ethics Committee usually involves somthing more complex than a DNR order. It involves the whole spectrum of medical care and I still contend that this is the fundamental flaw in the DNR legislation. It isolates DNR orders from the remainder of the spectrum of care; it treats them in a very heavy-handed and prescriptive way, rather than encouraging hospitals to develop flexible policies. No other treatment requires anywhere near the level of documentation and elaborate paperwork that is required to comply with the DNR law. Is this approach really, as it claims to be, in the best interests of patients?

DEBORAH DAMM O'BRIEN

ONE FAMILY'S EXPERIENCE WITH THE NEW YORK DNR LAW*

I would like to share some experiences that I had with my husband's family at the time of the death of their mother, in July, 1989. My mother-in-law, Mrs. O'Brien, was in a nursing home for several years. She was eighty-six years old and living in the nursing home because she was severely crippled by arthritis and confined to a wheelchair. She had had bouts of congestive heart failure and high blood pressure, but was in adequate health for a person her age.

When the Do-Not-Resuscitate law was enacted in 1988, the nursing home where Mrs. O'Brien resided presented her with information, as they did for all their residents, and held information sessions on the law. They discussed the implications of the law and what the decision to consent to a DNR order would mean. Mrs. O'Brien was a serious woman, so she took this, as she took many things, very, very seriously. She carefully reviewed all the information that was provided to her. She engaged each of her four children in serious discussions of the subject. It may be interesting to know that of her children, one is a physician who is a specialist in internal medicine, and another is a Roman Catholic priest. She discussed the subject of DNR orders, and the question of whether she should sign a consent to one, very carefully with all her children. She was a woman who had very deep religious convictions and a strong personal prayer life. She spent a lot of her time praying about the decision, and took into account what all her children had said to her. In fact, the discussions she had with her children made them more uncomfortable than it had made her.

Finally, she decided that she would sign a consent to a DNR order. When she told her children that she was going through with it, she told them that she was doing it for two reasons: one, she really did not want to have her life prolonged artificially; two, she felt very strongly that she did not want her children to have to make the decision to let her die "at a crisis point," as she put it. She was hoping to avoid both these types of discomfort for herself and her children. The nursing home at which she resided had her review the decision quite frequently, I believe every thirty

* Edited Transcript, Reprinted With the Consent of the Author.

R. Baker & M.A. Strosberg (eds.), Legislating Medical Ethics: A Study of the New York Do-Not-Resuscitate Law, 169–171.

days. This was something of a hardship in that for the first three or four times that she reviewed her decision, she called her children. She would ask them whether they thought anything had changed, or whether she should make a different decision. After the third or fourth time, she was much more comfortable that they were not unhappy or upset with the decision which she had made.

At approximately one A.M. on July 8, 1989, Mrs. O'Brien began to experience cardiorespiratory problems. She was still in the nursing home. The nursing-home personnel called the ambulance and emergency personnel responded quickly to the call. Shortly after they arrived, Mrs. O'Brien went into cardiac arrest and was described to us as "gone." The emergency crew who arrived with the ambulance wished to perform cardiopulmonary resuscitation [CPR] to revive her. They did not ask any questions about DNR consent. The nursing-home personnel had the presence of mind to point out that she had signed a DNR order. Confusion ensued. The emergency crew refused to respect the DNR order, insisting that it had not been signed recently enough, that is within the last seventy-two hours. They applied CPR and then took Mrs. O'Brien to the hospital. She did not regain consciousness. All the children were called to the hospital. She was non-responsive to voices or touch and was on a ventilator.

After several hours, we were all assembled, and a physician came in, called all of Mrs. O'Brien's children together and explained that she was gone and there really wasn't much hope for her recovery, given his best medical judgment. He added that if she were to maintain life in some sense, she would be unable to function, absent a miracle. He then asked the question which she had hoped to avoid having her children answer, which was whether they wanted the physician to continue supporting her life with extraordinary measures. The children all elected to have him discontinue the mechanisms and medications that were really keeping her alive, in some sense, but to have her remain on the ventilator. Unaware of her surroundings, she died at 8:30 P.M. that same day.

With the benefit of hindsight, I thought I'd share some of the feelings of that day and the following weeks. Because I work in New York State government, many of my family members have told me I should do something to "fix it" so that other families don't go through the same experience, as if I somehow had power over these things. One of the concerns which they kept reiterating was that they were angry that their mother had to go through all that she did. She had taken the prescribed legal steps to avoid it, but was forced to go through it anyway. The family experienced a great deal of psychological, spiritual, and physical pain from seeing Mrs. O'Brien in such a state. Also, I think that many of the family, in addition to the sadness of losing their mother, felt a sadness and an anger about having to make such a decision; Mrs. O'Brien had wanted to make that decision herself, and in fact had made and re-made it several times. And when all is said and done, they felt frustration and anger that there could be confusion about something that is so important to us as individuals. To make people sign a consent to a DNR order but have strings attached that make you look at the time and count the number of days seems absurd.

To this day, my family has many difficult thoughts and feelings with which to deal. Although our experience may be unique, we have no way of knowing whether other situations will arise in which there is confusion when emergency personnel are called. My family and I hope that by sharing this experience changes in the law will be considered.

[Editors note: Mrs. O'Brien's experience and those of others prompted a revision in the DNR law in 1991, that made DNR orders binding on emergency medical techhnicians, see discussion in this volume, pp. 9–31, pp. 439–445, and the amendments in this volume, pp. 445–454.]

TIMOTHY E. QUILL

WHEN THE AMBULANCE GOES HOME: A TRAGIC FLAW IN THE NEW YORK STATE DO-NOT-RESUSCITATE LAW

The Do-Not-Resuscitate (DNR) legislation attempted to anticipate commonly occurring situations where the decision about whether to initiate cardiopulmonary resuscitation (CPR) might occur, and give patients informed choice in the matter. Perhaps nowhere has the legislation been more troublesome than in the regulation of emergency medical technicians [EMTs] and other ambulance personnel. The clarification of the law by the New York State Health Department presented at this conference, and to be distributed subsequently (See Appendix, this volume, pp. 415–438), has helped insure that a DNR order issued in a nursing home will be honored by EMT personnel who are transporting patients to the hospital. The clarification will prevent the kind of tragedy and anguish experienced by Ms Damm O'Brien and her family (described in this volume, pp. 169–171), and countless others who had opted for DNR orders in a nursing home, yet had the misfortune of encountering ambulance personnel who did not recognize or honor such orders.

Unfortunately, similar transgressions are occurring regularly in people's homes because legislation does not guide EMT personnel in this domain, and, therefore, the "presumed consent" (to CPR) assumption overrides a patient's explicit request to the contrary. The law began as a consumer protection measure to ensure that patients were not arbitrarily excluded from the decision of whether or not to be resuscitated. In a conference filled with controversy, we have had a remarkable consensus about the importance of true informed consent. We all want patients to be in control of DNR decisions as much as possible.

We should all appreciate the extraordinarily meaningful and, at times, anguishing and painful discussions that patients, their families, and doctors engage in about prognosis, the very limited efficacy of CPR in chronic multi-system disease, and the patient's wishes and attitudes toward such treatments. We should all agree that the wish of an informed patient in favor of DNR should be honored, even when the odds of successful CPR are remote at best.

It is therefore disturbing, even outrageous, to read the following

R. Baker & M.A. Strosberg (eds.), Legislating Medical Ethics: A Study of the New York Do-Not-Resuscitate Law, 173–179.

directive from the Health Department intending to clarify the law as it applies to ambulances:

> Emergency personnel are not required to honor DNR orders for patients who are picked up at home. Emergency service personnel may honor DNR orders presented to them in a hospice patient's home when the order is written on hospice stationery or when there is telephone confirmation from the patient's physician or a physician at the receiving hospital. Emergency personnel are not encouraged to honor DNR orders in other situations (this volume, pp. 415–438).

As a strong believer in a patient's right to make informed decisions, including the right to refuse certain treatments, and as a former director of a home hospice program, I find a frightening disregard for patients' rights in the aforementioned statement. Outside of a hospice program where DNR orders "may" be honored presumably at the discretion of EMT personnel, there are explicit directives not to honor documents signed by the patient, family, and attending physician. Hospital DNR documents, often signed after extensive discussion and soul searching, are *not* to be recognized in the home. With increasing numbers of severely-ill patients being cared for at home, and with hospital stays being shortened considerably, this is a very prevalent problem.

In trying to determine if this is a theoretical or a real problem, I had no difficulty finding examples of people with very serious chronic and/or terminal illnesses being resuscitated against their will at home. Almost every attending physician I asked had some frightening account. In each case, the futile CPR was an assault against the patient's expressed wishes, and against the wishes of the family. The following real-life situations illustrate the problem.

Yates County is in a rural, economically-poor part of western New York State. The county has no certified hospice program, yet not surprisingly terminally ill patients are still cared for at home through the combined efforts of their families, the visiting nurses, aides, and primary care physicians. Many such patients know they are dying, and the objective of their care is to allow them to die with the most dignity and least suffering possible. When these patients are in the last moments of life, sometimes a family member panics and calls an ambulance. The request may be to confirm that the patient is dead, perhaps to transport the patient to the hospital because they would rather the actual death not be at home, or perhaps they are requesting some guidance about how to provide comfort.

The visiting nurses from Yates County had a myriad of stories of patients being resuscitated against their expressed wishes. In one instance, family members tried to stop the ambulance crew from "assaulting" their terminally-ill father who had wanted no such heroics with CPR. What ensued was a physical altercation between the family trying to protect their father from this unwanted intervention, and the EMT crew who feared the legal consequences of not performing CPR.

Another EMT crew, faced with the same dilemma, made the opposite decision. One of the EMTs knew the patient, who was in the terminal stages of lung cancer. This crew chose to honor the patient's and family's wishes, and did not initiate CPR. Instead, they helped the family provide comfort and confirmation that the patient was dying. These EMTs did what was morally correct (in respecting the patient's and family's stated wishes by not enforcing an invasive treatment), and also what made sense (CPR is ineffective and certainly not health restoring in that clinical situation). Note that in so doing they took considerable legal and professional risk. In fact, this crew was severely reprimanded for this decision, and almost lost their jobs. The ambulance companies, on advice of their legal counsel, have advised their personnel *never* to make an exception about initiating CPR. They fear a Health Department inquiry into cases such as this, but not into cases in which EMTs assault patients by forcing unwanted CPR on them. In fact, ambulance crews are instructed that the law requires that they do CPR no matter what the circumstances.

In Monroe County, where there is a certified home hospice program, similar problems exist. After many instances of CPR performed in the home against the expressed wishes of patients in the home hospice program, we finally have a signed agreement with most ambulance crews that they will honor DNR orders for certified Hospice patients. But the certified Hospice patients are only the tip of the iceberg. There are many terminally ill patients at home who do not qualify for this hospice program, which inevitably has limited enrollment anyway. Many patients are maintained through the efforts of their families, visiting nurses from other agencies, and aides. Most of these patients have requested and signed DNR documents in the hospital, and know they are in the process of dying. They have made a clear, informed choice about DNR that is *de facto* rejected by New York State law, the Health Department, and the

EMT personnel. If an ambulance is called, even if the patient is dead, CPR is initiated. The patient and the family are thereby assaulted and violated, and the EMT personnel must find this part of their work meaningless and demoralizing.

Another group that remains unprotected is the chronically ill, but still relatively independent, elderly patients who feel that they are ready to die, and don't want heroic measures. They have signed DNR documents in the hospital, and have made their wishes clear. (As one of my patients put it, "If you perform CPR on me, I will come back from the dead to haunt you. I am ready to go when my times comes.") In a hospital or in a nursing home, these patients' wishes would be respected. They could be transported from the nursing home to the hospital for conservative treatment of pneumonia without risking a CPR attempt should they arrest in transit. If such a patient is at home, with the same well-documented, expressed wishes, they are unprotected by the law. If an ambulance is called, and the patient has a cardiac arrest, they will be resuscitated no matter how clearly their wishes are documented. The only thing I can tell my patients who are at home and don't want CPR is that if they call an ambulance, their wishes won't be respected.

In an unclear situation, I still concur fully with the ambulance crew's imperative to initiate CPR first, and sort out the questions later. Delaying CPR for a few minutes to sort things out may mean the difference between death and life. People also can change their mind at the last minute. If there is considerable uncertainty about the patient's wishes, then CPR should be initiated. Treatment initiated in this circumstance can be withdrawn later if it proves futile, or if it turns out to be against the patient's clearly documented wishes.

Yet there are also clear situations in the home in which CPR is not indicated. A terminally-ill patient treated at home with a comfort-oriented approach should not receive CPR no matter what the circumstances. There needs to be adequate documentation, and clear concordance of patient, family, and attending physician about the patient's wishes. But if these criteria are satisfied, then it is a violation of human rights to initiate CPR. Similarly, patients who request and meet the criteria for DNR orders in the hospital should have similar options for their home. At present, such orders and informed requests, no matter how well documented, are systematically ignored by EMT personnel as directed by the State of New York.

Two solutions have been proposed by the Department of Health. The first was in response to a letter (I sent two years ago) alerting them to the problem. Through their counsel, Peter Millock, they suggested that EMT personnel can call the "medical control physician" at the Emergency Department who can then designate a DNR order. This solution is unrealistic for multiple reasons. First, if CPR is to be initiated at all, it must be initiated immediately. The five or ten minutes spent trying to reach an emergency physician, quite possibly busy with another emergency, would mean that the opportunity for life-saving intervention would be lost. If CPR is initiated in the interim while awaiting word from the emergency physician, then CPR has been initiated on a patient for whom it is inappropriate and specifically not requested, and the patient and their family have been unnecessarily assaulted for that period. Second, emergency physicians would be rightly reluctant to issue such an order for a patient that they don't know well. In such a case, the only no risk order would be to proceed with CPR. This is clearly not a realistic mechanism for overcoming the problem of EMT reluctance to respect a DNR decision in the home.

The second solution, proposed by the Director of EMT Services at the Health Department, is to educate the public not to call an ambulance if they don't want CPR. While on the surface this seems reasonable, it is, in fact, a rather callous response that seems to put the onus of solving a procedural problem of the Department of Health on families in distress. Panicked families will still call ambulances, but this call does *not* necessarily mean they are requesting CPR. As stated previously, it may be a request for confirmation that a patient has died, or perhaps a frightened question about oxygen or other technical matters, or even a request for transportation to the hospital.

Clearly, if a patient can be transferred from a nursing home to the hospital without the threat of CPR in cases where there is proper documentation, then there is no reason that similar options can't be made available to patients at home. There are some better potential solutions. First let me add the proviso that I would still recommend that CPR be initiated if the patient's wishes about CPR are unclear. I am not looking for EMT personnel to make on-the-spot decisions about whether or not to initiate CPR. What is needed is a clear system for identifying patients who clearly do *not* want CPR.

1. There is the need for an officially recognized DNR document for the home. A similar document has been developed for patients on certified

hospice programs. This approach must be broadened to include all patients who have made an informed decision to forego CPR. Possible candidates for this document would include the hospice DNR documents, the official hospital DNR forms, or perhaps a document developed and recognized by the State of New York.

2. All patients receiving organized health care might be given the option of selecting DNR or full CPR when their initial treatment plan is developed. If they have consented to DNR in the hospital, they might be asked if they want to be granted similar status at home.
3. Finally, there has been discussion about a regional register of DNR patients at home that could be made available to the ambulance companies.

As the DNR legislation is understood and clarified, it is clear that many patients are appropriately being given the option of foregoing CPR, particularly in situations where it is likely to be ineffective. The law provides the patient with protection and the opportunity to make an informed decision, rights that are respected in the hospital, the nursing home, and in transit between these facilities. Once the patient goes home, all of this careful, informed, decision making, consumer protection, and effort to humanize and individualize care is lost. The law as written is bad for patients at home, and bad for EMT personnel. It is hard to imagine a more humiliating experience for patients, families, and EMTs than performing futile CPR on terminally-ill patients who have no chance of recovery, and have explicitly stated their wishes not to be treated in such fashion. Yet unless the patient is in a certified hospice program, this is what will happen if an ambulance is called.

How can New York State allow this to happen? How can a law that was born out of a desire to protect consumers of health care violate their rights in such a flagrant way? Everyone with whom I have spoken in the Health Department, the legislature, and the Medical Societies agree that this is not the intent of the legislation. The problem is that the legislators did not consider these situations, and therefore made no provision for them. (In their defense, it is unrealistic to expect legislators to anticipate every aspect of such a complex process.) It is now unclear who has the authority to make decisions in this domain. The Health Department apparently is not empowered to make policy on these matters, so it seems that no one can correct this oversight in the law.

In the interim, patients are being violated with CPR against their expressed and documented wishes, if they or their families happen to call an ambulance. This so fundamentally violates the patient's right to decline treatment autonomously, as well as the beneficence which underpins the medical profession, that it must be addressed. If the Health Department cannot resolve the problem by revising its policies and recommendations, then the legislation must be rewritten and reenacted. The theoretical risk that some of the gains that the legislation has promoted may be lost is outweighed by the real and immediate risks experienced by patients at home who are forced to undergo CPR against their expressed wishes. Legislation cannot anticipate all eventualities. Yet if it is not flexible enough to be responsive to unanticipated bad effects, then perhaps the entire process of legislating health care decisions should be rethought.

Editors' Note: In 1991 The New York DNR law was amended and non-hospital DNR orders were given formal legal status. (See this volume, pp. 445–454).

CAROL CLAY

IMPLEMENTATION OF THE NEW YORK STATE DNR LAW AT A COMMUNITY HOSPITAL

Ellis Hospital is a large community hospital with 352 acute care beds and 82 skilled nursing beds. Since the inception of the New York State Do-Not-Resuscitate (NYS DNR) law in 1987, the staff has grappled with a wide variety of issues and questions on interpretation of the law. This case history will demonstrate how far awry things can go when an attempt is made to apply rigid rules to an area calling for judgment, compassion, and tolerance of individual differences. Since the question of initiating CPR arises in widely varying situations, and since there is a felt need to protect the public from potentially unscrupulous behavior by health care workers, ethical dilemmas surrounding this treatment arise with surprising frequency.

Ellis Hospital had established an Ethics Committee and drafted its own DNR policy two years prior to enactment of the law. Therefore, a significant amount of discussion and resolution of philosophical and ethical issues had already occurred. Initially, we thought it would be relatively easy to meld the current policy and New York State law. We have found, however, that for a variety of legal, regulatory, and emotional reasons, this assumption was not true. Despite numerous hours of discussing, arguing, and explaining, the number of questions does not appreciably diminish and problem resolution seems very slow. Everyone involved feels caught in the complexity of the legal and regulatory system which has been created.

Physicians feel caught when they try to use their best professional judgment but are faced with a bureaucracy of forms and rigid procedures. (In developing the policy and procedure, we tried to "simplify" the process for physicians by creating a documentation form for each scenario which includes a fill-in-the-blank for every required component. These forms total eight in number – one each for adult with capacity, adult without capacity with surrogate, adult without capacity without surrogate, and so on.) Nurses feel caught because they are ultimately responsible for deciding to initiate the code and are frequently faced with a situation of being forced to do this because some appropriate piece of paperwork has not been completed. Chaplains, social workers, and other health care team

R. Baker & M.A. Strosberg (eds.), Legislating Medical Ethics: A Study of the New York Do-Not-Resuscitate Law, 181–186.

members feel caught as they try to support patients and families through this emotionally intense time and are forced to include explanations about bureaucratic rules in what would seem to be most inappropriate circumstances. Finally, families and significant others feel caught when they are helpless to prevent distress in this final stage of life for a loved one.

Hospitals and hospital attorneys have been challenged for creating the rigid policies, procedures, and forms alluded to above. Unfortunately, our litigious society tends to foster a desire in most health care professionals for specific, clear guidelines which are not subject to a wide scope of interpretation. Furthermore, our health care regulatory environment requires clear documentation of meeting the various requirements of the State health code, the Joint Commission on Accreditation of Health Care Organizations, the Occupational Safety Health Administration, the Center for Disease Control, and on and on. Relying on four-hundred physicians and seven-hundred nurses to remember the details of documentation for legislation as complex as that governing the DNR law leaves one feeling quite vulnerable. Therefore, although the law did not mandate the development of eight forms, I believe there are not many individuals in the field of health care who would argue the necessity of some mechanism to ensure documentation of compliance.

Some examples of difficulties encountered in the implementation of the NYS DNR law are the following:

(1) No allowance for orders to be telephoned in by a physician;
(2) No provision for documentation of a DNR decision made prior to hospitalization;
(3) No provision for a DNR order to remain in effect over a succession of admissions for the same terminal illness;
(4) No allowance for telephone consent by a surrogate.

One cause of the above is the pervasive belief that a DNR order must be the product of a carefully considered decision resulting from a dialogue between patient, physician, and family and "long distance" or previously considered decisions do not support this dialogue. In practice, however, physicians often have discussed this possibility with patients and family members at some point prior to hospitalization. People with a terminal illness often choose to remain at home until a crisis precipitates hospital admission. To be required to wait until the physician can write an order for DNR, or until the surrogate can get to the hospital to sign a form, puts the process "on hold" during the very time period that an individual is most likely to be resuscitated, and does this even when the open discussion that the law is supposed to encourage has taken place. The situation can lead to anxiety, frustration, guilt, and blame for health care givers and a sense of overwhelming helplessness for families. A handbook distributed in September, 1990, co-authored by the New York State Department of Health, the Hospital Association of New York State and the New York State Medical Society (see this volume, pp. 415–438.) has addressed some of these issues in a question and answer format, but still leaves several areas open to interpretation.

The most difficult case related to the DNR law, that I have experienced, centered around a series of communication problems and underlying philosophical differences. The patient involved was a young man admitted from an Office of Mental Retardation and Developmental Disabilities (OMRDD) facility whom I will call Jim. The case was particularly distressing because of the emotional impact on family, care givers and, probably, Jim himself.

Jim was admitted on a Friday afternoon. He was 30 years old with a mental age of 30 months, due to Down's Syndrome. Chief complaints were cough, fever, and inability to eat. He had a long history of repeated pneumonias and was a hepatitis B carrier. He was admitted on service to a new attending physician who had recently begun practicing in New York State. The physician was familiar with the DNR law but was under the impression that it was the same for everyone and did not know that the OMRDD facility had to be notified of DNR orders for its residents.

At the time the history was taken and physical performed, it became apparent that Jim was very ill. He had a right lower lobe pneumonia with a greatly elevated white cell count, had markedly abnormal liver function tests, and had a systolic blood pressure of 80 which rapidly elevated with hydration. The initial impression was documented as pneumonia with early sepsis, although the progress note stated that he looked surprisingly well, in view of his abnormal laboratory values. Shortly after admission, Jim vomited a small amount of blood but the bleeding quickly stopped. Broad spectrum antibiotics were prescribed and infectious disease and gastroenterology consults requested. Except for several episodes of respiratory distress, one requiring suctioning, Jim remained stable for 24–36 hours. Three sisters and one brother were present during this time. The sister who had power of attorney was returning from the Bahamas. Jim's mother had died approximately six months previously after a long hospitalization with attempts at resuscitation, and the family was in agreement that they did not want the same course for their brother. The attending physician discussed DNR with family members because, in view of the multiple medical problems, he felt cardiopulmonary resuscitation (CPR) would impose an extraordinary burden on the patient. The family agreed that they wanted everything except CPR done for their brother. Therefore the order was written. A few hours later, the Medical Director of the OMRDD facility called the attending to check on Jim's condition and was told of the DNR order. There was confusion over who had authority to determine that the patient lacked capacity to make a DNR decision and during a twelve to twenty-four hour period many phone calls were exchanged. The facility Director objected to the order, but the attending physician insisted that the family wanted the DNR order and they had a valid right to have an order written.

The OMRDD Medical Director finally called the Nurse Manager, who functions as administrator-on-site over the weekend. The Nurse Manager called the administrator-on-call, who relayed the information that the DNR order would have to be rescinded until the Ethics Committee could be convened. This was done and, because the attending physician believed there was a high risk of respiratory arrest, the patient was transferred to ICU. At 4 a.m. that Monday morning, Jim experienced a respiratory arrest, was intubated, and placed on a ventilator.

The Ethics Committee, comprised of physicians, clergy, a nurse, a social worker, and an ethicist, was convened on Monday with family members, the attending physician, the OMRDD Medical Director, another OMRDD physician, and an administrator from the facility. A long, emotional, and somewhat hostile discussion occurred in which the family reiterated that they had seen their mother go through this situation and did not want a repetition for their brother. They stated that they were very impressed by the concern and care of the attending physician and other hospital staff and could not understand why OMRDD was "interfering."

The OMRDD staff saw Jim as one of their healthiest residents and felt that he had a chance at life. Although unstated, they seemed to believe that the DNR order was being contemplated just because Jim was developmentally disabled.

The attending physician was upset that his integrity and medical judgement were being questioned – that this order was truly imposing an extraordinary burden on his patient. He was also angry that he had been "harassed by phone" all weekend, yet no OMRDD physician had come in to see how sick Jim really was.

At the conclusion of this discussion, the Ethics Committee decided that the DNR order was appropriate. The OMRDD staff returned to their facility to confer; they had the following options: (1) accept the DNR order; (2) request that Jim be transferred to another physician; or (3) obtain a court order to revoke the order. Within two hours, they called to say they would not challenge the order. At this point, however, DNR was a moot point, since Jim was on a ventilator and unlikely to experience cardiac arrest. Therapy continued for approximately one month, during which Jim was subjected to many diagnostic and therapeutic procedures. He was started on TPN, had paracentesis, thoracentesis, insertion of a Swan-Ganz central line and a femoral shunt for dialysis. He was on aggressive antibiotic therapy and required vasopressors to maintain renal blood flow and ultimately to maintain his blood pressure. He was also maintained on an aggressive pulmonary toilet including suctioning and postural drainage. A large mass was found in his liver which was eventually found to be an abscess. Jim began to go into renal failure and a nephrology consult resulted in a recommendation for hemodialysis. The family did not want this, but the physician felt it was necessary in view of the decreased renal output. The family, therefore, began court proceedings to stop treatment. This avenue was not pursued because within a few days, dialysis was no longer possible, due to severe hypotension. Five days later, Jim died.

Because of the controversy over the DNR order, everyone who came in contact with Jim agonized with him and his family. For the majority who were responsible for inflicting all this aggressive "therapy" on Jim, causing unknown pain and fear, our thoughts were, "please, if this were me, my brother, my son – please don't ever let this happen to one of my loved ones." We felt we were forced to create an undue hardship on Jim because he was developmentally disabled.

His family felt overwhelming helplessness and frustration at being unable to protect their loved one from what they considered to be a tortured death. In contrast, the OMRDD staff's fear that developmental disability colors caregivers' thinking is ever present.

The events surrounding Jim's illness and death were extremely difficult for everyone involved. A tangled web of legal regulations, conflicting medical opinions, and assumptions about motivations contributed to a general sense of anger, frustration and helplessness. I believe that continued education and dialogue should be pursued aggressively to develop methods which will optimally integrate the expertise and concerns of all involved in such decisions.

BIBLIOGRAPHY

1. New York State Department of Health, New York State Medical Society and the Hospital Association of New York: 1990, *Do Not Resuscitate Orders: Questions and Answers for Heath Care Professionals* (this volume, pp. 415–438).

LAWRENCE R. FAULKNER

THE NEW YORK DNR LAW AND THE DISABLED: THE EXPERIENCE OF THE NEW YORK STATE OFFICE OF MENTAL RETARDATION AND DEVELOPMENTAL DISABILITIES

The experience of the New York State Office of Mental Retardation and Developmental Disabilities (OMRDD) with the New York State Do-Not-Resuscitate statute, Public Health Law Article 29-B (DNR statute), and the regulations issued by the New York State Department of Health (DOH) to implement the statute ([6], §405.43), can be divided into two general areas. The first of these areas of concern is the relationship between OMRDD-licensed or operated facilities, including those administered by the State of New York and those administered by the private sector, and acute care hospitals and other health care providers not licensed by OMRDD. The second area of concern is the development and implementation of a process governing the issuance of do-not- resuscitate (DNR) orders in facilities operated or licensed by OMRDD.[1]

New York State Programs for Care of the Disabled

A basic understanding of the nature of the programs regulated and operated or licensed by OMRDD is necessary before the impact of the DNR statute on persons served within the OMRDD system can be understood, and those provisions of the DNR statute important to such persons reviewed. Over the past two decades, New York State has gradually moved away from the large institution as the model for the provision of care to the mentally retarded and developmentally disabled.[2] At the present time, the state operates several large facilities, referred to as developmental centers or in the DNR statute as "schools," and, hundreds of smaller community-based residential and day facilities. In addition, private providers, the vast majority being not-for-profit corporations, operate similar community based facilities. The types of residential facilities currently operated or licensed by OMRDD range from those providing residential care for developmentally disabled individuals with serious medical involvement, to those providing only supportive services. By name, the residential programs include intermediate care facilities (ICF), specialty hospitals, community residences (CR), supervised apartments, supportive apartments, private schools, summer camps, and

R. Baker & M.A. Strosberg (eds.), Legislating Medical Ethics: A Study of the New York Do-Not-Resuscitate Law, 187–203.

family care. All of these programs, whether operated by the state or the private sector, are governed by state laws and regulations,[3] as are those programs receiving federal funds or subject to some type of special oversight.

Each of the above programs is designed to provide care to a class of individuals with certain levels of disabilities and certain habilitative needs. Staffing requirements, including medical staff, are determined by regulations which are drafted with the needs of those individuals in mind. The ICFs, which include the developmental centers or "schools," are designed for the most medically demanding disabled individuals.

Legal Control of the Health Care of the Disabled

Certain legal considerations concerning consent to professional medical care must also be reviewed before the OMRDD experience with the DNR statute can be understood. New York State law does not give the director of an OMRDD-licensed or operated facility the authority to consent to medical care on behalf of a disabled resident of that facility. The one possible exception, as stated in OMRDD regulations, provides that:

> Medical, dental, health, and hospital services may be rendered to a person of any age without seeking informed consent when, in the physician's judgment, an emergency exists creating an immediate need for medical attention. In such cases, the supplier of the proposed professional medical treatment may accept the authorization of the chief executive officer of the individual's residential facility to render such professional medical treatment.[4]

The authorization of the chief executive officer, provided for in that regulation, is actually redundant in light of a provision in the Public Health Law which provides that consent for medical treatment is unnecessary where "an emergency exists and the person is in immediate need of medical attention and an attempt to secure consent would result in delay of treatment which would increase the risk to the person's life or health."[5]

The DNR statute does not change the situation regarding the lack of authorization, with the one exception of emergencies, of the OMRDD-operated or licensed facility director to consent to medical treatment for a resident. The Public Health Law governs who does have the authority to give medical consent. It provides that consent for medical, dental, health, and hospital services may be secured from the competent individual patient if he or she is over 18, is the parent of a child or has been married; from the parent of a child for that child; or from a pregnant individual for prenatal care ([10], §2504). Thus, the Public Health Law, prior to passage of the DNR statute or Health Care Proxy statute, did not provide for any surrogate health-care decisionmaking beyond that of a parent for a child. Not only do the statutes and regulations fail to confer upon the director of a mental hygiene facility the authority to give consent for professional medical care, with the one exception discussed above, but, in addition, several court decisions have given specific directions concerning the type of care to be given to an individual without the capacity to make his/her own decision. The courts have directed that life-sustaining treatment must be extended to such a patient in the absence of clear and convincing evidence of the patient's refusal of such treatment when they had capacity to make health care decisions ([2], [5]). All surrogate decisionmakers, including facility directors, are governed by these decisions.

The law in New York in the area of medical-care decision making is based on the presumption that all patients have the right to make their own medical-care decisions so long as they have the capacity to make such decisions ([13], [2], [1]). The decision itself cannot determine capacity; each individual has the right to make idiosyncratic decisions or decisions others might consider inappropriate. The issue to be determined is whether particular patients have the capacity to make medical-care decisions.

Defining what constitutes the capacity to make medical-care decisions is not easy. OMRDD has attempted to define such capacity as "the ability to adequately understand [sic] and appreciate the nature and consequences of such professional medical treatment, including the benefits and significant risks and alternatives to such treatment so as to be capable of making a decision thereto in a knowing and voluntary manner." The same OMRDD regulations warn against using the decision itself to judge the person's decision-making ability: "A person's decision relative to the proposed professional medical treatment shall not, in and of itself, be the exclusive basis for the determination of capacity" ([7], §633.99(j)).

The idea that individuals with capacity have the right to make their own medical-care decisions can also be found in Department of Health Memoranda[6] and regulations, which provide that a patient has the right to refuse medication and treatment ([6], §414.14(4)). OMRDD regulations provide that, if an individual is over the age of 18 and has the capacity to understand appropriate disclosures regarding a proposed medical treatment, such treatment can only be initiated upon receiving such person's informed consent ([7], §633.11(a)(1)(iii)(c)).

The courts in New York have consistently restated the position that adult individuals must consent to their own medical care. That position can be found in cases dating back to at least 1914. In that year, the New York Court of Appeals held that: "Every human being of adult years and sound mind has a right to determine what should be done with his own body..." ([13] at 125, 129). More recently the Court of Appeals ruled that: "It has long been the common law in this state that a person has the right to decline medical treatment, even if life saving, absent an overriding state interest" ([3] at 528).

The Problem of Incapacity to Consent

When an individual does not have the capacity to make his or her own medical-care decisions, another approach for making such decisions must be found. Actually, the law has developed three general approaches toward resolving the dilemma of delivering needed medical care to those persons incapable of consenting to such care. These three general approaches can be classified as *parens patriae*, legislative design, and previous decisions by the incapacitated person when he/she had capacity.

The concept of *parens patriae* reflects the obligation of the state to act in a person's best interest when such an individual cannot make decisions for him or herself. It has historically been used by the courts to fashion relief for situations, including those involving medical care, where an individual does not have the ability to care for him or herself and no specific statute exists to govern decisions about such care [3]. It is also the doctrine underlying or justifying those legislatively designed and sanctioned programs providing both voluntary and involuntary care to incapacitated persons.

New York State has developed several legislative approaches to provide medical care to individuals who lack the capacity to make medical-care decisions. Examples of such legislative approaches include provisions of the Public Health Law which permit a parent to give effective medical consent for a child ([10], §2504(2)), and surrogate medical-care decisionmaking committees ([9], art. 80). Public Health Law provisions allowing for treatment without consent in times where such treatment is considered a medical emergency ([10], §2504), provisions authorizing the appointment of a guardian with authority to consent to medical treatment for an incapacitated person,[7] and the DNR legislation ([10], art. 29-B) are other examples of such a legislative approach. In addition, OMRDD has developed regulations which govern who can consent to medical care. These regulations provide that a lawfully empowered guardian; an actively involved spouse, parent or adult son or daughter; a surrogate decisionmaking committee; or a court can give effective consent for medical treatment when an individual does not have the capacity to give such consent ([7], §633.11). However, these regulations, like those OMRDD regulations concerning emergency care, do not govern the actions of a doctor or hospital, both of which are governed by regulations of the Department of Health and not those of New York State.

Finally, the previously expressed opinions and decisions of an individual can be used to control medical-care decisions which must be made after that person loses the ability to make such decisions. In 1988, the New York State Court of Appeals expressed this position in the *O'Connor* decision, restating the position it had taken in 1981 [5]. In *O'Connor*, the Court held that a "hospital or medical facility must respect [a person's right to decline medical treatment] even when a patient becomes incompetent, if, while competent, the patient stated that he or she did not want certain procedures to be employed under specified circumstances" ([2] at 528).

The Court of Appeals in both the 1981 *Storar* case and the 1988 *O'Connor* case held that, without clear and convincing proof that a person would decline life-prolonging treatment (in the form of statements or written documents executed while the individual had the capacity to make medical-care decisions), it would presume that the individual wanted all forms of such treatment. The Court in *O'Connor* said:

> Every person has a right to life, and no one should be denied essential medical care unless the evidence clearly and convincingly shows that the patient intended to decline the treatment under some particular circumstances....This is a demanding standard, the most rigorous burden of proof in civil cases. It is appropriate here because if an error occurs it should be made on the side of life ([2] at 531).

The Court of Appeals has, in effect, limited discretion or choice in the application of the *parens patriae* standard in cases involving the withdrawal or withholding of life-sustaining or death-delaying treatment. Its holdings stand for the proposition that, absent clear and convincing proof that a person, while having the capacity, gave specific instructions in this area of medical care, and absent specific legislative directives, the doctrine of *parens patriae* will always act to require aggressive treatment. Thus, prior to the passage of the Do-Not-Resuscitate[8] statute, there was no mechanism in New York State for a surrogate to make the decision to withhold CPR for a person who lacked the capacity to make his or her own medical-care decisions, unless that person once had such capacity and at that time was very specific in his or her instructions.

The DNR statute changed this rule. It provides that a surrogate may consent to the withholding of potentially life- sustaining treatment. Because of the significance of such a decision, the DNR statute and the regulations implementing the statute precisely circumscribe the medical conditions necessary before such an order can be issued. The law and regulations also carefully outline the process by which the capacity to make one's own decision is determined[9] and specify the relationship of the surrogate empowered to make the decision to the incapacitated individual ([10], §2965; [6], §405.43(f)(4)).

The Effect of the DNR Statute on the Care of the Disabled

The statute authorizes the director of the mental hygiene facility, from which the disabled person was removed to the hospital or nursing home, to intervene when necessary to safeguard the interests of the disabled individual. The facility director is not given the authority to consent to the issuance of the order or to concur with the correctness of any particular DNR order mandated by the statute. Rather, the statute was drafted to: (1) insure notice to the facility director at several critical junctures; (2) give the facility director the authority to intervene to insure that a determination concerning the capacity of an individual who is developmentally disabled was appropriately diagnosed; and (3) give the facility director an opportunity to oppose the issuance of a DNR order.

The statutory and regulatory requirements for notice are fundamental to the protection of the rights of the mentally disabled hospital patient. Notice of a decision by the treating physician that such a person lacks capacity to make decisions concerning a DNR order must be given to the director of the mental hygiene facility where such person resided before hospitalization. Notice of that decision concerning capacity must also be given to the person highest on the list of surrogates provided for in the DNR statute and to the patient, with one exception ([10], §2963(4); [6], §405.43(d)(4)). This notice alerts the facility director that a decision may be made by someone other than the patient and that a DNR order is under consideration. Unless the facility director was involved in supplying a concurring opinion regarding capacity, this may be the first formal notice that a DNR order is under consideration. This notice not only alerts the facility director to the fact that a DNR order is being considered, but also permits the facility director to object through the dispute-mediation system where he/she feels that the patient has the capacity to make such a decision.[10] Thus, the individual and staff who should have the most knowledge about the patient and the extent of the patient's disability can judge the patient's capacity and intervene, if necessary, on behalf of the patient, asserting the patient's right to make his/her own decisions.

Notice must also be given to the director of the mental hygiene facility where the individual resided before hospitalization when such individual consents on his/her own behalf to a DNR order ([10], §2964(4); [6], §405.43(e)(4)). Notice under such circumstances permits the director to object through the dispute-mediation process where he/she feels that the patient does not have the capacity to make such decisions. In both of the above cases, the notice requirement permits the facility director to challenge a decision concerning capacity.

Finally, notice must be given to the director of the mental hygiene facility which formerly was the patient's residence when a DNR order is consented to by a surrogate. Such notice must also be given when a DNR order is issued without consent of a surrogate or the patient in situations where cardiopulmonary resuscitation is judged to be medically futile ([10], §§2965(6)(c), 2966(2); [6], §§405.43(f)(6)(iii), (g)(2)). Upon receipt of notice in either of those situations, the facility director is free to contest the order through the dispute-mediation system.

These requirements for notice to the facility director of the decisions concerning the capacity of the individual allow the director, presumably a professional with an understanding of the individual as well as his/her disability, the opportunity to challenge a decision concerning capacity. The director can therefore protect those who do not have capacity and protect the individual liberty of those who do have capacity. Requirements for notice to the facility director of surrogate consent to a DNR order, or its issuance without consent, gives the facility director the opportunity to object where the patient does not have one of the enumerated medical conditions.

From the perspective of the disabled patient, the second important component of the law is the requirement that, when the treating physician determines that lack of capacity to consent to a DNR order is due to a developmental disability, a concurring opinion concerning the reason for lack of capacity must be secured from a professional *with training and experience in the treatment of persons who are developmentally disabled.* Specifically, the law requires that the concurring opinion be secured from

> a physician or psychologist employed by a school named in section 13.17 of the mental hygiene law, or who has been employed for a minimum of two years to render care and service in a facility operated or licensed by the Office of Mental Retardation and Developmental Disabilities, or who has been approved by the commissioner of mental retardation and developmental disabilities in accordance with regulations promulgated by such commissioner. Such regulations shall require that a physician or psychologist possess specialized training or three years experience in treating developmental disabilities ([10], §2963(3)(c); [6], §405.43(d)(3)(iii)).

This requirement helps to assure that persons are not classified as incapable of deciding issues concerning a DNR order simply because of a diagnosis of developmental disabilities. Many persons suffering from such disabilities can still make important decisions concerning their personal health care. Without this provision, persons with capacity might be denied the right to make such decisions because a physician, who lacks experience with the disabled, incorrectly assumes a lack of capacity.

Indirectly, the provisions of the law and regulations which require a written clinical opinion, in all cases, of a lack of capacity[11] before a surrogate can consent to the issuance of a DNR order, help insure that decisions concerning capacity do not ignore possible developmental disability. Thus, reliance upon expertise in the field is encouraged.

Finally, the statute and regulations provide that the director of the facility may take unresolved objections to a dispute-mediation system, and, if necessary, appeal to a court ([10], §2972; [6], §§405.43 (m), (n)). In this fashion, the director is given legal authority to appeal any objections he/she has concerning capacity and/or the medical appropriateness of the proposed DNR order.

These three concepts – notice, concurring opinion on capacity, and access to dispute mediation – are the foundations in the statute for the protection of disabled persons and the areas of most concern for facility directors. It should be recalled that the term 'facility director' in the law refers to directors of both state and privately operated facilities, so long as the latter are licensed by the state. In many cases the state may not be the apellant; the director of a privately operated facility will be the participant in the system.

Evaluation of the DNR Statute

In general, the procedures established by the statute have worked well in the short time they have been in operation. The directors of OMRDD developmental centers have provided appropriate staff for a concurring opinion when requested and received appropriate notices. The problems that have arisen apparently come more from a lack of experience with the provisions of the statute than from problems with the requirements contained therein.

The most significant issue that has arisen concerns the proper role for the physician or psychologist providing the concurring opinion on capacity as mandated in the DNR statute ([10], §2963(3)(c); [6], §405.43(d)(3)(iii)). When the DNR statute became operational, hospitals began using the first of the three alternative sources for securing the concurring opinion on capacity, by requesting that the directors of the developmental centers provide a staff physician or psychologist to render an opinion concurring on the lack of capacity of an individual who was developmentally disabled. OMRDD staff was apparently used for this purpose because the commissioner of OMRDD had not yet established a list of qualified persons to render the concurring opinion, and because securing the assistance of persons employed in the private sector would take additional efforts and time. The developmental-center directors were instructed by the commissioner of OMRDD, and advised by counsel at OMRDD, to have a qualified professional available on a 24-hour basis to visit patients and render the requested opinion. The problem that arose was that neither the professionals rendering the concurring opinion nor the hospitals requesting it were clear that the opinion provided for in the statute only concerned the capacity of the patient to render his/her own opinion concerning a DNR order, and whether such person was incapacitated by reason of developmental disability. Both the hospital staff and the professionals sent by the facility often thought that incapacity was assumed for a patient diagnosed as mentally retarded or developmentally disabled and that the concurring opinion called for in the statute concerned the appropriateness of the proposed DNR order.

This situation was troublesome for several reasons. First, and most importantly, the law does not give the facility director, or his delegated professional staff, the authority to consent to any professional medical treatment, including a DNR order. The one exception to this rule, the emergency provision, has been discussed earlier. Second, when professionals, believing they were responsible for offering an opinion on the appropriateness of the DNR order, delayed giving advice on the DNR order or disagreed with the hospital physician, the facility director was often accused by the hospital of impeding a hospital-based medical-care decision or placing OMRDD clients in a special class distinct from others in the hospital. In most cases, this misunderstanding concerning the nature of the opinion being requested has been corrected through training of OMRDD staff and meetings with hospital-based staff.[12]

A second problem that has arisen concerns the nature of the alleged incapacity requiring a second opinion from the physician or psychologist with employment or experience in treating persons with developmental disabilities. The statute provides that such a professional must be called in to render an opinion on capacity when "the attending physician determines that a patient lacks capacity because of a developmental disability..." ([10] §2963(3)(c); [6], §§405.43(d)(3)(iii)). The fact that a patient has been diagnosed as developmentally disabled is not sufficient reason to call for the concurring opinion from the professional with experience in treating developmentally disabled individuals. The concurring opinion on capacity is only required from such a professional if the incapacity to render a decision concerning a DNR order is due to such a disability. If a developmentally disabled patient is believed, by the treating physician, to lack capacity to decide questions concerning the issuance of a DNR order due to a different medical condition, such as a coma, then the concurring opinion can come from another physician authorized by the hospital to render such opinions.

The final problem that has occurred concerns the availability of professionals to render the concurring opinion on capacity when requested. There have been objections by some hospitals to having to rely upon OMRDD-employed professionals when the OMRDD facility is located at some distance from the hospital or the professionals provided by OMRDD lack privileges at the hospital. Two actions have been taken to remedy this perceived problem. The directors of the OMRDD developmental centers have been authorized to develop lists of qualified professionals in cooperation with area hospitals. These lists, approved by the commissioner of OMRDD, should give the hospitals direct access to physicians and psychologists not employed by OMRDD, who are authorized to render the concurring opinion on capacity required by the statute. In addition, hospitals have been advised that there is a third category of professionals authorized by the statute to review capacity, those employed outside of the developmental centers with minimum levels of experience, which can be accessed to render the necessary concurring opinion.

There have been several other issues which have arisen on an anecdotal basis at particular hospitals. The most troublesome of these has been the occasional hospital which has confused two of the medical diagnoses which allow for a DNR order, medical futility or that "resuscitation would impose an extraordinary burden on the patient in light of the patient's medical condition and the expected outcome of resuscitation for the patient" ([10], §§2965(5)(c)(iii), (iv); [6], §§405.43(f)(5)(iii)(c), (d)), with the patient's underlying diagnosis of developmental disability. The value of the developmentally disabled person's life is not a factor to consider under the DNR statute. The medical condition placing a patient's life at risk and the acute incident which might lead to resuscitation efforts are the subjects of the legislation.

Study of the Reaction of OMRDD Employees to the DNR Statute

A survey questionnaire was sent to the local offices of OMRDD (Developmental Disabilities Services Offices (DDSO's)) in March, 1990, asking them to review their experiences with the DNR process through April 1, 1990.[13] While the confused nature of some of the responses renders many of the findings questionable, some interesting statistics arise.

In only one case was a DDSO notified that a former resident had capacity to make his/her own decision concerning the issuance of a DNR order. Fifteen DDSO's had been asked to render concurring opinions on lack of capacity on 86 separate occasions. In 81 of these cases, the DDSO concurred that the individual lacked capacity. Since there was confusion concerning the nature of the concurring opinion and, as discussed earlier, whether it involved only questions about capacity or whether it also included a judgment on the appropriateness of the DNR order, the remaining five cases could either be cases where the DDSO concluded that the patient had capacity to make his/her own decision or where there was disagreement between the hospital and the DDSO over the issuance of the DNR order. While only reporting 86 requests for a concurring opinion, the facilities report 112 cases in which a DNR order was issued for patients without capacity. The largest number of these were consented to by a parent (42) or a brother or sister (23). The DDSO's report that the extraordinary burden diagnosis was used in 37 cases to justify the order, the terminal condition diagnosis was used in 30 cases, and the medically futile diagnosis was used in 20 cases. They report only four cases of a DNR order being issued without consent due to both a diagnosis of medical futility by two physicians and the unavailability of a surrogate. In only four cases is an actual appearance before some type of dispute- mediation system reported.

The DOH DNR regulations were in effect for two years at the end of the survey period. The survey indicates that OMRDD-operated or licensed facilities are continuing to develop a working relationship concerning the issuance of DNR orders with local acute-care hospitals and with nursing homes. Problems concerning the role of the physician or psychologist offering the concurring opinion on capacity continue to need attention, but this can be rectified with proper training and discussion. The results of the survey indicated that the system is working fairly well. The directors are receiving notices required by the statute and responding as required. In most cases, consent is secured from a close relative, as intended by the statute, and the limited number of disputes going before the mediation system would appear to be evidence of the informal resolution of disputes when they arise.

Regulations authorizing OMRDD developmental centers to issue DNR orders became effective December 1, 1989 ([7], §633.18). Therefore, OMRDD had considerably less experience with the issuance of such orders for persons residing in its developmental centers or the care of persons returned from hospitals to the developmental centers with such orders than for its hospitalized former residents when the survey was conducted. The OMRDD regulations parallel the DOH regulations in most respects.

Within the OMRDD system, only developmental centers may issue DNR orders or maintain such orders for persons transferred thereto from acute-care hospitals or nursing homes. OMRDD interpreted the statute to apply only to the developmental centers. It based this limitation upon an interpretation of the meaning of the term 'hospital' in the statute, because the statute specifically authorized a "school named in section 13.17 of the mental hygiene law" to issue DNR orders ([10], §2961(7)), and because the developmental centers, being large ICFs, have the most extensive medical staff and were therefore deemed most capable of administering a DNR order. The restriction of the availability of DNR orders to developmental centers has caused some concern. Several persons have commented that patients admitted to a hospital from a community facility should be allowed to "return home" to die peacefully if the hospital issued a DNR order. To some extent this problem was resolved by the issuance of DOH Memorandum 89–59 on July 13, 1989. This document provides that a patient residing in the community may have an effective DNR order if the patient is enrolled in a hospice program and a written DNR order has been issued by that program. The survey results indicate that only five developmental centers had issued a total of 14 DNR orders. None of these report finding that the resident had the capacity to render his/her own decision concerning the DNR order. The developmental centers report that in seven cases a parent consented, in two cases a brother or sister consented, and in one case a close friend consented. The source of the remaining consents is unclear. In seven cases the reason for the DNR order is listed as the conviction that resuscitation would be an extraordinary burden upon the patient. In four cases, the resident was determined to have a terminal condition. In three cases, the resident was permanently unconscious, and, in one case, resuscitation was considered to be medically futile. Ten developmental centers reported receiving a total of 49 residents transported to the developmental center with a DNR order. In 20 cases, the DNR was reissued and in 29 it was canceled.

Experience with the DNR statute in developmental centers and in community-based facilities where the resident is a patient under the care of a hospice program was limited when the survey was conducted. There are clearly some issues needing resolution. Among these are the question of why 29 out of 49 DNR orders were canceled when residents returned from hospitals. Such a high rate of cancellation would appear to indicate very different beliefs about the conditions under which a DNR order is appropriate between acute-care hospitals and developmental centers.

Conclusion

The DNR statute represents a significant forward step in medical care policy for New York State. It is the first modern piece of legislation in New York that specifically authorizes a surrogate, appointed after the onset of mental disability, to make certain critical life-determining medical care decisions for an adult. The Health Care Proxy legislation, recently passed by the New York legislature, provides further accessibility to such decisionmaking for persons without capacity. However, neither the DNR statute nor the Health Care Proxy legislation address a critical problem for the disabled person who never had the capacity to issue a proxy or make health-care decisions. If such an individual is faced with a medical care decision, concerning the withholding of intensive life-prolonging care or removing same, not of withholding resuscitation, there is no procedure, authorized by law, which will permit the cession or refusal of such treatment. For such a person, future legislative solutions are necessary.

Notes

[1] The New York State Department of Health regulations governing the issuance of DNR orders under the statute are contained in [6], §405.43. These regulations, originally at §405.42, were effective April 1, 1988 and govern the application of the DNR statute in hospitals and nursing homes, as well as psychiatric centers and OMRDD facilities. The statute provides that OMRDD is to develop its own specific regulations governing the application of the DNR statute in OMRDD facilities. OMRDD did not have those governing regulations in effect until December 1, 1989 ([7], §633.18). Most of the references in this paper reflect Department of Health requirements because the OMRDD regulations mostly parallel the Department of Health regulations and because OMRDD had limited experience with its own regulations at the time of the survey.

[2] According to figures supplied by OMRDD, fewer than 7,000 New Yorkers with developmental disabilities now live in developmental centers, while more than 23,000 live in the community. This is a reversal of the situation as recently as 1975 when 20,000 persons with developmental disabilities lived in the developmental centers and only about 1,000 lived in the community [4].

[3] Article 16 of the Mental Hygiene Law (MHL) of the State of New York authorizes the Commissioner of the Office of Mental Retardation and Developmental Disabilities to issue regulations reasonably necessary to implement the requirements of the law ([9], §16.00). Examples include regulations found in New York's Administrative Code governing the operation of ICFs, ([7], part 681), community residences ([7], part 686), family care homes ([7], part 687) and specialty hospitals ([7], part 680). In addition to specific regulations governing the operation of specific classes of facilities, OMRDD has

issued regulations with often cut across facility types. Thus, regulations governing client rights and protection are located in [7], part 633 and those covering reportable incidents and abuse are contained in [7], part 624.

4 [7], §633.11(a)(1)(ii). The reference to "person" and "individual's" in the regulation, and other OMRDD regulations, is to "a child or adult with a diagnosis of developmental disability, who has been or is being served by a state, private, or voluntary operated facility certified by OMRDD. This shall include children or adults who have applied to or have been screened for services and for whom a clinical record is maintained or processed by such a facility." ([7], §633.99(ii), (yy)).

5 [10], §2504. The OMRDD regulation, discussed previously, authorizing the director of a facility to consent to medical treatment on behalf of a disabled person in the limited circumstances of a medical emergency may be of limited value both because of the public health law authorization to treat without consent in an emergency and because OMRDD regulations do not govern the operation of acute care hospitals or physicians.

6 An example of Department of Health Memoranda concerning a patient's right to decline offered medical care can be found in D.O.H. Memoranda 89–84 which concerns a patient's right to refuse nutrition and hydration.

7 [11]. There is considerable controversy over the authority of a guardian appointed pursuant to Article 17-A of the Surrogate's Court Procedure Act to consent to medical treatment on behalf of a ward where the appointing court has not specifically authorized such authority. Recent decisions, including [12], have held that medical treatment may not be administered over the objections of the individual, in the case of *Rivers* three women found to be mentally ill and in need of involuntary care and treatment, unless a court of law has specifically found that the individual does not have the capacity to make medical care decisions. The earlier finding that the three women in the *Rivers* case were mentally ill was not sufficient, in itself, to override their objections to medical treatment. That line of reasoning may also hold that a guardian appointed pursuant to section 17-A of the Surrogate's Court Procedure Act only has the authority to consent to medical treatment on behalf of a ward where the appointing court has reviewed the capacity of the disabled individual to make personal medical care decisions and has found such capacity to be lacking.

8 While the passage of the DNR legislation permitted a surrogate for the first time to make the decision to withhold possible life-sustaining treatment, it only applies to CPR. The Health Care Proxy Statute, effective in January 1991, permits an individual with capacity to appoint a proxy to make all healthcare decisions should that person later lose capacity. In that respect, the Health Care Proxy statute is considerably broader then the DNR legislation.

9 [10], §2963; [6], §405.43(d). The issues concerning determining capacity for individuals who resided in a facility operated or licensed by OMRDD before admission to a facility covered by the statute are discussed latter in this article. For others, a determination that an individual lacks capacity shall be made by a physician. At least one additional physician must concur with that determination. If the reason for the lack of capacity is considered to be mental illness, the concurring opinion must come from a physician certified or eligible to be certified by the American Board of Psychiatry and Neurology.

10 [10] §2972; [6], §405.43(m). The Dispute Mediation System is a system which must be established by the hospital, nursing home or developmental center to resolve disputes

arising under the statute. It is authorized to mediate any dispute challenging an issuance of a DNR order including disputes concerning decisions on capacity and disputes between surrogates on the list. The regulation spells out the composition of the system and persons with standing to appear before it with a dispute. An order not to resuscitate can be issued by the facility if a dispute has not been resolved within 72 hours of its submission.

[11] [6], §405.43(d)(2). The regulations require that the determination be in writing, shall include the physician's finding concerning the cause, nature, extent and probable duration of the lack of capacity, and shall be included in the patient's medical chart.

[12] OMRDD program staff and attorneys from its Office of Counsel have offered training on the implementation of the DNR statute to state and voluntary operated facility staff in several locations throughout the state. The author of this article has participated in many of these and continues to schedule such training upon request. In addition, the author, along with other OMRDD staff, has met with staff at several hospitals to review implementation of the DNR statute. Finally, attorneys representing hospitals have participated in programs sponsored by the New York State Bar Association which included sections on the DNR statute.

[13] There are 20 Developmental Disabilities Service Offices (DDSO) covering New York State. Originally each one contained a large state-operated institution known as a Developmental Center. As community facilities have replaced the developmental center as the model for services the centers have closed, or are scheduled for closure. However the area once served by the center remains the geographic area for local services within the OMRDD organizational framework. Each of the 20 DDSOs received a questionnaire in March, 1990. They were asked to review their relationship with area hospitals and nursing homes as that relationship related to DNR orders and where the developmental center remained open, as it did in most cases, they were asked to answer questions concerning the operation of the DNR process in the developmental center. The questions on the survey covered all aspects of the DNR legislation. Since regulations governing the operation of the statute in developmental centers had only been in effect for four months the responses to that area of inquiry were limited. The DDSOs surveyed were: Bernard Fineson in Queens, Bronx, Brooklyn, Broome; J.N. Adam in Perrysburg; Letchworth in Thiells, Long Island, Manhattan, Monroe, Newark; O.D. Heck in Schenectady, Rome, Staten Island; Sunmount in Tupper Lake, Syracuse, Wassaic, Westchester, Wilton and West Seneca. Each DDSO returned the questionnaire.

BIBLIOGRAPHY

1. *In re Harvey U.*, 116 A.D. 2d 351, 501 N.Y.S. 2d 920 (3d Dept. 1986).
2. *In re O'Connor*, 72 N.Y. 2d 517 (1988), 531 N.E. 2d 607, 534 N.Y.S. 2d 886 (1988).
3. *In re Weberlist*, 79 Misc. 2d 753, 360 N.Y.S. 2d 783 (1974).
4. Journal of the New York State Office of Mental Retardation and Developmental Disabilities: 1991, Editorial, *Journal of New York State Office of Mental Retardation and Developmental Disabilities* **5**, 2.
5. *Matter of Storar*, 52 N.Y. 2d 363, 420 N.E. 2d 64, 438 N.Y.S. 2d 266 (1981), *cert. denied*, 454 U.S. 858 (1981).

6. New York State Administrative Code, title 10.
7. New York State Administrative Code, title 14.
8. New York State Department of Health Memorandum 89–84.
9. New York State Mental Hygiene Law.
10. New York State Public Health Law.
11. New York State Surrogate's Court Procedure Act, Article 17-A.
12. *Rivers v. Katz*, 67 N.Y. 2d 485, 495 N.E. 2d 337, 504 N.Y.S. 2d 74 (1986).
13. *Schloendorff v. Society of New York Hospital*, 211 N.Y. 125, 105 N.E. 92 (1914).

†DAVID FINLEY

STRIKING A BALANCE

Physicians do not represent a morally or ethically homogeneous group. Although the education and training may be structured similarly, the experience of that training and the motives, purpose, and rewards for pursuing a medical career are highly individualized. Each physician interprets his or her role differently: some as "healers"; some as "care providers."

In medical school, students learn the appropriate treatments, tests and interventions for every disease state. In the process, they are lead to believe that every medical issue can be reduced to a true/false or most correct multiple choice answer format.

In clinical practice, physicians develop experience and insight into the risks and benefits of a particular management plan. They also come to learn that there are no "correct" answers and that management decisions are not unilateral. The art of the doctor-patient relationship is in negotiating a care plan that balances the physician's judgment, experience, and insight with the patient's values, beliefs, and preferences. The role of the physician is evolving from the paternal, protective "captain-of-the-ship" model to that of a counselor and guide. Even in routine clinical practice, there are conflicts between doctors and patients related to what is medically possible and individually permissible.

Recently, a family was referred for counseling. Initially admitted for acute myocardial infarction, the 86 year-old patient had sustained two sequential cerebral infarctions during her critical care course. The patient was comatose, in renal failure, and clinically septic. The family was certain that the patient would never want these treatments under these circumstances. Their question was both simple and relevant: "Why are they doing this?" After reviewing the chart, I spoke with the attending of record regarding the withdrawal/withholding of treatment and DNR status. Indignantly he replied, "I am in the business of saving lives – not taking them!" When I pressed the issue as to whether he and his private patient of five years had ever discussed her preferences related to care, his response was "No, how could I predict that this could happen?"

How we reflect on the death and dying process draws on a much

R. Baker & M.A. Strosberg (eds.), Legislating Medical Ethics: A Study of the New York Do-Not-Resuscitate Law, 205–212.

broader network of values. It is the reflection of who we are and what we believe in, in the most elemental form. Some physicians believe that death is an inevitable consequence of life; others believe that death constitutes the ultimate failure of medical care. For the former; their purpose is to provide comfort and dignity throughout the dying process. For the latter, their purpose is to prolong, protect, and preserve life, without imposing a judgment about the quality of that life.

This plurality of moral and ethical behaviors within the medical community stems from our individual values and beliefs. Although that diversity best meets the needs of varied patients, it demands some general organizing principles to assure that the conflicts which inevitably arise from differences in moral and ethical values can be resolved. These organizing principles have evolved from both internal mechanisms (standards of care/policy and procedures) as well as from external influences (bioethics, regulation and legislation).

In attempting to strike a balance between physicians and patients, the New York State law on DNR orders has established an overall uniformity of process that individual, hospital-based policies could not. Hospital policies developed by the respective medical boards of each institution would be expected to represent the predominantly held medical views unique to each hospital. The views and the policies developed would vary from hospital to hospital. Key issues that would likely be affected would include the consent process, the scope of disclosure, the determination of capacity, the determination of futility, and the role of a surrogate. The law addresses all these issues and provides substantial support for patients by encouraging open discussion and individual decisionmaking.

The ideal model for healthcare decisionmaking would balance the physician's judgment, skill, and experience and the patient's values, beliefs, and personal preferences related to treatment. Treatment plans should be negotiated.

The DNR law supports this process without interfering with the patient/physician relationship in any way. The basis of decision-making requires an informed and insightful consent, but the nature and the content of that process is not addressed by the law. The law protects the patient's right to self-determination by specifying that the patient is the primary focus for decisionmaking, unless the patient will suffer immediate and severe injury from the discussion or is incapacitated and unable to participate. Even under the two conditions noted, decisions about CPR should be based on the patient's wishes to the extent that they can be known.

In an acute care environment, treatment decisions are frequently based on the medical indications for treatment. The principal limitation of the medical indications approach is that it fails to address issues of pain/suffering, burden/benefit, or the quality of the outcome from the patient's perspective. When decisions to initiate treatment or to continue treatment are made out of context and without incorporating the patient's preferences into the treatment plan, the patient can become the passive, non-participatory recipient of care.

At a time when acute care resources are critically limited, it seems appropriate to identify those patients who would not choose to receive that care if given a choice. The New York State DNR law lends support to the public and professional need to identify issues early, discuss them openly, and take appropriate action. In most cases, patients welcome the opportunity to participate in the decisionmaking process. In the setting of acute illness, patients often feel vulnerable and victimized. The open discussion of issues and options gives them an opportunity to exercise control over their further care. The concerns that I hear expressed are not about the inevitability of death, but the uncertainty of the dying process.

Patients need to know that they will be treated with dignity and that every effort will be made to relieve their pain and suffering. Even when curing is no longer an option, the caring continues. Tremendous fear and distrust evolve from the uncertainty related to the dying process. People want to know what to expect. Medicine is too often limited in offering alternatives to aggressive end of life care. More reasonable options should exist for patients who refuse relentlessly aggressive management.

There are circumstances in which survival may not be the most desirable outcome, nor is it, necessarily, the best measure of success. The public continues to express concern that hospital centers have become sophisticated, depersonalized diagnostic centers. They are no longer meeting, and may not even know, the needs of the communities they serve. The sought after dream of dying in one's sleep has been eroded by images of isolation, depersonalization, and dehumanization. Critical care has been soundly criticized for prolonging the dying process without offering a chance for cure or hope of recovery. Much like a game of Pac Man or pinball, it wasn't whether you win or lose but how long you played the game that's important. Patients desperately need the support of legislation to be able to negotiate effectively within the environment we have developed. While the law cannot assure the patient's right to a participatory role, it certainly promotes that right.

I do not agree that discussions about end-of-life care are depressing, self-fulfilling, or unreasonable. To the contrary, patients are encouraged and empowered by direct participation in the decisionmaking process. Patients are often much more open to the discussion of end-of-life care than their doctors. A physician's insecurity or uncertainty about death limits the opportunity for open discussion. Too often then, alternatives for end-of-life care are never discussed. Honesty, integrity, and openness are essential ingredients to an effective physician-patient relationship.

For both partners in the physician-patient relationship, it would be ideal if these discussions took place electively and well before a moment of crisis. The physician must know patient preferences related to end-of-life care; the patient must know whether the physician can and will honor those requests. A catastrophic event is not the time to identify an irreconcilable philosophical and normative difference.

There is general agreement, both publicly and professionally, that a competent, well-informed adult has the capacity to make decisions regarding treatment options. If an attending physician determines that an adult patient lacks capacity, the cause, nature, extent, and probable duration of the patient's incapacity must be documented. Again, the DNR law seeks to protect patient's rights to the extent possible. But, the law does not interfere with the medical determination of incapacity. The law creates a uniform approach and standard.

There may be some misunderstanding among health care professionals with regard to the presumed consent clause. The law simply states that in the absence of information to the contrary, most patients would consent to CPR if it is indicated, appropriate and likely to be beneficial. The presumed consent standard does not create a duty or obligation to provide resuscitation to patients for whom those efforts would be inappropriate, medically unwarranted or futile. The law has been interpreted by some to imply that, in the absence of a properly documented DNR order, there is an absolute obligation to attempt resuscitation in any circumstance, without regard to benefit.

The decision to initiate resuscitation, as well as the decision to terminate resuscitation, should be based on the medical assessment of the likelihood of patient benefit. In an emergency situation, without the benefit of patient direction, CPR should be initiated, even if the outcomes may be marginal, but not futile. The physician responsible for conducting the code is professionally responsible for the treatment decisions. Like any other medical decision, the decision to initiate, terminate or forgo resuscitation should be informed and insightful.

The law does not interfere with the medical assessment of individual risk/benefit assessments or the standards of medical practice. Quite the contrary, the law protects physicians for not implementing resuscitation in those cases of medical futility provided he or she has informed the patient or surrogate and followed the other procedures under the law.

It is the physician who must make the determination of futility and document it in the medical record. A competent patient must be informed of the determination of futility and the basis of that decision. If the patient has a surrogate, the surrogate must be informed. If there is no surrogate available, willing or competent, medical futility and the absence of a responsible surrogate must be documented in the medical record by two physicians. Once properly documented, a DNR order can be written.

The patient and surrogate must be informed of the determination of medical futility and the consequences of the determination. As with every other aspect of the DNR process, disagreements can be referred for dispute mediation. What the law supports is that decisions should be well-reasoned, appropriate and defensible. It promotes the physician's professional role and responsibility for making, documenting, and communicating decisions of medical futility.

Conflicts arise when physicians or nurses interpret the law as mandating that all patients under any circumstance or condition *must* be resuscitated in the absence of a properly executed DNR order. Another conflict arises when healthcare providers present issues regarding CPR to medically futile patients or their surrogates as if there is a choice to be made – and there isn't.

The determination of medical futility is a professional issue. We routinely assess the risks and benefits of every diagnostic test, medical treatment or intervention required for good patient care. We don't ask patients to agree with any other medical diagnosis or determination. Based on the history, physical and database, we inform patients of our assessment and the recommended plan for treatment. We then attempt to broaden their understanding and acceptance through education regarding the consequences, options and outcomes related to the medical circumstance.

As physicians, we have a responsibility to guide patients' decision-making using our judgment, experience, and insight. The law does not mandate that physicians provide care contrary to the reasonable practice of medicine. It requires that patients be informed of the physician's judgment regarding their capacity and the determination of medical futility.

I believe that we are all better off for the implementation of the DNR law. The law specifies responsibility for decisionmaking, communication and documentation, supporting the rights of both patients and physicians in the DNR process. The key to the New York State law on DNR is open discussion, full disclosure and clear documentation. One advantage it affords is the opportunity to de-mystify the dying process and to give patients the right to make informed decisions about their end-of-life care.

There are many thoughtful, caring, and open physicians. For those who include the patient's values, beliefs, and preferences in the management plan, there should be no difficulty in complying with a law that supports their basic standard of practice. For the few who do not, there is a clear performance expectation that must be upheld.

I do not share the view that nearly identical outcomes could be achieved through hospital-based, institutional policies. First, there is very little information available on how well institutional policies work or whether they meet their intended goals. Second, physicians are divided on many of the critical issues: their role and responsibility related to the dying patient, the significance and appropriateness of patient participation in end-of-life decisionmaking, and the role of surrogate participation. Further, some physicians are still reluctant to discuss death and dying openly with their patients. Subtle differences in philosophical orientation will result in differences in both policy and practice at each hospital.

Without statewide policies it is likely that there would be as much variation in practice based on individual hospital policy as there was when individual practitioners defined their own policy in the absence of institutional guidance. Patients should have consistent rights everywhere within the healthcare system. Their rights must be protected regardless of the physician's personal standard of practice or the policies defined by the medical board of the hospital with which the physician is affiliated.

In many ways, patients have seen the DNR law as a "balance of power" issue. In knowing their rights, many expect and some demand to be heard. I remember well an elderly woman who refused admission to the critical care unit until she was assured that her advance directive would be recognized, recorded, and respected. More than autonomy, the DNR law has provided patients and those close to them with a sense of confidence and authority.

The DNR law cannot, will not, and was not intended, to make attempted CPR more appropriate. As healthcare providers, we must support outcome research to identify those patients unlikely to benefit from CPR. Based on these studies of efficacy, we should develop standards that address the quality and the appropriateness of aggressive care. Outcome monitoring is the best means of establishing an objective relationship between the care provided and patient benefit.

Most of the negative comments that I have heard about the DNR law deal with concerns that it is cumbersome, complicated, or difficult to complete. The confusion seems to arise when people tend to focus more on the language of the law than its intent. Most of the frustration arises from systems and operational issues unique to each institution – where the documentation sheets are kept, how they are filed, how they are coded; how the local policies were developed; who was inserviced, and by whom. These issues must be evaluated on an individual institutional basis. What these problems suggest is not that the law is cumbersome, but that implementation strategies and systems need to be improved.

The DNR law is an important effort to address an area of tremendous public concern. It attempts to create a structured system that balances the patient's rights and the physician's responsibility. It is not the answer to all of the problems of health care. It won't make physicians more sensitive, considerate, or compassionate. It won't change the willingness of physicians to spend the time it takes to understand, not just the patient's decision for or against CPR, but the basis upon which that decision rests.

Nor can the law assure that patients are always insightful or that they will make the best choices for their further care. It can not insure that the information provided to the patient regarding the risks and benefits of treatment, risks and benefits of nontreatment, and of alternatives, is accurate and clearly presented.

All the law can do is to provide a uniform approach to the consent and documentation process and create an expectation in the public's good. The expectation is that as a patient approaches decisions related to end-of-life care, the physician will include the patient's values in structuring the management plan.

One of the most important consequences of the New York State law on orders not to resuscitate is it's implication for public and professional education. Education, insight, and direction are needed for a decision-making process that was previously unilateral, poorly documented, and difficult to defend. As we plan for our education, our relationships and our financial well-being, we should also consider how we might wish to be treated in the face of catastrophic illness. End-of-life planning should be considered as important as any other life planning process.

Although the focus for decisions related to CPR and life-sustaining treatment is often the elderly, the debilitated and the chronically ill, these are critical issues for all of us. Whether to be the victim or the participant in the "magic of medicine" may be entirely dependant upon our awareness of our individual choices and our right to make these choices for ourselves.

The conclusion that the New York State law has been effective will be supported by more frequent and more open discussion of resuscitation with patients and families and a uniform decisionmaking process. The law does not easily change the physician-patient relationship, the ethical practice of medicine, or the standard of medical care. But the law opens the door to a world of opportunity that will require increased assessment of healthcare outcomes which we hope will ultimately lead to more rational and efficient care. This venture will require a consensus concerning both professional and public concerns that should in time be reflected in effective public health policy.

PART IV

RESEARCH

ROBERT ZUSSMAN

THE DO-NOT-RESUSCITATE ORDER AS RITUAL

I should acknowledge from the start a certain skepticism, not only about the New York State Do-Not-Resuscitate (DNR) law but about DNR orders more generally. As contributors to this volume also suggest, I want to argue that if we think of DNR orders as decisions or of the new state law as a means of enforcing a certain type of decision-making process, we will not get very far. I am sceptical about the law because of research I conducted in the ICUs of two large teaching hospitals, one in New York, the other in Massachusetts. While the research was conducted before the enactment of the DNR law, both insitutions had policies in place similar to the policies required by the law. My research suggests that DNR orders are not records decisions, but symbolic representations of decisions. The writing of a DNR order is, then, in language that I fear is more familiar to sociologists than to health care professionals, a type of ritual. I do not, however, invoke the notion of ritual in order to dismiss the new law. Quite to the contrary, I invoke the notion of ritual to suggest that the new law has made an important contribution to social change – albeit one significantly different from that envisioned by the law itself.

Let me first explain my skepticism. In the first instance, there is considerable question about the effectiveness of CPR. Although there is considerable variation, depending on how extensively CPR is attempted, most research shows that it effectively restores cardiac and respiratory function in only one out of three patients and that – of those who are resuscitated – no more then 30% (and probably significantly less) survive to discharge from the hospital ([2]; [8], pp. 234–235). Thus, while I in no sense mean to denigrate the significance of those attempts at resuscitation that do succeed, we should recognize that in at least a large majority of cases the DNR order is little more than a recognition of the work that nature has already done, and the limits of medicine in the face of this work. In this sense the decision to write a DNR order is not (at least not usually) a life-and-death decision. It is a decision about how much effort will precede death.

Second, the decision not to attempt resuscitation is only one of many issues confronting medicine at the end of life. And it is by no means apparent that the decision to withhold CPR is more significant than, for

R. Baker & M.A. Strosberg (eds.), Legislating Medical Ethics: A Study of the New York Do-Not-Resuscitate Law, 215–225.

example, decisions to withhold blood products, decisions not to intubate or initiate dialysis, or decisions concerning the withdrawal of treatment. From my point of view, it is as interesting to ask why DNR orders have been singled out for so much attention as to ask anything about the way the decisions are made.

Third, even after a DNR order has or has not been written, there is considerable room for variation. On the one hand, as the New York legislation stresses, the decision on DNR orders should be made independently of other treatment decisions. Thus, in some cases, a DNR order is accompanied by a general reduction of therapeutic efforts. In others, it is accompanied by what is, in all other respects, a "full court press." On the other hand, even when a patient or a patient's family objects to a DNR order, there may be an informal agreement among the physicians that certain treatments are futile and legitimately withheld on grounds of clinical indications.

Finally and most importantly, virtually every set of policies for issuing DNR orders emphasizes the priority of the patient's right to autonomy and self-determination and provides, in the absence of a competent patient, for often remarkably elaborate procedures for the recognition of a surrogate. The New York legislation, for example, lists no less than seven categories of potential surrogates in order of priority, in addition to a set of procedures to be followed in the event no surrogate is available. Yet, with all of these guidelines, there is often an enormous gap between formal and substantive procedures. To be sure, there are many cases in which physicians demonstrate a genuine respect for the wishes of a patient or the patient's family. It will come, I suspect, as no surprise that, in interviews I conducted with house staff, resident after resident insisted that decisions to write a DNR order are, for the most part, made in effect by physicians who then shape the responses of the prescribed surrogate. One resident related that:

> Most families don't want to know the gory details of what you would do to these patients if you didn't let them die. I think the doctor has to assess the likelihood of this person surviving and what kind of life they're going to have if they survive. And then with that thought, the doctor should bring up with the family what he or she has decided....I find that, if you really made a medically sound decision about whether or not they should have extensive measures taken, most families will agree that enough is enough.

Another said:

> When we try to convince someone [a surrogate] to make a patient a no-arrest page, we'll say, do you want us to pump on his chest? That doesn't terrify them. "Sure, doctor." But they don't understand the full implications of that. "Do you want us to put him on a breathing machine, you know, and keep him alive even when the rest of him is dead?" and they understand that quite well.

Although I doubt that two brief quotations will convince those who do not already agree with me, I should also point out that these findings are entirely consistent with a larger and more systematic body of research. In many cases, but not in all cases, language about "the wishes of the patient" and, more often, "the wishes of the family," are simply the language in which a decision is expressed, although the decision has, in substance, been made by physicians. Given all this, it comes as little surprise that in the fascinating research by Kamer, McClung and their colleagues, they found that the new law has had a great deal of effect on the documentation of decisions not to resuscitate but precious little effect on the decisions themselves ([4], [6], see this volume, pp. 227–234.).

What I would like to suggest is that DNR policies make only limited sense if we think of them as means for making decisions. But they make considerably more sense if we think of them in a way that is perhaps less congenial to conventional medical modes of thought; that is, if we think of DNR orders as a medical ritual. From this point of view the significance of DNR orders is not the decisions they codify, but that, in writing them, physicians are representing, symbolically, a set of values about the relationship between patients and physicians and about the role of medicine in contemporary American society.

Let me anticipate an objection to this line of thought: that writing a note has nothing to do with values and is little more than a cynical response to legal formalities. As one New York resident told me, the DNR "note itself is not written for the other house staff. I don't think the house staff really cares what is in your note. They only care what the status of the patient is...." She suggested, moreover, that the note is written, instead, "for anyone who may review the chart," and that the "only one who would review the chart would be a lawyer or a medical review board." The special character of DNR notes was entirely explicit in one Massachusetts intern's comments about a note she had written. Ann had begun her note for Mr.

N., a 74-year-old man with metastatic cancer: "Family (wife – Janet N.) & 2 daughters discussed code status requesting that [spelled 'pt'] not be resuscitated." But she had crossed out 'pt' and written above, 'patient,' spelled out fully. When I ran into Ann later, I asked her why she had done this. I expected her to find the question strange (an occupational hazard of sociology), but she surprised me. She said she was trying to get out of the habit of using abbreviations, particularly in DNR notes because they are subject to review and lots of people, even nurses, don't always know what abbreviations stand for. Moreover, she stressed, this is particularly important in DNR notes because they are particularly likely subjects of litigation. Given this, there is a temptation to dismiss DNR orders as, at best, a mere formality and, at worst, obscurantist. There is a temptation to dismiss the DNR order as little more than a cynical response to the requirements of law, without any meaning to physicians except as an effort to protect themselves in the event of litigation.

But this, I think, would be a mistake. In one case, for example, I had asked an attending physician, just before one of his final conversations with the family of a patient who had had a protracted stay in the ICU, why it mattered so much to him that they should agree to a DNR order, especially as the attending himself thought it highly unlikely they would be able to resuscitate her successfully. But the attending told me that the DNR order itself was not the point: "It tells us something about the family. I might not bronch her." It would, he added, be a sign of good faith on their part. The Do-Not-Resuscitate order – as a formal order, appropriate for a chart note – had taken on a symbolic character.

The symbolic character of DNR orders recasts their significance as legal documents. In invoking legal considerations, I would suggest – albeit speculatively – that the Intensive Care medical staffs are not expressing a concern about potential penalties, themselves something of a chimera, so much as they are searching for direction in an area that they find troubling and difficult. In invoking the law, the ICU physicians are invoking a system that is itself a system of symbols – a formal, codified representation of a normative order. This is not, of course, the language of physicians themselves. Yet, it is very much their meaning. The DNR order, one resident told me, is "a medical-legal decision [and] should be documented as such." Moreover, he added, "I don't think it's changed policy in any way." Still, while he groped for a way to express himself, he thought that formal procedures and formal notes had much of value: "It's just, it's made things a lot clearer for everyone, although initially there was a lot of resistance to it....It makes life a lot easier for everyone, from attendings down to the nurses." In this sense, physicians invoke formal procedures and the law as a means of reassuring themselves, as a means of coping with the uncertainty endemic to medicine.

The symbolic character of DNR and other orders is perhaps most apparent in their language [7]. If DNR orders were simply written pragmatically, we would expect their language to be prosaic and unadorned. But often it is not. While some of the notes state simply and explicitly that "no resuscitative efforts be made in the event of an arrest," that language is often supplanted by more metaphorical formulations. Consider, for example, the following note:

> Spoke to son about further use of extraordinary measures. Son expressed wish for father (patient) not to be subject to CPR or any further heroic measures should the need arise. Patient reportedly expressed this wish prior to his hospitalization....It was understood that pt would be treated medically aggressively short of heroics – CPR, shock, etc.

The note does, to be sure, specify that the patient is not to be resuscitated. But the note also specifies that the patient is not to be "subject" to resuscitation, a term that suggests an evaluation. Moreover, the note alludes to "heroic measures" and "extraordinary measures," terms that contain an evaluation embedded in an implicit distinction between what is routine (and therefore can be expected of physicians) and what is not routine (and, therefore, cannot be expected). These terms suggest a moral quality that goes well beyond the mere recording of an order.

Chart notes represent a recognition of the rule of law in medicine. That recognition is not explicit so much as it is implicit in the very fact that the notes are written. But other matters are explicit.

In the first instance, chart notes acknowledge the rights of patients and their surrogates. In the Massachusetts hospital I studied, responsibility for decisions is usually ascribed to family:

> Discussed dismal prognosis [with] pt's daughter who has decided [with] agreement of her sisters [on] a DNR status for their mother – no chest compressions, defibrillation, cardioversion – *They will* further *discuss* options re fluid, blood and pressor support *and inform us* today. [*Emphasis* added.]

In the New York hospital I studied, responsibility is also ascribed to the family, but, in response to the stricter standards of New York State law, more often formulated in terms of the family's representation of the wishes of the patient himself or herself:

> Discussed status and prognosis with family. The wife and daughter feel that given his current poor state and prognosis, *that he would not want* and they do not want CPR performed should he suffer a cardiac arrest. All other therapy will be continued. [Emphasis added.]
>
> After detailed discussion about pt's overall medical/neurological condition, his family has agreed that the use of further "heroic" measures would be meaningless. *They feel that the pt would never have wanted to be kept alive in this manner*. We will not perform CPR or resuscitate by chemical/pharmacological means. [Emphasis added.]

We may, of course, be rightly skeptical that the wishes of the patient or family are always as clear or autonomous as they seem. The wishes of the patient or family, as I suggested earlier, are frequently beside the point of the actual decision-making process. Similarly, the formula, invoked frequently in New York, that a surrogate is merely expressing the wishes of the patient is itself usually something of a fiction. Particularly in cases in which patients had not expressed wishes, the invocation of such wishes is often merely the language in which the family's preference is recorded. This the New York housestaff openly admit. One intern remembered "distinctly" writing a DNR order that said:

> "Had a long talk with patient's family, someone who was *non compos mentis*. The family feels that superhuman or heroic treatment at this point would not be advisable, therefore...." And I say, "oh oh" and start all over and wrote, "the family feels that the patient would not want heroic measures done at this point"....We sort of use the family in whatever role we want to, as either speaker for the patient or speaker for themselves or guardian or whatever.

The chart notes, then, at least in regard to the wishes of patients' and their families, cannot be read as literal truth. They can, however, be read as symbolic truth.

Only an occasional note identifies either the patient or a member of the patient's family by name. More often, both are identified only as part of a general category. Even when names are included, it is only after they have been situated in a category. Thus, in the notes just cited, there are references to "wife," "daughter," and, without any specification, "family." Other notes refer simply to "husband," "son," "sister, or "brother." And, in some notes, even the patient is not mentioned by name. By assigning responsibility to a category of person rather than to a specific, named person, the notes move beyond the level of specific cases to the level of principle.

Thus, DNR orders and other chart notes express an ideal. Invocations of patients' or families' wishes are, in many cases, fictions. However, if they were merely fictions, we might expect physicians to treat DNR orders lightly, as little more than a nuisance. But they do not take the orders lightly, precisely because they approach the wishes of patient with all due seriousness. DNR orders evoke the value – if not the reality – of the patient's and family's rights. They should not be read as a statement of the patient's or family's wishes – although they may be such – but as an affirmation that those wishes *should* be assigned priority.

Beyond recognizing the rights of patients and the rule of law, DNR orders and other chart notes are an affirmation that physicians have reached a decision and that they agree about that decision. This is not a trivial matter. For example, the following note, referring to "agreement" among housestaff and attendings, followed intense, week-long disagreements between housestaff and attendings over whether or not to continue transfusions for a 50-year-old man with an intractable gastrointestinal bleed.

> In discussions [with] pt's family in light of pt's condition & poor prognosis, it was their wish that in the event of catastrophe or cardiopulmonary arrest, pt should have no heroic measures performed, i.e., no CPR. *The medical housestaff & attendings remained in agreement with their decision.* [*Emphasis* added.]

Indeed, there is often intense disagreement, among housestaff, between housestaff and attendings, and between physicians and nurses over how aggressively to treat patients. The simple statement in the chart that a patient is not to be resuscitated is an affirmation that, in regard to at least one type of aggressive treatment, the staff has resolved its disagreements.

At the same time, the DNR order affirms the sometimes complex lines of authority within medicine. The following note refers to the agreement of consultants and Dr. Taylor, the patient's private physician: it is an acknowledgement of the right of private physicians to follow patients into the Intensive Care Unit and the priority of their responsibilities.

> Have discussed pt [with] family (husband), Dr. Taylor, & consultants fully. Husband has asked that no further aggressive or invasive measures be taken & that the major focus be on the pt's comfort alone. Dr. Taylor agrees [with] above decisions by husband that no cardiopulmonary resuscitation or aggressive measures be done.

However, aside from references to private physicians, references to the agreement of named medical personnel (like references to named family) are notably absent. Thus, while Dr. Taylor is named, "consultants" are mentioned generically. Consider also the following note:

> Discussed overall situation at length w/ patient's sister, niece (closest relatives). Family understands that patient has terminal illness and prognosis is grave. They request that CPR not be initiated for cardiac arrest & that medicines to support blood pressure (pressors) not be administered. All other supportive care to continue. *The staff of the MICU supports the decision*. Therefore, the patient is a no arrest page. [*Emphasis* added.]

Here, responsibility is detached from any particular person and vested, instead, in the "staff of the MICU [Medical Intensive Care Unit]" as a corporate whole. Such a formulation insists on both the agreement of the staff and the rights of that staff, regardless of the individuals involved. In this sense, the DNR order is a reaffirmation of the lines of authority in medicine – whether the authority of the private physician based on a distinctive relationship to a particular patient or the collective authority of the ICU staff based on a position in the medical division of labor.

Perhaps most importantly, the DNR order represents a recognition that there are limits to what medicine is required to do. This, too, is no small matter. Medicine is caught between two sometimes conflicting values: on the one hand, an ethic of intervention and treatment; on the other hand, an injunction to do no harm. The DNR order expresses, symbolically and however partially, a resolution of that conflict. It is an affirmation that there are at least some instances in which potentially therapeutic intervention may be withheld. This affirmation is made, in part, to those who might review the chart and, in part, to the patient or the patient's surrogate. But, more importantly, it is made among physicians themselves. It is an affirmation that active treatment is not the only value of medicine but one to be balanced against concerns of comfort and humanity.

Yet, at the same time that the formal chart note ordering termination of treatment acknowledges the limits of medicine, it defies those limits. Phillippe Aries, French social historian, has argued in his magisterial study of Western attitudes toward death that, at least in the years since World War II, we have stripped death of its moral and spiritual significance [1]. Not for us is Little Eva ascending toward heaven, or Ivan Illich pondering the ultimate meaning of life in the face of death, nor even are family and friends gathered around the deathbed for the moment of final benediction. For us the good death has become simply the painless death, the death that comes in sleep and allows us to say, "at least he didn't suffer." We have made death, argues Aries, a technical matter, something to be managed. We can see the effort to manage death, in part, in the work of social scientists like Elizabeth Kubler-Ross who lay out regular stages of a "dying process" and turn on them with an analytic eye [5]. And we can see it even more clearly in our removal of death from the home and its relocation to the hospital or the hospice where it can be contained, postponed and orchestrated with all the skills of contemporary medicine. "Try to make it through the night," one attending physician suggested to the housestaff about a 67-year-old woman who had already been made DNR: "I wouldn't like it for the family if she expired just after I talked to them. It'd be nice psychologically, for me and for them."

Yet, death cannot be contained or postponed indefinitely. This the physicians at both hospitals I studied are intensely aware of. "[M]y feeling," one resident told me, "is that when they have made somebody DNR it hasn't really changed the outcome." Death is a nasty business which insists on its own way and its own timing despite the best efforts of contemporary medicine. To contemporary medicine, insistent on an ability to manage illness, it is the ultimate reproach.

The DNR order is an answer to this reproach. It represents an insistence that death is not simply something that happens, but something that is allowed to happen, something about which a decision is made. It is in this respect that the complex provisions of DNR policies concerning who is to decide and in what circumstances make perhaps the most sense. For they are an insistence that, even in the face of death, it is possible to impose order, rationality, and technique. In this sense, then, even at the moment that it represents a recognition of medicine's limits, the DNR order is also an affirmation of the powers of medicine and the powers of management.

We are accustomed to thinking of ritual as something draped in tradition, something that grows empty or hollow – that becomes *mere* ritual – as the values that once animated the words, symbols, and gestures lose touch with current realities. We are accustomed also to thinking of ritual as something that grows crescively out of a social situation and is then elaborated slowly and incrementally. Neither of these images holds true for the DNR order. Rather, the DNR order is something we might think of as a ritual from above. It does not simply grow out of the values of medicine. It does not simply take values already found in medical practice and then attempt to represent them symbolically. Rather, it is also an attempt to shape the values of medicine – to invite the recurrent affirmation of both the appropriateness of withholding treatment and, at the same time, of patients' rights. If the new DNR legislation does not exactly change the way anyone makes decisions, it may do something even more valuable. It may require physicians not only to share in but also affirm a culture in which the rights of patients are reconciled with the traditional values of medicine.

Notes

[1] For a discussion of rituals in medicine more generally, see [3].

BIBLIOGRAPHY

1. Aries, P.: 1981, *The Hour of Our Death*, Knopf, New York.
2. Bedell, S.E., Delbanco, T. and Cook, E.F.: 1983, 'Survival After Cardiopulmonary Resuscitation in the Hospital', *New England Journal of Medicine* **309**, 569–76.
3. Bosk, C.: 1980, 'Occupational Rituals in Patient Management', *New England Journal of Medicine* **303**, 71–76.
4. Kamer, R. S. *et al.*: 1990, 'Effects of New York State's Do-Not-Resuscitate Legislation on In-Hospital Cardiopulmonary Resuscitation Practice', *American Journal of Medicine* **88**, 108–111.
5. Kubler-Ross, E.: 1969, *On Death and Dying*, MacMillan, New York.
6. McClung, J.A. and Kamer, R.S.: 1990, 'Legislating Ethics: Implications of New York's Do-Not-Resuscitate Law', *New England Journal of Medicine* **323**, 270–272.

7. Nolan, K.: 1987, 'In Death's Shadow: The Meanings of Withholding Resuscitation', *Hastings Center Report* **17**, 9–14.
8. President's Commission for the Study of Ethical Problems in Medicine and Biomedical and Behavioral Research: 1983, *Deciding to Forego Life-Sustaining Treatment*, U.S. Gov't Printing Office, Washington, D.C.
9. Zussman, R.: 1992, Intensive Care: *Medical Ethics and the Medical Profession*, University of Chicago Press, Chicago, IL.

RUSSELL S. KAMER AND JOHN A. McCLUNG

NEW YORK'S DO-NOT-RESUSCITATE LAW: BURDEN OR BENEFIT?*

In 1987, New York State became the first jurisdiction to enact legislation governing the withholding of cardiopulmonary resuscitation (CPR). Other states are watching New York's initiative to see if it will serve as a model for them to follow. In view of the far-reaching consequences of codifying the process of medical decisionmaking in statutory law, a debate has emerged about both the need for legislative intervention and its effectiveness. To address these questions, we will first review the confluence of events that lead to the drafting of the law. It will then be possible to understand how circumstances unique to New York State may have engendered practices that depart from the usual methods of making medical decisions.

HISTORICAL BACKGROUND

The technique of closed-chest massage was first described thirty years ago after which it gradually entered clinical practice as a specialized therapy for the treatment of victims of sudden cardiac arrest ([3], [5]). Six years later, the National Research Council of the National Academy of Sciences recommended instructing all medical as well as paramedical and allied health-care personnel in CPR [10]. In 1973, a national conference on standards for cardiopulmonary resuscitation and emergency cardiac care was convened which recommended that training in basic life support techniques should be expanded to include the general public. These recommendations were published in a monograph issued in 1974, which goes on to state explicitly that, "the purpose of cardiopulmonary resuscitation is the prevention of sudden, unexpected death. Cardiopulmonary resuscitation is not indicated in certain situations, such as in

* Adopted with permission from information appearing in *New England Journal of Medicine*, "Legislating Ethics: Implication of New York's Do Not Resuscitate Law" **323**, 270–272, 1990.

R. Baker & M.A. Strosberg (eds.), Legislating Medical Ethics: A Study of the New York Do-Not-Resuscitate Law, 227–234.

cases of terminal, irreversible illness where death is not unexpected" [11]. In cases where the patient is hospitalized, the conference recommended documentation of a decision not to resuscitate in the patient's progress note as well as an explicit written do-not-resuscitate (DNR) order, "for the benefit of nurses and other personnel who may be called upon to initiate or participate in cardiopulmonary resuscitation" [11].

Despite these recommendations to withhold CPR from the terminally ill, these patients with irreversible illness were often subjected to CPR. Moreover, when the decision was made to withhold CPR, the decision was not always written in the patient's chart. Each hospital developed its own system of surreptitious codes that indicated a patient was not to be resuscitated. For example, the letters *NTBR* could be written on a patient's chart. These initials would signify to the staff that the patient was *not to be resuscitated.* If there was an investigation into why this patient did not receive CPR, the physician could attempt to avoid responsibility by saying that the letters NTBR actually meant *no temperatures by rectum*!

In 1976, the year of the *Quinlan* decision, an editorial in the *New England Journal of Medicine* noted that the withholding of life-sustaining therapy, including CPR, from the terminally ill was an "open secret" in the profession [1]. The editorial was written in response to the publication of two policies governing the withholding of therapy instituted at the Massachusetts General Hospital and the Beth Israel Hospital, both in Boston, Massachusetts ([6], [15]). Massachusetts General Hospital's policy established a series of therapeutic categories into which patients could be placed. The physician was responsible for assigning patients into the categories which determined the level of treatment which they received. All patients were to receive CPR unless explicitly stated to the contrary in the medical record. In a fashion similar to the national conference recommendations, the physician's only interactive duty was to answer questions raised by patient and family. Active consultation with the family, but not the patient, was required only for acts of comission, such as discontinuation of ventilators.

By contrast, the Beth Israel policy allowed for a patient-initiated refusal of CPR regardless of medical justification. It further mandated that the patient formally consent to the issuance of a DNR order, even if it was medically indicated and required a surrogate consent for patients lacking decision-making capacity. In this latter category, DNR decisions were not to be issued unless death was expected within two weeks' time. This approach was endorsed in part by the Massachusetts Appeals Court two years later in a decision which sanctioned explicit DNR orders while at the same time reserving them for "irreversibly, terminally ill" patients and then only with the express consent of patient and family [2].

DNR ORDERS IN NEW YORK STATE

In New York, there was very little activity in this area until 1981, when the death under mysterious circumstances of a woman in a Queens hospital intensive care unit sparked a grand jury investigation that lasted two years. Among the issues investigated was the Institution's failure to offer the patient CPR, because of a covert system according to which purple dots were affixed to the charts of patients who were not to be resuscitated. The system had apparently been conceived in response to a staff decision against the use of explicit DNR orders in order to "minimize legal exposure." Among the justifications offered for this practice was a statement by the physician who designed it to the effect that the purple dots "were nothing more than suggestions, if you will, to the nurse who is perfectly at liberty to call the code if she desires to call the code" [17].

Partly in response to this incident, the Medical Society of the State of New York in 1982 released a series of guidelines for the withholding of CPR that were similar to those adopted by Beth Israel Hospital of Boston in 1976 [18]. Over the next few years, a number of hospitals in the state began independently formulating policies governing the issuance of explicit DNR orders.

In 1984, the grand jury issued its report, citing the covert designation of resuscitation status as an example of "shocking procedural abuses" and calling for procedural safeguards that were virtually identical to those issued previously by the State Medical Society. In addition, it was suggested that these findings demonstrated an "urgent need for regulations by the state government" [17]. The New York State Task Force on Life and the Law was convened by the Governor in 1985 to recommend policy on a variety of issues, including the question of cardiopulmonary resuscitation. A proposal specifying the procedure by which DNR orders could be issued was subsequently presented to the State Legislature, was enacted in July of 1987 and became effective in April 1988 [12].

Aside from the political ramifications of the grand jury report, there was another driving force behind the perceived need for legislative action.

Over the years, New York has developed a body of common law that limits the right of surrogates to refuse life-sustaining treatment on behalf of incapacitated persons who have not previously expressed their wishes on the subject [8]. The DNR legislation therefore provided a vehicle for the legal authorization of such decision making with respect to the withholding of CPR in a state that had and continues to have a judicial tradition of opposition to substituted judgement [7].

CLINICAL CONSIDERATIONS

From a clinical standpoint, there is very little difference between the procedures outlined in the New York State law and those previously described in the medical literature. Despite the complaint of many New York physicians that the requirements are cumbersome, they represent little more than the legislative codification of recommended policy, past and present [9], [15], [18]). It has also been argued that the law imposes a new duty to resuscitate all patients for whom the proper DNR forms have not been completed – in effect leading to more resuscitative efforts ([13], [16]). This perception persists in the medical community, despite clear explanation by lawyers that the legislation's presumption of consent to resuscitate does not mandate resuscitation in patients without DNR orders for whom it is the "well grounded judgment" of a physician that CPR will be futile [19].

In fact, no evidence presented to date suggests any increase in the number of CPR attempts since the law took effect. Our own experience in one New York tertiary care hospital has been that the law's only statistically significant effect was to increase the number of formal DNR orders appearing on order sheets. There was no change in either the overall number of resuscitation attempts or in the already prevalent (97%) practice of including patients or family members in discussions about DNR status [4]. Although these observations demonstrate no active harm stemming from the legislation, it is important to realize that virtually the same results were reported by another New York Hospital one year before the law was enacted, simply in response to the creation of a formal institutional DNR policy [14].

Although the law requires that all inpatients be informed of their right to request DNR status, our findings suggest that it has not increased patient's autonomy. Patients are involved in DNR decisions only 13 to

28% of the time, and surrogate involvement is required in the remainder – an observation made consistently before the law was passed and not changed as a result of its passage, as far as we can document [4]. This observation is not necessarily surprising, since it is often only after serious hemodynamic or neurologic instability occurs that many patients are considered candidates for DNR status, and such instability may render a patient incapable of making an informed decision.

THEORETICAL CONSIDERATIONS

If, in fact, there is no clinically measurable benefit conferred by legislation, over and above that engendered by a formal internally generated hospital policy, is there a normative justification for legislative intrusion in this area? Why should DNR orders be different from all other orders? Why should the issuance of DNR orders require a special statute? To answer these questions, we must first try to discern in what ways CPR appears to differ from other medical interventions in order to understand why it is considered deserving of special treatment. Stuart Youngner has identified what we have classified as five factors which may be considered by some to imbue CPR with special significance [20].

First, it is a dramatic intervention which is perceived by many as "life saving." This perception is rarely accurate. There is no doubt that CPR is potentially life-*preserving*, but it is the unusual person whose life is "saved" simply by the application of CPR. In most cases, CPR serves as a means of allowing a patient to survive long enough to benefit from more definitive therapy directed at the primary disease entity. These definitive therapies are arguably as life-saving as CPR, and yet decisions regarding their use are not necessarily considered in need of a legislatively designed protocol.

Second, it is correctly observed that CPR requires immediate application in order for it to be successful. It is therefore critical that a carefully planned decision regarding its use be made in advance of its necessity. Be that as it may, this observation in no way serves to separate this procedure from a host of other procedures (for example emergency intubation, emergent tracheostomy, the Heimlich maneuver) each of which would then, by extension, require its own set of legislatively generated protocols designating in what fashion it would be employed or withheld. The ensuing legislative burden alone would probably dissuade even the most ardent lawmaker.

Third, failure to perform CPR results in a virtual 100% mortality. This observation serves to differentiate CPR from most other therapies. This difference, however, does not alter the way in which the decision to use or to withhold CPR is made. As with all medical decisions, the relative risks and benefits of the procedure need to be evaluated.

Fourth, education of the general public in the techniques of basic life support has lead to the belief that CPR falls under the rubric of fundamental first aid. As such, CPR appears to be more in the public domain than other medical interventions. Although this certainly may account for some of the political interest in this procedure, it is questionable whether additional weight ought to be assigned to an intervention based upon who has the capacity to perform it, rather than upon whom it is performed.

This brings us to the fifth consideration. Every human being, without exception, will die. As such, every person will one day find himself or herself in a state of affairs wherein CPR might be employed. This realization may account for the substantial public interest in this issue and may perhaps be one of the forces which mobilizes legislative action. Although this observation may explain the extent of public interest, it does not thereby justify approaching the decision-making process in a totally different fashion.

It would appear then that there is no substantive difference between the decision-making process surrounding CPR and that which surrounds any other medical therapy. Barring idiosyncratic political and judicial influence, either all these therapies require legislative protocols, or none of them do.

CONCLUSIONS

New York's DNR law stands largely as a legislative enshrinement of a communal approach to medical decision making that has dominated the literature since the 1976 publication of the DNR policy of Beth Israel Hospital in Boston. Although there are no data to suggest that it has had a negative effect on patient care, the clinical evidence that a nearly identical outcome can be achieved by policies generated at the institutional level suggests that the law's specifics are redundant, inefficient, and unnecessary.

The thrust of every DNR policy published in the past decade has been that the physician is responsible for providing adequate information to the patient, or an appropriate surrogate, so that informed decisions about CPR can be made. These policies respecting patient autonomy have replaced the former model of decision making where the physician alone retained control of medical decisions, without the need for any protocol or consultation. This shift away from the principle of beneficence and towards the principle of patient autonomy as the primary motive force behind patient care decisions is, of course, not unique to the issue of CPR. The changing way in which DNR decisions are made reflects the change in the way all medical decisions are made.

New York State's law has had little effect on clinical practice. Given the evidence that a nearly identical outcome can be achieved by policies generated at the institutional level, New York State's law appears to be unnecessary. If this is so, then the current New York State initiative is the result of the political and judicial climate of this jurisdiction rather than a model for other legislatures to follow.

BIBLIOGRAPHY

1. Fried, C.: 1976, 'Terminating Life Support: Out of the Closet!', *New England Journal of Medicine* **295**, 390–391.
2. *In re Dinnerstein*, 380 N.E. 2d 417 (1978).
3. Jude, J.R. and Elam, J.O.: 1965, *Fundamentals of Cardiopulmonary Resuscitation*, F. A. Davis, Philadelphia.
4. Kamer, R.S. *et al.*: 1990, 'Effect of New York State's Do-Not-Resuscitate Legislation on In-Hospital Cardiopulmonary Resuscitation Practice', *American Journal of Medicine* **88**, 108–111.
5. Kouwenhoven, W.B., Jude, J.R. and Knickerbocker, G.G.: 1960, 'Closed-Chest Cardiac Massage', *Journal of the American Medical Association* **173**, 1064–1067.
6. Massachusetts General Hospital – Clinical Care Committee: 1976, 'Optimum Care for Hopelessly Ill Patients', *New England Journal of Medicine* **295**, 362–364.
7. *Matter of O'Connor*, 72 N.Y. 2d 517 (1988).
8. *Matter of Storar*, 52 N.Y. 2d 363 (1981).
9. Miles, S.H., Cranford, R. and Schultz, A.L.: 1982, 'The Do-Not-Resuscitate Order in a Teaching Hospital', *Annals of Internal Medicine* **96**, 660–664.
10. National Academy of Sciences – National Research Council: 1966, 'Cardiopulmonary Resuscitation: A Statement by the Ad Hoc Committee on Cardiopulmonary Resuscitation', *Journal of the American Medical Association* **198**, 372–379.
11. National Conference Steering Committee on Cardiopulmonary Resuscitation and Emergency Cardiac Care: 1987, 'Standards for Cardiopulmonary Resuscitation (CPR) and Emergency Cardiac Care (ECC)', *Journal of the American Medical Association* **257**, 833–868.

12. New York State Public Health Law, Article 29-B, Statute 413-A.
13. Praeger, K.M.: 1989, 'How CPR Can Threaten the Desperately Ill', *Wall Street Journal* March 9, 1989, 16.
14. Quill, T.E., Stankaitis, J.A. and Krause, C.R.: 1990, 'The Effect of a Community Hospital Resuscitation Policy on Elderly Patients', *New York State Journal of Medicine* **86**, 622–625.
15. Rabkin, M.T., Gillerman, G. and Rice, N.R.: 1976, 'Orders Not To Resuscitate', *New England Journal of Medicine* **295**, 364–366.
16. Rosner, F. and Hotchkiss, E.J.: 1988, 'Must We Always Offer the Option of CPR? The Law in New York', *Journal of the American Medical Association* **260**, 3129.
17. Sullivan, R.: 1984, 'Hospital's Data Faulted in Case of Terminally Ill', *The New York Times*, March 21, 1984, B1.
18. Sullivan, R.: 1982, 'Standards Issued on Resuscitation of Dying Patients', *The New York Times*, September 19, 1982, A1.
19. Swidler, R.N.: 1989, 'The Presumption of Consent in New York State's Do-Not-Resuscitate Law', *New York State Journal of Medicine* **89**, 68–72.
20. Youngner, S.J.: 1987, 'Do-Not-Resuscitate Orders: No Longer Secret, But Still a Problem', *Hastings Center Report* **17**, 24–33.

JUDITH C. AHRONHEIM, SATHYA MAHESWARAN AND CARL ROSENBERG

DOES THE NEW YORK STATE DNR LAW PREVENT MEDICALLY INAPPROPRIATE DNR?

The designers of New York State's Do-Not-Resuscitate (DNR) law endeavored, among other things, to create a means of preventing medically inappropriate resuscitation – that is, resuscitation that "will probably fail or succeed only to the extent that the patient is repeatedly resuscitated in a short time period before death" ([10], pp. 6–8). The word "fail" is not further defined, but the law permits the physician to make the decision to withhold CPR in cases of "medical futility," which is defined as a situation in which CPR would be "unsuccessful in restoring cardiac and respiratory function" or that the patient would "experience repeated arrest in a short time period before death occurs" ([8], §2970). To this end, the law would provide immunity to doctors who wrote DNR orders in good faith, and means would be devised to overrule families who insisted on resuscitation that would clearly be medically futile. Although it is doubtful that regulations mandated and delineated by state law have any advantages over existing practices [6], another, and possibly primary purpose of the law was to prevent covert DNR orders. To this end, the law would require a process whereby consent *not* to resuscitate would have to be obtained from the patient or surrogate in all but a few, highly exceptional circumstances. The law as it was written and the regulations governing its implementation were viewed by some as restrictive and cumbersome, difficult to comply with, and likely to increase the rate of inappropriate cardiopulmonary resuscitation (CPR). Fear had been voiced after the law went into effect that CPR was on the rise rather than on the decline. A well-known physician-ethicist from another state, echoing this concern, was quoted as saying, "We've reached a point where almost no one is allowed to die in a U.S. hospital without resuscitation" [11].

Having heard these fears voiced by a number of our colleagues locally, we decided to look further into this question. We conducted a retrospective study of patients who died on medical services in three New York City hospitals, in which we examined the proportion of patients undergoing CPR during the year before and the year after the law went into effect on April 1, 1988. We were surprised to find no evidence of an

R. Baker & M.A. Strosberg (eds.), Legislating Medical Ethics: A Study of the New York Do-Not-Resuscitate Law, 235–240.

increase in CPR, and, within the limits of our sample size of nearly 1000 charts, the study could not rule out the possibility that CPR was, rather, on the decline. In a preliminary analysis, the use of CPR prior to death was shown to decline slightly, from 40.1% in the year prior to the law to 35.7% in the year immediately after the law went into effect, but this change was not statistically significant. The methods and results of our study have been published elsewhere in detail [1]. The 3 hospitals studied – Bellevue, New York University (Tisch), and the Manhattan Veterans Hospital – differed greatly in their socioeconomic composition, distribution of disease and age at death, and sex distribution. The absence of a statistically significant difference was maintained after we controlled for these potentially confounding variables, and after we controlled for disease severity. Thus, our study showed no evidence that the law produced either an increase or decrease in CPR, although a much larger study might have been able to detect a change. An ideal study would view practices beginning several years before 1988, and continue on for several years after to see if the law produced any trends that had not already begun in the past, independent of the law. Still, it would be difficult to measure the phenomenon of *inappropriate* resuscitation.

Although we were unable to measure the elusive phenomenon of inappropriate resuscitation, some data that we gathered raises concern over how it should be defined.In a separate analysis, we found that, of patients who died, 25.2% with advanced cancer and 30.3% with AIDS underwent CPR at least once prior to death. In most other disease categories, the proportion was considerably higher (see Appendix 1). A multivariate analysis revealed that, regardless of disease severity, the proportions undergoing CPR did not change between 1987 and 1989 [1]. Thus, despite the implementation of a law that hoped to reduce inappropriate resuscitations, CPR was the final procedure performed in a large proportion of gravely ill patients, and was frequently performed even in conditions where survival is not expected. It is well established that hospitalized patients in many disease categories who undergo CPR rarely survive to discharge ([4], [3], [2], [13]). Although we know of no specific data on AIDS patients, virtually zero survival has been consistently reported in advanced cancer. A category with a better prognosis than general medical patients is the group with unexpected cardiac arrest or primary cardiac arrhythmia without severe myocardial disease ([15], [14]). Their prognosis is more favorable than general medical patients because they are medically distinct – in them, CPR is directed towards the affected organ (the electrical conducting system of the heart); it restores electrical activity of the heart and when successful *is* successful because vital organs, including the myocardium (heart muscle) and the lung, are capable of functioning normally or at least adequately once cardiac conduction, and thereby circulation, is restored. In these patients, the presumption of consent for CPR is appropriate because the procedure is suitable for the medical situation and is therefore potentially life-saving.

Under New York State law, however, *all* patients are presumed to consent. This often includes patients in whom CPR has a dismal prognosis, but who may not *in all opinions* fit the strict legal definition of "medical futility." It is presumably for this reason that the law has required the hospital to appoint a second physician to concur on the futile prognosis before CPR can be withheld without a DNR order ([7], p. 14). This cumbersome requirement is imposed in the very cases in which CPR may not "fail", but when "successful" is death-prolonging rather than life-saving; this is the case because CPR is a procedure that is *not* effective in directly restoring the function of diseased vital organs. In people who are terminally ill, or in those who merely have serious chronic medical disease, cardiac arrest is the disease's conclusion and not an intercurrent event. Where CPR is performed on this background of vital organ dysfunction or failure, one may argue that it is *not* medically appropriate. Although the presumption of consent may not constitute an absolute duty to resuscitate [12], the Union College study has demonstrated that the interpretation of futility is one of the most misunderstood and contested aspects of the law.

What is appropriate is to ask whether the presumption of consent in these situations is truly in the interest of the patient or is rather a safeguard for the health care system, fearful of legal liability.

A possible argument in favor of liberal use of CPR is that it is someone's only chance, and that therefore it "can't hurt" to try, but, of course, it can hurt. If a patient is dying and CPR restores consciousness, the intervention has the effect of not only prolonging the dying process but making it more anguishing. Patient surrogates placed in the position of requesting termination of life support sometimes feel they are the agents of their loved one's death. To compound the problem in New York State, more stringent legal standards govern the termination of life support than the institution of DNR [5]. Approaching the competent patient for his or her opinion, namely, obtaining consent for DNR, seems a simple solution. However, if the patient is clearly dying and has not initiated a DNR discussion, obtaining refusal of CPR (that is obtaining consent for DNR), can be very problematic. It can produce fear and anxiety in a patient whose clinical and emotional state require calm and comfort, but the law permits the avoidance of this discussion only in cases that are unrealistically extreme – namely, when two physicians have determined that "severe and immediate injury" such as a heart attack or suicide ([9], 10(C), §405.43) would result from the discussion. A young AIDS patient is hardly likely to suffer a heart attack, nor is someone dying with metastatic cancer likely to have the energy to commit suicide over a discussion of CPR. However, in these situations it is more appropriate to engage the patient in a discussion of what *can* be done (for example, pain control, sedation, visitation) rather than seeking permission to avoid the assault of the code team, a frightening specter. A sensitive DNR discussion could of course be an encounter of great comfort, but unfortunately a DNR law hardly guarantees that such a discussion will take place. In someone who will not survive for long, such a discussion can lead to the misunderstanding that death can be prevented. This creates a fiction that death (as opposed to treatment) is something governed by one's "right to choose." We must ask if we are here respecting the principle of autonomy or whether we are sometimes exploiting the principle for the purpose of reducing our responsibilities as health professionals.

Although our two-year chart review could not answer these troubling questions, it did strongly suggest that the law had the potential of leading to more paper work, not a desirable outcome in today's bureaucratically overburdened health care system. DNR status is generally documented as a chart note or as a formal order on the order sheet or both. Before the law, formal orders were written for only 32.7% of patients who were designated DNR but after the law went into effect formal orders were written for 83.9%. This change was particularly dramatic for the University Hospital, a private, not-for-profit institution, in which the percentage leapt from 9.5 % to 100%. Thus, although actual use of CPR did not change, at least one form of documentation increased significantly on April 1, 1988, in accordance with the law. The law requires that the DNR order be reviewed every three days for patients in acute hospitals, and local hospital policies have generated different degrees of administrative burden to comply with this law. More paperwork is likely to be viewed as onerous to an overburdened hospital staff and of questionable value to the patient.

The law and increasing awareness nationally of DNR has probably succeeded in preventing secret DNR orders. Although a patient or surrogate's participation in medical decision making is essential, we must acknowledge that it does not prevent the medical outcome when death is inevitable, and we must give heed to the possibility that obtaining permission for death may add to the trauma of the dying process for many patients and their loved ones. We must also acknowledge that, although the DNR law hoped to prevent inappropriate resuscitation, we ought to clarify our definition of medical inappropriateness with illustrative examples (not legal specifications): CPR instituted in the setting of irreversible illness such as advanced cancer, chronic failure of liver, kidney, heart, or lung, and advanced brain disease. It would also be helpful if the State of New York were to adopt more realistic standards to facilitate the removal of artificial life support in the many situations in which CPR fails. Most importantly, we must ask how well the DNR law, or any law that purports to serve patients' rights, actually serves the patient, for which it is ultimately designed, or whether it sometimes serves the health care system at the expense of the patient.

BIBLIOGRAPHY

1. Ahronheim, J.C., Maheswaran, S. and Rosenberg, C.: 1992, 'Impact of Do-Not-Resuscitate Legislation on the Use of Cardiopulmonary Resuscitation in Three Teaching Hospitals', *New York State Journal of Medicine* **92**, 281–185.
2. Applebaum, G.E., King, J.E. and Finucane, T.E.: 1990, 'The Outcome of CPR Initiated in Nursing Homes', *Journal of the American Geriatric Society* **38**, 197–200.
3. Bedell, S.E. *et al.*: 1983, 'Survival After Cardiopulmonary Resuscitation in the Hospital', *New England Journal of Medicine* **309**, 569–576.
4. Hershey, C. and Fisher, L.: 1982, 'Why Outcome of Cardiopulmonary Resuscitation in General Wards is Poor', *The Lancet* **1**, 31–34.
5. *In re Westchester County Medical Center* (O'Connor), 72 N.Y. 2d 517, 534 (1988). N.Y.S. 2d 886, 531 N.E. 2d 607 (1988).
6. McClung, J.A. and Kamer, R.S.: 1990, 'Legislating Ethics. Implications of New York's Do-Not-Resuscitate Law', *New England Journal of Medicine* **323**, 270–272.
7. Medical Society of the State of New York, New York State Department of Health and Hospital Association of New York State: 1990, *Do Not Resuscitate Orders. Questions and Answers for Health Care Professionals.*
8. New York Public Health Law Article 29-B, ch. 818. 'Orders Not To Resuscitate'.
9. New York State Codes, Roles and Regulations.
10. New York State Task Force on Life and the Law: 1988, *Do Not Resuscitate Orders. The Proposed Legislation and Report of the New York State Task Force on Life and the Law*, 2nd edition, Albany, New York.
11. *New York Times*, October 14, 1990: A-1, B-20.
12. Swidler, R.N.: 1989, 'The Presumption of Consent in New York State's Do-Not-Resuscitate Law', *New York State Journal of Medicine* **89**, 69–71.

13. Taffet, G.E., Teasdale, T.A. and Luchi, R.J.: 1988, 'In Hospital Cardiopulmonary Resuscitation', *Journal of the American Medical Association* **260**, 2069–2072.
14. Timerman, A., Piegas, L.S. and Sousa, J.E.: 1989, 'Results of Cardiopulmonary Resuscitation in a Cardiology Hospital', *Resuscitation* **18**, 75–84.
15. Tresch, D.D. *et al.*: 1984, 'Long-Term Survival After Prehospital Sudden Cardiac Death', *American Heart Journal* **108**, 1–5.

APPENDIX 1

Table 1. Patients undergoing CPR prior to death [1]

Disease Category [2]	Underwent CPR	All Patients	Percent
Advanced Cancer	110	437	25.2
AIDS	95	314	30.3
Cardiac	88	98	89.8
Chronic vegetative [3]	1	6	16.7
Collagen-vascular	14	16	87.5
Delirium tremens	1	2	50.0
Gastrointestinal bleed	3	8	37.5
Hepatic encephalopathy	13	24	54.2
Iatrogenic	1	1	100.0
Infection	78	119	65.5
Metabolic [4]	5	8	62.5
Neurologic [5]	11	21	52.4
Respiratory	13	14	92.9
Unexpected Arrest	6	7	85.7
Other [6]	9	13	69.2
All Deaths	448	1,088	41.2

[1] Data from 3 hospitals, April 1, 1987, through March 31, 1989, which included 88 patients who underwent CPR and survived prior to issuance of a DNR order, and 48 patients who neither underwent CPR nor were designated DNR but were listed as having been found dead in bed. These 136 patients were excluded from the published analysis (see [1]).
[2] Underlying disease that led to death.
[3] rofound global neurologic impairments of various etiologies.
[4] Almost all chronic renal failure.
[5] Neurologic impairments less severe than "chronic vegetative" (e.g. hemiparesis).
[6] Hypothermia, anaphylaxis, volvulus, hip fracture, ruptured aneurysm.

TIMOTHY E. QUILL AND NANCY M. BENNETT

THE EFFECTS OF A HOSPITAL POLICY AND STATE LEGISLATION ON RESUSCITATION ORDERS FOR GERIATRIC PATIENTS*

In 1986, we reported the effect of a do-not-resuscitate (DNR) policy on the ordering and performance of cardiopulmonary resuscitation (CPR) in a population of elderly patients hospitalized at a community hospital [9]. A nonsignificant increase in the explicit ordering of DNR and a nonstatistically significant decline in the actual performance of CPR was found. In 1987, New York State passed legislation requiring that all New York hospitals create and implement DNR policies within mandated guidelines that went into effect on April 1, 1988 [6]. This legislation has been criticized as being cumbersome and unnecessarily restrictive [10]. Adapting our flexible, successfully implemented DNR policy to the New York State guidelines was difficult because of the increased, seemingly unnecessary documentation requirements and stipulations. This study emanated from our concern that the legally mandated requirements would create new barriers that would discourage physicians from engaging in discussions about DNR options with patients and their families.

The study population of patients older than 79 years who died in the hospital was chosen in part because it was the subject of our original inquiry [9]. It is an excellent population for study about DNR issues because of reports suggesting the near futility of CPR in the hospitalized elderly ([1], [3], [5], [7], [12]) and because of our experience that many elderly patients, when given information about CPR and its low probability of success, choose not to have it. Our policy advocates giving patients information and choice rather than arbitrary restrictions based on age or other factors.

The following questions were posed in this study: (1) Would the hospital DNR policy that we initiated in 1983 exert a lasting effect on DNR ordering for patients older than 79 years who died in the hospital? (2) Would the alteration of the hospital DNR policy to comply with New York State DNR legislation influence physician DNR ordering in our hospital for this population? (3) Did the institution of a hospital DNR

---

* Reprinted with permission from the *Archives of Internal Medicine* **152**, 569–572 Copyright 1992, American Medical Association

R. Baker & M.A. Strosberg (eds.), Legislating Medical Ethics: A Study of the New York Do-Not-Resuscitate Law, 241–250.

policy improve the success rate of CPR in our geriatric patients, compared with published outcome studies, by selecting those with a higher likelihood of survival? (4) Was there documentation in patient charts that decisions about DNR or CPR in geriatric patients reflected the patient's actual wishes?

PATIENTS AND METHODS

The study was carried out at The Genesee Hospital, Rochester, NY, a 384-bed teaching hospital associated with the University of Rochester School of Medicine and Dentistry. The Genesee Hospital DNR policy (TGH policy), fully described in our original article [9], was instituted in January, 1983. The policy required a note in the chart assessing the patient's wishes and prognosis before issuing a DNR order. Before that time there was no formal policy to guide physicians or their patients who wished to have limitations placed on therapeutic efforts.

On April 1, 1988, New York State legislation governing DNR (NYS law) went into effect [8]. According to our interpretation of NYS law, one of five sets of DNR forms, each ranging in length from two to six pages, had to be completed before a DNR order was issued (depending on whether the patient was competent, incompetent with a surrogate, incompetent without a surrogate, etc.). With both TGH policy and NYS law, if no DNR order was issued, the patient was treated as if CPR had been ordered in the event of a cardiopulmonary arrest.

Study populations were identified by death records from our hospital database. In our original study, we identified and reviewed charts of all patients over 79 years old who had died in the hospital in the last 6 months of 1982, before TGH policy (period 1), and compared them with all patients over 79 years old who had died in the last 6 months of 1983 (6 months after the institution of TGH policy). The original report was restricted to patients who had the diagnosis of cerebrovascular accident, dementia, or cancer.

In the present study, we applied no diagnostic restrictions. We reviewed a comparable 6-month period in 1984 and stopped regular monitoring when it appeared that the changes were stable. The combination of these two 6-month periods in 1983 and 1984 after TGH policy constitute period 2. After the revision of TGH policy to comply with NYS law effective April, 1988, we reviewed all deaths of patients older than 79 years for three additional 6-month periods (July 1, 1988, through December 31, 1988; July 1, 1989, through December 31, 1989; and January 1, 1990, through June 30, 1990). The combination of these three periods after NYS law constitute period 3. All identified charts were reviewed for age, DNR order in the order sheet, DNR form completion (in the last three study periods after the legal mandate), and actual performance of CPR. For the groups in 1989 and 1990, we looked for evidence in the chart that the patient's actual wishes were being taken into account, including current or previously stated wishes, or evidence of an attempt to try to understand what incompetent patients would want, given knowledge of their condition and prognosis.

To define a study group of patients who received CPR in 1988, we used the hospital procedure summary sheets completed at discharge or death to identify all patients who were coded as having CPR. With the use of the computerized billing records, the identified patient records were then reviewed for age, diagnosis related group (DRG), and status at the end of hospitalization. We included all patients admitted to the hospital, excluding only those who received CPR and died in the emergency department. Because of previous data suggesting that CPR was most successful in those with ventricular arrhythmias [7], we divided patients into primary cardiac and primary noncardiac DRGs. Outcomes were defined as the status at the end of hospitalization (discharge home or to another health care facility versus death). Unfortunately, comparison data about CPR attempts and outcome from before our DNR policy was initiated in 1983 were unobtainable.

We calculated 95% confidence intervals for all proportions. In addition, the Mantel-Haenszel chi^2 test [2] was used to compare the percentages of patients for whom a DNR order was written in the periods before and after TGH policy and the NYS law. Similar analyses were used to compare actual CPR attempts in those with CPR orders for the same periods and to compare CPR survival rates in relation to age and cardiac versus noncardiac DRGs for 1988.

RESULTS

The increased explicit issuing of DNR orders reported in our original study persisted (Table 1). In both periods 2 and 3, the percentage of patients with DNR orders increased relative to period 1. The increase from period 1 to period 2 was significant ($P<.001$), but the increase from period 2 to 3 was of borderline significance ($P=.053$).

Table 1. CPR and DNR Ordering in Patients Older Than 79 Years Who Died*

Period	1: No Policy	2: TGH Policy	3: NYS Policy
Time Intervals	7/82–12/82	7/83–12/83, 7/84–12/84	7/88–12/88, 7/89–12/89, 1/90– 6/90
Total No. of Deaths	107	178	231
DNR Ordered, %	21 (13–29)	76 (70–82)	84 (79–89)
No CPR When DNR Or'd, %	91 (79–103)	97 (95–100)	99 (98–101)
CPR Att'd Without DNR Order, %	29 (19–39)	56 (41–71)	92 (83–101)

* CPR indicates cardiopulmonary resuscitation; DNR, do not resuscitate; TGH, The Genesee Hospital; and NYS, New York State. Numbers in parentheses are 95% confidence intervals of population percentages.

There were no statistically significant differences between the three periods in the percentage of patients with DNR orders who died without CPR attempts. The percentage increased slightly during the three periods but was already more than 90% in period 1. However, CPR was performed when ordered in 29% of patients in period 1, increasing to 56% in period 2 ($P<.01$), and to 92% in period 3 ($P<.001$). Within the two 6-month intervals of period 2, there was a statistically significant increase in the performance of CPR when ordered, from 42% in 1983 to 74% in 1984 ($P<.05$).

The success rates of CPR for 1988 are summarized in Table 2. The chances of surviving CPR were significantly higher for patients who had cardiac DRGs than for those with noncardiac DRGs for all age groups ($P<.01$). The chances of surviving CPR when the patient had a primary cardiac DRG did not change with age. The chance of surviving CPR when the DRG was primarily noncardiac appeared to decline steadily with age, but the small numbers of patients resulted in wide overlapping confidence intervals for the estimates of percentage survival.

Table 2. Analysis of 1988 CPR survival rates by age and DRG[1]

DRG	CPR ATT'pts No.	% Survival	Age, y	No. of Attempts	Survival, No. (%)
Cardiac	115	50 (41–59)[2]	<70	55	31/55(56) (43–69)[2]
			70–79	30	11/30(37) (20–54)
			>79	30	16/30(53) (35–71)
Noncardiac	50	26 (14–38)	<70	19	7/19 (37) (15–59)
			70–79	18	5/18 (28) (7–49)
			>79	13	1/13 (8) (7–22)

[1] DRG indicates diagnosis related group; CPR, cardiopulmonary resuscitation.
[2] The 95% confidence intervals for population percentages.

Chart documentation associated with DNR orders for patients older than 79 years who died in the hospital showed evidence of direct patient participation (during the hospitalization or through a previous directive) only 22% and 27% of the time during 1989 and 1990, respectively (Table 3). When families were consulted, the families' own wishes rather than their perception of the patient's wishes were recorded in the chart the majority of the time (86% versus 14% in 1989 and 75% versus 25% in 1990).

Evidence of the patient's informed consent to CPR was present in the chart in only one of the 14 patients over 79 years old in the 1990 study group who had CPR ordered before their death. For the other 13 patients, no discussion about CPR or DNR was documented in seven, unresolved discussions with the families occurred in three, and statements that "the family wants everything" were recorded in the remaining three.

Table 3. Origin of do-not-resuscitate order in patients older than 79 years who died

	% of Patients	
	1989 (n=46)	1990* (n=70)
Patient's direct request (past or present)	22	27
Family/surrogate assessment of patient's wishes	9	14
Family/surrogate wishes	52	43
Attending decision	2	6
No documentation	15	10

* Differences between years are not statistically significant.

COMMENT

The DNR policy instituted by The Genesee Hospital in 1983 has been associated with a significant and persisting increase in the explicit ordering of DNR by physicians for patients over 79 years of age who died in the hospital (21% in period 1 versus 76% in period 2; $P<.001$). The NYS law was certainly not associated with a decreased tendency to issue DNR orders compared with our original TGH policy, as we had originally hypothesized, and in fact was associated with a small, non-statistically significant increase in DNR orders (84% in period 3). With both the TGH policy and the NYS law, CPR is implicitly ordered when there is no DNR order. There was a significant increase in the actual performance of CPR in the subgroup without DNR orders after the TGH policy and another significant increase after NYS law (period 1, 28%; period 2, 56%; period 3, 92%; $P<.01$ for all differences). Thus, the NYS law requiring rigid DNR documentation certainly did not inhibit and may even have enhanced the actual performance of CPR when no DNR order was issued, compared with TGH policy alone.

There was no significant change in the high rate of adherence to DNR orders due to TGH policy or NYS law (>90% before TGH policy). Regardless of explicit DNR orders, the population of patients who died and who underwent CPR went from 22% in period 1, to 12% to 16% in periods 2 and 3, suggesting that TGH policy and NYS law in part made explicit a preexisting covert method for withholding CPR. One result of the policy and the law was that patients who do not have DNR orders at the time of an in-hospital cardiac arrest are now likely to receive CPR. Thus, careful selection and informed consent are critical.

Although total numbers were small, the success rate of CPR for patients older than 69 years (39% overall) summarized in Table 2 was remarkable compared with other published reports suggesting the survival rate is less than 5% ([1], [3], [5], [7], [12]). Particularly significant are the comparable survival rates for CPR in patients at all ages with primary cardiac DRGs. Although survival for noncardiac DRGs appeared to decline with age and the confidence intervals were wide due to the small sample, the rates of survival appear better than in previous reports ([1], [3], [5], [7], [12]). We attribute this difference to better selection of patients for CPR and to the removal of patients with a poor prognosis from the pool of patients receiving CPR (84% of patients older than 79 years who died in period 2 had DNR orders). Our data suggest that properly selected elderly patients, particularly those with cardiac DRGs, have reasonable odds of surviving CPR to leave the hospital.

The final question that we addressed was whether DNR or CPR orders reflected actual patient wishes. As seen in Table 3, only 22% and 27% of DNR orders in 1989 and 1990 study groups were based on the past or present explicit request of a competent patient. There was documentation of the family or surrogate's attempt to assess the patient's wishes in another 9% and 14%, respectively. The largest source of DNR orders was the family or surrogate's statement of *their own wishes* for the patient, without any assessment of how those wishes reflected their perception of the patient's wishes. In the hierarchy of informed decision making, the decision of an informed, competent patient has priority. If the patient is incompetent to make such a decision, it is the duty of the surrogate decisionmaker to exercise "substituted judgment," which means using knowledge of the patient's values and beliefs to decide as the patient would if he or she were able [4]. It appears from the chart review that families and other surrogates are deciding what they would want for the patient rather than assessing what the patient would want for himself or herself.

One flaw of the NYS law and of our 1983 TGH policy is that they "presume consent" to CPR in all circumstances when no other order is explicitly stated or documented ([9], [11]). Although appropriate for occurrences of sudden death or accidents in the community when the patient's condition is unknown, the presumption that elderly patients with irreversible medical conditions and poor prognoses want CPR may be grossly inaccurate and misleading. The current process of discussing prognosis and possible DNR is highly dependent on the physician and, if the patient is incompetent, on a surrogate to help make decisions in the patient's best interest. If a patient's physician or surrogate is reluctant to make an explicit DNR decision, the patient is presumed to consent to CPR by default. Our 1990 review of the 14 patients older than 79 years who died after receiving CPR in the first 6 months of 1990 was particularly disturbing in this regard. Only one of 14 charts showed evidence of an active, adequately informed decision in favor of CPR. Seven charts had no documentation that the question was considered, or that the patient (or the surrogate) was informed of the prognosis or of the option of DNR. Three charts had documentation that a discussion was initiated with the patient or family because of a deteriorating medical situation and a poor prognosis, but since there was no formal decision, the patient was given CPR. Finally, three charts had statements that the "family wants everything" in the face of a very poor prognosis, without any documentation of the patient's wishes, or of what specific interventions were implied by "wanting everything." It seems that the presumption of consent may force some patients to undergo CPR when uninformed or when there are breakdowns in communication. Since those who do not have DNR orders are now more likely to have CPR in the event of a cardiac arrest than before the policy or the law, active informed patient decision making is paramount.

There are several limitations to the current study. First, we did not collect data from 1985 through 1987. It is therefore hard to determine if the significant changes in CPR rates for those with CPR ordered are due to the effects of TGH policy over time or due to the implementation of NYS law. It seems clear in either event that NYS law, despite its rigid documentation requirements, did not exert an adverse effect on our hospital policy in terms of the outcomes measured. Second, although our CPR success rates in 1988 were much higher than those in previous reports, these rates were based on a relatively small number of attempts and successes. In addition, we had no control groups, either contemporary or historical, to prove that the relatively high rate represents better selection of patients as a result of the policy or the law. Systematic CPR records were not kept before 1988, and there was no reliable way to assess CPR attempts and outcomes. Although only 15% of the deaths of patients older than 79 years in our study group were in patients who had CPR ordered in 1988, there is no clear evidence that the remaining 85% who were not resuscitated would not have survived resuscitation if it had been attempted (although they did have to meet NYS law criteria for a DNR order, which includes a poor prognosis). Finally, a chart review was used to assess patient and family participation in medical decision making. Chart documentation may underestimate the extent to which efforts were made to elicit the patient's wishes, although it probably does reflect those aspects of the decisionmaking process that the physicians believe are most important.

The generalizability of our results may be questioned because of the sequential interventions of policy and law, and because The Genesee Hospital is a community hospital in which the implementation of DNR changes was physician generated and reinforced. The effects might be considerably less in a less supportive environment. Finally, the generalizability and comparability of our 1988 CPR survival data are uncertain because of small numbers and the highly evolved selection criteria, but these data do suggest that CPR is not necessarily futile in properly selected geriatric patients.

In summary, our DNR policy seems to have a long-lasting effect on physicians' willingness to issue DNR orders in hospitalized geriatric patients. Patients with DNR orders were almost always spared CPR if they suffer an in-hospital cardiac arrest. A higher percentage of elderly patients appeared to receive DNR orders as a result of the hospital DNR policy, and those who do not have DNR orders now tend to have CPR much more frequently in the event of in-hospital cardiac arrest. The fact that the performance of CPR when implicitly ordered has increased from 29% before the hospital DNR policy to more than 90% the last 3 years suggests that a preexisting covert system of DNR ordering has now been replaced by an explicit system. This explicit system has the potential to promote a more careful application of CPR to those patients who want a procedure in the event of a cardiac arrest, and who have a significant chance of benefiting from it. The NYS DNR law has not adversely affected, and may even have enhanced, the effects of our hospital policy. To the extent that such legislation forces all hospitals to implement DNR policies, it may promote better patient selection and increased patient choice about CPR and DNR. Our 1988 review of all CPR attempts suggests that carefully selected elderly patients, particularly those with primary cardiac DRGs, may have better odds of surviving CPR than in previously published reports. However, despite our long-standing DNR policy and the NYS law, our chart review suggests that the majority of decisions in this domain still do not reflect the wishes of an informed patient, or a careful attempt by a family or other surrogate to decide what the patient would want. The challenge of future DNR policies is to make decisions about both CPR and DNR more reflective of the choices of an informed patient, and not to presume consent in either direction without a thorough assessment of the patient's prognosis and wishes.

BIBLIOGRAPHY

1. Bayer, A.J., Ang, B.C. and Pathy, M.S.: 1985, 'Cardiac Arrests in a Geriatric Unit', *Age and Aging* **14**, 271–276.
2. Dean, A.G. *et al.*: 1990, *Epi Info, Version 5: A Word Processing, Data Base and Statistics Program for Epidemiology on Microcomputers*, USD, Inc., Stone Mountain, GA.
3. Gulati, R.S., Bhan, G.L. and Horan, M.A.: 1983, 'Cardiopulmonary Resuscitation of Old People', *The Lancet* **2**, 267–269.
4. The Hastings Center: 1987, *Guidelines on the Termination of Life-Sustaining Treatment and the Care of the Dying*, The Hastings Center, Briarcliff Manor, NY.
5. Linn, B.S. and Yurt, R.W.: 1970, 'Cardiac Arrest Among Geriatric Patients', *British Medical Journal* **2**, 25–27.
6. McClung, J.A. and Kamer R.: 1990, 'Legislating Ethics: Implications of New York's Do Not Resuscitate Law', *New England Journal of Medicine* **323**, 270–272.
7. Murphy, D.J. *et al.*: 1989, 'Outcomes of Cardiopulmonary Resuscitation in the Elderly', *Annals of Internal Medicine* **111**, 199–205.
8. New York Public Health Law, Article 29-B, Statute 413-A, Effective, April, 1988.
9. Quill, T.E., Stankaitis, J.A. and Krause C.R.: 1986, 'The Effect of a Community Hospital Resuscitation Policy on Elderly Patients', *New York State Journal of Medicine* **86**, 622–625.
10. Rosner F. and Hotchkiss E.J.: 1988, 'Must We Always Offer the Option of CPR? The Law in New York', *Journal of the American Medical Association* **260**, 3129.
11. Swidler, R.N.: 1989, 'The Presumption of Consent in New York State's Do-Not-Resuscitate Law', *New York State Journal of Medicine* **89**, 69–72.
12. Taffet, G.E., Teasdale, T.A. and Luchi, R.J.: 1988, 'In Hospital Cardiopulmonary Resuscitation', *Journal of the American Medical Association* **260**, 2069–2072.

NORTON SPRITZ

THE NEW YORK STATE DNR LAW: VIEWS OF THE MEMBERS OF THE NEW YORK CHAPTER OF THE AMERICAN COLLEGE OF PHYSICIANS

When the New York State law governing the placing of patients on Do Not Resuscitate (DNR) status went into effect on April 1, 1988, New York became the first state to regulate this process by specific legislation. The process leading to enactment of the DNR statute began in March, 1985, when Governor Cuomo established the New York State Task Force on Life and the law. There was concern that patients were being placed on DNR status without their consent or that of their surrogates. There was also the concern that the opposite was happening – patients were being subjected to CPR when, had they been given the opportunity to do so, they might have rejected it as an unwarranted and intrusive extension of the dying process.

Optimal utilization of DNR orders was being inhibited by uncertainty on the part of physicians and other health professionals about their legal liability when they withheld cardiopulmonary resuscitation (CPR). Abuses of the DNR process came into public focus as a result of legal actions against several hospitals in the state. Courts and grand juries, confronted with these allegations of abuse, commented on the need for reform. The Task Force framed the DNR statute which, with alterations, became law on April 1, 1988 [10].

SURVEY OF THE MEMBERSHIP

Since the DNR law concerns itself with issues directly involved in medical practice, the New York State Chapter of the American College of Physicians became interested in the views of its members about the legislation and the ethical issues underlying it.

In December of 1989, twenty months after the institution of the law, a questionnaire was sent to 1600 members of the Chapter. Seven hundred and fifty-nine (47.4%) were completed and returned. Fifty-two percent of the respondents identified themselves as subspecialists; 34% were Associates of the College – medical residents and fellows. Nineteen percent selected academic medicine to describe their professional

R. Baker & M.A. Strosberg (eds.), Legislating Medical Ethics: A Study of the New York Do-Not-Resuscitate Law, 251–261.

activities. The rest were primarily in clinical practice; 55% carried out their professional activities in New York City; the rest in other communities in New York State. Forty-two percent had graduated from medical school after 1981; 27% before 1960.

Can we accept the responses of the 47% who completed the questionnaire as a valid indicator of the views of the membership of the Chapter? The consistency of the responses among subgroups of respondents supports this view. Whether analyzed separately by age, type of practice, size of community, or specialization, no significant differences in view could be detected. Of the 753 responses, 200 resulted from a second mailing to those who had not responded initially. This subset similarly did not differ significantly from the total group of responders, adding further support to the suggestion that those who failed to respond did not, as a group, hold views different from the responders.

RESULTS OF THE SURVEY

1. *General Aspects of the Law*

The law establishes the legal framework for the DNR process. It grants civil and criminal immunity to those who withhold or administer CPR in good faith accordance with its regulations. The fundamental premise on which the law rests is that of patient autonomy. In essence, it places no limitations on the right of the patient with capacity to take the decision to accept or reject CPR.

As indicated in Table 1, the respondents largely favored these general aspects of the law. A substantial number of all respondents, and a majority of those with an opinion, stated that the law had a "beneficial" effect on DNR policy in their hospital. Clear majorities held that the law clarified the placing of patients on DNR status and provided legal protection to those who did so. A majority rejected the contention that the procedural requirements of the law operated in such a way as to harm the interests of the patient.

Table 1. General Aspects of the DNR Law

1. What is the effect of the DNR law, as instituted in your hospital, on policy concerning resuscitation?

Beneficial 45% *Detrimental* 30% *None* 11% *No Opinion* 14%

2. The DNR law has reduced uncertainty about the rights and obligations of patients, their families and health care providers about resuscitation decisions:

Agree 57% *Disagree* 50% *No Opinion* 15%

3. The DNR law has made it too difficult to enter a DNR order and is thereby harming the interests of patients:

Agree 33% *Disagree* 50% *No Opinion* 17%

4. The DNR law has made it more likely that I will raise the issue of DNR status with my patients:

Agree 68% *Disagree* 30% *No Opinion* 2%

5. The DNR law has made it more likely that my patients and/or their families will raise the issue of DNR status with me:

Agree 40% *Disagree* 46% *No Opinion* 14%

6. The DNR law has enabled health care providers to issue lawful DNR orders without undue fear of liability:

Agree 54% *Disagree* 24% *No Opinion* 22%

2. *Therapeutic Exception*

The clearest application of the principle that the patient and not the physician will control decisionmaking with respect to DNR is seen in the way that the law handles the issue of the "therapeutic exception." In certain situations the physician is given the privilege of placing a patient on DNR status without obtaining consent because, in the view of the physician, the patient would suffer significant injury by having to confront the realities of prognosis and quality of life that influence the DNR decision. This traditional exercise of discretion by the physician is, to a great extent, eliminated by the New York DNR legislation. In order to invoke the "therapeutic exception" in writing a DNR order in New York State, the physician must establish that the injury that the patient would suffer through a discussion of the DNR option would be "immediate and severe." The Task Force further tightens this criterion by insisting that the potential injury be "life-threatening"; they give fatal arrhythmia and the immediate threat of suicide as examples of instances in which the physician may invoke the exception [12].

In order to establish the consensus on the Task Force's narrow therapeutic exception, the respondents were asked to choose from among the following three options the one most closely in accord with their own view:

Option 1: I agree with the position taken in the DNR law. With rare exceptions the possibility that such discussions will lead to an adverse effect is overcome by the importance of the patient's making an informed decision about CPR.

Option 2: I agree that in most instances patients should participate in the DNR decision. I feel, however, that exceptions should be broader than permitted under the law, and that a significant number of patients will be harmed by having to deal directly with this issue.

Option 3: Discussions of DNR status generally have an adverse effect on patients and/or the doctor-patient interaction. There should be no requirement in the law to place these issues before patients.

The respondents selected among the three options as follows:

Option 1: 45%;
Option 2: 47%;
Option 3: 9%.

The Associate members supported the DNR law and the importance of patient participation even more strongly than did their senior colleagues. They voted as follows:

Option 1: 52%;
Option 2: 46%;
Option 3: 2%.

3. *DNR Status and Procedures other than CPR*

The New York State DNR law is explicit in defining the right of patients on DNR status to treatments other than CPR. Eighty percent of the respondents expressed agreement with this position. When asked to apply this principle to specific measures, 69% would include chronic dialysis, and 61% care in the Intensive Care Unit among those procedures to which patients on DNR status should continue to be entitled.

Seventy-seven percent felt that in the hospitals in which they operate, patients on DNR status do, in fact, receive treatments other than CPR which are appropriate for their condition. Only 22%, however, credit the DNR law for making it more likely that hospitals adhere to this policy.

4. *The DNR Law and "Medical Futility"*

The law does not require CPR in every instance in which a patient dies without a DNR order in place [15]. It does not, however, permit the physician to place his patient on DNR status because he considers CPR to be "futile" or inappropriate, in the absence of written consent by the patient or surrogate. The survey indicates that a substantial majority of the respondents are in fundamental disagreement with this principle. Seventy-seven percent of the respondents agreed with the following statement:

> There are situations in which resuscitation is so clearly inappropriate or futile on medical grounds that physicians should be permitted to institute DNR status based on clinical judgment, without obtaining consent.

The differences between the views of the respondents and those underlying the DNR law become more striking when the respondents are given the opportunity to define the limits of their concepts of 'futility' and 'inappropriateness.' This was accomplished by asking about two specific clinical examples:

Case 1: A 74-year-old patient with terminal cancer has the capability of making decisions. He is receiving only palliative therapy and his physician believes that prompt resuscitation might enable him to live a few days but without hope of real improvement or discharge from the hospital. There is a 50% risk that resuscitation will leave him on a respirator or in a chronic vegetative state.

Case 2: An 85-year-old patient suffers from Alzheimer's disease. He is not oriented to his surroundings, does not recognize his family and hardly communicates. He is transferred to your care for the treatment of pneumonia.

Seventy-seven and seventy-five percent, respectively, of the respondents felt that it would be proper for the attending physician to place that patient on DNR status without having to obtain consent from the patient or his surrogate. The perception that CPR is frequently administered inappropriately was reinforced when the respondents were asked about practice in their hospitals. In the strongest consensus revealed in the entire survey, 88% felt that, in the hospital in which they practiced, patients dying without a DNR order would undergo some effort at resuscitation, whether or not it was "appropriate." Forty-three percent felt that the DNR law made such resuscitation more likely and 37% felt that the law made it less likely that such efforts at resuscitation would occur.

5. *Life-sustaining Measures other than CPR*

The respondents were asked whether they were opposed on moral or religious grounds to the withholding or discontinuation of mechanical ventilation or nutritional support from patients in a persistent vegetative state. For mechanical ventilation, only 11% answered "yes"; for nutritional support, the number rose to 28%. Those who opposed withdrawal either of ventilation or nutrition did not hold views different from those of their colleagues concerning issues related to DNR.

DISCUSSION

The New York State DNR law has provided a unique opportunity to study the attitudes of a group of physicians about the issues underlying the application of CPR together with their response to legislative regulation of this procedure. The participating physicians, members of the New York Chapter of the American College of Physicians, constitute the majority of internists in New York and provide care for patients throughout the state at both a primary and consultative level.

Their view of the law can best be described as ambivalent. As a group, the members of the New York State Chapter of the American College of Physicians do not concur with the published view of some New York physicians who find the law to be an unwarranted and destructive imposition on medical practice [13].

Adoption of the New York DNR law was stimulated by publicly portrayed evidence that the DNR process in New York hospitals was often carried out in a deceptive way, with uncertainty about its legal status, and in clear violation of the mandate for patient involvement in decisionmaking. The positions expressed by the respondents indicated that major segments and, in many instances, the majority of the polled physicians shared these concerns and were accepting of a regulatory process that acted to alleviate them.

The respondents expressed, in several ways, their support for the involvement of patients or surrogates in decision making about CPR. By greater than a 2:1 margin, they credit the law with having increased the likelihood that they and their patients will communicate about DNR status. More than 90% of respondents rejected the idea that, in general, discussion of prognosis and life values necessary to make informed decisions about CPR had a sufficiently adverse effect on patients to preclude their participation in the process. This position is in accord with that of a group of nationally prominent physicians published in 1984 [18].

Although 42% of all respondents and a majority of the Associate members concurred with the very narrow limits of the therapeutic exception as defined in law, nearly half felt that adherence to this narrow exception led them to discuss DNR in instances in which it was harmful to their patients. This view has been expressed in at least two reports by New York physicians who describe instances in which they felt that harm to patients had resulted from adherence to the law ([14], [19]).

The clearest conflict between the views of the respondents and the DNR law concerns the issue of "medical futility." A large majority of the respondents would allow physicians to place patients on DNR status without obtaining consent when they consider CPR to be futile on medical grounds. The law not only largely forbids unilateral actions by physicians based on the concept of "medical futility", it defines futility in a much narrower way than would the majority of respondents.

As defined by the DNR law, "futility" is limited to circumstances in which resuscitation will not accomplish its goal of restarting cardiac or respiratory function. The respondents would broadly extend this definition to permit physicians the prerogative to withhold CPR unilaterally when it becomes inappropriate. In case 1 (given above), the inappropriateness stems from poor prognosis and the decreased effectiveness of CPR in the presence of a major underlying illness – in this case metastatic malignancy. In the second case, the inappropriateness of CPR is a product of reduced quality of life (and perhaps age), whereas prognosis for duration of life is not a pertinent consideration.

Faber-Langendoen has proposed that terminal patients with metastatic malignant disease, like Case 1 in the questionnaire, be placed automatically on DNR status [4]. Hacker and Murphy have suggested that nursing home patients be placed on DNR status without consent ([5], [9]). Their justification would, in general, apply to Case 2. The right of physicians to impose DNR orders based on their medical judgments has also been justified on the basis of a "humane paternalism" that sees a role for physicians in protecting the patient from inappropriate and adverse procedures that have been mandated by the patient's surrogate [3].

The views of the respondents concerning the imposition of DNR status without consent conflict not only with the DNR law but a large and probably dominant body of bioethical thought [6]. Patient control of decisions that involve issues of quality of life has been reinforced by the recent studies of Uhlmann and Pearlman [16]. They found that the physicians' perception of quality of life of elderly patients differed consistently from that expressed by the patients themselves.

In a commentary concerning the DNR law, Tracy Miller, counsel for the Governor's Task Force, refers to the therapeutic exception as a "loophole." She depicts limitations to patient or surrogate control based on medical futility as "exceptions [that] will swallow the rule" [8]. By so doing, she raises an important question common to all regulations designed to control physician behavior: Is it possible to write laws that permit desirable limitations on absolute control by patients of the decisionmaking process without undermining the fundamental intent of the legislation? It is likely that the limitations on physician prerogative embodied in the DNR law reflect, in addition to a strong commitment to patient autonomy, concern over this issue.

In addition to control of decisionmaking in choices about life-prolonging measures, the need to communicate with patients or surrogates has been emphasized as a separate responsibility of physicians. For instance, in the recent recommendations by the American Medical Association, physicians could impose DNR status without specific consent, but only if they are acting in accord with the patients' values that they have established by communication with the patient [2]. The survey of the membership of the New York Chapter does not specifically address the respondents' views about the requisite communication before they impose DNR status without consent in the two instances cited. It is likely, however, that in view of their general support for those aspects of the law that enhanced communication, even those who favored DNR without consent would have communicated such decisions to the patient in Case 1 and the family in Case 2. The overwhelming support by the respondents of the principle that patients on DNR status do not forgo their right to appropriate procedures other than CPR would suggest that, while the physicians would wish to place the patients in question on DNR status, they would not give up an active professional involvement in their care.

McClung and Kamer, and Ahronheim *et al.* have shown that while the DNR law seems to have enhanced documentation and communication about CPR, it has not affected the actual practice of resuscitation in New York ([1], [7]). In the largest consensus in the study, the respondents concur. Eighty-seven percent feel that, when patients die without a DNR order in place, resuscitation is usually attempted even when inappropriate, and that the DNR law, if anything, has made this more likely. In order to deal effectively with this issue, we shall have to await a fuller understanding of the factors that lead to patients dying without having expressed their wishes about resuscitation. Actions throughout the country at both the state and federal levels to encourage advanced directives may have an important impact on this issue ([11], [17]).

Several state legislatures, following the lead of New York, have enacted laws that either require their Departments of Health to develop protocols for the establishment of DNR status or, as in Georgia, define circumstances, as in the New York DNR law, under which CPR can legally be withheld. Since ultimately these legislative initiatives are played out in the patient-doctor interaction, the views of the involved physicians must be understood and reconciled with the intent of the legislative action for the regulations to succeed.

ACKNOWLEDGEMENTS

I am deeply indebted to the Executive Office of the New York State Chapter of the American College of Physicians under the direction of Adrienne Rosoff, and to the Philadelphia Office of the College, with particular gratitude to Lois Snyder, Esq. I also wish to acknowledge with gratitude the statistical analyses carried out by Mr. Thomas M. Terp.

The study was carried out while I was President of the New York State Chapter. I am also grateful to the Officers and Council of the New York Chapter for their support, and particularly to those members who took the time to complete the questionnaire.

BIBLIOGRAPHY

1. Ahronheim, J.C., Maheswaran, S. and Rosenberg, C.: 1992, 'Impact of Do-Not-Resuscitate Legislation on the Use of Cardiopulmonary Resuscitation in Three Teaching Hospitals', *New York State Journal of Medicine* **92**, 181–185.
2. American Medical Association Council on Judicial and Ethical Affairs: 1991, 'Guidelines for the Appropriate Use of Do-Not-Resuscitate Orders', *Journal of the American Medical Association* **265**, 1868–1871.
3. Brennan, T.A.: 1987, 'Do-Not-Resuscitate Orders for the Incompetent Patient in the Absence of Family Consent', *Law Medicine and Health Care* **14**, 13–19.
4. Faber-Langendoen, K.: 1991, 'Resuscitation of Patients With Metastatic Cancer. Is Transient Benefit Still Futile?', *Archives of Internal Medicine* **151**, 235–239.
5. Hackler, J.C. and Hiller, F.C.: 1990, 'Family Consent to Orders Not to Resuscitate: Reconsidering Hospital Policy', *Journal of the American Medical Association* **264**, 1281–1283.
6. Lantos, J.D. *et al.*: 1989, 'The Illusion of Futility in Clinical Practice,' *American Journal of Medicine* **87**, 81–84.
7. McClung, J.A. and Kamer, R.S.: 1990, 'Legislating Ethics: Implications of New York's Do-Not-Resuscitate Law,' *New England Journal of Medicine* **323**, 270–272.
8. Miller, T.E.: 1989, 'Do-Not-Resuscitate Orders: Public Policy and Patient Autonomy,' *Law Medicine and Health Care* **17**, 245–254.
9. Murphy, D.J.: 1988, 'Do-Not-Resuscitate Orders: Time for Reappraisal in Long-Term-Care Institutions', *Journal of the American Medical Association* **260**, 2098–2101.
10. New York Public Health Law, Article 29-B, Statute 413-A, effective April 1, 1988.
11. New York Public Health Law, Health Care Proxy Act, § 2980–2994, 1991.
12. New York State Task Force on Life and the Law: 1988, *Do Not Resuscitate Orders: The Proposed Legislation and Report of the New York State Task Force on Life and the Law*, 2nd edition, Albany, New York.
13. Praeger, K.M.: March 9, 1989, 'How CPR can Threaten the Desperately Ill', *Wall Street Journal*, 16.

14. Swendler, P.T.: 1989, 'Reflections of the New York Do-Not-Resuscitate Law,' *New York State Journal of Medicine* **89**, 57.
15. Swidler, R.N.: 1989, 'The Presumption of Consent in New York State's Do-Not-Resuscitate Law', *New York State Journal of Medicine* **89**, 69–72.
16. Uhlmann, R.F. and Pearlman, R.A.: 1991, 'Perceived Quality of Life and Preferences for Life-Sustaining Treatments in Older Adults,' *Archives of Internal Medicine* **151**, 495–497.
17. United States Congress: December 1991, 'Patient Self-Determination Act'.
18. Wanzar, S.H. *et al.*: 1984, 'The Physician's Responsibility toward Hopelessly Ill Patients', *New England Journal of Medicine* **310**, 955–959.
19. Zugar, A.: 1989, 'High Hopes', *Journal of the American Medical Association* **262**, 2988.

ROBERT BAKER, MARTIN A. STROSBERG, JOSEF SCHMEE, I. ALAN FEIN, VIRGINIA JONAS DERSCH, JONATHAN BYNUM AND PHILIP OATES

THE 1988 DNR REFORMS: A COMPARATIVE STUDY OF THE IMPACT OF THE NEW YORK DNR LAW AND THE JCAHO ACCREDITATION REQUIREMENTS

The DNR reforms of 1988, a coincident trial of both the legislative and the self-regulatory routes to reform, provide an ideal vehicle for assessing the impact of bioethical reform. They can be construed as inadvertant "natural experiment," a comparative trial of the effects of reforming DNR practices by means of an amendment to the state's public health law, or by means of a change in the accreditation policies of the Joint Commission on Accreditation of Health-Care Organizations (hereafter, JCAHO). In the study described below, we attempt to assess the impact of these two different routes to mandatory bioethical reform: the JCAHO's latitudinarian professional self-regulative approach; and New York's use of a statute enforced by the state department of health and the law courts.

Methodological Issues

One reason for the paucity of empirical research on medical ethics is the difficulty of mounting any empirical investigation of moral phenomena – especially on a wide-scale. Even basic empirical data is elusive. For example, the Zimmerman-Knaus multi-institutional study of DNR orders, (the best account we have of the prevalence of such orders) involves only 19 ICUs in 13 hospitals (10 teaching) and makes no pretences at being either regionally or nationally representative. Problems arise because most standard methodologies – direct observation, interview, chart analysis – can only be instituted for a relatively small number of individuals or institutions [21]. To surmount these limitations, we turned to an innovative strategy: We surveyed a large population of informants (primarily ICU directors) familiar with DNR practices at the institutions in which they work.

This strategy presupposes that ICU directors are familiar with DNR practices at the institutions in which they work and could serve as representatives for the views of their colleagues. To assure ourselves of the correctness of these assumptions (and to garner background information to interpret responses to open-ended questions) we conducted on-site

R. Baker & M.A. Strosberg (eds.), Legislating Medical Ethics: A Study of the New York Do-Not-Resuscitate Law, 263–301.

personal interviews with the medical director, the nursing director, and most of the medical and nursing staff of a surgical intensive care unit in an over-600-bed urban teaching hospital and also with their counterparts at the single ICU of a small (under 150-beds) community non-teaching hospital. Our initial assumptions were only partially correct: for while the characterization of DNR policy and practice given by the *medical* director coincided with that of the fellows, residents, and other *physicians* who work on the ICU; it differed from those offered by critical care *nursing* directors and the nurses. Similar differences surfaced in the questionnaire responses. We therefore present the responses of these two types of critical care directors separately. This caveat aside, throughout this study we treat both ICU medical and nursing directors as reliable representatives of the perceptions of their fellow physicians and nurses.

In the New York section of this study we also surveyed hematologist-oncologists. H/Os stand in a different relationship to the hospital and to their patients than ICU directors. Whereas ICU directors have a long-term administrative relationship with the hospital but usually only a short-term relationship with most of their patients, H/Os have a long-term and often deeply personal relationship with their patients, but seldom have a long-term administrative relationship with the hospital. Unfortunately, the relative lack of administrative responsibilities may have affected H/O response rates. ICU directors responded to our survey, in part, because they consider it their administrative duty to undertake such tasks. H/O's were under no such obligation – which may explain their lower response rates. These lower rates may over-represent strong positive or (more likely) negative reactions to DNR reform.

Studying DNR practices prior to 1988 is difficult for the very reasons that prompted bioethical reform. The often covert, poorly documented, non-standardized DNR orders given at medical institutions which lacked formal policies make pre-reform, post-reform comparisons problematic. The post-reform environment further complicates the issue: to ask physicians whether they themselves performed activities later declared illicit, courts distortion [1]. These difficulties are not uncommon in empirical research on morality; to address them we adapted questionnaire techniques developed by James Rest and other moral psychologists [15].

More specifically, we attempted to measure the perceived impact of bioethical reform by means of a multi-part questionnaire which, in addition to standard closed-ended and open-ended questions, presented 16 third person pre/post questions to practitioners in randomized order.

These questions took the form: *Please indicate your assessment (on a scale of 0% to 100%) of the likelihood that individual clinicians on the ICU at which you work would have performed the following action in March 1988______and April 1989/90______.*

1) *Discussing DNR orders with patients at risk for CPR;*
2) *Discussing DNR orders with the families of incompetent patients at risk for CPR;*
3) *Writing a DNR order at the request of a patient;*
4) *Writing a DNR order for a terminal patient with the patient's consent;*
5) *Writing a DNR order for an incompetent patient with family consent;*
6) *Giving an undocumented verbal DNR order for a terminal patient without informing the patient or the family;*
7) *Writing a DNR order without informing the patient or the family;*
8) *Writing a DNR order after informing the patient but without consent;*
9) *Interpreting a DNR order as a "signal" not to initiate life-sustaining interventions other than CPR;*
10) *Interpreting a DNR order as a "signal" to discontinue life-sustaining interventions (e.g., ventilators, naso-gastric feeding tubes).*
11) *Writing DNR orders for patients who may benefit from resuscitation;*
12) *Failing to write a DNR order because of family ambivalence;*
13) *Failing to write a DNR order for a terminal, developmentally disabled patient because of the attitude of an institution or guardian;*
14) *Failing to write a DNR order for a terminal patient because of bureaucratic technicalities;*
15) *Administering futile CPR to irreversibly terminal patients;*
16) *That terminal patients and their families will be treated humanely and decently with respect to DNR.*

By asking practitioners to compare estimated likelihoods of *actions*, we obtained reports on activities that leave no documentary trail, e.g., discussion with patients, slow/show-coding , etc.; by making the questions *retrospective* we were able to assess perceptions of policies and practices both before and after the 1988 DNR reforms. By using the *third person* (i.e. by asking the likelihood that *clinicians* would have performed certain actions on the ICUs at which they work) we avoid asking clinicians to directly indict *themselves* of wrong-doing. Finally, since we are attempting to measure *change*, we have arranged for responses to be given in the form

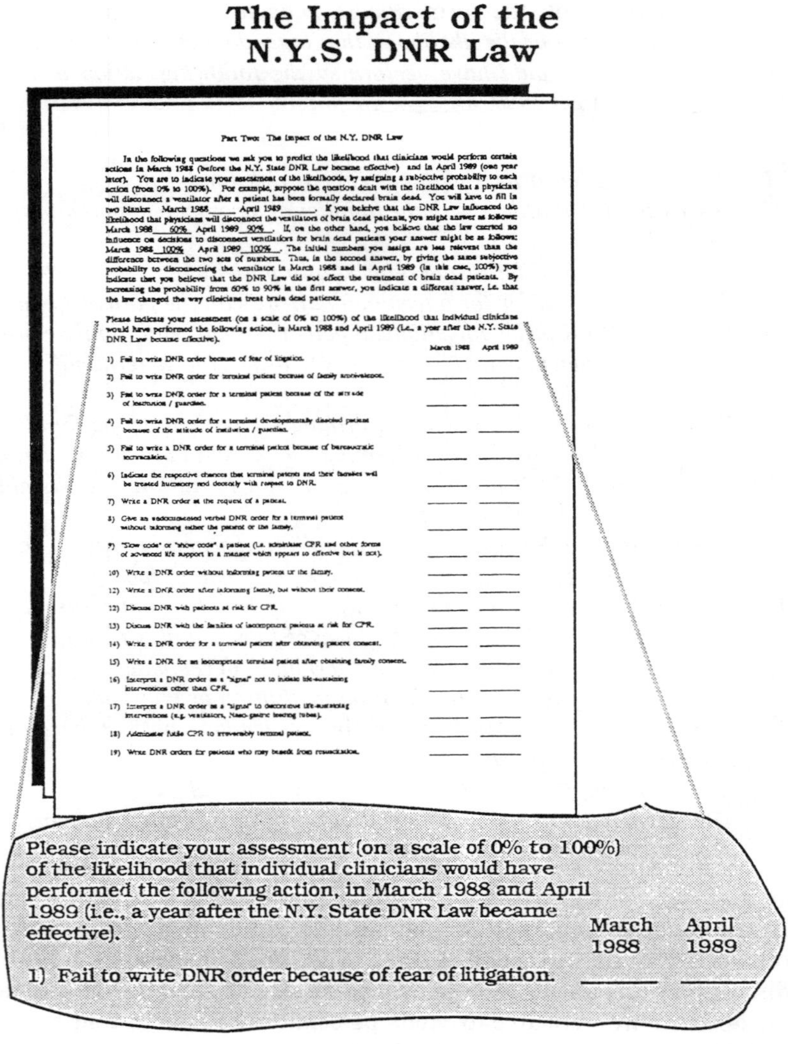

The Impact of the N.Y.S. DNR Law

Part Two: The Impact of the N.Y. DNR Law

In the following questions we ask you to predict the likelihood that clinicians would perform certain actions in March 1988 (before the N.Y. State DNR Law became effective) and in April 1989 (one year later). You are to indicate your assessment of the likelihoods, by assigning a subjective probability to each action (from 0% to 100%). For example, suppose the question dealt with the likelihood that a physician will disconnect a ventilator after a patient has been formally declared brain dead. You will have to fill in two blanks: March 1988______ April 1989______. If you believe that the DNR Law influenced the likelihood that physicians will disconnect the ventilators of brain dead patients, you might answer as follows: March 1988__60%__ April 1989__90%__. If, on the other hand, you believe that the law exerted no influence on decisions to disconnect ventilators for brain dead patients your answer might be as follows: March 1988__100%__ April 1989__100%__. The initial numbers you assign are less relevant than the difference between the two sets of numbers. Thus, in the second answer, by giving the same subjective probability to disconnecting the ventilator in March 1988 and in April 1989 (in this case, 100%) you indicate that you believe that the DNR Law did not effect the treatment of brain dead patients. By increasing the probability from 60% to 90% in the first answer, you indicate a different answer, i.e. that the law changed the way clinicians treat brain dead patients.

Please indicate your assessment (on a scale of 0% to 100%) of the likelihood that individual clinicians would have performed the following action, in March 1988 and April 1989 (i.e., a year after the N.Y. State DNR Law became effective).

	March 1988	April 1989
1) Fail to write DNR order because of fear of litigation.	______	______
2) Fail to write DNR order for terminal patient because of family ambivalence.	______	______
3) Fail to write DNR order for a terminal patient because of the attitude of institution / guardian.	______	______
4) Fail to write DNR order for a terminal developmentally disabled patient because of the attitude of institution / guardian.	______	______
5) Fail to write a DNR order for a terminal patient because of bureaucratic technicalities.	______	______
6) Indicate the respective chances that terminal patients and their families will be treated humanely and decently with respect to DNR.	______	______
7) Write a DNR order at the request of a patient.	______	______
8) Give an undocumented verbal DNR order for a terminal patient without informing either the patient or the family.	______	______
9) "Slow code" or "show code" a patient (i.e. administer CPR and other forms of advanced life support in a manner which appears to effective but is not).	______	______
10) Write a DNR order without informing patient or the family.	______	______
12) Write a DNR order after informing family, but without their consent.	______	______
12) Discuss DNR with patients at risk for CPR.	______	______
13) Discuss DNR with the families of incompetent patients at risk for CPR.	______	______
14) Write a DNR order for a terminal patient after obtaining patient consent.	______	______
15) Write a DNR for an incompetent terminal patient after obtaining family consent.	______	______
16) Interpret a DNR order as a "signal" not to initiate life-sustaining interventions other than CPR.	______	______
17) Interpret a DNR order as a "signal" to discontinue life-sustaining interventions (e.g. ventilators, Naso-gastric feeding tubes).	______	______
18) Administer futile CPR to irreversibly terminal patient.	______	______
19) Write DNR orders for patients who may benefit from resuscitation.	______	______

Please indicate your assessment (on a scale of 0% to 100%) of the likelihood that individual clinicians would have performed the following action, in March 1988 and April 1989 (i.e., a year after the N.Y. State DNR Law became effective).

	March 1988	April 1989
1) Fail to write DNR order because of fear of litigation.	______	______

Fig. 1.

of two percentages, a pre-reform 1988 percentage (e.g., 60%) and a post-reform 1989 percentage (e.g., 90%). The percentages given as responses are amenable to quantitative analysis by the Wilcoxon Signed-Rank test ([14], [18]), which weighs both the *proportion* of respondents reporting a decrease, or (as in the example cited) an increase, in an activity, as well as the *extent* of the change (in this instance 30 points, i.e., the difference between 60% and 90%). For reasons of clarity, the information we present in illustrative tables is simplified and may contain only one dimension of the data (either the direction of change or the extent of change) our significance tests, however, always use full data.

In 1988-89 we conducted a telephone survey of New York acute care hospitals and found that 281 had ICUs (exclusive of neonatal, perinatal and pediatric ICUs – which we did not survey because they deal with special problems). Six-hundred and twenty-six board-certified H/Os were listed by the American Board of Medical Specialties. Questionnaires were mailed to the entire population of both groups at the beginning and end of the summer of 1989. Cumulatively, 223 (98 CCMD, 125 CCND) responses were received from the medical and/or nursing directors at one or more of the ICUs at 127 (49%) of New York's acute care hospitals. Twenty-eight percent of H/Os (172/626) responded. The responses to the two mailings were not significantly different. The ICU director responses were from 56% of Upstate-rural hospitals, 52% of Upstate-urban and 43% of N.Y.C-Metropolitan hospitals. As Table 1 illustrates, this distribution in each sample approximates the geographic distribution of the populations from which they were drawn.

We did not attempt to replicate the New York survey on a national scale; instead we build upon it by *constructing* a set of Non-New York ICU medical directors comparable in age, experience, etc. to the New York medical director population. (We chose *medical* directors because, for reasons which will become apparent shortly, they were the most representative.) To garner our comparison sample we placed a modified version of the assessment questionnaire in the registration packet for the May 1990 (San Francisco) meeting of the Society of Critical Care Medicine. Convention questionnaires generate low yields (in this case 144 responses, or approximately 14% of the estimated attendees) but, as anticipated, after culling out nurses, pediatric intensivists and New Yorkers (19% of the respondents), we had a sample of 81 non-New York critical care physicians from 39 states, 56% of whom were medical

Table 1. Geographic Distribution of Responses

	NYS Acute Care Hospitals with ICU's			
	Downstate	Upstate-Urban	Upstate-Rural	Total
Hospital Population	130 (46%)	90 (32%)	61 (22%)	281 (100%)
Hospital Sample	56 (41%)	47 (34%)	34 (25%)	137 (100%)

	NYS Board-Certified H/O's			
	Downstate	Upstate-Urban	Upstate-Rural	Total
H/O Population	471 (77%)	130 (21%)	12 (2%)	613 (100%)
H/O Sample	131 (76%)	36 (21%)	6 (3%)	173 (100%)

directors. Henceforth we shall refer to this group as the "national comparison group," or the "national sample."

To be useful, the national sample of 81 medical intensivists had to be comparable to the New York sample of 98 medical directors, not only in size, but also in age and critical care experience. It was: 46% of New Yorkers and 49% of the national sample were between thirty-one and forty years old; 35% of New Yorkers and 36% of the national sample were between forty-one and fifty; 58% of New Yorkers and 62% of the national sample had between six and fifteen years critical care experience; exactly the same percentage of both samples, 19%, had over fifteen-years experience. Moreover, their experience with writing DNR orders was also comparable: 69% of the national comparison group and 59% of New Yorkers work on ICUs where one or more DNR orders were written per week.

One possibly significant difference between the two groups is that the national comparison group works at larger hospitals: 82% work at ICUs in hospitals with over 300 beds, compared to 51% of New Yorkers. This may bias the national sample in favor of DNR reform, for in New York, medical directors at large teaching hospitals responded more favorably to DNR reform – they were not, however, any less likely to report the problems attendant upon reform (see Dersch's analysis in the next chapter).

1988 DNR reforms Impact on Discussion, Consent and Documentation of DNR

Table 2. New Yorkers' Estimated Likelihood of Discussion/Consent/Documentation

	Clinicians Reporting Change	At Institutions Whose Practices Change After DNR Reform			At Institutions With No Change
		1988 (A) +	Change (B) =	1989 (C)	1988/9 (D)
Discussion					
Q1. Discussing DNR with patients at risk for CPR.					
CCND **	66%	37.3%	38.5%	75.8%	50.5%
CCMD **	66%	35.5%	30.7%	66.2%	57.8%
H/O **	70%	34.9%	39.6%	74.5%	55.4%
Q2. Discuss DNR with families of incompetent patients at risk for CPR.					
CCND **	73%	41.1%	41.4%	82.6%	64.1%
CCMD **	66%	44.9%	32.8%	77.7%	75.8%
H/O **	67%	47.2%	36.7%	83.9%	79.3%
Consent					
Q3. Writing a DNR order at the request of a patient.					
CCND **	66%	45.5%	44.4%	89.9%	85.7%
CCMD **	37%	58.9%	26.6%	85.3%	85.3%
H/O **	33%	46.8%	41.2%	88.8%	85.3%
Q4. Writing a DNR order for terminal patient with patient consent.					
CCND **	67%	47.5%	42.8%	90.3%	94.0%
CCMD **	47%	44.9%	33.3%	78.9%	96.8%
H/O **	42%	43.1%	45.9%	89.0%	89.3%
Q5. Writing a DNR order for incompetent patient with family consent.					
CCND **	64%	48.8%	43.2%	92.0%	92.5%
CCMD **	48%	48.3%	34.0%	82.9%	92.7%
H/O **	69%	45.9%	43.8%	89.7%	88.6%
Non-Disclosure					
Q6. Giving an undocumented verbal DNR for a terminal patient without informing the patient or the family					
CCND **	62%	57.8%	–50.4%	7.5%	8.4%
CCMD **	59%	36.6%	–29.7%	6.9%	5.0%
H/O **	71%	50.9%	–42.6%	8.3%	7.9%
Q7. Writing DNR order without informing the patient or the family.					
CCND **	50%	48.0%	–43.0%	5.0%	6.7%
CCMD **	53%	34.8%	–30.3%	4.5%	12.6%
H/O **	34%	42.2%	–37.0%	5.2%	3.0%

Table 2. New Yorkers' Continued

	Clinicians Reporting Change	At Institutions Whose Practices Change After DNR Reform			At Institutions With No Change
		1988 (A) +	Change (B) =	1989 (C)	1988/9 (D)
Q8. Writing DNR order after informing the family but without consent.					
CCND **	49%	53.2%	–45.4%	7.9%	1.0%
CCMD **	43%	36.1%	–31.9%	4.2%	12.0%
H/O **	55%	43.1%	39.3%	3.8%	10.7%
Interpreting DNR as a Signal to Discontinued Other Life-Support					
Q9. Interpreting a DNR order as a 'signal' not to initiate life-sustaining interventions other than CPR.					
CCND §	47%		[No Significant Change]		43.2%
CCMD §	57%		[No Significant Change]		45.6%
H/O §	71%		[No Significant Change]		43.7%
Q10. Interpreting a DNR order as a 'signal' to discontinue life-sustaining interventions (e.g., ventilators, naso-gastric feed tubes).					
CCND §	53%		[No Significant Change]		20.0%
CCMD §	63%		[No Significant Change]		26.4%
H/O §	67%		[No Significant Change]		25.3%

** = p≤01; * = p≤05; § = Not Satisfically Significant
Sample Size: CCND's = 113; CCMD's = 83; H/O's = 154

What was the impact of the mandatory DNR reforms of 1988? As the responses in Tables 2 and 3 indicate, both nationally and in New York, *the reforms achieved their objectives with respect to disclosure, documentation and consent – and even with respect to discussion.* There is unanimous agreement, in all categories of clinician surveyed, in both New York and in the national comparison group, that consequent to the 1988 reforms there was a substantial increase in the likelihood that DNR orders would be *discussed* with patients at risk for CPR, and with their families (Q1, 2), and that any DNR orders implemented would have *patient-family consent* (Q3-5). On the specific issue of direct *discussion of DNR orders with patients*, they report that the likelihood of such discussions occurring on the ICUs on which they worked *doubled* (Q1). Conversely the relatively standard practices of so-called "slow" and "show codes" (defined as administering CPR and other forms of ACLS in a manner which appears to be effective but is not) and other covert, undocumented DNR orders decreased to the point of non-existence (Q6-8).

EVIDENCE THAT THE LAW WORKS

(NEW YORK: DNR WITHOUT DISCUSSION AND/OR CONSENT)

Likelihood of "Slow Code" or "Show Code" a patient (i.e., administering CPR and other forms of ACLS in a manner which appears to be effective but is not)

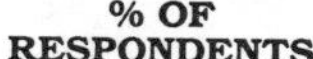

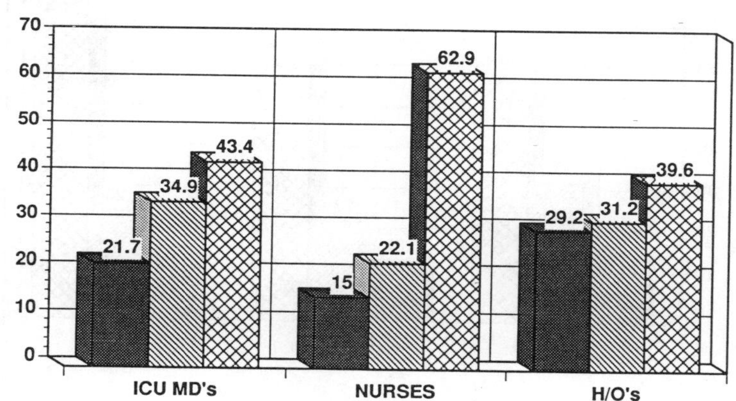

% OF CLINICIANS WHO THOUGHT THAT LIKELIHOOD HAD:

INCREASED
NO CHANGE
DECREASED

Fig. 2a.

EVIDENCE THAT THE LAW WORKS

(NEW YORK: DNR WITHOUT DISCUSSION AND/OR CONSENT)

Likelihood of giving an undocumented verbal DNR order for a terminal patient without informing either the patient or family

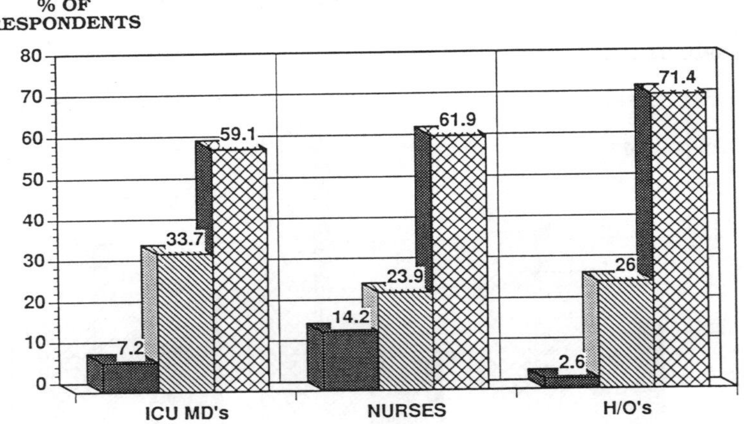

% OF CLINICIANS WHO THOUGHT THAT LIKELIHOOD HAD:

INCREASED

NO CHANGE

DECREASED

Fig. 2b.

EVIDENCE THAT THE LAW WORKS

(NEW YORK: DISCUSSION OF DNR)

Likelihood of writing a DNR order without informing patient or family

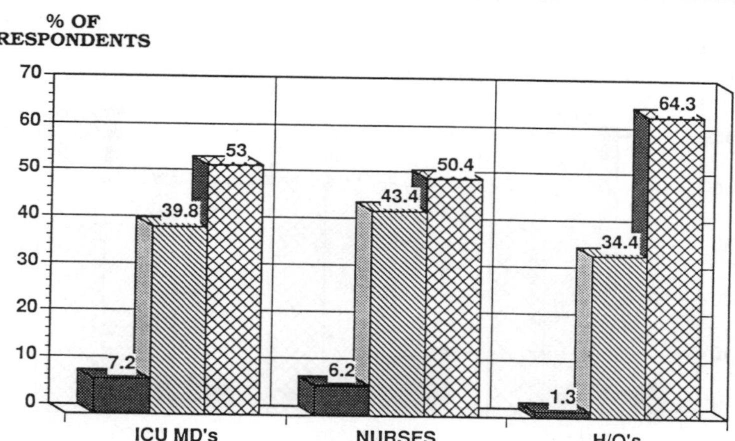

% OF CLINICIANS WHO THOUGHT THAT LIKELIHOOD HAD:

- INCREASED
- NO CHANGE
- DECREASED

Fig. 2c.

EVIDENCE THAT THE LAW WORKS

(NEW YORK: DNR WITHOUT DISCUSSION AND/OR CONSENT)

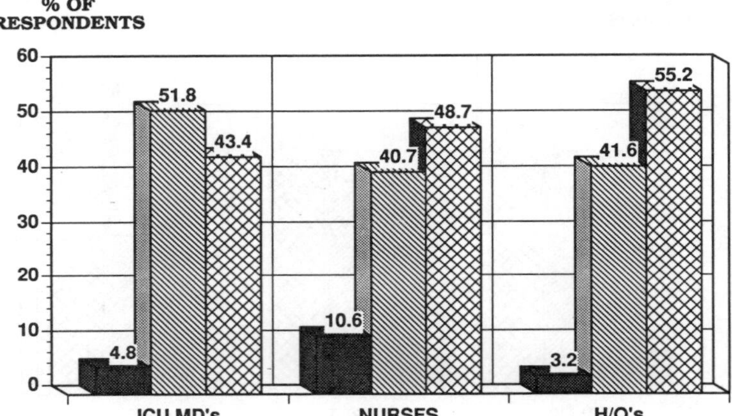

Fig. 2d.

EVIDENCE THAT THE LAW WORKS
(NEW YORK: DISCUSSION OF DNR)

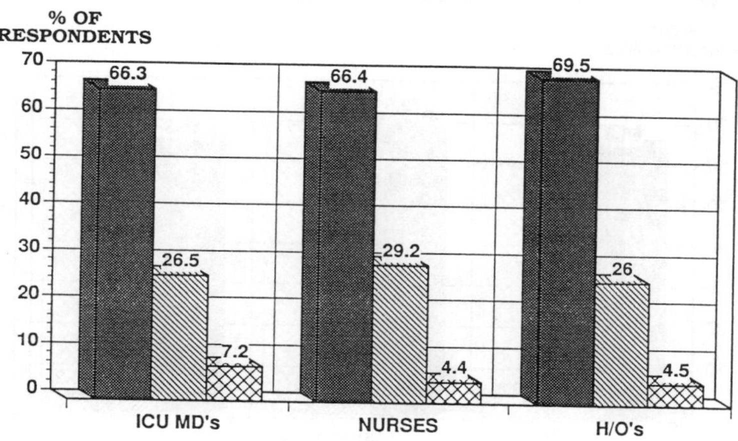

Fig. 2e.

EVIDENCE THAT THE LAW WORKS

(NEW YORK: DISCUSSION OF DNR)

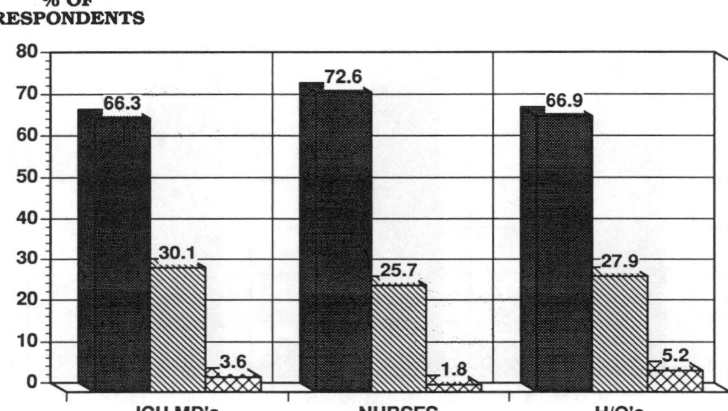

% OF CLINICIANS WHO THOUGHT THAT LIKELIHOOD HAD:

INCREASED

NO CHANGE

DECREASED

Fig. 2f.

EVIDENCE THAT THE LAW WORKS

(NEW YORK: DISCUSSION OF DNR)

Likelihood of writing a DNR order at the request of a patient

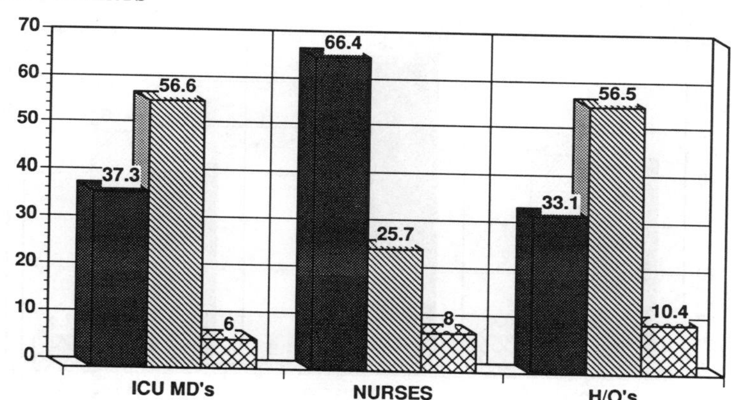

% OF CLINICIANS WHO THOUGHT THAT LIKELIHOOD HAD:

- INCREASED
- NO CHANGE
- DECREASED

Fig. 2g.

EVIDENCE THAT THE LAW WORKS

(NEW YORK: DISCUSSION OF DNR)

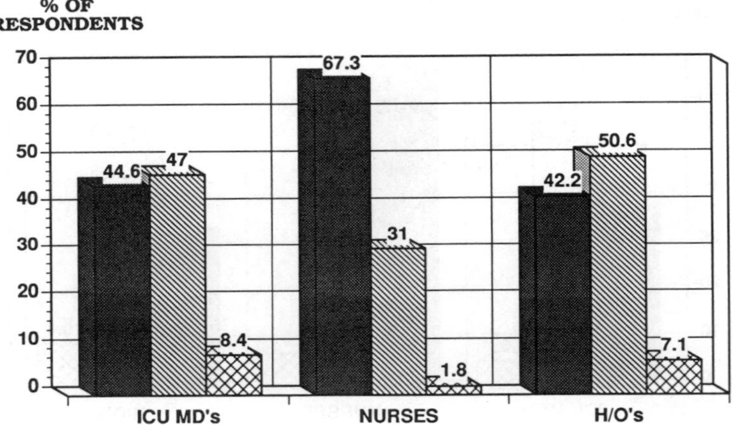

Fig. 2h.

EVIDENCE THAT THE LAW WORKS

(NEW YORK: DISCUSSION OF DNR)

Likelihood of writing a DNR order for an incompetent terminal patient after obtaining family consent

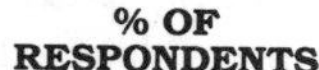

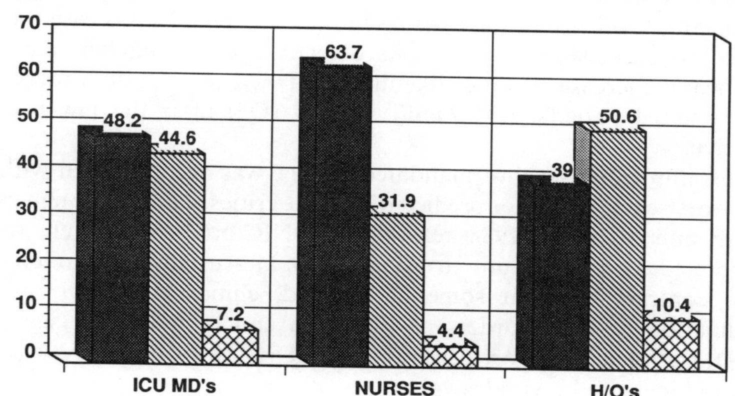

% OF CLINICIANS WHO THOUGHT THAT LIKELIHOOD HAD:

INCREASED
NO CHANGE
DECREASED

Fig. 2i.

The significance of these findings comes into focus if one recalls that the major studies of physician-patient-family *discussion* prior to 1988 had found that physicians *almost never* discussed DNR orders directly with patients, and were even reluctant to do so with families ([2]. [3], [8], [12], [13]).

One of the most important changes effected by the law in New York was the introduction of true legal surrogacy, that is the legal right of a family member to act as a surrogate for a patient in making a DNR decision, even in those cases where the patient left no "clear and convincing" evidence of their wishes in these matters. In this case too the DNR law successfully achieved its objective, since clinicians report a significant increase in the likelihood of writing DNR orders for incapacitated patients *with family consent* (Q5) after the law became effective.

This impressive level of mandated change was accomplished without the "worst-case" scenarios predicted by some critics. Thus, although, both before and after the 1988 reforms, a DNR order was likely to be interpreted as a *signal* not to initiate new life-sustaining interventions (Q9), contrary to what some had feared, clinicians *do not see* the legitimation of DNR orders as the "thin end of a wedge" signaling *withdrawal* of life support other than CPR (Q 10), since there was not reported increase in withdrawal.

The Equal Effectiveness of both Professionally and Legally Mandated Reforms

Comparing the percentages in the post-reform 89/90 columns in Table 3 will immediately make evident, that both the JCAHO reforms and the New York DNR law were equally effective. The mechanism of DNR reform in New York was an amendment to public health law (enforced by the Department of Health and the law courts); the JCAHO reforms were professional standards enforced as accreditation requirements; *yet the level of compliance with bioethical ideals of discussion, documentation and consent achieved by both the JCAHO and the New York DNR law reforms appears to be comparable.* It would appear, therefore, that, in this particular instance, professional self-regulation by accreditation standards was as effective an instrument of mandatory bioethical reform as external legal regulation.

Table 3. Effectiveness of 1988 DNR Reforms

	Likelihood of DNR Discussion, Consent, & Disclosure							
	NYS DNR Law				JCAHO Regulations			
	1988	Change	1989	No Change	1988	Change	1990	No Change
Discussion								
Q1.	35.5%	30.7%	66.2%	57.8%	30.5%	25.3%	55.8%	54.4%
Q2.	44.9%	32.8%	77.7%	75.8%	39.6%	24.6%	64.3%	64.0%
Consent								
Q3.	58.9%	26.6%	85.3%	85.3%	61.4%	20.9%	82.3%	89.7%
Q4.	44.9%	33.3%	78.9%	96.8%	58.8%	24.7%	83.4%	90.6%
Q5.	48.3%	34.0%	82.9%	92.7%	60.0%	22.9%	82.9%	93.3%
Non-Disclosure								
Q6.	36.6%	–29.7%	6.9%	5.0%	43.7%	–25.9%	17.8%	11.2%
Q7.	34.8%	–30.3%	4.5%	12.6%	27.4%	–18.4%	9.0%	12.5%
Q8.	36.1%	–31.9%	4.2%	12.0%	32.3%	–18.6%	13.7%	9.9%

Only the statistically significant direction of change is reported.
Significance corresponds to $p \leq .05$ per the Wilcoxon Signed Rank Test.

The Impact of Reform on Delaying DNR and Increasing Futile CPR

The near unanimity in response to the questions about the efficacy of DNR reforms reported to this point dissolves when we turn to questions about the *negative* effects of reforms – delayed DNR orders, increased futile CPR., etc. (see Tables 4 and 5). In New York, H/Os, in particular, report that the DNR law frustrates writing DNR orders for terminal patients by making them contingent on the approval of ambivalent families (Q 20) and reluctant guardians (Q13), and hostage to bureaucratic technicalities (Q14). They also report a highly significant increase in futile CPR (Q15), which decreases the likelihood that cancer patients and their families will be treated humanely with respect to DNR (Q16). Their fellow *physicians*, the medical directors concur, although they hesitate to condemn the law as inhumane (Q16). Nursing directors, in marked contrast, report *none* of these problems. They believe the DNR law *increases* the likelihood that patients and families will be treated humanely and decently with respect to DNR (Q16).

New Yorkers' conflicted reactions to the 1988 reforms are reflected by the graph in Figure 1: 83% of nursing directors thought patients were better off because of the law; 79% thought clinicians are better off; but, as

Table 4. New York: DNR Law's Impact on Writing DNR Orders

		Percentage of Respondents Reporting		
		Increase	Decrease	No Change
Q11. Writing DNR orders for patients who may benefit from resuscitation.				
CCND	**	17.7%	7.1%	75.2%
CCMD	**	15.7%	8.4%	75.9%
H/O	§	13.6%	12.3%	74.0%
Q12. Failing to write a DNR order because of family ambivalence.				
CCND	§	34.5%	21.2%	44.2%
CCMD	**	43.4%	19.3%	37.2%
H/O	**	44.2%	13.0%	42.9%
Q13. Failing to write a DNR order for a terminal, developmentally disabled patient because of the attitude of institution or guardian.				
CCND	§	31.9%	20.4%	47.8%
CCMD	§	34.9%	24.1%	41.0%
H/O	**	40.9%	11.7%	47.4%
Q14. Failing to write a DNR order for a terminal patient because of bureaucratic technicalities.				
CCND	§	37.2%	27.4%	35.4%
CCMD	**	57.8%	20.5%	21.7%
H/O	**	57.8%	16.9%	25.3%
Q15. Administering futile CPR to irreversibly terminal patients.				
CCND	§	38.9%	33.6%	27.4%
CCMD	*	43.0%	22.0%	35.0%
H/O	**	52.6%	26.6%	20.8%
Q16. That terminal patients and their families will be treated humanely and decently with respect to DNR.				
CCND	**	38.9%	8.0%	53.1%
CCMD	§	24.1%	16.9%	59.0%
H/O	*	18.2%	36.4%	45.5%

Sample Size: CCND's = 113; CCMD's = 83; H/O's = 154
** = ≤01; * = p≤05; § = Not Statiscally Significant

Figure 1 shows, only 58% thought the law provided humane DNR. At the other extreme, 61% of H/Os believe patients would be better off *without* the law, 67% believe that clinicians would be better off without it, and 53% believe DNR was *not* humane under the law. Medical directors assessments are even more conflicted: 55% believe patients are better off and 52% believe clinicians are better off, because of the law. On the question of whether the law permits humane DNR, 44% thought it did,

Table 5. NY and Non-NY Perceptions of DNR Reform's Impact on DNR Orders

	Percentage of Respondents		Estimated Likelihood of Action			
	Increase	No Change	1988	Change	1990	No Change
Q12. Failing to Write a DNR Order because of family ambivalence.						
• NY	43%	37%	44.7%	36.7%	81.4%	57.4%
• Non-NY	–	69%	[Not Significant]			69.4%
Q14. Failing to write a DNR order for a terminal patient because of bureaucratic technicalities.						
• NY	58%	22%	32.8%	35.8%	68.6%	41.4%
• Non-NY	28%	70%	49.2%	–22.0%	27.2%	34.5%
Q15. Administering futile CPR to irreversibly terminal patients.						
• NY	43%	35%	22.5%	42.4%	64.6%	32.8%
• Non-NY	44%	53%	47.7%	–24.6%	23.1%	41.7%
Q16. That terminal patients and their familites will be treated humanely and decently with respect to DNR.						
• NY	–	59%	[Not Significant]			71.0%
• Non-NY	32%	65%	59.8%	22.9%	82.6%	87.5%

Only the statistically significant direction of change is reported.
Significance corresponds to $p \leq .05$ per the Wilcoxon Signed Rank Test.

43% that it did not – 13% did not answer. (For further analysis of the conflicted reactions of New York clinicians to the law, see both the Introduction, and the next chapter.)

In striking contrast to their New York peers, the national comparison group sees DNR reform as *consistently* beneficial (see Table 5). They report no increase in delayed DNR due to family ambivalence (Q12), and they believe DNR reform significantly *decreases* failures to write DNR orders due to bureaucratic technicalities (Q14), significantly *lessening* the extent of futile CPR (Q15) and increasing the likelihood that patients and families would be treated humanely with respect to DNR (Q16). The numerical differences between the New Yorker medical directors and the national comparison group are impressive: whereas 58% of New York medical directors report an *increase* in "failure to write a DNR order because of bureaucratic technicalities," only 1% of the national comparison group reports such an increase. Forty-three percent of New

Yorkers report an increase in the likelihood of "administering futile CPR to irreversibly terminal patients"; by contrast, only 3% of the national group report an increase. To sum up: Whereas *New York physicians perceive legally mandated DNR reform as delaying DNR orders, increasing futile CPR, and diminishing the humanism of the DNR decision, the JCAHO's professionally mandated DNR reforms were perceived as unequivocally beneficial by the national equal comparison group.*

THE NY LAW'S PROBLEMS

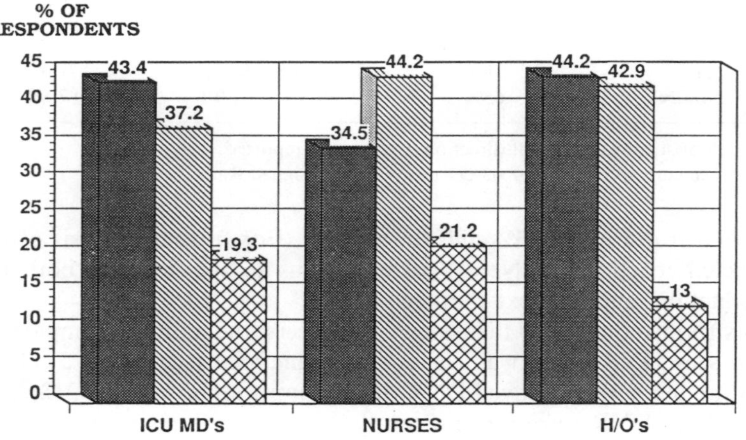

Fig. 3a.

THE NY LAW'S PROBLEMS

Likelihood of failing to write a DNR order for a terminal developmentally disabled patient because of the attitude of institution/guardian

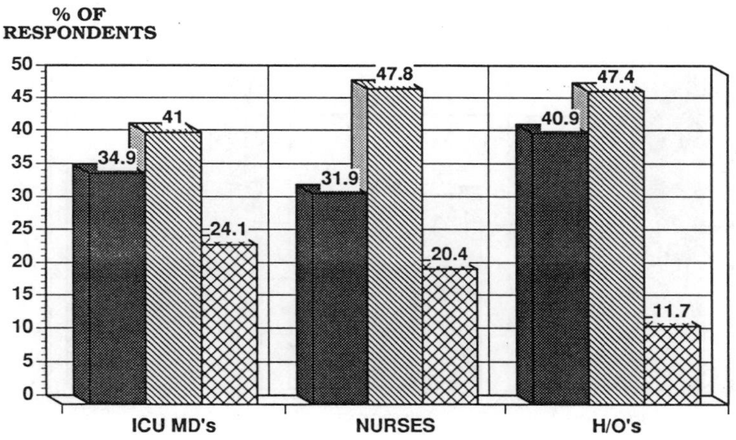

% OF CLINICIANS WHO THOUGHT THAT LIKELIHOOD HAD:

INCREASED

NO CHANGE

DECREASED

Fig. 3b.

THE NY LAW'S PROBLEMS

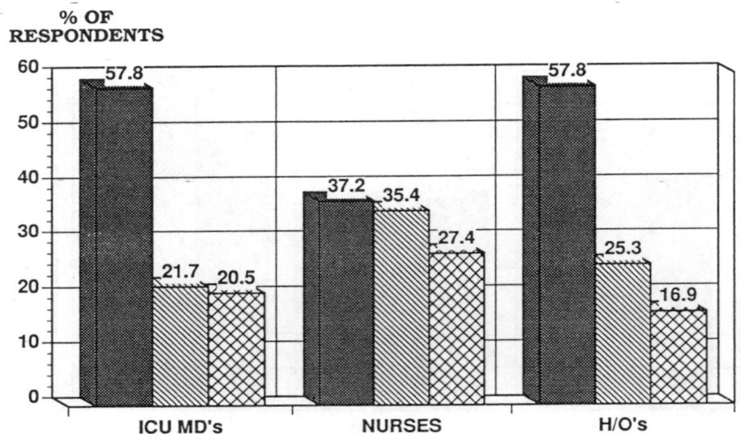

Fig. 3c.

Why New York's Reforms were Perceived Differently than the JCAHO Reforms

What accounts for the difference between the unequivocal welcome accorded DNR reform by the national sample, and the conflicted and often hostile reaction of New York physicians? Part of the answer is to be found in different routes to reform taken outside of New York. The JCAHO accreditation standards are latitudinarian; they permit each medical institution to determine for itself how best to protect the patient's rights, to document the patient's decisions, and so forth. As the responses to closed-ended questions in our survey indicate, institutions took advantage of the latitude permitted them and instituted a range of different policies. Most (87%) policies require patient or surrogate consent for a valid DNR order (which may, however, be oral (85%)), but only 32% require patient consent to be witnessed, and only 16% have such a requirement for surrogate consent. Only 14% report the need for any type of second physician concurrence to a DNR order – except in determinations of incapacity, for which 73% report that a second physician's opinion is necessary. As mandated by the regulations, all DNR orders are entered in patients' medical records; but 36% permit DNR orders to be initially given by phone.

On the sensitive issue of "futile" DNR, half of the national comparison group (51%) responded affirmatively to the question: "In situations where it is impossible for you to comply with the requirements of the DNR policy, is it permissible for you to withhold CPR on the grounds of medical futility?" Only 32% of New Yorkers answered "Yes" to the same question.

There are some significant differences in the policies regulating DNR orders for New Yorkers and for the national comparison group. At the time the survey was conducted, most of the physicians in the national sample could initiate a DNR order over the telephone; they were also free to issue DNR orders without consulting a second physician, or obtaining witnesses, or securing written documentation in the form of a patient or surrogate consent, and about half could write a DNR order on the basis of futility. New Yorkers lacked these freedoms (although the July, 1991, amendment of the DNR law eased restrictions, eliminating entirely the need for signed surrogate consent). Thus part of the protest against the law was a function of stringency of the New York regulations.

Yet about half of the national comparison group report policies that are equally stringent in limiting physicians ability to deal with futile CPR. *And none of the these physicians report the type of problems that exasperate New York physicians.* Why are they more tolerant of constraints on their practice than New York physicians? One factor would appear to be that the policies constraining DNR practices outside of New York were devised by the staff of the physician's *own* institution; the underlying rationale of these policies are thus likely to be both affirmed and understood by those who implement them. Moreover, should any aspects of the policy which prove unreasonable or unworkable in practice, it can be eliminated, revised or reinterpreted at the institutional level. New Yorkers, in contrast, lacked the ability to control or revise policy at the institutional level.

Just as importantly, the professionally mandated accreditation requirements of the JCAHO, are given in an easily comprehended paragraph which leaves the explicit interpretation and implementation of DNR reform (i.e., "insur[ing] patients' rights," giving families "a role in the decision," documenting decisions in the medical record, etc.) to individual medical-nursing committees. However, the vehicle of legally-mandated reform, Article 29-B of New York's Public Health Law, is a statute, and it reads like one. Here, for example, is the governing section regulating surrogate consent to DNR orders (that is, the most common form of DNR consent).

> § 2965.5 Standards for surrogate decision-making....
> (c) A surrogate may consent to an order not to resuscitate on behalf of an adult patient only if there has been a determination by an attending physician with the concurrence of another attending physician selected by a person authorized by the hospital to make such a selection, given after personal examination of the patient that, to a reasonable degree of medical certainty:
> (i) the patient has a terminal condition; or
> (ii) the patient is permanently unconscious; or
> (iii) resuscitation would be medically futile; or
> (iv) resuscitation would impose an extraordinary burden on the patient in the light of the patient's medical condition, and the expected outcome of resuscitation for the patient.

Not surprisingly, the plaint of "incomprehensibility" is an almost universal characteristic of New York clinicians comments on the law. As one New York medical director put the point, the "language is too complicated ...simplify, use normal English [and] educate MDs on how the law covers them." Note the suggestion that physicians misunderstand the law. The written comments continually remark on the pervasive misinterpretation of the law. Thus one H/O reported, "[The law] is an incredible nuisance...lack of knowledge by residents leaves them trying to get patient's signatures." It is striking that not one of the responses in the national comparison group complains about the language or comprehensibility of DNR policies.

New York Clinicians' Comprehension of the DNR Law

How knowledgeable are New York clinicians about the DNR law? To assess their comprehension, we had the Task Force Counsel prepare fourteen questions. Better than 90% of clinicians knew the basic requirements of the law, e.g., that DNR orders for patients with decision-making capacity require witnessed consent. Only 3% believed, mistakenly, that consent required notarization. *Nursing* directors had the most accurate knowledge of the law. Two-thirds knew that it was permissible to honor DNR orders written at another institution; by contrast, only 38% of *medical* directors and 26% of H/Os answered this question correctly. Certain aspects of the law, however, confused almost all clinicians. The law mandates review of DNR orders every three days, but also states, "Failure to comply...shall not render an order not to be resuscitated ineffective" (§ 2970.1). Yet 60% of nursing directors, 61% of H/Os and 62% of medical directors treated "non-review" as "non-renewal", and responded that DNR orders which had not been reviewed were invalid.

The most common misunderstandings of the law involved "over-interpretations," that is, reports of non-existent requirements. For example, the law explicitly states: "Every adult shall be presumed to have capacity to make a [DNR] decision,"(§2963), that is, "determinations" of capacity are *not* required by the New York DNR law. Yet 72% of nursing directors, 71% of H/Os and 69% of medical directors report that to honor a patient's request for a DNR order, a physician must first determine the patient's "capacity" to make such a request. Worse yet, 53% of nursing directors, 48% of H/Os and 47% of medical directors believe that such determinations require second physician concurrence. Unfortunately these misreadings of the law often cause real problems. Thus one medical director complained bitterly that seeking second physician concurrence to

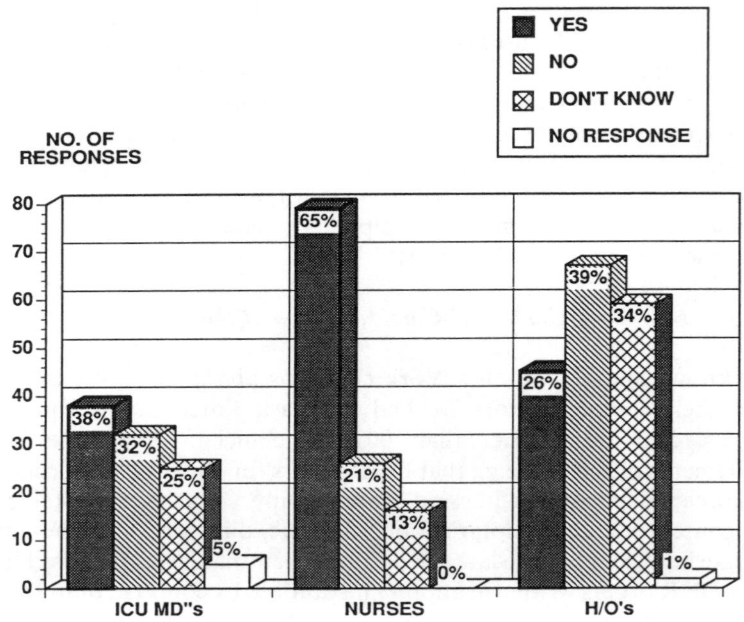

Does the law allow you to honor a DNR order that was written at another facility? **Correct Answer: (YES)**

Fig. 4a.

determine patient capacity to make DNR decisions "has delayed DNR decisions to the detriment of the patient/family/hospital."

The most tragic over-interpretation is the one the H/O corrected in his residents – making patients *sign* DNR consent forms. There is no such requirement in the statute, which explicitly states that patients may "express a decision consenting to an order not to resuscitate *orally*" (§ 2964.2). Yet 59% of nursing directors, 51% of medical directors, and 43% of H/Os stated that the law requires patients to sign their own DNR orders. This misreading of the law generated the most poignant objections to it on the part of clinicians protesting the "inhuman[ity]" of requiring patients to "sign their own life away." As the nursing director who wrote this observed: "people just can't deal with this emotionally."

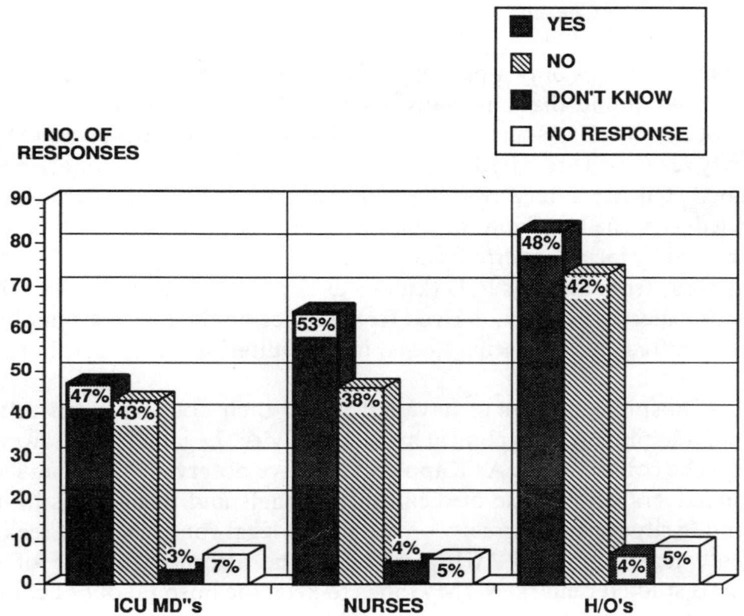

For a patient who appears to have decisionmaking capacity, must a second doctor be involved in determining the patient's condition, etc? Correct: (NO)

Fig. 4b.

Consent Forms and the Role of Lawyers

Language provides only a partial explanation of clinician misreadings of the law. We found that clinicians seldom commented on the New York DNR Statute itself. As one H/O wrote: "I was not aware there was a DNR law. My responses are based on hospital policies which I assume are based on law." On-site interviews confirm that most clinicians derive their knowledge of the law from the consent forms used by their hospital – as interpreted by local "experts." The expert used by the surgical ICU studied was a nurse from another ICU (known as the "DNR maven"). The DNR maven's expertise, in turn, derived from service on the Ethics Committee, which drafted the consent forms in consultation with the hospital attorney.

Most hospitals appear to have developed their consent forms in this manner – acting on both clinical and legal advice. Legal advice, however, tends to be conservative. As Kapp and Lo have observed, "attorneys and risk managers who advise medical professionals and institutions in life-sustaining situations err greatly on the side of legal conservatism...seeking absolute legal immunity" ([10], p. 179). The attorney for one of the hospitals studied remarked, "My job is to keep the hospital out of court." Thus attorneys who normally consider it legally prudent to get notarization for surrogate signatures, naturally recommended it for surrogate DNR consent (hence the report of a notarization requirement by 3% of clinicians). Similarly, since signatures are excellent legal documentation, and since signed forms are required for surrogate consent, symmetry and legal prudence suggested that patients too should sign DNR consent forms. The result, to quote the written comments of one CCMD, was that: "Our institution's implementation has been created to demonstrate to a review-type body that the patient had due process – not humane consideration." Clinician over-interpretations of the DNR law would thus appear to reflect "protections" built into hospital DNR consent forms on the advice of hospital attorneys.

Attorney over-interpretations of the DNR law, in turn, were prompted by a lack of interpretive guidance from the New York Department of Health and were actively cued by the language of the statute, which stipulated legal rather than medical documentation conventions for surrogate DNR decisions, viz:.

> A surrogate shall express a decision consenting to an order not to resuscitate in writing, dated, and signed in the presence of one witness eighteen years of age or older who shall sign the decisions. (§2965.6a)

This now infamous requirement – which clinicians condemn as the "death warrant" clause – is important, not only because the act of *signing* a legal document requesting non-resuscitation (in front of witnesses, etc.) takes on symbolical significance when performed at "the death bed," but also because, by replacing medical with legal documentation, it *forced* hospitals turn to their attorneys in order to draft consent forms. The attorneys, not surprisingly, acted like the lawyers they were trained to be, and advised hospitals to draft "liability-proof" DNR consent forms. The inadvertent but sad consequence of replacing medical standards of documentation with legal standards are summed up in the following comment from a nursing director.

> [E]mphasis is placed on obtaining signatures on multiple forms rather than the physical and emotional needs of the dying patient and his family.... In order to meet the letter of the law we address the need to get consent forms signed. The programs that I have attended address the consent process, not the dying process. I feel that the signing of consent forms has put new meaning into the cliche 'signing your life away.' The guilt feelings for some must be overwhelming.

On analysis, much of the differential impact of the professionally mandated JCAHO reforms and the legally mandated N.Y. DNR reforms can be traced to the fact that, unlike the JCAHO regulations, the New York reforms were implemented by a statute, written in a language alien to clinicians, which substituted legal for medical documentation conventions, and required interpretation by lawyers – who, in "doing their job," tended to be over-protective of the hospital to the detriment of families and patients. *Thus one of the clearest lessons to be drawn from New York's experience with the DNR law is that when legal regulation of professional behavior is necessary* (as it clearly was in New York, given the recalcitrance of the courts), *statutes should attempt to preserve and utilize the professional self-regulatory process, keeping alterations to a minimum.* The New York Task Force inadvertently deviated from this precept when they drafted a statute that substituted legal for medical documentation conventions – thereby setting in motion a process which, to their dismay, initially undermined many of the benefits of the DNR reforms.

A second lesson to be learned from New York's experience is the importance of state bioethics agencies, like the New York Task Force on Life and the Law. The Task Force staff diligently attempted to correct what they considered misreadings and over-interpretations of the law and to combat the bureaucratization of the dying process that lawyers implemented in the name of the law. They cooperated with academic assessment teams (like that directed by the authors), and they carefully analyzed the DNR law's problems. Working with the Department of Health, they ultimately persuaded the legislature to revise the most problematic feature of the statute. It is too early to contemplate assessing the impact of these revisions; it is our best guess, however, that were we to conduct another survey next year, clinicians assessments of the law would be overwhelmingly favorable – except, perhaps, on the issue of "futile CPR."

The Language of Futility

Frustration and outrage over being forced to administer "medically inappropriate" or "futile" CPR were common in the answers given to open-ended survey questions. Moreover, as their answers to closed-ended questions indicate , 70% of the national comparison group and 57% of the New York medical directors surveyed believe that physicians should be empowered to write DNR orders based on a medical determination that CPR would be futile, irrespective of patient/family wishes. Ninety six percent of the national sample and 87% of New Yorkers also hold that if a futility-based DNR order is written, patients/families should be informed of the order. In answer to a second question, the same 96% and 87% believe that the patient/family has "a right to a second opinion" before a DNR order is implemented.

What do physicians have in mind when they use such expressions as "medically inappropriate" or "futile" CPR? As Diana Crane reported in her classic study, *The Sanctity of Social Life*[6]. American clinicians conceptualize life in terms of capacity for social interaction. This means, as our data show, that they have a broad conception of futility. Thus, in response to closed-ended questions, about half of all nursing directors , almost two-thirds of medical directors (both in New York and in the national sample) and over 70 percent of H/Os surveyed consider CPR to be futile *if the patient will not survive hospitalization or will survive but in a coma.* When clinicians, especially physicians, speak of administering "futile" CPR, therefore, they are not merely talking about CPR which will be *inefficacious*, in the sense that it will fail to resuscitate patients, but also about CPR which will be *efficacious but meaningless* because the patients resuscitated will never have a conscious post-hospital existence.

In contrast, the DNR statute, following accepted legal and bioethical usage, defines medically futility *narrowly*, so that CPR is futile only if it is *inefficacious*, in the sense that it fails to restore cardiopulmonary function (§2961). These semantic differences tend to confuse the discussion of the New York DNR law, and (as we argued in the Introduction) the discussion of DNR in general. Thus in an article in the *New York State Journal of Medicine*, Robert Swidler replied to clinicians complaints that the DNR law required them to administer futile CPR as follows.

> The view that the presumption of consent [in the DNR statute] constitutes an absolute duty to resuscitate is at odds with what the statute says, what the drafters and legislators intended, and what good medical practice requires ([17]. p. 70.)

Our survey was conducted a half year after Swidler's article was published. Nonetheless, 66% of nursing directors, 57% of H/Os, and 47% of medical directors replied "No" to the question: "In situations in which it is impossible for you to comply with all the procedural requirements of the DNR law, is it lawful for you to withhold CPR on grounds of medical futility alone?" Many knew Swidler's article, yet few physicians, and none of the hospital attorneys interviewed found his argument persuasive.

Why not? In part because of the semantic confusions noted earlier, but in large measure because Swidler's analysis presumes a use of not initiating CPR which is meaningless in the hospital context. Hospital protocol treats cardiopulmonary arrests as medical emergencies which automatically require a staff response, CPR, unless there is a countermanding order. To utter "an order not to attempt cardiopulmonary resuscitation in the event a patient suffers cardiac or respiratory arrest," however, is to give a DNR order as defined in NY law (§2961). So, while Swidler's analysis might establish that solo physicians in non-hospital contexts may refrain from administering futile CPR, it is inapplicable in hospitals – where physicians must voice an order to staff to cancel CPR, and are thus inescapably bound by the DNR statute.

Even were Swidler's analysis applicable to the hospital context, it would still fail to address the problem of "futile" CPR that bothers most New York clinicians. For once the DNR conversation has been initiated, the New York DNR law requires CPR *unless* the patient or surrogate explicitly declines it. However, what troubles New York clinicians most (in their written comments) was "futile" CPR administered, not to new admissions or in the emergency room, but by "default," because patients or their families are undecided, ambivalent, or had yet to officially declare a DNR decision. One medical director's crude comments epitomize clinician opinion on the subject of being mandated to administer futile CPR by default.

> [T]he law is...backwards...[we are] caught between family desires and actuality, and when [they] have doubts, [we] resuscitate. Make the law that CPR [is] instituted only at patient/family request, not its opposite.

Notice that these comments, like those of the medical director quoted earlier, indicate a willingness to accept the administration of "futile" CPR, *provided that it is expressly requested by a patient or surrogate*. Physicians seem willing to yield to the patient or the surrogate's express desires, even to the point of administering "futile" CPR. What they find objectionable is administering "futile" CPR when neither patient nor surrogate have expressly requested it, that is CPR by default. As one nurse remarked (during an interview): "Do the people who write these laws understand the sort of brutal assault they ask us to inflict on patients – just because no one can make up their mind? "

Thus, in addition to the two different conceptions of "futile CPR" described earlier, there would appear to be four different albeit interrelated issues falling under the rubric "futile CPR" ([11], [16], [19]): (i) administering "futile" CPR in the emergency room and other contexts in which circumstances preempt the determination of patient-surrogate wishes with respect to CPR; (ii) administering "futile" CPR by default because patients or families, although consulted about CPR/DNR, have yet to officially declare a desire for either; (iii) offering CPR as an intervention in cases in which physicians believes it to be"futile" [4]; (iv) administering "futile" CPR at the explicit request of a patient/surrogate. At present there appears to be a bioethical [7], medical and legal consensus on only one aspect of the issue – the absence of an obligation to administer "futile CPR," in the narrow bioethical-legal sense (i.e.,

CPR that will not restore cardiac function) to patients in the ER and for new admissions.

Conclusion

What can we learn from the 1988 DNR reforms? Perhaps the most important lesson is that they were impressively effective. For the most part, by 1988, physicians appear to have accepted the bioethical ideal of a patient-physician partnership for medical decision-making about life-sustaining treatments like CPR. Given the pervasiveness of clinician acceptance of bioethical ideals it is only superficially surprising that both the stringent New York and the latitudinarian JCAHO DNR reforms appear to have been equally effective. Had clinicians been resistant to bioethical ideals, they might have taken advantage of the latitude permitted them by the JCAHO. In fact, however, the American College of Physicians survey found that only 9% of internists believe that there is no need to discuss DNR decisions with their patients (see this volume, pp. 251–261).

It appears that a consensus has decisively emerged, and the long debate over the patient's role in decisions to refuse life-sustaining treatment initiated in the 1970s (most notably by the Quinlan case) has been authoritatively settled by 1983 President's Commission Report. The JCAHO accreditation requirements, and the statute introduced by New York DNR law, therefore, effectuate *previously* accepted ideals; their impact was to make practical what had already accepted at the level of principle. The New York law, in particular, struck down legal barriers which inhibited physicians from discussing DNR with patients and (especially) surrogates, and which seemed to prohibit documenting the consequent decisions in the medical record. Thus the DNR reforms of 1988 did not, for the most part, change physicians' minds about the right way to act, rather they removed barriers and created a context in which could easily act in a manner that they already believed to be proper. In retrospect, therefore, there is little to be surprised about in the success of the 1988 reforms.

What is surprising, however, is the extent to which new barriers to "doing the right thing" were raised by the New York DNR law. For the most part, these barriers were an artifact of a desire to *protect patients against medical paternalism* (except in the case of OMRDD patients, where the motivation was to protect developmentally disabled patients from discrimination). Protectionism not only led to stringent consent and consultation requirements; it also led to the introduction of *legal*, as opposed to *medical* standards of documentation – to *consent forms*, as opposed to the documentation of consent in the patient's medical record. These extra-medical forms and stringent consultation requirements became the bane of the New York DNR law (prior to the reforms of July 1991). Ironically, in striving to protect patients by substituting legal for medical standards of consent and documentation, the law reinsinuated lawyers into the DNR decision-making process. The lawyers, in turn, projected their natural concern to protect hospitals against litigation into consent forms. The forms tended to require even more protections then the law itself – bureaucratizing the dying process by requiring patient signatures and even notarization for DNR orders.

Yet, for the most part, concerns about medical paternalism appear to have been unfounded. In 1983 they were probably legitimate concern. By 1988, however, most physicians accepted the bioethical ideal of shared patient-physician decisionmaking in which they provided the medical *facts*, as it were, allowing patients to decide matters according to their own *values*. Consequently, as our data indicate, the stringently enforced New York reforms were no more effective in implementing bioethical ideals than the latitudinarian JCAHO accreditation reforms (or earlier voluntary reforms implemented at individual hospitals – such as those reported by Quill and Bennett in this volume, pp. 241–250). The New York reforms were, however, burdened with onerous (and apparently unnecessary) protections which generated hostile reactions which were unheard of nationally.

On one issue, however, the 1988 reforms sparked a truly national debate – the question of futility. Our analysis suggests that the debate is at least partially *semantic*. Bioethicists tend to consider CPR to be "futile" if it will not restore cardiopulmonary function, or will restore it for only a short period (on the order of a few hours). Our findings – which are consistent Diana Crane's classic study of ICU clinician language, and with the scenario responses to the ACP survey – is that clinicians, especially physicians, extend the meaning of futile to embrace those cases in which CPR effectively restores cardiorespiratory function, but the patient nonetheless does not survive long enough to be discharged from the hospital and/or in which the patient's cognitive function is not restored (so that the patients survives but in an irreversible coma or a persistent vegetative state).

These usages undercut the division of labor presupposed by the bioethical ideal of shared patient-physicians decisionmaking, because the clinician's broad conception of "futility" incorporates judgments about the *value* of extending existence in a coma, in a vegetative state, or in a hospital ward. There is thus no clear distinction between value judgments and factual judgments. Hence what from the clinical perspective appears to be a "medical" determination of the *fact* of futility, will be seen as a paternalistic *value* judgement from the perspective of the bioethicist. Conversely, when bioethicists attempt to constrain physicians against imposing their values on patients (by unilaterally issuing a DNR order on the grounds of medical futility), they will be perceived by clinicians as interfering with the practice of medicine by forcing the administration of CPR which, from the clinical perspective, is properly deemed futile.

Semantic problems demand linguistic solutions. Since discussions of "futility" seem inextricably confused, it would appear that the debate over "futility" ought properly to be resolved by appealing to a usage without any history in this area. We propose the distinction between *efficacious* and *inefficacious* CPR. CPR should be considered *inefficacious* if it will not restore cardiopulmonary functioning. Judgments about the efficacy of CPR are entirely and properly *medical*, and physicians have no more obligation to seek patient or surrogate consent about the decision to administer inefficacious CPR than they do about decisions with respect to any other medically inefficacious intervention. If, in their medical judgement, an intervention is inefficacious it should not be administered. If, however, CPR is likely to be *efficacious*, but would leave the patient in a persistent vegetative state, or would merely prolong the dying process, then, as all other decisions about the *value* of life-sustaining treatment, the determination of value ought to be made by the patient or the patient's surrogate.

If, as we believe, physicians are willing to accept the bioethical ideal with respect to life-sustaining interventions, but unwilling to accept bioethical intrusions on their *medical* expertise, they should be willing to accept that their power to write DNR orders without patient or surrogate consent is limited to those cases in which CPR is *inefficacious*. Conversely, if bioethicists acknowledge that the patient's right to decide is restricted to decisions which are primarily about the value of life extension, they should be willing to limit the patient's right to consent to DNR orders to those cases in which it is *effective*, and recognize the propriety of physicians' writing DNR orders *without patient consent* in those cases where it will be *ineffective*. Once the semantics of the situation are clarified there is, in our view, no substantial conflict between patients rights and physicians powers with respect to CPR and DNR. In principle, it appears possible to resolve the present policy impasse by clarifying the terminology of the debate.

ACKNOWLEDGEMENTS

We are grateful to the Dana Foundation, the Union College Humanities Faculty Development and College Research Funds, and The Critical Care Education Foundation of the Albany Medical College for their generous support, and to the national and the New York Society of Critical Care Medicine, as well as Dr. Charles Reilly, for assisting with the distribution of the DNR Assessment questionnaires. We would also like to thank Tracy Miller, Executive Director of the New York State Task Force on Life and the Law, and Robert Swidler, former Counsel to the Task Force, for their unstinting cooperation and for their thoughtful responses to the findings in this study. Deborah Atwood, Lawrence Ponemon, Eugene Spanguolo and Sean Hornbeck were also part of our research team. We would like to thank them, as well as our administrative assistants, Elizabeth Cole, Rhonda Sheehan and, most especially, Marianne Snowden.

REFERENCES

1. Baker, R., Dersch, V. and Strosberg, M.: 1989, 'Physicians' Attitudes Towards Using Deception', *Journal of the American Medical Association* **262**, 2233.
2. Bedell, S. and Delbanco, T.: 1984, 'Choices About Cardiopulmonary Resuscitation in the Hospital', *New England Journal of Medicine* **310**, 1089–1093.
3. Bedell, S. *et al.*: 1986, 'Do-Not-Resuscitate Orders for Critically Ill Patients in the Hospital: How Are They Used and What Is Their Impact?' *Journal of the American Medical Association* **256**, 233–237.
4. Blackhall, L.: 1987, 'Must we always use CPR?' *New England Journal of Medicine* **317**, 1281–1284.
5. Brody, B.: 1990, 'Quality of Scholarship in Bioethics', *Journal of Medicine and Philosophy* **15**, 161–178.
6. Crane, D.: 1977, *The Sanctity of Social Life*, Transaction Books, New Brunswick, NJ.
7. Hastings Center: 1987, *Hastings Center Guidelines on the Termination of Life-Sustaining Treatment and the Care of the Dying*, Indiana University Press, Bloomington, IN.

8. Jonsson, P., McNamee, M., Campion, E.: 1988, 'The Do Not Resuscitate Order: A Profile of its Changing Use', *Archives of Internal Medicine* **148**, 2373–2375.
9. Kamer, R., Dieck, E., McClung, J., *et al.*: 1990, 'Effect of New York State's Do-Not-Resuscitate Legislation on In-hospital Cardiopulmonary Resuscitation Practice', *American Journal of Medicine* **88**, 108–111.
10. Kapp, M., Lo, B.: 1986, 'Legal Perceptions and Medical Decision Making', *Millbank Quarterly* **64**, Suppl. 2,163–202.
11. Lantos, J, Singer, P, Walker, R., *et al.*: 1989, 'The Illusion of Futility in Clinical Practice', *American Journal of Medicine* **87**, 81–84.
12. Lo, B., McLeod, G., Saika, G.: 1986, 'Patient Attitudes to Discussing Life-sustaining Treatment', *Archives of Internal Medicine* **146**, 1613–1615.
13. Longo, D., Warren, M., Roberts, J., Dunlop, G.: 1988, 'Extent of DNR Policies Varies Across Healthcare settings', *Healthprogress*, June 1988, 66–73.
14. Moses, L., Emerson, J., Hosseini, H.: 1984, 'Analyzing Data From Ordered Categories', *New England Journal of Medicine* **311**, 442–448.
15. Rest, J.: 1979, *Moral Development: Advances in Research and Theory*, Praeger Publishers, New York.
16. Schneiderman, L, Jecker, N, Jonsen, A.: 1990, Medical Futility: Its Meaning and Ethical Implications, *Annals of Internal Medicine* **112**, 12–36.
17. Swidler, R.: 1989, 'The Presumption of Consent in New York State's Do-Not-Resuscitate Law', *New York State Journal of Medicine* **89**, 69–72.
18. Wilcoxon, F.: 1945, 'Individual Comparisons by Ranking Methods', *Biometrics* **1**, 80–83.
19. Youngner, S.: 1988, 'Who Defines Futility?' *Journal of the American Medical Association* **260**, 2096–2097.
20. Youngner, S.: 1990, 'Futility in Context', *Journal of the American Medical Association* **264**, 1295–1296.
21. Zimmerman, J.E., Knaus, W.A., Sharpe, S.M. *et al.*: 1986. 'The Use and Implications of Do Not Resuscitate Orders in Intensive Care Units', *Journal of the American Medical Association* **255**, 351–356.

VIRGINIA JONAS DERSCH

DIFFERENCES IN CLINICIANS' REACTIONS TO THE NEW YORK STATE DNR LAW

In this essay, there is further analysis of responses of Medical and Nursing Directors and Hematologist-Oncologists to the Union College Survey. Two general research questions are addressed: (1) How do perceptions of the New York State DNR Law vary among these three professional groups? (2) How can the variability be explained?

THEORETICAL FRAMEWORK

Social Role Theory

The theoretical framework which informs this discussion is social role theory, with emphasis on the professional roles of health care providers. The concept of "social role" is well-established in the sociological literature [10]. A social role may be defined as the cluster of attitudes, behaviors, rights, obligations, privileges and expectations (of both the self and others) that pertain to, and are associated with each social status, or position in the social network of society. Roles allow people to formulate their behavior mentally in order to shape their actions in appropriate ways, i.e., in order to be able to carry out their role performance in societally approved ways. Statuses and roles are, for sociologists, the foundation of social structure in that they shape the pattern of relationships between individuals, and the patterns of interaction within social organizations. Social roles are learned during the socialization process in which individuals are taught, both on a conscious and unconscious level, how to perform their future roles. For the three clinician categories considered here, a relevant form of socialization is their medical or nursing school training.

Components of role theory of interest here are: (1) Role Conflict which occurs when an individual is confronted with conflicting expectations stemming from the simultaneous occupancy of two or more statuses, e.g., a police officer having to arrest his/her own child. (2) Role Ambiguity, which occurs when an individual is not sure how to perform their role.

R. Baker & M.A. Strosberg (eds.), Legislating Medical Ethics: A Study of the New York Do-Not-Resuscitate Law, 303–321.

This could be because of lack of knowledge or experience, e.g., new house staff on July 1, or it could be because of a change in regulations which mandates new attitudes, expectations, and behaviors. (3) Role Failure which occurs when a role incumbent becomes, for whatever reason, unable to perform core component(s) of the role, e.g., a surgeon who loses his eyesight.

Professional Roles

In the classical sociology literature, a professional occupation possesses certain characteristics: a service orientation, a lengthy and highly structured training period, significant autonomy in many areas of its role performances, e.g., in selection and training of neophytes [6, 8].

Freidson points out that the physician is, sociologically speaking, the "dominant professional" in the health care setting ([6]). As Hingson *et al.* note, doctors "sit atop the medical hierarchy. They exercise a high degree of autonomy in their work and are answerable to no higher professional authority" ([8], p. 244). In addition to the high degree of autonomy of the medical profession, a core characteristic of the physician's role is his or her sense of "medical responsibility." Becker *et al.*, note that "Medical responsibility is responsibility for the patient's well-being, and the exercise of medical responsibility is seen as the basic and key action of the practicing physician. The physician is most a physician when he exercises this responsibility" ([2], p. 224).

Further, Freidson in discussing the "values of physicians," notes the high value put on action, independence and autonomy when he writes that physicians' "action orientation. . .relies on first hand experience and is supported by both a will to believe in the value of one's actions, and a belief in the inadequacy of general knowledge for dealing with individual cases" ([6]. p. 178). In other words, the role of the physician, as presented and internalized in medical school, is characterized by a high degree of autonomy, a deep sense of personal responsibility for treatment of patients, and an orientation to independent action based on the physician's own personal knowledge and experience. As Mintzberg notes, the professional works autonomously, close to clients, but fairly independently of colleagues. S/he is subject to controls by the profession, but only minimally by the professional organization where s/he works, e.g., the hospital [4,] [12].

The role of the nurse, on the other hand, is less independent and autonomous, primarily because nurses' technical knowledge, their training, and their work is under the control of physicians, i.e., nurses are trained to follow "doctor's orders." Most often, nurses perform their work in hospitals, where they work under hierarchical control, i.e., they report "upwards" in the hospital chain of command.

The responsibility they have traditionally borne toward patients, unlike the autonomous medical responsibility of the physician, is the administration of round-the-clock, hands-on, personalized care of the total patient, i.e., nurses have been trained to deal with not only the patient's physical condition, but also with his emotional state. Another part of their traditional role performance has been to interact, on the physician's behalf, with family members, informing them about the patient's condition, reassuring them, advising them and the like. Nurses tend to see themselves as Patient Advocates, placing patient needs above all other considerations and channelling information between doctors, patients, and their families ([1], [5], [11], [14]).

Mintzberg calls the hospital a "professional bureaucracy," wherein the organization's structure is "bureaucratic, yet decentralized." It "relies for coordination on the standardization of skills, which is achieved primarily through formal training. It hires duly trained specialists – professionals – for the operating core, then gives them considerable control over their own work" ([12], p. 175). The work done by professionals is highly complex, requiring many steps and sequences, combined with application of professional judgment which has been honed over years of experience. Thus professionals who work in organizations are really "collections of independent individuals who come together only to draw on common resources and support services" ([12], p. 189).

The ICU Medical Director

The 1989 *JCAHO Accreditation Manual for Hospitals* lists as responsibilities of the ICU Medical Director (M.D.):

> implementing policies established by the medical staff for the continuing operation of the unit; making decisions, in consultation with the physician responsible for the patient, for the disposition of a patient when patient load exceeds operational capacity; assuring that the quality, safety and appropriateness of patient care services provided within the unit are monitored and evaluated on a regular basis and that appropriate actions based on the findings are taken [9].

Although JCAHO requires a medical director to do these things, as Strosberg, *et al.*'s 1990 study of medical director availability found, there are two types of ICU medical directors: "working directors" and "paper directors." Working directors spend appreciable time in the ICU and take an active role in managing all of the unit's resources. Paper directors, on the other hand, although they "may chair JCAHO-mandated committees," they may "...take little part in the day-to-day operation of the unit, except in the course of providing treatment for their own patients" ([13], p. 452). Hence, it appears that the JCAHO-mandated responsibilities of the ICU medical director may not always be exercised by that individual.

By default, these responsibilities generally fall to the nursing director who, along with house staff, typically directs the day-to-day functioning of the unit. As Zussman notes, "whatever stability is to be found among intensive care personnel" is provided by ICU nurses. Further as he notes, ICU nurses and Nursing Directors possess high levels of technical skills which set them apart from rank-and-file floor nurses ([14], p. 64). For the nurse who becomes an ICU Nursing Director there is an increase in both autonomy and responsibility, with scant, if any lessening of the traditional R.N. role of Patient Advocate.

Mintzberg notes that, regardless of its source, innovation is problematic for the professional bureaucracy because it "runs" on standard approaches to problems, which he terms, "pigeonholing." Because innovation requires reordering of the pigeonholes, the breaking away from old routines or standards, resistance may be at a high level [12].

The New York State DNR Law can be conceptualized as an innovation imposed by the administrative fiat of outsiders (the New York State Legislature) on the basically autonomous professionals who carry out the mission of the hospital.

Application of Social Role Theory

The Nursing Director (N.D.) is first and foremost, a nurse whose training and experience of bedside care, plus interaction with patients and their families, has cast him or her into the role of Patient Advocate. However, as pointed out above, in the ICU's with "paper directors," much responsibility for the day-to-day functioning and overall stability of the unit falls to the Nursing Director. Hence Nursing Directors can be expected to approve the law, perceiving it as beneficial for patients and their families because it empowers them, and for health care professionals because it offers them legal guidelines and protection.

Hematologist-Oncologists are community-based physicians who bear primary medical responsibility for their gravely ill and often highly dependent private patients. Their role could be termed that of trusted guide for patients through their dying trajectory. Given the almost complete autonomy in decision making to which they are accustomed, and the intimate nature of their relationships with patients and their families, the Hematologist-Oncologists can be expected to dislike the DNR Law as an intrusion into their medical practice.

Medical-Directors are physicians whose additional role obligations as ICU director have been mandated by the JCAHO. Still, as noted earlier, ICU Medical Directors involve themselves in the day-to-day operation of the unit on varying levels. Those whose involvement is heaviest can be termed "working directors," while those who are less involved may be termed "paper directors." Given that the sample of medical directors surveyed here most likely contains both kinds of directors, the expectation here is for some ambivalent and/or conflicting attitudes toward the New York State DNR Law. More specifically, one might expect that paper directors would hold attitudes similar to those of other physicians (e.g., the hematologist-oncologists), while working directors would hold attitudes similar to those of nursing directors.

To reiterate, social role theory provides deeper understanding of the perspectives of these three players in the drama of the ICU. Because each of these professionals stands in a different role relationship to the ICU patient, it follows that there will be variation in their attitudes, behaviors, rights, and obligations.

DATA ANALYSIS

Data utilized here have emerged from responses to both structured and open-ended questions. The questions asked were: "Would patients be better off had the New York State Legislature not passed the DNR Law?" and "Why?"; "Would clinicians be better off had the New York State Legislature not passed the DNR Law?" and "Why?"; "Does the New York State DNR Law provide humane DNR?"

Table 1 presents a comparison of attitudes of the three care-giver categories. This data is based upon answers to the three structured

Table 1. Perceptions of the DNR Law for Three Clinician Categories

	Nursing Directors		Medical Directors		Hematologist-Oncologist		
	% Who Agree	N	% Who Agree	N	% Who Agree	N	P Value
Clinicians have Benefitted	79%	(117)	54%	(90)	31%	(157)	.001
Patients have Benefitted	91%	(108)	57%	(92)	36%	(163)	.001
The law provides humane DNR	67%	(105)	51%	(83)	42%	(158)	.001

questions presented above. Chi-square tests of statistical significance were performed.

Analysis of this table reveals that, in general, Nursing Directors, the Patient Advocates, may be said to overwhelmingly "approve" of the New York State DNR Law, given that almost all feel that patients have benefitted from the law, and that 79% feel that clinicians have benefitted from it. Only one-third feel that it does not provide humane DNR. Medical Directors, in contrast, display ambivalent attitudes toward the DNR Law, with approval levels hovering at about half on each of these three measures. Hematologist-Oncologists the Patient Guides, report the lowest levels of approval of the DNR Law, with less than half supporting it on any of the three measures.

In summary, responses of the three clinician categories reveal the attitudes one would expect them to display given the social role responsibilities and attitudes previously discussed. Deeper understanding of these attitudes has been sought in two further ways:

(1) through answers to the open-ended questions of "why" respondents feel that clinicians and patients have or have not benefitted from the DNR Law. These perceived advantages and disadvantages are presented in Tables 2 and 3.
(2) through application of control variables within each care-giver category group. These results are presented in Tables 4, 5, 6 and 7.

Table 2. Advantages of the DNR Law

	Nursing Directors (N=54)*	Medical Directors (N=18)*	Hematologist-Oncologists (N=18)*
For Clinicans:			
provision of guidelines	27%	14%	6%
legal protection	21%	8%	4%
For Patients:			
clarification of patient and family rights	40%	3%	3%
promotion of awareness, discussion, participation of patients and families	21%	15%	9%

* Respondents permitted more than one response, percents may exceed 100.

Table 3. Disadvantage of the DNR Law

	Nursing Directors (N=69)*	Medical Directors (N=47)*	Hematologist-Oncologists (N=109)*
For Clinicians:			
bureaucratic red tape	24%	34%	43%
procedural problems	26%	12%	16%
uwelcome interference by lawyers and politicians in the medical sphere	–	25%	11%
For Patients:			
personal stress	–	10%	34%
family stress/conflict	11%	25%	31%
For Both Clinicians & Patients:			
patient lack of understanding of CPR and/or DNR	11%	7%	8%
more inappropriate DNR	6%	25%	19%
unwelcome interference with doctor-patient relationship	–	22%	34%
reluctance of M.D's to discuss and/or write DNR order	33%	-	–

* Respondents permitted more than one response, percents may exceed 100.

Table 4. ICU Experiences of Medical Directors Who Think That the DNR Law Provides Humane DNR.

	% Who Agree	Total N	P Value
Under 2/3 time spent in ICU	46%	(69)	
Over 2/3 time spent in ICU	71%	(14)	.05

Table 5. Impact of Hospital Control on Medical-Directors' Perceptions of the DNR Law

	Community		University		P Values
	% Who Agree	Total N	% Who Agree	Total N	
Clinicians have benefitted	44%	(55)	86%	(21)	.01
Patients have benefitted	48%	(56)	85%	(21)	.01
The law provides humane DNR	45%	(51)	63%	(19)	–

Table 6. Impact of Hospital Size on Medical-Directors' Perceptions of the DNR Law

	Under 300 Beds		Over 300 Beds		P Values
	% Who Agree	Total N	% Who Agree	Total N	
Clinicians have benefitted	44%	(43)	65%	(46)	.05
Patients have benefitted	40%	(43)	73%	(48)	.001
The law provides humane DNR	38%	(42)	63%	(41)	.05

Table 7. Impact of Hospital Location on Medical-Directors' Perceptions of the DNR Law

	Upstate		Downstate		P Values
	% Who Agree	Total N	% Who Agree	Total N	
Clinicians have benefitted	43%	(51)	64%	(39)	.05
Patients have benefitted	45%	(51)	68%	(41)	.05
The law provides humane DNR	35%	(47)	69%	(36)	.01

OPEN-ENDED QUESTIONS

Within each of the three clinician categories, about two-thirds chose to answer either, or both, of the open-ended questions about advantages or disadvantages they perceive: 69% (84/121) of the Nursing Directors; 62% (59/95) of the Medical Directors; and 67% (116/173) of the Hematologist-Oncologists. In the following tables, (Tables 2 and 3), the percents shown are based upon smaller numbers because not all answered both open-ended questions. In light of the varying and overall smaller numbers of respondents who chose to answer these questions, no tests of statistical significance have been performed on this data.

Differences between the three groups of respondents are highlighted in Table 2 which reports on opinions which were volunteered by respondents in response to the question of why they thought patients and/or clinicians had benefitted from the DNR Law. As can be noted, many Nursing-Directors perceive benefits of the law, but few Medical-Directors or Hematologist-Oncologists do. This table is based upon answers given by the few respondents who mentioned advantages of the law: 64% of the Nursing Directors; 31% of the Medical Directors and 14% of the Hematologist-Oncologists.

Altogether, 61% of the Nursing-Directors specifically cite approval of the law on basis of its advantages for patients: "The law has made the subject public – patients are more aware and have more voice in the decision. More M.D.s are forced to really discuss DNR with the patient"; "Individuals have the right of self-determination in regards to terminal disease"; "M.D.s should not have the responsibility over an individual's fate or control whether he lives or dies"; "The law has helped patients and families in making the decisions"; "The law allows peaceful death"; "Death with dignity is a definite possibility now". These comments, and many others clearly demonstrate the continued salience of the role of Patient Advocate for the Nursing Directors. About half (48%) of this group mention that the law has aided them in their role as ICU Nursing Director by providing guidelines for DNR and legal protection to the clinician: "the law protects the practitioner from accusations"; "the law has provided a framework and legal documentation for the patient as well as the M.D."; "The law probably protects the clinician more than the patient".

Some comments by those Medical-Directors who see benefits in the law: "Patients are more aware now"; "the law has increased the public's awareness"; "the law encourages the patient to be an active participant in his own care and management"; it "clarifies legalities so that all is clearer for the doctor and patient"; "the formalization of DNR makes it doctor-friendly and reduces risk of litigation".

Hematologist-Oncologists' favorable comments include: "Patients feel more comfortable (now) that the state has approved these discussions"; "the single most valuable aspect of the law has been to increase the dialogue between doctor, patient and family on the subject of CPR"; "doctors can feel more comfortable ordering a DNR now that it is permissible by law"; "it may offer us some protection".

This table has provided insight into why Nursing-Directors tend to approve of the law so unanimously. That is, it confirms that these Nursing-Directors' nursing school socialization into the role of Patient Advocate retains its power even when the nurse later takes on the additional role of ICU administrator (in which role, the law is approved of because it provides legal guidelines and protection.) In contrast, only about half as many of the Medical Directors mention specific benefits of the law; even fewer Hematologist-Oncologists do.

Table 3, like Table 2, reports on opinions which were volunteered by the three groups of respondents. Here, answers to the question of why they thought patients and clinicians would have been better off without the DNR Law are presented. This table is based upon answers given by the large numbers of respondents who pointed out problems they had with the law, i.e., 82% of the 84 Nursing Directors; 80% of the 59 Medical Directors; and 94% of the 116 Hematologist-Oncologists.

As can be seen, a number of problems with the law have been mentioned by respondents. Notable here is the 94% of Hematologist-Oncologists who have volunteered multiple reasons why both they and their patients would have been better off without the law. Medical-Directors have lower levels of complaints; Nursing-Directors have the lowest level of all. Objections to the law fell into three broad areas: those focused on problems for the clinician; those focused on perceived adverse impact on patients and families; those whose impact falls on both patients and clinicians.

Of interest here is the recognition that Nursing-Directors (i.e., nurses), and doctors, whether Medical-Directors or Hematologist-Oncologists, perceive several separate and distinct problem areas with the law. For example, one-third of Nursing-Directors report that they have problems because many physicians are reluctant to discuss DNR with patients, and to write a DNR order. Typical comments are: "Many doctors use the regulation to meet their own beliefs on DNR. At times, doctors do not give enough information to patients and families to make an appropriate decision"; "some doctors do not morally agree with DNRs and say things to families like 'How can you do this?' How can anyone sign a paper after listening to that?"; "Doctors rebel against discussing DNR status with critical patients when nurses ask them to"; "There is no recourse for the family of a patient who wishes a DNR but the doctor refuses it"; "Some doctors have a problem discussing death and treatment options." Again, the power of the role of Patient Advocate is demonstrated.

For the Medical-Directors and Hematologist-Oncologists, there are different concerns. Both of these physicians resent interference in their medical workplace environment. The Hematologist-Oncologists, whose relationship with their dying private patients is that of guide, especially resent interference with the doctor-patient relationship. Comments include: "the law diminishes the delicate interpersonal patient/physician relationship necessary to arrive at these decisions"; "the law is too rigid – does not take into account hopeless situations and psychological trauma involved"; "it interferes with the physician assisting patients in making very difficult decisions"; "the law is an intrusion into doctor/family/patient relationships"; "the law does not allow doctors to handle the situation gently and humanely"; "it destroys the warm and personal relationship between patient and doctor which should exist"; "we can no longer individually practice medicine – cookbook medicine is inhumane"; "Doctor is retained to make medical decisions. It should be left to his judgment".

In contrast, the Medical-Directors are more vexed by interference with their decisionmaking powers and prerogatives: For example, "too much law in the hands of people outside the medical profession is problematic"; "the law antagonizes most of the medical community and produces a counter reaction against it"; "DNR is a technical decision (mainly) and not a philosophical one"; "the law only produces stumbling blocks"; "I foresee a never-ending state intrusion into medical practice"; "Damn armchair quarterbacks!".

Some Medical-Directors and Hematologist-Oncologists state that they disapprove of the law because of the stress on patients who are now forced to discuss their own impeding demise. As one would expect, given that the patients they must (under the law) talk to about DNR are their own private patients, many Hematologist-Oncologists object to the law on that basis, e.g., "not all patients want to confront their own mortality. Even those who know they have a terminal illness may deny to the very end and cannot deal with the DNR consent"; "nobody wants to die"; "telling a patient he is dying increases stress and guilt in families".

Similarly, objections to the law, because of family stress and conflict, are mentioned more by Hematologist-Oncologists and Medical-Directors than by Nursing-Directors. The different relationships that these three groups have with ICU patients play a role here, i.e., for the Hematologist-Oncologist, as noted above, these are private patients whose family members are undoubtedly known to him/her. For the Nursing-Director and Medical-Director however, theirs is not a personalized relationship of long-standing, but a medical and administrative one which often has begun only when the patient entered the ICU.

Other problems cited were objections to the practical, rather than to the philosophical components of the law, e.g., the red-tape and the sequencing of procedures. As can be seen, those in all three clinician categories raise these objections, with Hematologist-Oncologists hating the red-tape more than anyone else. Nursing-Directors cite problems with procedures more often. This undoubtedly because as non-physicians, Nursing-Directors must seek physicians' signatures and approval as part of the entire DNR process.

Another problem was the reported increase in inappropriate DNR since the law's inception. All three clinician groups note this, but Medical-Directors mention it more frequently than either of the other clinicians. Comments include: "too many patients get coded because of cumbersome paperwork"; "patients who are hopelessly ill are being resuscitated because the physician did not obtain a DNR consent"; "another ventilator victim of legislative imprisonment". As Tables 2 and 3 reveal, the three clinician categories surveyed here have differing reasons for liking or disliking the DNR Law. Nursing Directors' answers reveal their orientation as Patient Advocates. Hematologist-Oncologists' answers reveal resentment of interference with their professional relationships with patients and their families for whom they perceive the law as causing stress.

The range of answers given by Medical Directors reveal the broader range of their approval and/or disapproval of the law. As one might expect, these more "bureaucratized" physicians are troubled by the law's interference in the medical sphere and by their perception that the law has increased inappropriate DNR. However, in these answers one also glimpses the physician who is caring for his/her own patients and who therefore echoes the concerns of the Hematologist-Oncologist that the law's disadvantages include interference with doctor-patient relationships and elevation of stress levels of patients and families. Perhaps the two kinds of Medical Directors discussed above (i.e., "working" and "paper" directors) can be discerned here; however, this data set does not permit further investigation of the matter.

A number of respondents made suggestions about how the DNR Law's "problems" could be solved. These focus on three areas:

(1) correction of its bureaucratic and procedural problems (which has largely been accomplished);
(2) education of the public regarding: (a) CPR, its nature, use, and effectiveness, and (b) DNR, what it means, when it may be appropriate, and (c) the need for families to discuss and set guidelines for DNR in advance of a crisis;
(3) education for health care professionals regarding: (a) ways to discuss death with patients and families, and (b) ways to more effectively counsel patients and families about how to deal with guilt, and how to reach agreement regarding DNR orders.

CONTROL VARIABLES

In an attempt to determine whether clinicians' reactions to the law are a function of personal characteristics or of the context in which they work, a series of cross-tabulations were done. Control variables utilized were of two types:

(1) Personal Characteristics: age; gender; years of ICV experience, percent of work time spent in ICU;
(2) Structural Factors: Size of hospital as measured by number of beds; control of hospital as measured by being a community or a university hospital; location of hospital as measured by designation of "downstate," or "upstate." ("Downstate" includes the New York City metropolitan area.)

For the Nursing Directors, application of the control variables revealed no clusters of attitudes which were related to either the personal characteristics or the structural factors, nor were any expected, given the high level of agreement among this group.

For the Hematologist-Oncologists, the only characteristic which was found to have an impact on attitude was age, i.e., 41% of those over the age of forty think that the DNR Law provides humane DNR, but only 29% of those under the age of forty think that it does. This difference was not statistically significant.

When control variables are applied to the Medical Directors' responses, several patterns are revealed. Among the personal variables, one aspect of these Medical Directors' ICU experience has been found to have significant impact on their perceptions of whether or not the law provides for humane DNR; the percentage of work time (under 2/3 time vs. over 2/3 time) that is currently spent in the ICU. These results are presented in Table 4. A Chi-square test has been performed.

It is clear that the ICU experience of these Medical Directors have impact on their opinions about whether or not the law provides for humane DNR. In the above table, finding a positive relationship between perceptions of the law as humane and percent of their work time spent in the ICU is readily understandable, given the distinction between working directors and paper directors. Nearly three-fourths (71%) of the Medical Directors who spend more time in the unit think that the law does provide for humane DNR. This is very close to the 67% of Nursing Directors who report that attitude (see Table 1). In contrast, only 46% of Medical Directors who spend less time in the unit think that the law is humane – a percentage close to the 42% of Hematologist-Oncologists who report that attitude (see Table 1).

Among the structural variables, three factors have been found to have significant impact on the attitudes of Medical Directors toward the DNR Law: (1) the size of the hospital (under 300 beds vs. over 300 beds); (2) the form of control it is under (community vs. university); and (3) its location (upstate vs. downstate). In the following three tables, these are presented. Again, Chi-square tests of significance have been performed for each.

Analysis of these three tables reveals that attitudes of these Medical Directors are influenced by the nature of the hospital in which the ICU which they direct is located. Table 5 shows that Medical Directors who direct ICU's in university hospitals report the highest approval levels found, with 85% feeling that both patients and clinicians have benefitted from the DNR Law, while slightly under half of those who work in community hospitals feel that way. Differences between these two groups about the perceived "humaneness" of the DNR provided under the law are less striking, although more in the university setting feel that it is humane.

Table 6 examines impact of hospital size on ICU Medical Directors' attitudes. Those who work in larger hospitals report overall higher approval levels, with some two-thirds saying that clinicians have benefitted, and almost three-fourths saying that that patients have benefitted. In smaller hospitals, fewer see the law's benefits, with only 40% feeling that patients have benefitted. Those in larger hospitals are more likely to feel that the law provides humane DNR.

Table 7 reflects the impact of the hospital's location within New York State on Medical Directors' attitudes. Those who work in downstate hospitals report higher approval levels on all three measures than do those who work in upstate hospitals, where less than half think that clinicians and patients have benefitted from the law. Regarding whether the law provides humane DNR, those working in downstate hospitals are twice as likely to think that it does.

To summarize these findings, it is clear that characteristics of the hospital in which the ICU is located have powerful impact on Medical Directors' attitudes and opinions about the DNR Law. Those who direct ICU's in larger hospitals (many, but not all of which are downstate) are more likely to portray the DNR Law as helpful to both themselves and their patients. Similarly, they are more likely to feel that the DNR it provides is humane than are those who work in smaller upstate hospitals. Those who direct the ICU's in university hospitals, whether upstate or downstate, report the most favorable attitudes toward the law, feeling that it has benefitted both clinicians and patients. Regarding the humaneness of the DNR provided under the law, community and university hospital ICU Medical Directors are fairly close in attitude.

The common finding in these three tables is the contrast between attitudes of ICU Medical Directors who work in larger, university, and/or downstate hospitals, and attitudes of those who work in the smaller, community and/or upstate hospitals. Overall, the picture which emerges from the application of control variables upon the attitudes of Medical Directors is that approval of the law is higher among those who spend more of their working time there. The units in which they work tend to be located in large university hospitals. On the other hand, those who report lower approval levels are those who actually spend less of their working time there. These respondents tend to work in units which are located in smaller community hospitals.

As noted in Tables 4, 5, 6, and 7, utilization of control variables has enhanced the understanding of Medical-Director attitudes toward the DNR Law. Factors which have been found to have significant impact are those which focus on some aspect of the work site, e.g., location, size, control of the hospital, rather than on personal characteristics such as age or gender.

CONCLUSIONS

Differences in reactions to the New York State DNR Law for three groups of clinicians have been presented. Analysis of answers to open-ended questions has been undertaken, and control variables have been utilized in an effort to explain why these clinicians' attitudes vary.

Social Role theory, with its recognition that different positions in the social network evoke different attitudes, behaviors, and expectations, has been found to have considerable explanatory power.

The Nursing Directors' responses indicate overall approval of the New York State DNR Law. These nurses who, despite their added and administrative responsibilities in the ICU, and despite the recognition of some problems, (most notably the reluctance of some MD's to discuss DNR with patients) by and large, are pleased with the law. These Patient Advocates note that because the law forces doctors to discuss DNR with patients and families, it effectively removes total responsibility from doctors through the mandating of some level of patient self-determination. Further, although they recognize that some older, less-educated patients may not desire this decision-making power, other younger, more highly educated patients and their families do. In short, these nurses reveal their primary attitudinal and behavioral orientation as Patient Advocate in their support of the New York State DNR Law.

The Hematologist-Oncologists, on the other hand, express a high level of disapproval of the law. These physicians, by virtue of both their medical school training and their experience as community-based physicians, perceive themselves to be autonomous care-givers who, as patient guides, bear virtually complete medical and decisionmaking responsibility for their gravely ill patients. Their dislike for the law can be explained on several levels. First, because the law was imposed by administrative fiat, and not as a result of the exercise of professional judgement, one would expect to encounter some serious resistance from these autonomous professionals, e.g., "lawyers cannot comprehend such problems"; "the state now dictates medical practice."

Several components of role theory may provide further insight: (a) Role Conflict may be present because of the Medical Director's orientation toward action, in this case, CPR. This orientation may be thwarted by the patient or family who requests that a DNR order be written. (b) Role Ambiguity may be present as well, due to the newness (at the time of the study) of the law and its requirements. (c) Role Failure may be perceived by these Medical Directors who now must abrogate their previously-held, some may even say paternalistic power to make medical decisions in the best interests of patients without their input or that of their families. A number of comments by Hematologist-Oncologist point up perceptions of role problems: "cookbook medicine in inhumane because the law does not distinguish on basis of what caused the patient to arrest"; "the law undermines the primary care physician"; "we dedicate our lives to these problems"; "the law says in effect that 'we don't trust you'"; and thus, it "takes the thrill out of medical care." In short, many of these Hematologist-Oncologists reveal in their comments that they "oppose" the law because it, in their view, prevents them from performance of a core component of their role as Patient Guide, i.e., "making good and appropriate decisions for patients."

Between these two extremes of high approval of the law by Nursing Directors and basic disapproval of it by Hematologist-Oncologists, fall the opinions of ICU Medical Directors. Their midrange levels of approval for the DNR Law have been explored by means of open-ended questions and by application of control variables. As a result of these analyses, two subpopulations of Medical Directors have been noted: (a) those who generally approve of the law, thus somewhat resembling the Nursing Directors in their attitudes, and (b) those who generally oppose the law, thus somewhat resembling the Hematologist-Oncologists.

Those who demonstrate higher levels of approval of the law spend over two-thirds of their working hours on the unit and they work in large downstate university hospitals. These may in fact be the so-called "working" directors whose greater presence in the unit may cause them to perceive the same benefits of the law that Nursing Directors mention. In effect, they may, by virtue of increased patient and family contact, become, like nurses, "patient advocates."

Those Medical Directors who disapprove of the law tend to spend less than two-thirds of their working hours in the unit and they work in smaller upstate community hospitals. These may be the so-called "paper" directors who, while they do from time to time perform the administrative duties that the JCAHO mandates, by and large, they delegate these duties to others in the unit. One reason why they may dislike the law is because, as an innovation, it has created more work by necessitating the creation of new "pigeonholes," i.e., the reordering of old categories, routines and standards. Secondly, having been imposed from "above" by administrative fiat, the law would likely be seen as an assault on their autonomy ("I foresee a never-ending state intrusion into medical practice"). Further, given that the primary role of these "paper" directors is, in fact, like the Hematologist-Oncologists, community-based physician treating his/her own patients (i.e., they are Patient Guides), they disapprove of the law on basis of its intrusion into, as one Medical Director noted, "the intimate heart of the M.D.-patient relationship." Finally, their disapproval, like that of the Hematologist-Oncologists, and of some nurses as well, may be due to their perception of an increase in futile CPR since the law was passed. As one Medical Director noted, the paperwork involved in a DNR order ultimately has consigned some patients to being coded without reasonable expectation of any subsequent quality of life, i.e., "another ventilator victim of legislative imprisonment."

The distinction between "paper" directors and "working" directors appears to have significant explanatory power. Although it has not been possible to fully explore this theoretical insight within the framework of this study, it has provided tantalizing clues regarding attitudes and behaviors of ICU Medical Directors.

ACKNOWLEDGEMENTS

The author wishes to thank her colleagues, Robert Baker and Martin Strosberg, for their extraordinary patience and good humor, and most importantly, for their generously shared knowledge of the dynamics of the hospital ICU and of bioethical reform. Truly, this chapter reflects their thinking as much as the author's.

BIBLIOGRAPHY

1. Aries, N. and Kennedy, L.: 1986, 'The Health Labor Force: The Effects of Change,' in P. Conrad and R. Kern (eds), *The Sociology of Health and Illness: Critical Perspectives* (2nd ed.), St. Martin's Press, NY, pp. 196–207.
2. Becker, H. *et al.*: 1961, *Boys in White: Student Culture in Medical School*, University of Chicago, Chicago, IL.
3. Bloom, S. and Wilson, R.: 1972, 'The Patient-Practitioner Relationship,' in H. Freeman, *et al.* (eds.) *Handbook of Medical Sociology* (2nd ed.), Prentice-Hall, Englewood Cliffs, NJ., pp. 315–339.
4. Croog, S. and VerSteeg, D.: 1972, 'The Hospital as a Social System,' in H. Freeman, et. al. (eds.), *Handbook of Medical Sociology* (2nd ed.), Prentice-Hall, Englewood Cliffs, NJ., pp. 274–314.
5. Davis, F.: 1972, *Illness, Interaction, and the Self*, Wadsworth, Belmont, CA.
6. Freidson, E.: 1970, *Profession of Medicine*, Harper and Row, NY.
7. Georgopoulos, B. and Mann, F.C.: 1972, 'The Hospital as an Organization,' in Jaco, E. G. (ed.), *Patients, Physicians and Illness* (2nd ed.), Macmillan, NY., pp. 304–311.
8. Hingson, R. *et al.*: 1981, *In Sickness and in Health: Social Dimensions of Medical Care*, Mosby, St. Louis, MO.
9. Joint Commission on the Accreditation of Healthcare Organizations: 1989, *Accreditation Manual for Hospitals*, Joint Commission on the Accreditation of Healthcare Organizations, Chicago, IL.
10. Linton, R.: 1936, *The Study of Man*, Appleton-Century-Crofts, NY.
11. Mauksch, H.: 1972, 'Nursing: Churning for Change,' in H. Freeman, et. al. (eds.) *Handbook of Medical Sociology* (2nd ed.), Prentice-Hall, Englewood Cliffs, NJ., pp. 206–230.
12. Mintzberg, H.: 1989, *Mintzberg on Management: Inside Our Strange World of Organizations*, Free Press, NY.
13. Strosberg, M. *et al.*: 1990, 'Nursing Perception of the Availability of the Intensive Care Unit Medical Director for Triage and Conflict Resolution,' *Heart and Lung* **19**, 452–455.
14. Zussman, R.: 1992, *Intensive Care: Medical Ethics and the Medical Profession*, University of Chicago Press, Chicago, IL.

PART V

RETROSPECTION AND REFLECTION

TRACY E. MILLER

AN ASSESSMENT OF THE UNION COLLEGE STUDY AND A RESPONSE TO ROBERT BAKER'S ANALYSIS OF THE DNR LAW

Since its inception, the Task Force on Life and the Law has welcomed comments from the public – health care professionals and administrators, patients and families, civic organizations and others. This dialogue with diverse organizations and individuals in New York State has been central to the Task Force's work. The Task Force members have also carefully examined studies of clinical practice that might shed light on the impact of the four laws now in place based on their recommendations. However, commentary on or studies about public policy are most useful when they are balanced and based on available facts or evidence. Unfortunately, the study by Baker *et al.*, "The 1988 Do-Not-Resuscitate Reforms: A Comparative Study of the Impact of the New York DNR Policy and the JCAHO Accreditation Requirments for DNR Policy" (this volume, pp. 263–301), and "The Legitimation and Regulation of DNR Orders", (this volume, pp. 33–301), fall short of both criteria.

This article comments specifically on two chapters in this volume (pp. 33–101 and pp. 263–301). It focuses on these two chapters for several reasons. First, the authors draw conclusions that are far more sweeping than those asserted by other authors in this volume. Second, many of their conclusions are not supported by the data in their study, or are directly contradicted by the studies of clinical practice. Finally, their principal arguments are inherently contradictory or incoherent. By addressing only the primary shortcomings in their arguments, this article does not intend to suggest agreement with other facts or arguments they assert.

Through the looking glass

In drawing conclusions about the DNR law, Baker (this volume, pp. 33–301), and Baker *et al.* (this volume, pp. 263–301, hereafter The Union College Study) rely solely on clinicians' perceptions about the impact of the DNR. They do so despite the studies of actual practice presented in this volume which show that those perceptions were inaccurate. As a result, their analysis of the law and its impact rest on false factual assumptions. This is most devastating to arguments on the critical issue of

R. Baker & M.A. Strosberg (eds.), Legislating Medical Ethics: A Study of the New York Do-Not-Resuscitate Law, 325–332.

futile CPR and the extent of "reform" achieved in New York and other states concerning discussion between patients and doctors about CPR.

The data presented in The Union College Study report on the perceptions of physicians and nurses about clinical practices before and after the DNR law. In contrast, Ahronheim *et al.* ([1], this volume, pp. 235–240), Kamer *et al.* (this volume, pp. 227–234), and Quill and Bennett (this volume, pp. 241–250) examined actual practices before and after implementation of the DNR law by evaluating patient records to determine the patient's medical condition, written DNR status, whether the order was based on patient consent and other variables. Their study results show the fault line between the perceptions of physicians and actual practice about several crucial factors. Among other findings, the data of practice show that futile CPR did not increase following implementation of the law and that physicians were not more likely to discuss the decision with patients. These findings directly contradict the two principal findings of The Union College Study of physician perception: that futile CPR increased as did consultation by physicians with patients about CPR.

Rather than address the disparity in the findings in the Union College Study and the other studies in this volume, both Baker and Baker *et al.* treat the data on perception as fact, largely ignoring the data on clinical practice. Throughout his article (pp. 33–101), Baker confuses perception and fact, suggesting that the Union College Study, in contrast to those by Ahronheim *et al.* and Kamer *et al.*, evaluated the law's "impact on the less readily detectable aspects of clinical practice: slow and show-coding; undocumented DNR orders; and, most importantly, clinician-patient discussion of the CPR/DNR decision" (Introduction, this volume p. xii). Yet, the studies by Ahronheim *et al.* and Kamer *et al.* as well as the Quill study cover precisely these aspects of practice.

Data about clinician perceptions can offer important insight: it can yield information about how clinicians understand law or professional guidelines, their attitudes about policies or practices, and the need for professional education. However, where clinicians' perceptions are directly contradicted by data about clinical practice, those perceptions cannot be used to gauge clinical practice or the impact of a law on practice, as Baker has done throughout the analysis [7], pp. 116–118).

The elusive meaning of futility

The national debate on medical futility has highlighted the wide range of meanings clinicians assign to the term futility and the need to define futility in order to discuss the issue intelligently. At the end of his article [2], Baker argues that physicians' authority to decide unilaterally about treatment should depend on how "futility" is defined. He distinguishes situations when "CPR is inefficacious, in which physicians have a legitimate right to determine the appropriateness of CPR; and those in which CPR is efficacious but the meaning and value of the effects are open to question." He then states that physicians who decide about CPR in the latter situations "violate the fundamental tenet of the bioethical revolution: that the right to determine the meaning and value of life properly resides with the patient" ([2] p. 96).

Remarkably enough, The Union College Study never defined "futility" for the respondents in the many questions it asked about the issue. It did, however, ask respondents how they would define the term: 70% of hematologists/oncologists, one-half of the critical care nurses and almost two-thirds of critical care doctors defined CPR as futile in situations when the patient would not leave the hospital following CPR or would be left in a coma. Baker *et al.* do not report further on the responses, but other clinicians undoubtedly defined the term more broadly. Hence, the overwhelming majority of respondents to the study defined futility in a way that Baker rejects as an unacceptable violation of patient or family choice.

Baker does not recognize this fact; he relies on data on physicians' perceptions about "futile" CPR and individual statements by doctors to condemn the law for leading to the provision of CPR that is "cruel" and "perverse." He also repeatedly presents physician rage about the requirement of patient or surrogate consent as justifiable and appropriate because it leads to "futile" CPR. He never acknowledges that physicians' understanding of futility is directly at odds with his own, or that patient or family consent in the vast majority of cases deemed "futile" by physicians is essential to prevent unilateral physician judgments about what he describe's as "the value and meaning of life."

Righteous protest?

One central thesis of Baker's analysis of the DNR law is the notion that physicians' protest against the law reflected weak not strong paternalism; physicians did not object to discussing CPR with patients or to the loss of professional discretion about this matter, but resented the provision of "futile" CPR. To support this argument, Baker repeatedly asserts that clinicians welcomed the DNR law as a way to empower patients, "... all three categories of respondents to the Union College survey overwhelmingly welcomed the DNR law because it gives the patient and family the decisive voice in making such a choice" ([2] p. 65).

This claim and the conclusions that rest upon it are contradicted by the data from his own study. Other clinical studies reported in the medical literature about physician practices in discussing CPR with patients also consistently contradict this conclusion [4]. The Union College Study did not ask clinicians directly whether they support patient autonomy or the law as a vehicle to enhance patient autonomy. Virginia Dersch's analysis of the responses to questions about the law's "advantages" and "disadvantages," although not statistically significant, offers the only insight available from the Union College Study on this question [5]. According to her analysis, nurses strongly favored the law because it empowered patients and families, while physicians, especially the hematologists/ oncologists, did not. In an open-ended question, 64% of nurses mentioned advantages of the law, 31% of medical directors did so, and only 14% of hemotologists/oncologists noted that the law had any advantages [5].

The majority of nurses note the advantages of the law for patients, often pointing out that the law gives patients a greater voice in the decision. In addition, nearly one-third of the nurses reported problems with implementing the law because many doctors are reluctant to discuss CPR with patients and to write a DNR order. In contrast, few hemotologists/oncologists responded to the question about benefits of the law, although many mentioned disadvantages. Dersch cited the following physician comments as typical: "M.D. is retained to make medical decisions. It should be left to his judgment." "Not all patients want to confront their own mortality. Even those who know they have a terminal illness may deny to the very end and cannot deal with DNR consent." Dersch concluded that medical directors resented most the interference "with their decision-making powers and prerogatives," while many hemotologists/oncologists objected specifically to the duty to talk with patients.

On what grounds then did Baker *et al.* conclude that "all three categories" of clinicians in their study support patient autonomy? Perhaps he inferred this conclusion from the data that clinicians perceived an increase in physician discussion about CPR with patients following implementation of the law. This inference cannot be sustained. The data on clinical practice show that no such increase occurred. Moreover, even if it had occurred, it would reflect physicians' compliance with or response to the law, not necessarily their support for patient autonomy.

In his article (this volume, pp. 33–101), Baker states "Normally, the physician orders and the staff acts – patients are not part of the chain of command." The DNR law changed this for decisions about CPR, requiring discussion with patients and their families. Far from "welcoming" this change, as Virginia Dersch's analysis [5] shows, many physicians deeply resented the interference in their clinical prerogatives and power, a factor that would have exerted a strong influence on all their responses about the law.

Medical futility and the Task Force position

Baker describes his position on policies for "futile" CPR at the close of his article (this volume, pp. 33–101). Essentially, he advocates that physicians should seek consent from patients or surrogates, unless CPR is physiologically futile, meaning that it will not restore cardiac or respiratory function. In these cases, he recommends that physicians inform the patient or surrogate of this fact and write the order. He neglects to mention that this is virtually identical to the New York State Department of Health (DOH) interpretation of the DNR law, and the Task Force's own explicit position on medical futility [7]. The DOH spelled out this interpretation in a memorandum and a guidebook for health care professionals distributed at the Union College Conference in 1990 (this volume, pp. 415–438). The Task Force endorsed this DOH interpretation at that time, and articulated its position and reasoning at length in its 1992 report, *When Others Must Choose* [8].

Instead of acknowledging the explicitly stated DOH and Task Force position, Baker insists that the law was intended to create a right to CPR, even when physiologically futile. He also rejects the DOH and Task Force position on another crucial point; the ability of physicians to make an appropriate medical judgement not to resuscitate at the time the patient arrests, even in the absence of a DNR order. Here too, the DOH and Task Force position were explicit. A 1988 DOH memorandum stated that the law did not change physicians' authority to decide about CPR at the time of arrest. Baker presents convoluted arguments to suggest that Robert Swidler and the DOH misunderstood or misinterpreted the statute on this point. Specifically, he asserts that this interpretation could not apply in hospitals because physicians could not "issue" an order not to "attempt" CPR at the time of arrest without following the requirements of the statute for orders written in advance ([3], p. 296).

This analysis is wrong. The statute by its clear intentions covers only DNR orders written in advance of an arrest. Indeed, this is precisely how Baker describes the common understanding of a DNR order, at the beginning of his article. The DNR law is silent on orders at the time of arrest, leaving DOH the authority as well as the responsibility to provide an interpretation consistent with legislative intent. The answer to his query of how the law could allow such decisions if it intended to promote advance discussion about CPR with patients and families is simple – neither DOH nor the Task Force believed that patients should be punished for physicians failure to raise the issue in advance.

Basically, Baker argues that the interpretation offered by the lawyers who drafted the law, by the Task Force that proposed it, and by the agency responsible for enforcing it should be ignored. In essence, after describing the "perversities" that lawyers "inflicted on the clinical context," Baker suggests his own legal perversity, one that denies physicians precisely the latitude he argues the law should have granted to avoid default CPR – CPR provided inappropriately because no DNR order had been entered. To bolster his argument, he quotes one hospital lawyer who was "outraged" that the DOH treated the law so "cavalierly," by issuing this interpretation (this volume, pp. 158–159). In the only allusion to the data on clinical practice, Baker notes parenthetically that this reaction could not have been too widespread. Nor should it have been. Poor legal judgment should neither be considered authoritative nor relied upon in matters that directly affect the well-being of patients.

On legislating morality

Baker asserts that one of the principal problems of the DNR law is that it "legislated morality" – it imposed an alien moral code on a "significant minority or majority of those affected by the law." His definition of legislating morality is odd, focusing on numbers or percent of those affected, rather than on the nature of the conduct proscribed or the proscription. But even taking the definition on its own terms, the argument is incoherent for the simple reason that he treats only doctors as "those affected by the law" – patients, families and others somehow dropped out of the picture.

Baker cites individual clinicians' comments and his data on physician perception to support the claim that the law imposed an "alien moral code" on an objecting public. He never mentions the large body of data on patient attitudes about CPR and the desire for discussion with doctors. In fact, the DNR law did constrain physicians, not patients or families (whom it sought to empower). Admittedly too, physicians are an important voice on bioethical concerns, and a significant political force, but they are not the majority or even a significant minority of those affected by the DNR law.

Baker draws upon an analogy to prohibition to make his point. This is inapposite; prohibition did restrain the conduct of a large segment of the public. A better analogy would be restrictions on self-referral to laboratories owned by doctors, caps on physician fees or laws protecting patient confidentiality, all of which restrain a small minority to promote the interests of the large majority. Laws against murder or corporate polluting would also improperly "legislate morality" under Baker's definition; he also imposes an "alien moral code" on those whose conduct they seeks to constrain.

Comparing New York to other states

As I remarked in my previous article (this volume, pp. 105–132), the data relied upon by Baker *et al.* in comparing the impact of New York's DNR law and reform by the Joint Commission on the Accreditation of Health Care Organizations in other states is too flawed to serve that purpose. One other observation about the comparison merits comment. As evidence of the success of the JCAHO's reforms (effective outside New York) in dealing with "futile" CPR, Baker asserts that the dissatisfaction which surrounded the DNR law in New York State was "nowhere in evidence in the medical literature" outside New York State. On the contrary, few issues have received as much sustained attention, and protest, in the recent medical/ethical literature as medical futility. While the comments focus on hospital policies or individual cases, not on a particular law, they hardly reflect resolution of the issue or suggest that it is somehow unique to New York State. Instead, the articles address the complex social and ethical issues that underlie the debate as it relates not only to CPR but to all medical treatments.

REFERENCES

1. Ahronheim, J., Maheswaran, S., Rosenberg, C.: 1992, 'Impact of Do-Not-Resuscitate Legislation on the Use of Cardiopulmonary Resuscitation in Teaching Hospitals', *New York State Journal of Medicine*, 92: 181–185. See this volume, pp. 235–240.
2. Baker, R.: 1995, 'The Legitimation and Regulation of DNR Orders', this volume, pp. 33–101.
3. Baker, R., Strosberg, M., Schmee, J. *et al.*: 1995, 'The 1988 DNR Reforms: A Comparative Study of the Impact of the DNR Law and JCAHO Accreditation Requirements for DNR Policy', this volume, pp. 263–301, also referred to as the, 'Union College Study'.
4. Council on Ethical and Judicial Affairs, American Medical Association: 1991, 'Guidelines for the Appropriate Use of Do-Not-Resuscitate Orders', *Journal of the American Medical Association* **265**, 1871.
5. Dersch, V.: 1995, 'Differences in Clinical Reactions to New York State DNR Law', this volume pp. 303–321.
6. Kamer, R., Dieck, E., McClung, J. *et al.*: 1995, 'Effect of New York State's Do-Not-Resuscitate Legislation on In-Hospital Cardiopulmonary Resuscitation Practice', *American Journal of Medicine* 88, 108–111.
7. Miller, T.: 1995, 'Taking Stock of Do-Not-Resuscitate Policies: Perceptions and Practice', this volume, pp. 105–132.
8. New York State Task Force on Life and the Law: 1992, *When Others Must Choose*, New York, N.Y.
9. Quill, T., Bennett, N.: 1995, 'The Effects of a Hospital Policy and State Legislation on Resuscitation, Orders for Geriatric Patients', this volume, pp. 241–250.

ROBERT BAKER

A REVIEW OF THE EMPIRICAL STUDIES OF THE DNR LAW AND A REJOINDER TO TRACY MILLER

Tracy E. Miller, Executive Director of the New York State Task Force on Life and the Law, charges that "studies of actual [clinical] practice presented in this volume...show that [the Union College Study] rest[s] on false factual assumptions" [12, p. 325]. These charges, and those she levels against the implications we draw from similar findings made independently by Dr. Norton Spritz [18], are serious, but they arise from fundamental misunderstandings about the nature of clinical phenomena and of the findings of the five empirical studies of the DNR law. In this chapter I will show that Miller's readings of the empirical studies are incorrect, that her charges are therefore unfounded, and that her misreading of the empirical studies obscures the extent to which the DNR law successfully empowered patients.

There have been five empirical studies of the DNR Law, Ahronheim *et al.*, ([1, 2]), Kamer *et al.* ([8] [9]), Quill and Bennett ([15, 16]), Spritz [18], and the Union College Study [5]. Miller believes that there is a fundamental difference between these studies: the first three "report on fact," the other two on "impressions." When studies of "fact" conflict with studies of "impressions," Miller argues, impressions must yield to fact. Thus, since Miller believes that there is a conflict between the findings of two "impressionist" studies, and the findings of the three "factual" studies, she argues that the findings of the Spritz and Union College studies cannot be used to measure the extent to which the DNR Law empowered patients. Her analysis rests on two assumptions: that one set of findings is about "facts" while the other is about "impressions"; and that the findings of the two types of studies are in conflict. To assess her critique, therefore, we need to examine carefully what was actually studied by the various research teams, and what the various research teams found.

What the researchers studied

Ahronheim and her colleagues studied reports of CPR documented in the *charts* of patients who died while on the medical services of three hospitals (Bellevue, New York University Hospital, and New York Veterans Hospital), during the 12 months prior to and following the enactment of the DNR law. Kamer and his colleagues reviewed the *charts* of all adult inpatients who died at the Westchester County Medical Center during the

R. Baker & M.A. Strosberg (eds.), Legislating Medical Ethics: A Study of the New York Do-Not-Resuscitate Law, 333–346.

three months prior to the implementation of the DNR law and during a three-month period a year later, for indications of CPR, for DNR orders, and for indications of discussions with patients and/or their families about DNR status. Quill and Bennett had authored a pre-versus-post study of DNR orders (written in the *charts*) for selected over-79-years-old inpatients at Genesee Hospital after that hospital adopted a formal DNR policy in 1983; using the first two periods as comparison points, they studied the *charts* of all 79-year-old patients during an eighteen-month period (after the passage of the DNR law) noting evidence of CPR, DNR orders, and DNR discussions. Spritz analyzed 759 *responses* he received to a questionnaire sent to 1,600 members of the New York Chapter of the American College of Physicians (47.4% response rate). The Union College Study analyzed *responses* to a closed-ended and open-ended questionnaire received from 98 medical directors and 125 nursing directors at critical care units from 49% of New York's hospitals, and from 172 hematologist/oncologists practicing in the state (172/626, or 28%). They also *interviewed* the medical director, the nursing director, and the medical and nursing staff, of a surgical intensive care unit at a large urban teaching hospital and their counterparts at a small community non-teaching hospital (a total of 71 interviews).

Thus, the three studies Miller characterizes as reporting "actual practice" were based on chart reviews, whereas the two she dismisses as reporting mere "impressions" were based on questionnaire responses and interviews with clinicians. Which type of study is more "factual"? Which yields a better picture of "actual practice"? As we noted in the Introduction, the Union College research team opted to use the questionnaire and interview techniques developed in the field of moral psychology because we believed that "slow- and show-coding, undocumented DNR orders, and...clinician-patient discussion of the CPR/DNR decision" are not "readily detectable" from medical charts. Miller rejects this assumption, asserting that "the studies by Ahronheim *et al.* and Kamer *et al.* as well as the Quill study cover precisely these aspects of practice" ([12], p. 326). The researchers in question, however, disagree. Ahronheim and associates state that "it is not possible to know," on the basis of data collected from medical charts, "if there were an increase in the use of a so-called 'slow-code' [because] in such cases chart notes presumably would have indicated that such patients had undergone CPR" ([1], p. 184). Ahronheim's point is that medical charts are not photographs of clinical activities, they are entries made by doctors, nurses, and other health care personnel. Sometimes these entries accurately depict a clinical event; sometimes, for example, in the case of 'slow-codes', they obscure what actually happened.

Complicating matters further, prior to the 1988 reforms there was neither a standard way of giving a DNR order, nor of entering it into the medical chart; nor was there a standard method for indicating the nature of a DNR discussion with a patient or a surrogate, nor any standard way of indicating whether the discussion had culminated in informed consent. It is even difficult to determine whether patients actually had been subject to a DNR order in the pre-1988 era, since many DNR orders were entirely oral and never formally found their way onto patients' charts. Mindful of the difficulty of detecting informal and oral DNR orders, both Ahronheim and associates, and Kamer and colleagues, looked beyond the "Doctors Orders" section of the chart for evidence of a DNR order: Ahronheim presumed that an oral DNR order was given, even if no such order is in the "Orders" section, if there was a progress note "that a DNR discussion had taken place with a patient or a surrogate and that a decision not to resuscitate had been made," ([1], p. 182), Kamer, too, uses "no heroic measure," "supportive care only" and other comments in the progress section as presumptive evidence of an oral DNR order ([8], p. 109). Nonetheless, many oral DNR orders probably eluded detection, and all slow- and show-codes falsely appeared as instances of CPR. Moreover, because pre-1988 discussions with patients and surrogates are so vaguely documented, as Kamer and colleagues observe, "A more detailed evaluation of the actual decisionmaking process involved in generating a DNR order was beyond the scope of this study" ([8], p. 110). In other words, one can not determine, from the pre-1988 charts, the nature of DNR discussions doctors had with patients, and/or surrogates; more importantly, one can not determine whether these discussions culminated in informed patient and/or surrogate consent.

It is precisely this type of detail about the DNR decisionmaking process that Spritz and the Union College questionnaires sought to tease out. Before turning to these questionnaires, however, I should like to discuss the work of the one empirical researcher whose name is not mentioned by Miller, Robert Zussman. In "The Do Not Resuscitate Order as Ritual" [19], Zussman, a medical sociologist, offers the only observational study in the literature of the *actual practice of writing DNR orders* in teaching hospitals in New York and Massachusetts in the pre-1988 era. His studies underline the artifactual nature of medical records: that they are the creations of doctors and nurses. In the pre-1988 era, the various notes written into the medical record (to quote one New York physician) were "not for other house staff," that is, not for other physicians in residence at the hospital, because these physicians do not "really care what is in your note. They only care what the status of the patient is...." For whom, then, did the house staff write DNR notes and orders? Answer: "For anyone who may review the chart," that is, for "a lawyer or a medical review board" ([19], p. 217). Zussman supports this claim by reporting on an incident in a Massachusetts hospital in which an intern wrote a DNR status note in a patient's medical record. The intern had crossed out the abbreviation 'pt' and replaced it with the word 'patient'. When Zussman queried her about the change she remarked that it was necessary because charts are subject to medical audit, and because DNR orders are likely to become subjects of litigation.

Probing more deeply into the nature of DNR notes and orders, Zussman found that those written in New York State are more or less consciously constructed to conform to the "clear and convincing evidence" standard required by New York law; that is, unlike Massachusetts DNR notes and orders, New York DNR notes and orders are constructed in terms of the wishes of the patient. The term 'construct' is used advisedly. Zussman reports an interview with a New York intern who started to write a DNR note using the language about the *family's* wishes, and then, realizing that this language would not be acceptable under New York State law, *changed* his language to conform to the law; that is, the note was rewritten in terms of the *patient's* wishes. Clinical reality, of course, had not changed – only the language used in the chart was modified. Zussman also notes that the language of pre-1988 DNR notes and orders is not that of reportage; the charts do not state that Mrs. Smith says this and Mr. Jones says that; the language is almost always abstract, it refers not to named individuals but, more abstractly, to "the patient," "the family," "the daughter," "the son." Zussman concludes that: "the chart notes...at least in regard to the wishes of patients and their families, cannot be read as literal truth" ([19], p. 220): "DNR orders and other chart notes express an ideal. Invocation of patients' or families' wishes are, in many cases, fictions" ([19], p. 221). Insofar as Zussman is correct, insofar as DNR notes and orders are fictions, insofar as they do not reflect literal truth, they provide inadequate "data" for studies of "actual practice" (especially prior to 1988) and call into question virtually all claims about DNR discussions with patients and/or surrogates based on the study of patients' charts.

It is thus ironic that Miller classifies the three chart review studies as "factual" studies. These studies, like all studies of clinical phenomena, are attempts to understand clinical reality, and, like all studies, they have their limits, especially with respect to pre-1988 DNR orders. The Spritz and Union College studies were designed to complement the chart-review studies in a variety of ways. Spritz used scenarios to determine physicians attitudes towards futile CPR; the Union College Study asked clinicians to estimate the likelihood of different actions occurring at least once at the critical care unit where they work in March 1988 and in April 1989. Unlike Spritz's questions, the Union College questionnaire is formulated without personal pronouns. Miller, however, charges that asking "physicians about their own practices [is] a more reliable estimate than the impressions of a general shift in the practice of all physicians measured by the Union College Study" ([11], p. 112). As we observed in the methodology section of our study, and as we have argued in the *Journal of the American Medical Association* [4], "to ask physicians whether they themselves performed activities later declared illicit, courts distortion" [5]. James Rest's comprehensive overview of the methodologies of moral psychology [17], shows that any questionnaire that requires respondents to indict themselves, or their associates, is unlikely to be valid. Mindful of this, the Union College Study used a questionnaire that avoided asking respondents to admit wrongdoing; it simply asks them to estimate the likelihood of events occurring on the ICU where they work.

The Union College study also constructed a national comparison group of 81 critical care physicians, whose age, medical experience, and number of DNR orders written per week, were comparable to the 98 New York ICU medical directors who responded to the DNR questionnaire . As we ourselves were careful to point out ([8], pp. 267–268), there are some differences between the groups: Whereas all the 98 New York critical care physicians were medical directors at the time of the survey, only 56% of the national group were directors at the time of the survey. Since there is frequent turnover in the position of medical director, and since we found no significant difference between the responses of medical directors' and other ICU physicians, we do not believe that this difference is significant. More importantly, 81% of the national comparison group work at ICUs in over-300 bed hospitals, compared to 51% of New Yorkers. Although there was no statistically significant difference between the responses from medical directors at large and small hospitals on questions 1 through 16 in either the New York or the national comparison group, our colleague,

Virginia Dersch [6] found a statistically significant correlation between hospital size and physicians' attitude towards DNR reform on two sets of closed-ended questions: Are clinicians or patients are better off because of the DNR law? Is DNR more humane (after the 1988 reforms)? Medical directors at over-300-bed hospitals are more likely to view the DNR law's impact on clinicians and patients favorably ([6], Table 6). Thus, as we point out, and as Miller reiterates as a "criticism," the national comparison group *may* be somewhat more favorably disposed towards DNR reform than the New York critical care medical directors we studied ([5]).

Miller's major criticism is that the national comparison group is unrepresentative: "The study essentially relies on an average of one or two critical care doctors from each state to assess the impact of the Joint Commission on Accreditation of Health Care Organizations (JCAHO) policy in all hospitals in the state and nationally. While these responses may provide anecdotal insight or opinions, they do not constitute 'data'" ([11], p. 123). Unfortunately, Miller misunderstands our methodology. We were *not* conducting a national survey, we were constructing a comparison group. Our hypothesis was that if the JCAHO reforms had an impact outside of New York comparable to the impact that the DNR law had in New York, an arbitrarily assembled group of critical care physicians from outside New York, comparable to the New Yorkers in age and experience, would perceive a comparable post-reform increase in DNR discussions, consent, and documentation. This hypothesis was *confirmed*. As Table 3, p. 281 ([5]) shows, the national comparison group perceived the same pattern of increase in consent, discussion, and documentation as the New York critical care medical directors. This confirmation can not be dismissed as a coincidence; it is statistically significant (p less than .05) on the Wilocoxon Signed-Rank test. Once we had established that both the New York and the national comparison group had a comparable experience with these aspects of DNR reform, it was reasonable to ask in what ways their experience differed. The answers to that question proved to be significant, as we shall see in the next section.

What the five empirical studies of the DNR law found

In the previous section we showed that the distinction Miller drew between "factual" and "impressionistic" studies was untenable, and that the methodological issues she raised were either trivial, or rested on misunderstandings about the methodologies employed. Her second charge, however, can be made quite independently: that the findings of the Union College Study must be rejected because they are contradicted by the three chart-review studies.

Are the findings of the five empirical studies of the DNR law inconsistent with each other? One point on which all three chart-review studies agree is that the level of documentation for DNR orders increased significantly after DNR reform. Ahronheim and associates report that: "Implementation of the [DNR] law was significantly associated with an increase in documentation. Before enactment, DNR status was more often indicated as a progress note without a formal order on the order sheet. The increase in the use of formal orders was significant" ([1], p. 182). Kamer and colleagues found that DNR orders on the order sheet increased from 22% pre-law to 93% post-law ([8], Table II, p. 109). Quill and Bennett found that when the Genesee Hospital adopted its formal DNR policy in 1983, DNR orders increased from 21% to 76%, post DNR reform, the level of DNR orders increased to 84%. ([16], Table 1, p. 244). Do these findings contradict the findings of the Union College Study? Questions 3, 4, and 5 address the issue of writing a DNR order at the request of a patient or with patient or family consent ([5], Table 2, p. 269). Question 6 asks about writing an undocumented verbal DNR order without informing patients or family. All three categories of clinicians surveyed reported a statistically significant increase in writing DNR orders and a correlative statistically significant decrease in undocumented DNR orders. Thus the findings of the Union College Study and of the chart-review studies coincide; all the studies corroborate each other.

Miller contends, however, that the chart-review studies "show that futile CPR did not increase following implementation of the law and that physicians were not more likely to discuss the decision with patients. These findings directly contradict the two principal findings of the Union College Study of physician perception: that futile CPR increased as did consultation by physicians with patients about CPR" ([12], p. 326). Are the findings contradictory? On the question of "consultation of physicians with patients" Kamer and colleagues found a statistically non-significant *increase* in discussions with patients from 13% to 16% ([8], Table 3); Quill and Bennett found a statistically non-significant *increase* in discussions with patients from 22% to 27% ([16] Table 3, p. 246). Spritz's survey found that, by a greater than 2:1 margin, physicians believe that there has been an *increase* in the level of DNR discussion with patients ([18],Table I, Question 4, p. 253) and the Union College Study found that all three categories of clinicians report a statistically significant *increase* in the likelihood of such discussions at the p less than .01 level ([5]. Table 2, Questions 2 and 3, p. 269). All four studies that addressed this question found an *increase* in DNR discussions with patients, however, only Spritz's survey and the Union College Study found the increase to be statistically significant. There is thus a difference in the findngs, but characterizing this difference as a "contradiction" appears to be an "overstatement", since the studies corroberate each other.

It is reasonable, however, to consider possible explanations for the difference in the significance levels of the findings. Kamer and colleagues, and Quill and Bennett, between them, studied the records of patients who died at *two* hospitals. Moreover, as Kamer and colleagues note, their "investigation focused only on mortalities" and "was conducted in an acute care tertiary referral center, and its results can not necessarily be extrapolated to other hospitals" ([8], p. 110). In contrast, the Spritz and the Union College studies were not limited to the subset of mortalities, i.e., to those patients who died; nor were these studies limited to two hospitals. They were statewide: The responses analyzed in the Union College Study came from adult critical care units in 137 hospitals (49% of the non-VA, non-pediatric hospitals with ICUs in New York State), including not only Upstate-Urban areas but also the Downstate-Urban and the Upstate-Rural areas ([5], Table 1, p. 268). Thus, one way of explaining the higher significance levels found in the Union College Study is that, like Spritz's survey, it drew upon a more representative sample of patients for whom DNR orders were written, and upon a larger more geographically representative sample of hospitals in all regions of New York State.

There is another even more sigificant difference. As Zussman's research shows, statements about patients wishes in the pre-DNR law charts are often, "fictions". The two chart-review studies, however, had no way of excluding fictional patient-discussion entries (constructed to conform with New York law), and would naturally tend to overstate patient participation in DNR decisionmaking in the pre-DNR law era. The clinician surveys used by Spritz and the Union College Study, on the other hand, were not likely to be distorted by fictional chart entries and thus probably represent more accurately the extent to which actual discussions with patients increased after the passage of the DNR law.

The second area in which Miller contends that the chart-review studies "directly contradict" the findings of the Union College Study involves "futile CPR." Miller asserts that the chart-review studies "show that futile

CPR did not increase following implementation of the law" whereas the Union College Study finds that it did increase. In order to claim that the Union College Study "directly contradicts" the chart studies, Miller misstates the findings of the three chart studies. They do not show that "*futile* CPR did not increase" because they did not analyze "futility." As Ahronheim and associates note, they had no method of assessing the "appropriateness" or "futility" of CPR ([2]); Kamer and colleagues make a similar disclaimer ([8], p. 110). What the chart-review studies show is that the level of CPR neither increased nor decreased after the implementation of the DNR law. To quote Ahronheim and associates: "This study has failed to demonstrate that the New York State law was associated with a significant change in the proportion of patients undergoing CPR before death" ([1], p. 183); Kamer and colleagues report their findings as follows: "Table 1 shows a nonsignificant decline in the use of CPR after the DNR law was implemented...There was no significant change in the number of patients undergoing CPR despite plans made to the contrary" ([8], p. 109). There is no mention of 'futility' in either of these findings and so they can not directly contradict any findings about futility in the Union College Study.

Kamer and colleagues' remark – "despite plans to the contrary" – is important. As the Task Force states in its Report, one purpose of the DNR law was to reduce "medically inappropriate resuscitation" by legitimating DNR orders and conferring legal immunity on physicians issuing DNR orders that conform to the law ([13], Section III). This strategy was partially successful because, as all the studies found, formal DNR orders *increased* after the law. Thus one would expect that, since there was an *increase* in formal DNR orders after DNR reform, *fewer* patients would receive CPR; in other words, there should have been a correlative *decrease* in the percentage of patients receiving CPR. Yet the three chart-review studies found no such decrease. Ahronheim and associates "found that, of patients who died [in the periods studied] 25.2% with advanced cancer and 30.3% with AIDS underwent CPR at least once prior to their death...A multivariant analysis revealed that, regardless of disease severity, the proportions undergoing CPR did not change between 1987 and 1989. Thus, despite the implementation of a law intended to reduce inappropriate resuscitations, CPR was the final procedure performed in a large portion of gravely ill patients, and was frequently performed even in conditions where survival is not expected" [2].

Thus, the real question about the New York DNR law is: Why did the

DNR law not *decrease* the level of medically inappropriate CPR, as it was intended to do? Kamer and associates suggest that the law may not have decreased CPR because it merely transformed oral orders, and orders written informally in the progress notes, into formal orders written in the "Orders" section of the medical chart. Thus while there were changes in documentation, the number of actual DNR orders remained constant and hence the level of CPR was not affected. This hypothesis is consistent with their data, but not with the findings of Ahronheim and associates (who found a significant increase in DNR orders at one of the hospitals studied). Moreover, the Kamer hypothesis leaves unanswered the following question: Why did not legalization prompt physicians to write more DNR orders? Why are 25% of terminal cancer patients and 30% of terminal AIDS patients still receiving CPR?

The case studies in Section Three and the Union College Study suggest one reasonable answer: Even though the DNR law encouraged physicians to write DNR orders, the law's extensive documentation requirements tended to frustrate their attempts to do so. Thus, The Union College Study found that 57.8% of critical care medical directors, and the same percentage of hematologist/oncologists, reported a statistically significant *increase* in the "failure to write DNR orders for terminally ill patients because of bureaucratic technicalities" ([5], Table 3, Question 14, p. 283). By contrast, 70% of the critical care physicians in the national comparison group reported *no change* in the difficulty of writing a DNR order following the JCAHO reforms, while 28% reported a statistically significant *decline* in the "failure to write DNR orders for terminally ill patients because of bureaucratic technicalities" ([5], Table 5, Question 14, p. 283). Thus the best explanation of why CPR did not decrease following the implementation of the DNR law would appear to be that the suppressive effect of the law's bureaucratic documentation requirements offset the advantages of legalization.

A similar explanation may also account for the finding in the Union College Study that Miller is most intent on challenging: that 43.4% of New York critical care medical directors and 52.6% of hematologist/oncologists report a statistically significant *increase* in futile CPR for irreversibly terminal patients, whereas 44% of critical care physicians in the national comparison group report a statistically significant *decrease* in futile CPR, while 53% report no change. Miller claims that this finding is contradicted by the chart studies. Ahronheim expressly denies this [2]. Quill and Bennett, go further, they document an *increase* in default CPR as a consequence of bioethical policy-making. Thus, they found that only 29% of patients who did not have a DNR order received CPR at the Gensee Hospital in the period before the Hospital implemented a DNR policy based on the New York State Medical Society Guidelines; this percentage climbed to 56% after the DNR policy was implemented; and to 92% after the DNR law was implemented ([16], Table 1, p. 244). Quill and Bennett interpret their findings as follows.

> One flaw of the New York State law and of our 1983 [DNR] policy is that they "presume consent" to CPR in all circumstance when no other order is explicitly stated or documented.
>
> ...the presumption that elderly patients with irreversible medical conditions and poor prognoses want CPR may be grossly inaccurate and misleading...Our 1990 review of the fourteen patients older than 79 years who died after receiving CPR in the first six months of 1990 was particularly disturbing in this regard. Only one of 14 charts showed evidence of an active, adequately informed decision in favor of CPR. Seven charts had no documentation that the question was considered, or that the patient (or surrogate) was informed of the prognosis or of the option of DNR. Three charts had indications that a discussion was initiated with the patient of family because of a deteriorating medical situation and a poor prognosis, but since there was no formal decision, the patient was given CPR. Finally, three charts had statements that the "family wants everything" in the face of a very poor prognosis, without any documentation of the patient's wishes, or of what specific interventions were implied by "wanting everything." It seems that the presumption of consent may force some patients to undergo CPR when uninformed or when there are breakdowns in communication...those who do not have DNR orders are now more likely to have CPR in the event of a cardiac arrest than before the policy or the law...([16], pp. 247–248).

Thus Quill and Bennett found that futile CPR *increased* because of the presumption of consent implicit in standard bioethical policy statements on DNR and explicit in the New York DNR law. Their findings and those of the Union College Study coincide – although both studies leave unanswered the question: "If the percentage of dying patients receiving futile CPR increased, and if the overall percentage of dying patients receiving CPR was not affected by the law, what type of CPR decreased?"

The five empirical studies of the New York DNR law do not resolve all the questions one might raise about the impact of the law, but taken together with the case studies (in Section Three) they form a coherent and consistent picture. To reiterate: Contrary to what Miller contends, there is no inconsistency, i.e., no "direct contradiction," between the findings of the five studies. According to the Task Force, the DNR law was designed to "respond to the dual concerns regarding issuance of DNR orders: (i) issuance of the order without the consent of the patient or the patient's family members and (ii) failure to issue the order when it is medically indicated and consistent with the wishes of the patient or the appropriate decisionmaker" ([13], p. 396). All five empirical assessment studies found that the DNR law did *not* achieve the latter goal, it did not remove the barriers to issuing a DNR order when DNR is medically indicated, *i.e.*, it did not reduce the level of medically inappropriate CPR. Moreover, the authors of all five studies (and of most of the Case Studies) also agree that one reason the DNR law did not reduce medically inappropriate CPR was the excessive consent and documentation requirements created by the law. Ahronheim, Quill and Bennett, and the authors of the Union College Study, have also argued that the default CPR that is implicit in the law, and that is presumed in most standard bioethical policy statements on CPR ([7], [10], [14]), was a major factor in the continuing high levels of medically inappropriate and futile CPR.

Turning to the first objective of the law, issuance of DNR orders without the informed consent of patients or their surrogates: All five studies found an increase in the discussion of DNR orders with patients and surrogates, but only Spritz and the Union College Study were able to establish that the increase was statistically significant. Only the Union College Study explicitly addressed the issue of informed consent. It found that all three categories of clinician studied reported a highly significant increase in informed consent by patients and families. Thus only the Union College Study was able to document the extent to which the Task Force succeeded in achieving its first and primary objective.

It is ironic, therefore, that the Executive Director of the Task Force, disturbed by the detailed description of the failings of the DNR law in the Union College Study, should challenge its findings, since the study also provides an equally detailed account of the DNR law's success. The Union College study shows that the DNR law *increased* physicians' discussions of DNR with patients and with their families; that the law *increased* the likelihood that a DNR order would be written at the request of patients and their families; that the law *increased* the likelihood that a DNR order would be written with the informed consent of patients and their families. More importantly, the Union College Study also shows that the Task Force accomplished its primary goal: eliminating the notorious "purple dots," that is, the issuance of undocumented DNR orders and DNR orders written "without the consent of the patient or the patient's family members." The DNR law significantly empowered patients and their families and, just as importantly, ended the judicial and legislative gridlock that had paralyzed bioethical reform in New York State. By legalizing true proxy consent in New York, the DNR law set the precedent for some of The Task Force's most significant efforts to date: New York's Health Care Proxy Law and the proposed Surrogate Consent law.

In conclusion, the Union College Study is the only empirical study to document the full range of the positive impact of New York's DNR law. Every researcher who participated in the study applauds the Task Force's accomplishments. As independent researchers, however, we are also duty-bound to inform the Task Force, and the bioethics community, of the failings of the DNR law. Our most significant finding was that these failings are really the failings of two decades of confused bioethical theorizing. All major bioethical policy statements recommend DNR policies that are biased in favor of CPR ([7], [10], [14]). While this bias was exacerbated by the Task Force's need to sell the DNR law to the New York State legislature as a form of consumer protection legislation (and, consequently, by the extensive documentation mandated by the law), ultimately the problem lay at the level of bioethical policy-making. New York's experience with the DNR law has thus been a dramatic revelation of the cruel consequences of the bias toward CPR in currently accepted bioethical policy. It demonstrates, to anyone who carefully reviews the empirical or the case studies, that when the bias towards CPR is enforced as law, the all too frequent consequence is inhumane CPR inflicted on uninformed and unconsenting patients. The Task Force, to its credit, acted immediately to minimize these unintended and undesired effects of the DNR law. By acting so swiftly, the Task Force set an example that the rest of the bioethical community would do well to emulate.

REFERENCES

1. Ahronheim, J., Maheswaran, S. Rosenberg, C.: 1992, 'Impact of Do-Not Resuscitate Legislation on the use of Cardiopulmonary Resuscitation in Three Teaching Hospitals,' *New York State Journal of Medicine* **92**, 181–185.
2. Ahronheim, J., Maheswaran, S. Rosenberg, C.: 1995, 'Does the New York State DNR Law Prevent Medically Inappropriate DNR?', this volume, pp. 235–240.
3. Baker, R., Strosberg, M., 1995, 'Introduction', this volume, pp. xiii–xvi.
4. Baker, R., Dersch, V., Fein I. A. *et al.*: 1989, 'Physicians' Attitudes Towards Using Deception', *Journal of the American Medical Association* **266**, 2233.
5. Baker, R., Strosberg, M., Schmee, J. *et al.*: 1995, 'The 1988 DNR Reforms: A comparative study of the New York DNR Law and the JCAHO accreditation requirements for DNR policy', this volume, pp. 263–301 (Also referred to as The Union College Study).
6. Dersch, V.: 1995, 'Differences in Clinician Reactions to the New York State DNR Law', this volume, pp. 303–321.
7. Hastings Center: 1987, *Guidelines on the Termination of Life-Sustaining Treatment and the Care of the Dying*, Indiana University Press, Bloomington, Indiana.
8. Kamer, R., Dieck, E., McClung, J., White, P.: 1990, 'Effect of New York State's Do-Not-Resuscitate Legislation on In-Hospital Cardiopulmonary Resuscitation Practice', *American Journal of Medicine* **88**, 108–111.
9. Kamer, R., McClung, J.: 1995, 'New York's Do-Not-Resuscitate Law: Benefit or burden', this volume, pp. 227–234.
10. Medical Society of the State of New York: 1982, *Guidelines for Hospitals and Physicians on 'Do Not Resuscitate'*, Lake Success, New York; reprinted, this volume, pp. 369–370.
11. Miller, T.: 1995, 'Taking Stock of Do-Not-Resuscitate Orders: Perception and Practice', this volume, pp. 105–132.
12. Miller, T.: 1995, 'An Assessment of the Union College Study and a Response to Robert Baker's Analysis of the DNR Law', this volume, pp. 325–332.
13. New York State Task Force on Life and the Law: 1986, *Do Not Resuscitate Orders: The Proposed Legislation and Report of the New York State Task Force on Life and the Law*, Second Edition, New York, N.Y., this volume, pp. 381–413.
14. President's Commission for the Study of Ethical Problems in Medicine and Biomedical and Behavioral Research: 1983, *Deciding to Forego Life-Sustaining Treatment: A Report on the Ethical, Medical, and Legal Issues in Treatment Decisions*, U.S. Government Printing Office, Washington, D.C. Excerpts in this volume, pp. 371–379.
15. Quill, T., Bennett, N.: 1992, 'The Effects of A Hospital Policy and State Legislation on Resuscitation Orders for Geriatric Patients', *Archives of Internal Medicine* **152**, 569–572.
16. Quill, T., Bennett, N.: 1995, 'The Effects of A Hospital Policy and State Legislation on Resuscitation Orders for Geriatric Patients', this volume, pp. 241–250.
17. Rest, J.: 1979, *Moral Development: Advances in Research and Theory*, Praeger Publishers, New York, N.Y.
18. Spritz, N.: 1995, 'The New York State DNR Law: Views of the members of the New York Chapter of the American College of Physicians', this volume, pp. 251–261.
19. Zussman, R.: 1995, 'The Do-Not-Resuscitate Order as Ritual', this volume, pp. 215–225.

APPENDICES: THE GENEALOGY OF NEW YORK STATE'S DO-NOT-RESUSCITATE LAW

ARTICLE 29-BL. 1987, CH. 818. EFFECTIVE APRIL 1, 1988* ORDERS NOT TO RESUSCITATE

Section

2960. Legislative findings and purpose.
2961. Definitions.
2962. Presumption in favor of resuscitation; lawfulness of order; effectiveness of order; duty to provide information; no duty to expand equipment.
2963. Determination of capacity to make a decision regarding cardiopulmonary resuscitation.
2964. Decision-making by an adult with capacity.
2965. Surrogate decision-making.
2966. Decision-making on behalf of an adult patient without capacity for whom no surrogate is available.
2967. Decision-making on behalf of a minor patient.
2968. Effect of order not to resuscitate on other treatment.
2969. Revocation of consent to order not to resuscitate.
2970. Physician review of the order not to resuscitate.
2971. Interinstitutional transfers.
2972. Dispute mediation system.
2973. Judicial review.
2974. Immunity.
2975. Effect of order not to resuscitate on insurance and health care services.
2976. Judicially approved order not to resuscitate.
2977. Regulations.
2978. Rights to be publicized.

Section 2960. Legislative findings and purpose.
The legislature finds that, although cardiopulmonary resuscitation has proved invaluable in the prevention of sudden, unexpected death, it is

* To assist the reader, this selection contains subsection titles, numeric section references and some indentation not found in the statute itself but borrowed from The Task Force Report.

R. Baker & M.A. Strosberg (eds.), Legislating Medical Ethics: A Study of the New York Do-Not-Resuscitate Law, 349–367.

appropriate for an attending physician, in certain circumstances, to issue an order not to attempt cardiopulmonary resuscitation of a patient where appropriate consent has been obtained.

The legislature further finds that there is a need to clarify and establish the rights and obligations of patients, their families, and health care providers regarding cardiopulmonary resuscitation and the issuance of orders not to resuscitate.

Section 2961. Definitions.

The following words or phrases, as used in this article, shall have the following meanings unless the context otherwise requires:

1. Adult means any person who is eighteen years of age or older, or is the parent of a child, or has married.

2. Attending physician means the physician selected by or assigned to a patient in a hospital, who has primary responsibility for the treatment and care of the patient. Where more than one physician shares such responsibility, any such physician may act as the attending physician pursuant to this article.

3. Capacity means the ability to understand and appreciate the nature and consequences of an order not to resuscitate, including the benefits and disadvantages of such an order, and to reach an informed decision regarding the order.

4. Cardiopulmonary resuscitation means measures, as specified in regulations promulgated by the commissioner, to restore cardiac function or to support ventilation in the event of a cardiac or respiratory arrest. Cardiopulmonary resuscitation shall not include measures to improve ventilation and cardiac functions in the absence of an arrest.

5. Close friend means any person, eighteen years of age or older, who presents an affidavit to an attending physician stating that he is a close friend of the patient and that he has maintained such regular contact with the patient as to be familiar with the patient's activities, health, and religious or moral beliefs and stating the facts and circumstances that demonstrate such familiarity.

6. Developmental disability means a developmental disability as defined in §1.03(22) of The Mental Hygiene Law.

7. Hospital means a general hospital as defined in §2801.10 of this chapter and a residential health care facility as defined in §2801.3 of this chapter or a hospital as defined in §1.03(10) of the Mental Hygiene Law or a school named in §13.17 of the Mental Hygiene Law.

8. Hospitalization means the period during which a person is a patient in, or a resident of, a hospital.

9. Medically futile means that cardiopulmonary resuscitation will be unsuccessful in restoring cardiac and respiratory function or that the patient will experience repeated arrest in a short time period before death occurs.

10. Mental hygiene facility means a residential facility operated or licensed by the Office of Mental Health or the Office of Mental Retardation and Developmental Disabilities.

11. Mental illness means a mental illness as defined in §1.03(20) of the Mental Hygiene Law.

12. Minor means any person who is not an adult.

13. Order not to resuscitate means an order not to attempt cardiomonary resuscitation in the event a patient suffers cardiac or respiaratory arrest.

14. Parent means a parent who has custody of the minor.

15. Patient means a person admitted to a hospital.

16. Reasonably available means that a person to be contacted can be contacted with diligent efforts by an attending physician or another person acting on behalf of the attending physician or the hospital.

17. Surrogate means the person selected to make a decision regarding resuscitation on behalf of another person pursuant to §2965 of this article.

18. Surrogate list means the list set forth in §2965.4 of this article.

19. Terminal condition means an illness or injury from which there is no recovery, and which reasonably can be expected to cause death within one year.

Section 2962. Presumption in favor of resuscitation; lawfulness of order; effectiveness of order; duty to provide information; no duty to expand equipment.

1. Presumption in favor of consent to resuscitation. Every person admitted to a hospital shall be presumed to consent to the administration of cardiopulmonary resuscitation in the event of cardiac or respiratory arrest, unless there is consent to the issuance of an order not to resuscitate as provided in this article.

2. Lawfulness of order; effectiveness of order. It shall be lawful for the attending physician to issue an order not to resuscitate a patient, provided that the order has been issued pursuant to the requirements of this article.

The order shall be included in writing in the patient's chart. An order not to resuscitate shall be effective upon issuance.

3. Duty to provide information. Before obtaining, pursuant to this article, the consent of the patient, or of the surrogate of the patient, or parent or legal guardian of the minor patient, to an order not to resuscitate, the attending physician shall provide to the person giving consent information about the patient's diagnosis and prognosis, the reasonably foreseeable risks and benefits of cardiopulmonary resuscitation for the patient, and the consequences of an order not to resuscitate.

4. No duty to expand equipment. Nothing in this article shall require a hospital to expand its existing equipment and facilities to provide cardiopulmonary resuscitation.

Section 2963. Determination of capacity to make a decision regarding cardiopulmonary resuscitation.

1. Presumption of capacity. Every adult shall be presumed to have the capacity to make a decision regarding cardiopulmonary resuscitation unless determined otherwise pursuant to this section or pursuant to a court order. A lack of capacity shall not be presumed from the fact that a committee of the property or conservator has been appointed for the adult pursuant to article 77 or 78 of the Mental Hygiene Law, or that a guardian has been appointed pursuant to article 17-A of the Surrogate's Court Procedure Act.

2. Determination by attending physician. A determination that an adult patient lacks capacity shall be made by the attending physician to a reasonable degree of medical certainty. The determination shall be made in writing and shall contain such attending physician's opinion regarding the cause and nature of the patient's incapacity as well as its extent and probable duration. The determination shall be included in the patient's medical chart.

3. Concurrence.

(a) At least one other physician, selected by a person authorized by the hospital to make such selection, must concur in the determination that an adult lacks capacity. The concurring determination shall be made in writing after personal examination of the patient and shall contain the physician's opinion regarding the cause and nature of the patient's incapacity as well as its extent and probable duration. Each concurring determination shall be included in the patient's medical chart.

(b) If the attending physician of a patient in a general hospital determines that a patient lacks capacity because of mental illness, the concurring determination required by paragraph (a) of this subdivision shall be provided by a physician certified or eligible to be certified by the American Board of Psychiatry and Neurology.

(c) If the attending physician determines that a patient lacks capacity because of a developmental disability, the concurring determination required by paragraph (a) of this subdivision shall be provided by a physician or psychologist employed by a school named in §13.17 of the Mental Hygiene Law, or who has been employed for a minimum of two years to render care and service in a facility operated or licensed by the Office of Mental Retardation and Developmental Disabilities, or who has been approved by the Commissioner of Mental Retardation and Developmental Disabilities in accordance with regulations promulgated by such Commissioner. Such regulations shall require that a physician or psychologist possess specialized training or three years' experience in treating developmental disabilities.

4. Notice. Notice of a determination that the patient lacks capacity shall promptly be given

(a) to the patient, where there is any indication of the patient's ability to comprehend such notice, together with a copy of a statement prepared in accordance with §2978 of this article,

(b) to the person on the surrogate list highest in order of priority listed, when persons in prior subparagraphs are not reasonably available, and

(c) if the patient is in or is transferred from a mental hygiene facility, to the facility director.

Nothing in this subdivision shall preclude or require notice to more than one person on the surrogate list.

5. Limited effect of determination. A determination that a patient lacks capacity to make a decision regarding an order not to resuscitate persuant to this section shall not be construed as a finding that the patient lacks capacity for any other purpose.

Section 2964. Decision-making by an adult with capacity.

1. Duty to obtain consent.

(a) The consent of an adult with capacity must be obtained prior to issuing an order not to resuscitate, except as provided in subdivision 3 of this section.

(b) If the adult has capacity at the time the order is to be issued, the consent must be obtained at or about such time, notwithstanding any prior oral or written consent.

2. Decision by an adult; attending physician's obligation.

(a) During hospitalization, an adult with capacity may express a decision consenting to an order not to resuscitate orally in the presence of at least two witnesses eighteen years of age or older, one of whom is a physician affiliated with the hospital in which the patient is being treated. Any such decision shall be recorded in the patient's medical chart.

(b) Prior to or during hospitalization, an adult with capacity may express a decision consenting to an order not to resuscitate in writing, dated and signed in the presence of at least two witnesses eighteen years of age or older who shall sign the decision.

(c) An attending physician who is provided with or informed of a decision pursuant to this subdivision shall record or include the decision in the patient's medical chart if the decision has not been recorded or included, and either:

(i) promptly issue an order not to resuscitate the patient or issue an order at such time as the conditions, if any, specified in the decision are met, and inform the hospital staff responsible for the patient's care of the order; or

(ii) promptly make his or her objection to the issuance of such an order and the reasons therefor known to the patient and either make all reasonable efforts to arrange for the transfer of the patient to another physician, if necessary, or promptly submit the matter to the dispute mediation system.

(d) Prior to issuing an order not to resuscitate a patient who has expressed a decision consenting to an order not to resuscitate under specified medical conditions, the attending physician must make a determination, to a reasonable degrce of medical certainty, that such conditions exist, and include the determination in the patient's medical chart.

3. Therapeutic exception.

(a) In the event that the attending physician determines, in writing, that, to a reasonable degree of medical certainty, an adult patient who has capacity would suffer immediate and severe injury from a discussion of cardiopulmonary resuscitation, the attending physician may issue an order not to resuscitate without obtaining the patient's consent, but only after:

(i) consulting with and obtaining the written concurrence of another physician selected by a person authorized by the hospital to make such selection, given after personal examination of the patient, concerning the assessment of immediate and severe injury to the patient from a discussion of cardiopulmonary resuscitation;

(ii) ascertaining the wishes of the patient to the extent possible without subjecting the patient to a risk of immediate and severe injury;

(iii) including the reasons for not consulting the patient in the patient's chart; and

(iv) obtaining the consent of a surrogate pursuant to §2965 of this article, provided, however, that the consent of a surrogate shall not be required if the patient has previously consented to an order not to resuscitate pursuant to subdivision 2 of this section.

(b) Where the provisions of this subdivision have been invoked, the attending physician shall reassess the patient's risk of injury from a discussion of cardiopulmonary resuscitation on a regular basis and shall consult the patient regarding resuscitation as soon as the medical basis for not consulting the patient no longer exists.

4. Mental hygiene facility patients. If the patient is in or is transferred from a mental hygiene facility, notice of the patient's consent to an order not to resuscitate shall be given to the facility director prior to the issuance pursuant to this section of an order not to resuscitate. Notification to the facility director shall not delay issuance of an order not to resuscitate. If the facility director concludes that the patient lacks capacity or that issuance of an ordcr not to resuscitate may be inconsistent with the patient's wishes, the facility director shall submit the matter to the dispute mediation system of this article.

Section 2965. Surrogate decision-making.

1. Duty to obtain surrogate consent.

(a) The consent of a surrogate acting on behalf of an adult patient who lacks capacity or on behalf of an adult patient for whom consent by a surrogate is authorized by §2964.3 of this article must be obtained prior to issuing an order not to resuscitate the patient, except as provided in paragraph (b) of this subdivision or §2966 of this article.

(b) The consent of a surrogate shall not be required where the adult had, prior to losing capacity, consented to an order not to resuscitate pursuant to §2964.2 of this article.

2. Right to designate a surrogate. An adult with capacity has the right to designate a surrogate for the purpose of making a decision regarding cardiopulmonary resuscitation in the event the adult is subsequently determined to lack capacity.

3. Designation of surrogate; revocation. An adult with capacity may designate a surrogate either

(a) in writing, dated, and signed in the presence of two witnesses eighteen years of age or older who shall sign the designation or

(b) during the time the adult is a patient, orally in the presence of two witnesses eighteen years of age or older.

The two witnesses shall promptly inform an attending physician of the patient's designation of a surrogate. A designation may be revoked in the same manner as that provided in §2969 of this article for the revocation of consent to the issuance of an order not to resuscitate.

4. Surrogate list.

(a) One person from the following list, to be chosen in order of priority listed, when persons in the prior subparagraphs are not reasonably available, willing to make a decision regarding issuance of an order not to resuscitate, and competent to make a decision regarding issuance of an order not to resuscitate, shall have the authority to act as surrogate on behalf of the patient:

(i) a person designated by the adult pursuant to sub-division 3 of this section;

(ii) a committee of the person or a guardian appointed pursuant to article 17-A of the Surrogate's Court Procedure Act, provided that this paragraph shall not be construed to require the appointment of a committee of the person or guardian for the purpose of making the resuscitation decision;

(iii) the spouse;

(iv) a son or daughter eighteen years of age or older;

(v) a parent;

(vi) a brother or sister eighteen years of age or older; and

(vii) a close friend.

(b) After the surrogate has been identified, the name of such person shall be included in the patient's medical chart.

5. Standards for surrogate decision-making.

(a) The surrogate shall make a decision regarding cardiopulmonary resuscitation on the basis of the adult patient's wishes including a consideration of the patient's religious and moral beliefs, or, if the patient's wishes are unknown and cannot be ascertained, on the basis of the patient's best interests.

(b) Notwithstanding any law to the contrary, the surrogate shall have the same right as the patient to receive medical information and medical records.

(c) A surrogate may consent to an order not to resuscitate on behalf of an adult patient only if there has been a determination by an attending physician with the concurrence of another physician selected by a person authorized by the hospital to make such selection, given after personal examination of the patient that, to a reasonable degree of medical-certainty:

(i) the patient has a terminal condition; or

(ii) the patient is permanently unconscious; or

(iii) resuscitation would be medically futile; or

(iv) resuscitation would impose an extraordinary burden on the patient in light of the patient's medical condition and the expected outcome of resuscitation for the patient.

Each determination shall be included in the patient's medical chart.

(d) If a physician is designated by the patient to act as the patient's surrogate pursuant to this section, the physician shall not make the determination of the patient's medical condition required by paragraph (c) of this subdivision.

6. Decision by surrogate; attending physician's obligation.

(a) A surrogate shall express a decision consenting to an order not to resuscitate in writing, dated, and signed in the presence of one witness eighteen years of age or older who shall sign the decision.

(b) The attending physician who is provided with the decision of a surrogate shall include the decision in the patient's medical chart and, if the surrogate has consented to the issuance of an order not to resuscitate, shall either:

(i) promptly issue an order not to resuscitate the patient and inform the hospital staff responsible for the patient's care of the order; or

(ii) promptly make the attending physician's objection to the issuance of such an order known to the surrogate and either make all reasonable efforts to arrange for the transfer of the patient to another physician, if necessary, or promptly refer the matter to the dispute mediation system.

(c) If the patient is in or is transferred from a mental hygiene facility, notice of a surrogate's consent to an order not to resuscitate shall be given to the facility director prior to the issuance pursuant to this section of an order not to resuscitate. Notification to the facility director shall not delay issuance of an order not to resuscitate. If the facility director concludes that the patient has capacity or that issuance of an order not to resuscitate is otherwise inconsistent with this article, the facility director shall submit the matter to the dispute mediation system of this article.

(d) If the attending physician has actual notice of opposition to a surrogate's consent to an order not to resuscitate by any person on the surrogate list, or, if the patient is in or is transferred from a mental hygiene facility, by the facility director, the physician shall submit the matter to the dispute mediation system and such order shall not be issued or shall be revoked in accordance with the provisions of §2972.3 of this article.

7. Notice to patient. If a surrogate has consented to an order not to resuscitate, notice of the surrogate's decision shall be given to the patient where there is any indication of the patient's ability to comprehend such notice, except if a determination has been made pursuant to §2964.3 of this article. If the patient objects, an order not to resuscitate shall not be issued.

Section 2966. Decision-making on belhalf of an adult patient without capacity for whom no surrogate is available.

1. Standards and procedure. If no surrogate is reasonably available, willing to make a decision regarding issuance of an order not to resuscitate, and competent to make a decision regarding issuance of an order not to resuscitate on behalf of an adult patient who lacks capacity and who had not previously expressed a decision regarding cardiopulmonary resuscitation, an attending physician

(a) may issue an order not to resuscitate the patient, provided that the attending physician determines, in writing, that, to a reasonable degree of medical certainty, resuscitation would be medically futile, and another physician selected by a person authorized by the hospital to make such selection, after personal examination of the patient, reviews and concurs in writing with such determination, or

(b) shall issue an order not to resuscitate the patient, provided that, pursuant to §2976.1 of this article, a court has granted ajudgment directing the issuance of such an order.

2. Mental hygiene facility patients. If the patient is in or is transferred from a mental hygiene facility, prior to issuance of an order not to resuscitate pursuant to subdivision 1 of this section, notice of such order shall be given to the facility director. Notification to the facility director shall not delay issuance of an order not to resuscitate. If the facility director concludes that the patient has capacity or that issuance of an order not to resuscitate is otherwise inconsistent with this article, the facility director shall submit the matter to the dispute mediation system of this article.

3. Notice to patient. Notwithstanding any other provision of this section, where a decision to consent to an ordcr not to resuscitate has been made, notice of the decision shall be given to the patient where there is any indication of the patient's ability to comprehend such notice, except where a determination has been made pursuant to §2964.3 of this article. If the patient objects, an order not to resuscitate shall not be issued.

Section 2967. Decision-making on behalf of a minor patient.

1. Determination of capacity. An attending physician, in consultation with a minor's parent or legal guardian, shall determine whether a minor has the capacity to make a decision regarding resuscitation.

2. Duty to obtain consent; notify second parent.

(a) The consent of a minor's parent or legal guardian and the consent of the minor, if the minor has capacity, must be obtained prior to issuing an order not to resuscitate the minor.

(b) Where the attending physician has reason to believe that there is another parent or a non-custodial parent who has not been informed of a decision to issue an order not to resuscitate the minor, the attending physician shall make diligent efforts to notify that parent or non-custodial parent of the decision prior to issuing the order.

(c) If the minor is in or is transferred from a mental hygiene facility, notice of a decision to issue an order not to resuscitate the minor shall be given to the facility director prior to issuance of an order not to resuscitate. Notification to the facility director shall not delay issuance of an order not to resuscitate. If the facility director concludes that issuance of an order not to resuscitate is inconsistent with this article, the facility director shall submit the matter to the dispute mediation system of this article.

3. Prerequisite for parental decision-making. A parent or legal guardian may consent to an order not to resuscitate on behalf of a minor only if there has been a written determination by the attending physician, with the written concurrence of another physician selected by a person authorized by the hospital to make such selections given after personal examination of the patient, that, to a reasonable degree of medical certainty, the minor suffers from one of the medical conditions set forth in §2965.5(c) of this article. Each determination shall be included in the patient's medical chart.

4. Standard for parental decision-making; physician's obligation.

(a) A parent or legal guardian of a minor, in making a decision regarding cardiopulmonary resuscitation, shall consider the minor patient's wishes including a consideration of the minor patient's religious and moral beliefs, and shall express a decision consenting to issuance of an order not to resuscitate in writing, dated and signed in the presence of one witness eighteen years of age or older who shall sign the decision.

(b) The attending physician who is provided with the decision of a minor's parent or legal guardian, expressed pursuant to this subdivision, and of the minor if the minor has capacity, shall include such decision or decisions in the minor's medical chart and shall comply with the provisions of §2965.6(b) of this article.

(c) If the attending physician has actual notice of the opposition of a parent or non-custodial parent to consent by another parent to an order not to resuscitate a minor, the physician shall submit the matter to the dispute mediation system and such order shall not be issued or shall be revoked in accordance with the provisions of §2972.3 of this article.

Section 2968. Effect of order not to resuscitate on other treatment.

Consent to the issuance of an order not to resuscitate shall not constitute consent to withhold or withdraw medical treatment other than cardiopulmonary resuscitation.

Section 2969. Revocation of consent to order not to resuscitate.

1. Revocation by person. A person may, at any time, revoke his or her consent to an order not to resuscitate himself or herself by making either a written or an oral declaration to a physician or member of the nursing staff at the hospital where he or she is being treated, or by any other act evidencing a specific intent to revoke such consent.

2. Revocation by surrogate, parent or guardian. Any surrogate, parent, or legal guardian may at any time revoke his or her consent to an order not to resuscitate a patient by (a) notifying a physician or member of the nursing staff of the revocation of consent in writing, dated and signed, or (b) orally notifying the attending physician, in the presence of a witness eighteen years of age or older.

3. Obligation to cancel order. Any physician who is informed of or provided with a revocation of consent pursuant to this section shall immediately include the revocation in the patient's chart, cancel the order, and notify the hospital staff responsible for the patient's care of the revocation and cancellation. Any member of the nursing staff who is informed of or provided with a revocation of consent pursuant to this section shall immediately notify a physician of such revocation.

Section 2970. Physician review of the order not to resuscitate.

1. Obligation to review order. For each patient for whom an order not to resuscitate has been issued, the attending physician shall review the patient's chart to determine if the order is still appropriate in light of the patient's condition and shall indicate on the patient's chart that the order has been reviewed

(a) for the patient in a hospital, other than a residential health care facility, at least every three days;

(b) for a patient in a residential health care facility, each time the patient is required to be seen by a physician but in no case less often than every sixty days.

Failure to comply with this subdivision shall not render an order not to resuscitate ineffective.

2. Patient's condition improves; patient regains capacity.

(a) If the attending physician determines at any time that an order not to resuscitate is no longer appropriate because the patient's medical condition has improved, the physician shall immediately notify the person who consented to the order. Except as provided in paragraph (b) of this subdivision, if such person declines to revoke consent to the order, the physician shall promptly (i) make reasonable efforts to arrange for the transfer of the patient to another physician or (ii) submit the matter to the dispute mediation system.

(b) If the order not to resuscitate was entered upon the consent of a surrogate, parent, or legal guardian and the attending physician who issued the order, or, if unavailable, another attending physician at any time determines that the patient does not suffer from one of the medical conditions set forth in 2965.5(c) of this article, the attentding physician shall immediately include such determination in the patient's chart, cancel the order, and notify the person who consented to the order and all hospital staff responsible for the patient's care of the cancellation.

(c) If an order not to resuscitate was entered upon the consent of a surrogate and the patient at any time gains or regains capacity, the attending physician who issued the order, or, if unavailable, another attending physician shall immediately cancel the order and notify the person who consented to the order and all hospital staff directly responsible for the patient's care of the cancellation.

Section 2971. Interinstitutional transfers

If a patient for whom an order not to resuscitate has been issued is transferred from a hospital to a different hospital the order shall be effective upon receipt until:

1. a physician at the transferee hospital cancels the order; or
2. twenty-four hours have elapsed from the time of the patient's admission to the transferee hospital, whichever shall occur first, except that if the order has not been cancelled by a physician at the transferee hospital an attending physician at the transferee hospital, upon receipt of a copy of or written notice of the order, may presume that the order was validly issued and may issue an order not to resuscitate continuing the prior order.

Section 2972. Dispute mediation system.

1. Establishment of dispute mediation system.

(a) Each hospital shall establish a mediation system for the purpose of mediating disputes regarding the issuance of orders not to resuscitate.

(b) The dispute mediation system shall be described in writing and adopted by the hospital's governing authority. It may utilize existing hospital resources, such as a patient advocate's office or hospital chaplain's office, or it may utilize a body created specifically for this purpose, but, in the event a dispute involves a patient deemed to lack capacity pursuant to

(i) section 2963.3(b) of this article, the system must include a physician or psychologist eligible to provide a concurring determination pursuant to such subdivision, or a family member or guardian of the person of a person with a mental illness of the same or similar nature, or

(ii) section 2962.3(c) of this article, the system must include a physician or psychologist eligible to provide a concurring determination pursuant to such subdivision, or a family member or guardian of the person of a person with a developmental disability of the same or similar nature.

2. Authority. The dispute mediation system shall be authorized to mediate

(a) any dispute challenging consent to the issuance of an order not to resuscitate, including disputes regarding the determination of a patient's capacity, arising under this article

(i) between a patient and an attending physician or the hospital that is caring for the patient and, if the patient is a minor, the patient's parent, or

(ii) among an attending physician, a parent, non-custodial parent, or legal guardian of a minor patient, any person on the surrogate list, the hospital that is caring for the patient and, where the dispute involves a patient who is in or is transferred from a mental hygiene facility, the facility director, and

(b) any dispute submitted by a person on the surrogate list, challenging a decision by a surrogate not to consent to issuance of an order not to resuscitate.

3. Stay of order during dispute mediation. After a dispute regarding the issuance of an order not to resuscitate has been submitted to the dispute mediation system, an order not to resuscitate shall not be issued or shall be revoked and may not be reissued until

(a) the dispute has been resolved or the system has concluded its efforts to resolve the dispute or

(b) 72 hours have elapsed from the time of the submission of the dispute, whichever shall occur first. Persons participating in the dispute mediation system shall be informed of their right to judicial review.

4. Failure of mediation of dispute involving patient. If a dispute between a patient who expressed a decision rejecting cardiopulmonary resuscitation and an attending physician or the hospital that is caring for the patient is submitted to the dispute mediation system and either: (a) the dispute mediation system has concluded its efforts to resolve the dispute, or (b) 72 hours have elapsed from the time of submission without resolution of the dispute, whichever shall occur first, the attending physician shall either:

(i) promptly issue an order not to resuscitate the patient or issue the order at such time as the conditions, if any, specified in the decision are met, and inform the hospital staff responsible for the patient's care of the order; or

(ii) promptly arrange for the transfer of the patient to another physician or hospital.

5. Limitation on authority. Persons appointed pursuant to this section to participate in the dispute mediation system shall not have authority to determine whether a do not resuscitate order shall be issued.

Section 2973. Judicial review

1. Persons who may bring special proceeding; substantive standard. The patient, an attending physician, a parent, non-custodial parent, or legal guardian of a minor patient, any person on the surrogate list, the hospital that is caring for the patient and, in disputes involving a patient who is in or is transferred from a mental hygiene facility, the facility director, may commence a special proceeding pursuant to article 4 of the civil practice laws and rules, in a court of competent jurisdiction, with respect to any dispute arising under this article, except that the decision of a patient not to consent to issuance of an order not to resuscitate may not be subjected to judicial review.

In any proceeding brought pursuant to this subdivision challenging a decision regarding issuance of an order not to resuscitate on the ground that the decision is contrary to the patient's wishes or best interests, the person or entity challenging the decision must show, by clear and convincing evidence, that the decision is contrary to the patient's wishes including consideration of the patient's religious and moral beliefs, or, in the absence of evidence of the patient's wishes, that the decision is contrary to the patient's best interests.

In any other proceeding brought pursuant to this subdivision, the court shall make its determination based upon the applicable substantive standards and procedures set forth in this article.

2. Temporary restraining orders. In any proceeding brought pursuant to this section, the court may issue an order, pursuant to the standards applicable to the issuance of a temporary restraining order according to §6313 of the civil practice law and rules, which shall suspend the order not to resuscitate to permit review of the matter by the court.

3. When action may be commenced. Where a person or entity may invoke the dispute mediation systcm, no such proceeding shall be commenced until the dispute mediation system has concluded its efforts to resolve the dispute or 72 hours have elapsed from the submission of the dispute to the dispute mediation system, whichever shall occur first, provided, however, that the patient may commence an action for relief with respect to any dispute under this article at any time and provided further that the department of health or any other duly authorized state agency may commence an action or proceeding to enjoin a violation of this article at any time.

Section 2974. Immunity.

1. Immunity for carrying out decision. No physician, health care professional, nurse's aide, hospital or person employed by or under contract with the hospital shall be subject to criminal prosecution, civil liability, or be deemed to have engaged in unprofessional conduct for carrying out in good faith pursuant to this article a decision regarding cardiopulmonary resuscitation by or on behalf of a patient or for those actions taken in compliance with the standards and procedures set forth in this article.

2. Immunity for good faith resuscitation. No physician, health care professional, nurse's aide, hospital, or person employed by or under contract with the hospital shall be subjected to criminal prosecution, civil liability, or be deemed to have engaged in unprofessional conduct for providing cardiopulmonary resuscitation to a patient for whom an order not to resuscitate has been issued, provided such physician or person:

(a) reasonably and in good faith was unaware of the issuance of an order not to resuscitate; or

(b) reasonably and in good faith believe[d] that consent to the order not to resuscitate had been revoked or cancelled.

3. Surrogate, parent or legal guardian immunity. No person shall be subject to criminal prosecution or civil liability for consenting or declining to consent in good faith, on behalf of a patient, to the issuance of an order not to resuscitate pursuant to this article.

4. Mediator immunity. No person shall be subject to criminal prosecution or civil liability or be deemed to have engaged in unprofessional conduct for acts performed in good faith as a mediator in the dispute mediation system established by this article.

Section 2975. Effect of order not to resuscitate on insurance and health care services.

1. Life insurance. No policy of life insurance shall be legally impaired, modified, or invalidated in any manner by the issuance of an order not to resuscitate notwithstanding any term of the policy to the contrary.

2. Health insurance and health care services. A person may not prohibit or require the issuance of an order not to resuscitate for an individual as a condition for such individual's being insurcd or for receiving health care services.

Section 2976. Judicially approved order not to resuscitate.

1. Judicial decision when surrogate is unavailable. If no surrogate is reasonably available, willing to make a decision regarding issuance of an order not to resuscitate, and competent to make a decision regarding issuance of an order not to resuscitate on behalf of an adult patient who lacks capacity and who had not previously expressed a decision regarding cardiopulmonary resuscitation pursuant to this article, an attending physician or hospital may commence a special proceeding pursuant to article four of the civil practice law and rules, in a court of competent jurisdiction, for a judgment directing the physician to issue an order not to resuscitate where the patient has a terminal condition, is permanently unconscious, or resuscitation would impose an extraordinary burden on the patient in light of the patient's medical condition and the expected outcome of resuscitation for the patient, and issuance of an order not to resuscitate is consistent with the patient's wishes including a consideration of the patient's religious and moral beliefs or, in the absence of evidence of the patient's wishes, the patient's best interest.

2. Judicial approval of order. Nothing in this article shall be construed to preclude a court of competent jurisdiction from approving the issuance of an order not to resuscitate under circumstances other than those under which such an order may be issued pursuant to this article.

Section 2977. Regulations.

1. Health commissioner to establish regulations. Except as provided in subdivision two of this section, thc commissioner of health

(a) subject to the approval of the state hospital review and planning council by a majority vote of its members, shall establish such regulations as may be necessary for the implementation of this article and

(b) may provide suggested forms that may be used for the purpose of expressing a decision regarding cardiopulmonary resuscitation or for the purpose of designating a surrogate, pursuant to this article.

2. Mental hygiene facility patients. The commissioners of mental health and mental retardation and developmental disabilities, in consultation with the commissioner of health, shall establish such regulations as may be necessary for implementation of this article with respect to those persons in mental hygiene facilities.

Section 2978. Rights to be publicized.

1. Statement of rights. The commissioner of health, after consultation with the commissioners of mental health and mental retardation and developmental disabilities, shall prepare a statement summarizing the rights, duties, and requirements of this article and shall require that a copy of such statement:

(a) be furnished by the hospital to patients or to persons on the surrogate list known to the hospital at or prior to the time of admission to the hospital, and at the time of the first decision made pursuant to §§2964, 2965, 2966, or 2967 of this article or as soon thereafter as practicable and to each member of the hospital's staff involved in the provision of medical care; and

(b) is posted in a public place in each hospital.

2. Statement may be part of other statements of patient's rights. The statement of rights required by this section may be included in any other statement of patient's rights required by other provisions of this chapter.

GUIDELINES FOR HOSPITALS AND PHYSICIANS ON "DO-NOT-RESUSCITATE" – 20 SEPTEMBER 1982

The following are intended only to be guidelines for physicians and hospitals. Hospital medical staffs and governing bodies are encouraged to develop policies consistent with their respective by-laws and rules and regulations.

Definition

DNR (Do-Not-Resuscitate) means that, in the event of a cardiac or respiratory arrest, cardiopulmonary resuscitative measures will not be initiated or carried out.

Background

1. An appropriate knowledge of the serious nature of the patient's medical condition is necessary.

2. The attending physician should determine the appropriateness of a DNR order for any given patient.

3. DNR orders are compatible with maximal therapeutic care. A patient may receive vigorous support in all other therapeutic modalities and yet a DNR order may be justified.

4. When a patient is capable of making his own judgments, the DNR decision should be reached consensually by the patient and physician. When the patient is not capable of making his own decision, the decision should be reached after consultation between the appropriate family member(s) and the physician. If a patient disagrees, or, in the case of a patient incapable of making an appropriate decision, the family member(s) disagree, a DNR order should not be written.

R. Baker & M.A. Strosberg (eds.), Legislating Medical Ethics: A Study of the New York Do-Not-Resuscitate Law, 369–370.

Implementation

1. Once the DNR decision has been made, this directive shall be written as a formal order by the attending physician. A verbal or telephone order for DNR cannot be justified as a sound medical or legal practice.

2. It is the responsibility of the attending physician to insure that this order and its meaning are discussed with the appropriate members of the hospital staff.

3. The facts and considerations relevant to this decision shall be recorded by the attending physician in the progress notes.

4. The DNR order shall be subject to review at any time by all concerned parties on a regular basis and may be rescinded at any time.

PRESIDENT'S COMMISSION FOR THE STUDY OF ETHICAL PROBLEMS IN MEDICINE AND BIOMEDICAL AND BEHAVIORAL RESEARCH

DECIDING TO FOREGO LIFE-SUSTAINING TREATMENT (1983) EXCERPTED

Summary of conclusions

Building on a central conclusion of its report on informed consent [1] – that decisions about health care ultimately rest with competent patients – the Commission in this Report examines the situations in which a patient's choice to forego life-sustaining therapy may be limited on moral or legal grounds. In addition to providing clarification of the issues, the Report suggests appropriate procedures for decisions regarding both competent and incompetent patients and scrutinizes the role of various public and private bodies in shaping and regulating the process.

These aims are the only ones that this Commission believes to be within the scope of its role. The Report does not judge any particular future case nor provide a guidebook of the morally correct choice for patients and health care providers who are facing such a decision. Rather, the Commission intends to illuminate the strengths and weaknesses of various considerations and various instruments of social policy. Clarifying the relevant considerations and prohibitions may help decisionmakers, but it may also force them to confront painful realities more directly. The Commission hopes that this Report will help improve the process, but recognizes that an improved process will not necessarily make decisions easier.

The Report addresses a broad range of problems and patient situations. Serious questions about whether life should be sustained through a particular treatment usually arise when a patient is suffering from a known disease likely to prove fatal in the near future rather than in an unanticipated emergency (where any decisionmaking would necessarily have to be truncated). Life-sustaining treatment, as used here, encompasses all health care interventions that have the effect of increasing the life span of the patient. Although the term includes respirators, kidney machines, and all the paraphernalia of modern medicine, it also includes home physical therapy, nursing support for activities of daily living, and

R. Baker & M.A. Strosberg (eds.), Legislating Medical Ethics: A Study of the New York Do-Not-Resuscitate Law, 371–379.

special feeding procedures, provided that one of the effects of the treatment is to prolong a patient's life.

The issues addressed in this Report are complex and their resolution depends not only on the context of particular decisions but also on their relationship to other values and principles. Thus, it is exceptionally difficult to summarize the Commission's conclusions on this subject. The synopsis provided here should be read in the context of the reasoning, elaboration, and qualifications provided in the chapters that follow.

(1) The voluntary choice of a competent and informed patient should determine whether or not life-sustaining therapy will be undertaken, just as such choices provide the basis for other decisions about medical treatment. Health care institutions and professionals should try to enhance patients' abilities to make decisions on their own behalf and to promote understanding of the available treatment options.

(2) Health care professionals serve patients best by maintaining a presumption in favor of sustaining life, while recognizing that competent patients are entitled to choose to forego any treatments, including those that sustain life.

(3) As in medical decisionmaking generally, some constraints on patients' decisions are justified.

- Health care professionals or institutions may decline to provide a particular option because that choice would violate their conscience or professional judgment, though in doing so they may not abandon a patient.

- Health care institutions may justifiably restrict the availability of certain options in order to use limited resources more effectively or to enhance equity in allocating them.

- Society may decide to limit the availability of certain options for care in order to advance equity or the general welfare, but such policies should not be applied initially nor especially forcefully to medical options that could sustain life.

- Information about the existence and justification of any of these constraints must be available to patients or their surrogates.

(4) Governmental agencies, institutional providers of care, individual practitioners, and the general public should try to improve the medically beneficial options that are available to dying patients. Specific attention should be paid to making respectful, responsive, and competent care available for people who choose to forego life-sustaining therapy or for whom no such therapies are available.

(5) Several distinctions are employed by health care professionals and others in deliberating about whether a choice that leads to an earlier death would be acceptable or unacceptable in a particular case. Unfortunately, people often treat these distinctions – between acts and omissions that cause death, between withholding and withdrawing care, between an intended death and one that is merely foreseeable, and between ordinary and extraordinary treatment – as though applying them decided the issue, which it does not. Although there is a danger that relying on such labels will take the place of analysis, these distinctions can still be helpful if attention is directed to the reasoning behind them, such as the degree to which a patient is benefitted or burdened by a treatment.

(6) Achieving medically and morally appropriate decisions does not require changes in statutes concerning homicide or wrongful death, given appropriate prosecutorial discretion and judicial interpretation.

(7) Primary responsibility for ensuring that morally justified processes of decisionmaking are followed lies with physicians. Health care institutions also have a responsibility to ensure that there are appropriate procedures to enhance patients' competence, to provide for designation of surrogates, to guarantee that patients are adequately informed, to overcome the influence of dominant institutional biases, to provide review of decisionmaking, and to refer cases to the courts appropriately. The Commission is not recommending that hospitals and other institutions take over decisions about patient care; there is no substitute for the dedication, compassion, and professional judgment of physicians. Nevertheless, institutions need to develop policies because their decisions have profound effects on patient outcomes, because society looks to these institutions to ensure the means necessary to preserve both health and the value of self-determination, and because they are conveniently situated to provide efficient, confidential, and rapid supervision and review of decisionmaking.

Incompetent patients generally

(8) Physicians who make initial assessments of patients' competence and others who review these assessments should be responsible for judging whether a particular patient's decisionmaking abilities are sufficient to meet the demands of the specific decision at hand.

(9) To protect the interests of patients who have insufficient capacity to make particular decisions and to ensure their well-being and self-determination:

- An appropriate surrogate, ordinarily a family member, should be named to make decisions for such patients. The decisions of surrogates should, when possible, attempt to replicate the ones that the patient would make if capable of doing so. When lack of evidence about the patient's wishes precludes this, decisions by surrogates should seek to protect the patient's best interests. Because such decisions are not instances of self-choice by the patient, the range of acceptable decisions by surrogates is sometimes not as broad as it would be for patients making decisions for themselves.

- The medical staff, along with the trustees and administrators of health care institutions, should explore and evaluate various formal and informal administrative arrangements for review and consultation, such as "ethics committees," particularly for decisions that have life-or-death consequences for incompetent patients.

- State courts and legislatures should consider making provision for advance directives through which people designate others to make health care decisions on their behalf and/or give instructions about their care. Such advance directives provide a means of preserving some self-determination for patients who may lose their decision-making capacity. Durable powers of attorney are preferable to "living wills" since they are more generally applicable and provide a better vehicle for patients to exercise self-determination, though experience with both is limited.

- Health care professionals and institutions should adopt clear, explicit, and publicly available policies regarding how and by whom decisions are to be made for patients who lack adequate decision-making capacity.

- Families, health care institutions, and professionals should work together to make decisions for patients who lack decisionmaking capacity. Recourse to the courts should be reserved for the occasions when adjudication is clearly required by state law or when concerned parties have disagreements that they cannot resolve over matters of substantial import. Courts and legislatures should be cautious about requiring judicial review of routine health care decisions for patients with inadequate decisionmaking capacity.

Patients with permanent loss of consciousness

(10) Current understanding of brain functions allows a reliable diagnosis of permanent loss of consciousness for some patients. Whether or not life-sustaining treatment is given is of much less importance to such patients than to others.

(11) The decisions of patients' families should determine what sort of medical care permanently unconscious patients receive. Other than requiring appropriate decisionmaking procedures for these patients, the law does not and should not require any particular therapies to be applied or continued, with the exception of basic nursing care that is needed to ensure dignified and respectful treatment of the patient.

(12) Access to costly care for patients who have permanently lost consciousness may justifiably be restricted on the basis of resource use in two ways: by a physician or institution that otherwise would have to deny significantly beneficial care to another specific patient, or by legitimate mechanisms of policy formulation and application if and only if the provision of certain kinds of care to these patients were clearly causing serious inequities in the use of community resources.

Seriously ill newborns

(13) Parents should be the surrogates for a seriously ill newborn unless they are disqualified by decisionmaking incapacity, an unresolvable

disagreement between them, or their choice of a course of action that is clearly against the infant's best interests.

(14) Therapies expected to be futile for a seriously ill newborn need not be provided; parents, health care professionals and institutions, and reimbursement sources, however, should ensure the infant's comfort.

(15) Within constraints of equity and availability, infants should receive all therapies that are clearly beneficial to them. For example, an otherwise healthy Down Syndrome child whose life is threatened by a surgically correctable complication should receive the surgery because he or she would clearly benefit from it.

- The concept of benefit necessarily makes reference to the context of the infant's present and future treatment, taking into account such matters as the level of biomedical knowledge and technology and the availability of services necessary for the child's treatment.

- The dependence of benefit upon context underlines society's special obligation to provide necessary services for handicapped children and their families, which rests on the special ethical duties owed to newborns with undeserved disadvantages and on the general ethical duty of the community to ensure equitable access for all persons to an adequate level of health care.

(16) Decisionmakers should have access to the most accurate and up-to-date information as they consider individual cases.

- Physicians should obtain appropriate consultations and referrals.

- The significance of the diagnoses and the prognoses under each treatment option must be conveyed to the parents (or other surrogates).

(17) The medical staff, administrators, and trustees of each institution that provides care to seriously ill newborns should take the responsibility for ensuring good decisionmaking practices. Accrediting bodies may want to require that institutions have appropriate policies in this area.

- An institution should have clear and explicit policies that require prospective or retrospective review of decisions when life-sustaining treatment for an infant might be foregone or when parents and providers disagree about the correct decision for an infant. Certain categories of clearly futile therapies could be explicitly excluded from review.

- The best interests of an infant should be pursued when those interests are clear.

- The policies should allow for the exercise of parental discretion when a child's interests are ambiguous.

- Decisions should be referred to public agencies (including courts) for review when necessary to determine whether parents should be disqualified as decisionmakers and, if so, who should decide the course of treatment that would be in the best interests of their child.

(18) The legal system has various – though limited – roles in ensuring that seriously ill infants receive the correct care.

- Civil courts are ultimately the appropriate decisionmakers concerning the disqualification of parents as surrogates and the designation of surrogates to serve in their stead.

- Special statutes requiring providers to bring such cases to the attention of civil authorities do not seem warranted, since state laws already require providers to report cases of child abuse or neglect to social service agencies; nevertheless, educating providers about their responsibilities is important.

- Although criminal penalties should be available to punish serious errors, the ability of the criminal law to ensure good decisionmaking in individual cases is limited.

- Governmental agencies that reimburse for health care may insist that institutions have policies and procedures regarding decisionmaking, but using financial sanctions against institutions to punish an "incorrect" decision in a particular case is likely to be ineffective and to lead to excessively detailed regulations that would involve government reimbursement officials in bedside decision-making. Furthermore, such sanctions could actually penalize other patients and providers in an unjust way.

Cardiopulmonary resuscitation

(19) A presumption favoring resuscitation of hospitalized patients in the event of unexpected cardiac arrest is justified.

(20) A competent and informed patient or an incompetent patient's surrogate is entitled to decide with the attending physician that an order against resuscitation should be written in the chart. When cardiac arrest is likely, a patient (or a surrogate) should usually be informed and offered the chance specifically to decide for or against resuscitation.

(21) Physicians have a duty to assess for each hospitalized patient whether resuscitation is likely, on balance, to benefit the patient, to fail to benefit, or to have uncertain effect.

- When a patient will not benefit from resuscitation, a decision not to resuscitate, with the consent of the patient or surrogate, is justified.

- When a physician's assessment conflicts with a competent patient's decision, further discussion and consultation are appropriate; ultimately the physician must follow the patient's decision or transfer responsibility for the patient to another physician.

- When a physician's assessment conflicts with that of an incompetent patient's surrogate, further discussion, consultation, review by an institutional committee, and, if necessary, judicial review should be sought.

(22) To protect the interests of patients and their families, health care institutions should have explicit policies and procedures governing orders not to resuscitate, and accrediting bodies should require such policies.

- Such policies should require that orders not to resuscitate be in written form and that they delineate who has the authority both to write such orders and to stop a resuscitation effort in progress.

- Federal agencies responsible for the direct provision of patient care (such as the Veterans Administration, the Public Health Service, and the Department of Defense) should ensure that their health care facilities adopt appropriate policies.

(23) The entry of an order not to resuscitate holds no necessary implications for any other therapeutic decisions, and the level or extent of health care that will be reimbursed under public or private insurance programs should never be linked to such orders.

(24) The education of health care professionals should ensure that they know how to help patients and family make ethically justified decisions for or against resuscitation; those responsible for professional licensure and certification may want to assess knowledge in these areas.

NOTES

1. "A determination of this [adequate] level will take into account the value of various types of health care in relation to each other as well as the value of health care in relation to other important goods for which societal resources are needed" ([2], pp. 4–5).
2. "Decisionmaking guided by the best interest standard requires a surrogate to do what, from an objective standpoint, appears to promote a patient's good without reference to the patient's actual or supposed preferences" ([1], p. 179). See also [1], pp. 131–136.

BIBLIOGRAPHY

1. President's Commission for the Study of Ethical Problems in Medicine and Biomedical and Behavioral Research: 1982, *Making Health Care Decisions*, U.S. Government Printing Office, Washington, D.C.
2. President's Commission for the Study of Ethical Problems in Medicine and Biomedical and Behavioral Research: 1983, *Securing Access to Heath Care*, U.S. Government Printing Office, Washington, D.C.

DO NOT RESUSCITATE ORDERS – THE PROPOSED LEGISLATION AND REPORT OF THE NEW YORK STATE TASK FORCE ON LIFE AND THE LAW – 2ND EDITION, CONDENSED

I. PREFACE TO 1988 EDITION

Governor Cuomo convened the New York State Task Force on Life and the Law in March 1985. He charged the Task Force to make recommendations for public policy on issues posed by medical advances, including the determination of death, decisions about life-sustaining treatment, the issuance of do not resuscitate (DNR) orders, the treatment of disabled newborns, organ transplantation and the new reproductive technologies.

The Governor asked the Task Force to make the issuance of DNR orders a priority on its agenda because of confusion and uncertainty about the orders in New York State. This uncertainty, fueled in part by concerns over legal liability for openly documenting the orders, led to a host of unacceptable practices, ranging from secret codes and slow codes to the provision of resuscitation in cases where it was medically futile. Adult patients, even those fully capable of deciding for themselves about treatment, were often not consulted and included in the decision-making process.

While public attention to the problems associated with DNR orders initially focused on the acute care setting, questions about resuscitation also arose in long-term care facilities. Although most long-term care facilities do not provide full-scale CPR, they routinely decide which residents should be transported to the hospital in the event of arrest. Yet, as shown in a survey of health-care facilities conducted by the Task Force in September 1986, only 11% of the 174 nursing homes that responded to the survey had developed institutional policies on resuscitation decisions.

The Task Force concluded that legislation was needed to clarify the rights and obligation of patients, family members and health care professionals in the decision-making process. After considering how to contribute most effectively to public consideration of the issue, the Task Force developed a legislative proposal and a report that explained the policy choices embodied in the proposal.

R. Baker & M.A. Strosberg (eds.), Legislating Medical Ethics: A Study of the New York Do-Not-Resuscitate Law, 381–413.

The Task Force released its Report in May 1986. In February 1987, the Legislature held public hearings on the recommendations. Many organizations in the State presented testimony, including groups representing patients, physicians, nurses, social workers, hospitals and nursing homes. Representatives of numerous religious communities, the State and City Bar Associations and the Civil Liberties Union also attended.

On July 7, 1987, the Legislature enacted the bill, which was signed into law by Governor Cuomo on August 7, 1987. On April 1, 1988, the legislation became effective. It applies to hospitals, nursing homes and mental health facilities in the State. Experience to date suggests that many health care facilities and health care professionals support the basic principles in the law and welcome the guidance it provides. At the same time, some have found certain procedures cumbersome, such as those to determine a patient's decision-making capacity and to notify different individuals about the steps taken under the law.

Concerns also stem from misunderstanding about or an extremely cautious interpretation of certain provisions. For example, the presumption that all patients who do not have a DNR order consent to resuscitation in the event of cardiac arrest has caused anxiety among some health care professionals who believe the provision creates a new obligation to provide resuscitation. Yet, as explained in the Task Force's report, the presumption mirrors existing law – in the event of an emergency all patients are presumed to consent to needed treatment. The presumption protects health care professionals from liability for treating a patient without consent; it does not establish an obligation to provide treatment, especially in circumstances when treatment would be futile.

The legislation has also been interpreted to apply to all cases in the emergency room. Lacking time to issue an order formally, emergency room physicians have necessarily made decisions about resuscitation based on the patient's condition and the likelihood of benefit from the procedure. The statute does not require any change in this practice.

Further education of health care professionals about the legislation is needed. The Task Force supports the efforts now underway at the Department of Health to provide educational materials and additional guidance about the laws provisions.

This report explains the social, ethical and legal underpinnings for many of the policies established by this legislation, focusing on the decision-making process. While some particulars of the process proposed by the Task Force are different in the law, the ethical premises and broad outlines of the procedures are not: the requirement that physicians seek the informed consent of adult patients with decision-making capacity; the process to determine which patients are capable of deciding about resuscitation, highlighting the ethical and legal significance of this critical dividing line; the authorization of family members and others close to the patient to decide about resuscitation, subject to certain constraints; and protection for those patients who are most vulnerable because they are incapable of deciding and have no family members or others to decide on their behalf. The report also discusses the dispute mediation process and the ways in which the process can be structured.

New York State Task Force on Life and the Law
(August, 1988)

II. MEDICAL FACTS ABOUT RESUSCITATION

Cardiopulmonary resuscitation (CPR) is the restoration of heartbeat and/or breathing through medical intervention. Since cardiac arrest occurs at some point in the dying process of every person, regardless of the underlying cause of death, the decision about resuscitation is potentially relevant for every patient ([46], p. 235).

Basic resuscitation involves the initiation and maintenance of respiration and heartbeat through simple techniques such as mouth-to-mouth resuscitation and external chest compression which can be administered without equipment by any person trained in CPR. Advanced resuscitation requires more sophisticated techniques and is performed by trained medical personnel. Many of the techniques are highly complex and invasive. A defibrillator may be used to administer electric shock and stimulate cardiac contractions. Medications are often supplied through intravenous tubes or by direct injection to the heart. In extreme cases, intracardiac massage may be attempted. This procedure requires physicians to open the patient's chest and spread the patient's ribs in order to massage the heart directly.

Unless cardiac and respiratory function are restored within a short time of arrest, irreversible brain damage and death will occur. In order for CPR to be effective, basic techniques must be initiated within minutes of the arrest (ordinarily within 4–5 minutes), and must be followed immediately by advanced life support (within 10–12 minutes of the arrest) [8].

Cardiopulmonary Resuscitation: The Medical Outcome

CPR, when successful, restores heartbeat and breathing and enables a patient to resume his previous lifestyle. Less successful CPR efforts may fail altogether to restore basic life functions or may only partially succeed, leaving the patient brain damaged or otherwise impaired. Many patients who are resuscitated are so weak and ill that they never leave the hospital.

On average, in-hospital resuscitation restores cardiac and respiratory function in one out of three patients ([46], p. 234). For patients who are resuscitated, statistics regarding the percentage who survive to be discharged from the hospital range from 3% to 30% ([4], p. 570; [56]; [18], p. 32). Generally, lower rates are observed when CPR is administered without regard to unfavorable patient characteristics, while higher rates are associated with more selective application of CPR. The low survival rate reflects the devastating physical effects of cardiac and pulmonary arrest, the poor prognosis of many resuscitated patients, and the limited ability of CPR to reverse the course of death ([18], p. 33; [15], pp. 39, 43; [7]).

Do not Resuscitate Orders

A Do Not Resuscitate order is an order in the patient's medical chart to withhold resuscitation in the event of cardiopulmonary arrest. Although CPR is an emergency procedure, consideration and issuance of a DNR order occur prior to the actual cardiac or respiratory crisis. Thus, before the order is issued, there is an opportunity for a physician to inform the patient about CPR and to ascertain the patient's preferences.

The emergence of DNR orders stemmed from the widespread recognition that resuscitation was neither medically appropriate for nor consistent with the preferences of all patients. As experience with CPR increased, it became clear that for some patients it offered only a more violent death rather than a longer life.

The prevalence of DNR orders in hospitals has been the subject of numerous studies. One research effort found that DNR orders had been issued for 14% of the patients in a medical intensive care unit while another showed that orders had been issued or considered for 20% of all patients in a teaching hospital ([58], [13]).

III. THE NEED FOR CHANGE

It is widely recognized that, under certain circumstances, DNR orders are medically and ethically appropriate. Nonetheless, in the absence of clear public guidelines or judicial sanction, the medical profession remains uncertain and concerned about the legality of the orders. In response to this uncertainty, practices have emerged which fail to serve the interests of patients throughout the State. The problem is twofold: the issuance of DNR orders without the consent of patients or their family members, and the resuscitation of patients in circumstances where resuscitation is not medically indicated. While public concern has focused on the issuance of orders without consent and secrecy surrounding issuance of the orders, the second practice, medically inappropriate resuscitation, is at least as widespread and equally unsound.

Orders without Consent

The abuses associated with issuance of DNR orders captured public attention in New York as a result of a Grand Jury investigation conducted by a special prosecutor for the Attorney General's Office in 1982. The investigation was prompted by the death of an elderly patient in a Queens hospital who had not been resuscitated because of an unwritten DNR order, issued without consultation with the patient or the patient's family. The DNR order was indicated by a purple dot on the patient's chart, a system devised in response to a decision at the hospital that written DNR orders were "of doubtful legality" ([47], p. 13).

The Grand Jury investigation concluded that the covert system of issuing DNR orders led to a host of undesirable consequences: it invited clerical error, discouraged physicians from obtaining consent from the patient or the patient's family, and all but eliminated professional accountability ([47], p. 4). Indeed, as indicated by testimony before the Grand Jury, the only professionals who might be held accountable, the nurses who administered the dot system, bore no responsibility for the decision not to resuscitate the patient ([47], p. 16).

The Grand Jury investigation also found that procedural abuses stemmed from concern about civil and criminal liability for issuance of DNR orders despite the fact that the medical and ethical appropriateness of the orders in certain circumstances was indisputable. Although concern about legality of the orders was widespread in other states, the Grand Jury

Report noted that the prevalence of civil litigation in this State and the broad discretion vested in local prosecutors made the problem especially acute in New York ([47], p. 18).

While covert issuance of DNR orders was one response to the dilemma facing physicians, other responses developed: the "slow code" and the "show code." A "slow code" is the provision of resuscitation efforts in a manner which is generally designed to fail. Slow code procedures range from providing selective measures to moving more slowly to call the code team to the patient's bedside. The "show code" is activity conducted for the benefit of the patient's family which makes it appear as if resuscitation is being attempted.

The slow code, show code and dot system are all means of achieving the results of a DNR order without risking the legal liability associated with issuance of the order. Each of these practices violates the physician's professional obligations to patients and their families. Moreover, the furtiveness of these measures and the failure to obtain consent makes illicit and unethical what might otherwise be a medically appropriate decision.

Medically Inappropriate Resuscitation

The second problem associated with the provision of CPR is the resuscitation of patients when it is not medically indicated: when resuscitation will probably fail, or, at best, will succeed only to the extent that the patient will be subjected to intensive and repeated resuscitation before death inevitably occurs. Like DNR orders without consent, medically inappropriate resuscitation challenges the integrity of the medical system: it is the use of medical technology for reasons unrelated to the patient.

Resuscitation of patients when not medically indicated may occur for several reasons. Physicians may be reluctant to discuss resuscitation with patients or their families, and therefore do not obtain the consent needed to issue a DNR order. Even when the physician has obtained consent, fear of liability for issuance of the order may persist. Finally, family members may demand aggressive treatment for reasons other than a judgment about the benefits and burdens it poses to the patient. Guided by an unwillingness to accept the fact that the patient is dying, or an inability to resolve guilt feelings about care for the patient in other contexts, family members may insist upon resuscitation regardless of its likely outcome. Depending on the patient's condition, that outcome may be a more traumatic death rather than a prolongation of life. In some reported cases, persons have been resuscitated as many as 52 times within a four to six week period before death finally occurred ([21]; [20], p. 133).

Steps Toward Change

Public recognition of the abuses associated with the issuance of DNR orders has served as a catalyst for change. Following the Grand Jury investigation, some hospitals in the State adopted and implemented guidelines for the issuance of DNR orders. The Medical Society of the State of New York and the New York Academy of Medicine developed and publicized model guidelines for hospital use. Nonetheless, many hospitals still do not have formal policies regarding DNR orders and existing policies are not uniform throughout the State. The need remains for public guidance about some of the difficult issues which arise in seeking to make and implement resuscitation decisions.

IV. VALUES UNDERLYING RESUSCITATION DECISIONS

As technology creates new medical options, complex questions regarding those options arise. It is no longer clear that all available technology must be used to preserve life. Rather, in light of the increasing array of technologies to extend life, society has become more and more concerned about the individual's right to control how that technology is used.

In promoting the good of all, society seeks to provide the conditions which are needed to protect the life and foster the welfare of the individual, whose personal dignity and worth are absolute. Thus society has a compelling interest in protecting and preserving human life, especially in matters of life and death such as resuscitation decisions. At the same time, the dignity of each person requires a deep respect for the freedom and autonomy of the individual to make decisions about his own life.

Questions about individual autonomy and the preservation of human life have thrust medical decision making into the realm of public discussion. Society must provide standards for conduct and parameters within which the rights of patients, family members and health care professionals are defined. The embodiment of society's values in public policy must offer both a moral vision of the community and a concrete, practical framework for health care decisions.

In the health care context, autonomy means that the person is sovereign with respect to decisions about his own body and has the right not to be treated without consent. Autonomy has special significance for decisions about CPR. The benefit of extending life, often only for brief periods marked by suffering and disability, must be weighed against an earlier, more peaceful, death. Respect for autonomy recognizes the personal nature of the resuscitation decision and the patient's right to request or refuse CPR.

This recognition of patient autonomy is part of an historic shift in the physician-patient relationship. Medical decisions were traditionally made by the physician as medical expert. Today, as medical decisions are more clearly defined as decisions about values, decision-making responsibility is necessarily shifting from physician to patient.

A more cooperative model of the physician-patient relationship has emerged which recognizes the expertise of the physician and the personal responsibility of the patient as essential to medical decisions. While the physician provides needed information and guidance, decision-making authority ultimately rests with the patient. Although the patient places his treatment in the physician's hands, the need for dialogue and discussion remains.

Rather than clarify the moral content of decisions in the health care setting, a focus on autonomy often underscores our moral pluralism. In a pluralistic society, a patient's exercise of autonomy may conflict with the community's respect for human life. This reverence, central to our religious and moral beliefs, lies at the core of our medical tradition. The Hippocratic Oath has not lost its pertinence: the commitment to benefit the sick and relieve suffering is the foundation of medical practice.

On occasion, patients and physicians may disagree on the appropriate medical choice to be made. The patient's decision to reject resuscitation, rather than to prolong life, may conflict with the physician's personal convictions as well as the ethos of the profession and institution to which the physician is committed.

While the patient's autonomy must be respected, the physician cannot be forced to care for the patient in a way that violates his conscience. The physician therefore cannot be compelled to continue to treat a patient who has rejected resuscitation if the physician considers the provision of resuscitation for the patient a moral and professional obligation. The option to transfer care of the patient in such cases is an important recognition of the physician's rights.

A focus on autonomy also emphasizes individual rights at the expense of social obligations within the human community. On its own, autonomy fails to provide a basis for our moral obligations to one another beyond those established by contractual relationships. A commitment to absolute patient autonomy neglects the fact that the sick person is not totally independent, and overlooks human relatedness as a reality of the physician-patient relationship [55].

Moreover, while the principle of autonomy may justify a policy of non-intervention by the state, the medical community and the family, it fails to provide guidance for the patient in deciding whether to accept or refuse CPR. In a community that values personal autonomy and human dignity, it is a sign of respect and caring to assist others in exercising their freedom wisely.

Moral guidance for medical decisions is often provided by the family. For the patient with capacity to make health care decisions, family involvement can foster communication and provide care and support. Participation by family members in discussions about treatment may assist both physician and patient to select the best course of treatment.

The family's role, however, is a limited one. The privilege of confidentiality granted to the therapeutic relationship symbolizes the trust and privacy that exist between physician and patient. The frequency of physician consultations about resuscitation with family members rather than patients, even when the patient has decisional capacity, underscores the importance of defining familial participation when the patient's autonomy would be vitiated or denied ([3], [13]).

As the patient's capacity diminishes, the family's relationship with the physician and its role in decision making necessarily expand. The practice of relying on family members as substitute or surrogate decision makers for resuscitation and medical treatment generally also expresses a fundamental societal value. Family members are considered to be most knowledgeable of the lifestyle, preferences and values of the patient and best able to protect those interests. This is especially true when the patient is a child. Parental decisions about their children have long been included in the sphere of familial privacy and autonomy which is afforded special protection from state intrusion.

The presumption in favor of the family as decision maker is not, however, absolute. The delegation of authority to make health care decisions, especially where the decision may determine whether the person lives or dies, is critical. The family, or a particular family member, may not always be the best surrogate for the patient. The family member may have financial or other concerns which conflict with the patient's interests. In some cases, estrangement or feelings of guilt may adversely affect the quality of decision making. On the other hand, the limitation of familial participation in surrogate decision making poses additional questions. On what grounds may the state intrude into the sphere of familial privacy? If the state does intervene, who then speaks for the patient and on what basis?

In a pluralistic society it is a delicate and difficult task to balance competing values in laws and regulations that prescribe and prohibit human conduct. This is especially true when general rules must be fashioned to correspond to the very different realities of each person's dying process. However, legal standards must be informed by shared moral convictions in society. The challenge for public policy is to protect those shared values in a way that does not stifle individual choice. As stated by John Courtney Murray, "Law seeks to establish and maintain that minimum of actualized morality that is necessary for the healthy functioning of the social order" ([39], pp. 166–167).

Uniform substantive rules cannot possibly satisfy the myriad circumstances of the clinical experience nor can they reflect the personal nature of the resuscitation decision for each patient. Substantive rules must therefore be combined with procedures which protect patient autonomy while recognizing the need to balance other fundamental values, such as the preservation of life, in the health care setting.

V. LEGAL RIGHTS AND DUTIES

Duty to Provide Resuscitation

Under common law, once a physician-patient relationship has been established and the patient consents to treatment, the physician is obligated to preserve the patient's life by using the skills and means ordinarily applied by physicians in similar cases ([1], §201; [45]). Under such circumstances, a failure to treat the patient may give rise to the same liability as wrongful or negligent treatment ([1], §240).

Where emergency treatment is necessary, the patient's consent to treatment is presumed ([41], §2805-d(2) (a); [53]; [29], §18 at 117). Hence, unless proper consent to a DNR order has been obtained, the failure to provide CPR when it is medically indicated may subject a physician to civil liability, professional sanctions and, if sufficiently egregious, criminal penalties ([47]; [17], pp. 362, 366).

Right to Refuse Resuscitation

The right of a competent adult to refuse medical treatment has long been recognized in New York. In *Schloendorff v. Society of New York Hospital*, a 1914 decision, the Court of Appeals strongly affirmed this common law right. As stated by Judge Cardozo:

> Every human being of adult years and sound mind has a right to determine what shall be done with his own body; and a surgeon who performs an operation without his patient's consent, commits an assault, for which he is liable in damages.

In its 1981 decision in *Matter of Storar* the Court of Appeals again upheld the right of a competent adult to refuse medical treatment. As the Court explained, under existing law, the patient's right is paramount to the physician's obligation to provide medical care [34].

The Court recognized, however, that the common law right to refuse treatment is not absolute and may be overridden by compelling state interests: the elimination of a threat to public health, the protection of minor children or dependents, or the prevention of suicide [34]. With respect to the last interest, the Court, consistent with judicial decisions in other states, made clear that suicide relates only to self-inflicted harm and not to a decision to refuse life-sustaining treatment ([34], [30], [35], [54]).

After describing these state interests, the Court summarized existing law concerning the patient's common law right to refuse treatment as follows:

> To the extent that existing statutory and decisional law manifests the State's interest on this subject, they consistently support the right of the competent adult to make his own decision by imposing civil liability on those who perform medical treatment without consent, although the treatment may be beneficial or even necessary to preserve the patient's life [34].

Beginning with the 1976 New Jersey Supreme Court decision *In re Quinlan*

[26], a growing body of caselaw in state and lower federal courts has recognized a right to decline life-sustaining treatment based on the constitutional right to privacy ([54], [49], [35], [31], [24]). The right to privacy, although not expressly provided for in the United States Constitution, has been found by the courts to exist in the penumbra of specific guarantees of the Bill of Rights [16]. The Supreme Court has applied this right in matters relating to marriage, procreation, contraception, family relationships, child rearing and education; it has not yet addressed whether the right to privacy encompasses a right to decline life-sustaining treatment.

In *Eichner v. Dillon*, an intermediate level New York appellate court held that the constitutional right to privacy encompasses the right to refuse life-sustaining treatment [11]. Upon review, the Court of Appeals declined to rule upon the existence of a constitutional right to refuse treatment, explaining that the relief granted to the petitioner was adequately supported by common law principles [34].

Decisions on Behalf of Incompetent Adults

When a patient lacks the capacity to make a contemporaneous decision about withholding or withdrawing treatment, the critical issues are whether a substitute decision may be made by a family member or another person on behalf of the patient, and what substantive and procedural protections are necessary to protect both the patient's right to refuse treatment and right not to have his life foreshortened.

These issues were first confronted in the well-known case of Karen Ann Quinlan [26]. At the time of the 1976 court decision, Karen was 22 years old, comatose and supported by a respirator. The Court held that Karen did not, by losing her capacity, lose her right to decline treatment. It therefore permitted her father, as her guardian, to render his best judgment about whether she would exercise that right under the circumstances.

Since *Quinlan*, the principle of substitute decision making for life-sustaining treatment has been judicially recognized, albeit with certain important variations, in numerous other jurisdictions (e.g., [54], [51], [27], [35], [31], [24], [2], [14]). Moreover, the principle is now expressly embodied in eleven state statutes that specifically permit substitute decision making on behalf of incompetent patients.

In contrast, the New York Court of Appeals, in its 1981 decision in

Matter of Storar, declined to recognize the legality of substitute decision making [34]. *Matter of Storar* involved the review of two lower court decisions: the first concerned Brother Joseph Fox, an elderly member of a religious order, and the second involved John Storar, a middle-aged man, profoundly retarded since birth.

Brother Fox lapsed into a coma in October, 1979, and was placed on a respirator which maintained him in a vegetative state. Father Eichner, the director of the religious society to which Brother Fox belonged, initiated proceedings to obtain judicial approval to withdraw the respirator.

The Court of Appeals held that treatment for Brother Fox could be withdrawn based on "clear and convincing evidence" that Brother Fox had expressed his wishes about life-sustaining treatment prior to the time he became unconscious. By requiring a clear prior decision made by the patient himself rather than allowing a third party to make a substituted judgment on the patient's behalf, the New York Court of Appeals departed from the approach taken by most other states that have confronted this problem [28].

The Court also declined to address the process by which such decisions should be made except to note the availability of advance judicial review. In effect, the Court instructed physicians and families to obtain judicial approval for decisions to withdraw treatment in all but the clearest instances of patient approval or risk civil and criminal liability [34].

In its second opinion in *Storar*, the Court extended these principles and granted an application by a state facility to order blood transfusions for a 52 year old retarded man suffering from incurable cancer, over the objections of his mother, who was also his legal guardian. The Court explained that it was unrealistic to attempt to determine what John Storar would have wanted due to his mental impairment and refused to permit discontinuance of the treatment. This holding also departs from the approach taken by virtually all other courts that have addressed this issue, which permit decisions to be made for incompetent patients based on a best interests or substituted judgment standard.

Decisions in other states address substitute decision making for the issuance of DNR orders. In the leading case, *In re Dinnerstein*, the family and physician of a 67 year old woman who was terminally ill and in a vegetative state sought court approval for a DNR order. The court held that, under such circumstances, a physician, in consultation with the family, could issue a DNR order without judicial approval.

Decisions on Behalf of Minors

Decisions about the medical care of minors involve the separate rights and interests of the parents, the minor, and the state. The role of parents in such decisions is generally recognized as paramount [33]. Nevertheless, the state may – and often does – intervene to secure medical care for minors in cases where the parents are absent or fail to provide adequate medical treatment because of neglect, poor judgment, or religious beliefs.

Where the contemplated medical decision concerns the discontinuance of life-sustaining treatment, the interests of all three parties – the parents, the state and the minor – are great. The law in this State regarding their respective rights and obligations is not well-developed. Case law in other jurisdictions supports the conclusion that such decisions should be made in accordance with basic principles of substituted judgment: parents may decide to forego life-sustaining treatment on behalf of their minor child only where the child's medical prognosis is sufficiently poor, and where the decision reflects "as nearly as possible the actual interests and preferences" of the child ([9]; [23], [25]).

VI. THE PROPOSED LEGISLATION

Selection of the Legislative Option

Legislation is not the only means, nor is it always the best means, to establish public policy – especially where those policies involve sensitive and controversial moral questions. As the Task Force approaches each issue it has been charged to address, the question must be raised anew about the benefit of legislation as compared to other means of expressing public values and shaping human conduct: regulation, education, or judicial decision.

The Task Force has concluded that legislation is essential to establish clear, enforceable public standards concerning the issuance of DNR orders. Public standards are critically important to create uniform practices and to clarify the rights, authority and protections afforded patients, family members, and health care professionals in issuance of the orders.

Judicial precedents in the State regarding the withholding of treatment and the climate engendered by concerns about medical malpractice issues require that these standards be embodied in legislation. Unlike the courts in almost every other state, the New York Court of Appeals, in its decision in *Matter of Storar*, declined to recognize the authority of family members or other surrogates to consent to the withholding of care on behalf of patients who lack decision making capacity. Moreover, the Court also concluded that, in the absence of legislation, health care professionals and family members involved in decisions about the withholding or withdrawing of treatment have only two alternatives; they can either seek advance judicial approval in every case or face the possibility of civil and criminal liability. Finally, the Court made the need for legislative action clear by emphasizing the limitations of its holding and the need for judicial restraint in sensitive cases involving termination of treatment. As stated by the Court, "Unlike the legislature, the courts are neither equipped nor empowered to prescribe substantive or procedural rules for all, most, or even the more common contingencies."

Resuscitation decisions are now a "common contingency" in the delivery of care to severely ill patients. Moreover, the issues the Court of Appeals declined to address, procedures for substitute decision making and questions of liability for withholding treatment, urgently require resolution. Although the Commissioner of Health has the authority to promulgate regulations which address other aspects of resuscitation, the Task Force believes that legislation on this critical issue should be articulated and established in a unified and comprehensive proposal.

[T]he Task Force concluded that the DNR issue differs from other issues concerning the termination of treatment. The foundation for the acceptance of DNR orders is built upon two basic considerations: the intrusive nature of resuscitation and its medical futility for some patients. The assessment of the burdens and benefits of resuscitation therefore differs from that of other life-sustaining treatments.

While each form of life-sustaining treatment raises unique considerations, concerns about DNR orders and special factors relating to resuscitation warrant a separate legislative response. The Task Force will address issues relating to other life-sustaining treatments in subsequent reports and recommendations.

Purpose and scope of the legislation

The legislation proposed by the Task Force clarifies the rights and obligations of patients, their families, physicians and other health care providers regarding CPR and the issuance of DNR orders. It provides a means for patients with capacity to express their wishes and establishes a mechanism for decision making for patients without capacity. It also provides legal immunity to health care providers and persons making a decision on a patient's behalf who strive to act in accordance with the law. The proposed legislation thereby responds to the dual concerns regarding issuance of DNR orders: issuance of the order without the consent of the patient or the patient's family members and failure to issue the order when it is medically indicated and consistent with the wishes of the patient or appropriate decision maker.

The Patient with Capacity

The decision about resuscitation

Either the physician or the patient with decisional capacity may initiate a discussion about CPR and issuance of a DNR order. In the absence of a decision by the patient to refuse CPR, the proposed legislation explicitly affirms the presumption under existing law that all patients, in the event of cardiac or respiratory arrest, consent to CPR. Consistent with this presumption, the legislation requires the attending physician to obtain the consent of a patient with decisional capacity prior to issuing a DNR order, subject to the narrow therapeutic exception discussed in this section of the Report.

The proposed legislation also provides a means for the patient with capacity to express a decision to reject CPR. The right to decline CPR is an expression of the person's common law right, well-recognized in this State, to direct the course of one's own medical treatment, and not be treated without consent ([50], [34]). The proposed legislation does not limit exercise of that right to patients who suffer from specific medical conditions. Thus, patients may request a DNR order regardless of whether their illness is diagnosed as terminal.

This policy reflects the value of self-determination in the delivery of intrusive medical treatment. However, the Task Force recognizes the difficulty of balancing this value and other fundamental values, such as the preservation of life, in the health care setting. Most Task Force members believe that a person's right to self-determination outweighs other interests even when the decision to forego CPR may be ethically questionable. A few Task Force members believe that in certain circumstances, e.g., when the prognosis for recovery after CPR is excellent, a person's decision to forego CPR should not be honored because the decision is medically unjustifiable and ethically unsound.

The proposed legislation establishes a procedure for responding to conflicting decisions by patients and physicians. The procedure respects the right of physicians not to treat patients in a way which violates their own beliefs and is designed to enhance decision making by both patients and physicians.

If the attending physician is unwilling to abide by the patient's decision to refuse CPR, he may submit the issue to a hospital dispute mediation system required under the proposed legislation. While the dispute mediation system is not empowered to overrule the patient's decision, it may discourage decisions made without adequate information or deliberation.

The dispute mediation process also provides an opportunity to consider and perhaps reverse a physician's refusal to honor the patient's wishes. For some physicians, the availability of CPR creates its own imperative. Yet, the patient's right to refuse CPR demands great deference. During the resolution process, a physician may be persuaded by his colleagues, or by a better understanding of the patient's concerns, to honor the patient's wishes.

Under the proposed legislation, the physician also has the option of transferring care of the patient to another physician, after discussing the matter with the patient. The discussion itself may bring about a reconciliation of the patient's and physician's views. If it does not, the physician must make reasonable efforts to locate another physician who is willing to abide by the patient's wishes. Finally, if another physician cannot be identified to care for the patient or if the patient needs immediate care, the hospital may seek a court order overriding the patient's refusal of resuscitation.

The Task Force believes that resort to the courts will be very rare. The dispute mediation system will enhance the quality of decisions made by patients and physicians and minimize conflict. Only the highly improbable case of the otherwise healthy patient who might fully recover from resuscitation presents the kind of conflict which is likely to require judicial intervention. To date, there is no report of any such case in New York or other states in the nation.

Expression of the patient's wishes

The manner in which a person expresses a decision regarding resuscitation raises several concerns. The form of expression must convey the seriousness of the decision and ensure the authenticity of the person's statement. The formalities required, however, must not be so onerous that they unduly burden the ability of seriously ill patients to have their wishes honored.

The proposed legislation balances these objectives by providing that a person's wishes will be honored if expressed: (i) at any time prior to or during hospitalization in a writing signed and subscribed by two adult witnesses; or (ii) in an oral statement made during hospitalization in the presence of at least two adult witnesses. If the decision is expressed in an oral statement during hospitalization, one of the witnesses must be a physician affiliated with the hospital in which the patient is being treated. Since the authenticity and meaning of the oral statement must be evaluated by the attending physician, the fact that the statement was made in the presence of a hospital physician will greatly assist that evaluation and the attending physician's willingness to rely on the statement.

The patient may revoke consent to a DNR order at any time in a written or oral statement to a physician or nurse at the treating hospital, or by any other act evidencing a specific intent to revoke consent. Any medical staff member informed of revocation of the order is required to record the revocation in the patient's chart and to cancel the order immediately.

The physician's obligation

The proposed legislation requires an attending physician to obtain the consent of a patient with decisional capacity prior to issuing a DNR order except in those rare cases where the therapeutic exception applies. Thus, the physician's obligation to solicit the patient's wishes about resuscitation is only mandated when the physician decides that a DNR order would be appropriate; the physician is not required to consult all patients about resuscitation.

Nonetheless, the Task Force strongly urges the early initiation of discussions about CPR with all patients for whom there appears to be a substantial risk of cardiac or respiratory arrest. The Task Force believes that the difficulty the discussion poses for the physician, and possibly for the patient, is far outweighed by the benefits of openly ascertaining the patient's preferences in advance of an emergency.

Recent studies indicate the very limited extent to which physicians discuss resuscitation with patient. Even more startling, these studies also demonstrate the difference between physicians' opinions about patients' preferences and patients' actual wishes about CPR. In one study, one third of the patients who had been resuscitated and left the hospital stated unequivocally that they wished they had not been resuscitated and would not consent to resuscitation in the future ([3], p. 1091). Another study indicated that physicians are more reticent about discussing CPR with patients who are chronically ill, even when such patients have the capacity to make decisions regarding their treatment ([37], p. 710). Yet, it is precisely this group of patients for whom questions about resuscitation may be most relevant.

Although the legislation does not obligate the physician to discuss CPR with all patients, it does require hospitals to provide information about CPR and the rights and duties established by the proposed legislation. Currently, hospitals and nursing homes are required by State statute and regulations to inform patients generally about their rights by furnishing them with a copy of a statement called the "Patient's Bill of Rights" ([41], §2803-c; [40], vol. 10, §§405.25, 414.14). Under the proposed legislation, this statement would be expanded to include information about the rights of patients and others acting on behalf of patients with respect to issuance of DNR orders.

The proposed legislation does not specify the information which the physician must provide to ensure that the patient's consent to a DNR order is truly informed. In general, however, the patient must have the following information to give meaningful consent to a DNR order: his diagnosis and prognosis, an explanation of CPR and its likely outcome and the consequences of a DNR order.

If the patient initiates the discussion about withholding CPR and requests a DNR order, the attending physician must take one of three steps. He must issue the order or, if he objects to the order, must refer the matter to the dispute mediation system or make efforts to transfer care of the patient to another physician.

The option to transfer care of the patient is available to ensure that a physician is not compelled to issue a medical order that violates his conscience or professional ethos. The transfer option also protects the patient by imposing an affirmative obligation on the physician to identify another physician to care for the patient. The legislation requires the physician to make all reasonable efforts to transfer the patient and to do so promptly. While the physician is attempting to transfer the patient, he has a professional obligation not to abandon care of the patient.

The proposed legislation specifies that consent to issuance of a DNR order by the patient, or any person with authority to act for the patient, does not constitute consent to the withdrawal of other treatment. The obligation to provide appropriate medical treatment and care for the patient, including measures to provide comfort and relief from pain, is not diminished in any way by entry of a DNR order. Moreover, issuance of a DNR order can never justify discharging the patient from the hospital. Instead, since many patients for whom a DNR order is entered are terminally ill, there is a special obligation not to abandon these patients during their dying process.

Once a DNR order is issued, the attending physician is required to review the patient's chart at least every three days to determine the continued applicability of the order, and to record the outcome of that evaluation. For nursing home residents, the order must be reviewed every 30 days, a time frame which is consistent with the existing requirements for physician visits to nursing home residents ([40], §§415.1(d) (1), 415.5(b), 416.1(g) (h)). If more frequent visits are medically indicated, the appropriateness of the DNR order should also be reviewed during those visits.

Should the physician at any time determine that the patient's condition has improved and the DNR order is no longer medically appropriate, he has an obligation to notify the patient immediately. If the patient continues to refuse CPR, the physician must again choose to abide by the order, transfer care of the patient or refer the matter to the dispute mediation system.

The therapeutic exception

The medical imperative of "doing no harm," a central tenet of the Hippocratic Oath, gave rise to a practice of not talking to patients about the diagnosis or course of treatment where the physician determined that the discussion itself could harm the patient. This practice, commonly called the "therapeutic exception," excuses the physician from obtaining a patient's consent even if the patient has the capacity to make a decision about his own treatment.[1] Once applied broadly and routinely to include not only discussions about treatment but also information about diagnoses in cases of terminal illness, physician reliance on the exception has narrowed.

Where the decision relates to the withholding of life-saving treatment such as CPR, the rationale for the therapeutic exception is strained; a patient is spared the harm of a discussion about CPR and is thereby denied the right to insist upon or to refuse its application.[2] Moreover, physician reluctance to discuss resuscitation with patients heightens concern about the exception. Unless workable limits can be established, the exception will swallow the rule and deny persons with capacity the right to decide whether or not they will be resuscitated in the event of cardiopulmonary arrest.

The proposed legislation provides for a therapeutic exception limited to those rare circumstances when the discussion about resuscitation may be life-threatening. In all other instances, the exception is prohibited. The Task Force's proposal therefore makes clear that what is permissible for one purpose, the avoidance of harm to the patient, is unacceptable for another – the desire to avoid the difficult task of speaking with patients about their dying process.

The proposed legislation sets forth procedural and substantive limitations for reliance on the exception. First, the exception is applicable only if the attending physician determines that there is a strong likelihood that the patient would suffer "immediate and severe" harm from the discussion. The Task Force considered the circumstances which would meet this standard. Those circumstances include the patient with an arrhythmia for whom the discussion might trigger an arrest, and the patient with severe paranoid, depressive or suicidal tendencies who might suffer self-inflicted harm. Other conditions may justify reliance on the exception but they must be evaluated rigorously to determine if they meet the proposed standard.

The Task Force considered and rejected a broader standard for the exception that would have included general psychological harm to the patient. The Task Force recognizes that there are certain risks associated with allowing only a narrow therapeutic exception: medically appropriate DNR orders may not be entered because of physicians' reluctance to talk with patients, or because the discussion about CPR may impose a real and unwanted burden on the patient. The Task Force concluded that these risks did not outweigh the interests protected by requiring the consent of a patient with capacity to issue the order.

As proposed by the Task Force, if the physician determines that the patient would probably suffer severe and immediate harm from the discussion, he must seek a second opinion about the assessment of risk to the patient. If the second opinion confirms his own, he must still consult the patient to the extent possible without jeopardizing the patient's physical or emotional health. The purpose of the consultation is not to obtain consent, but to solicit the patient's wishes. The consultation may therefore be general; the discussion may refer to "aggressive" or "extraordinary" treatment. If the patient executed a written statement of wishes prior to hospitalization, the physician might allude to the statement and seek a direct or indirect affirmation.

If the patient had not previously expressed his wishes in writing, the physician must obtain the consent of a surrogate in accordance with the procedures and requirements for surrogate decision making. The proposed legislation imposes two additional requirements when the therapeutic exception is invoked. First, the physician must document the reasons for not consulting the patient in the patient's chart. Second, the physician must assess the patient's risk of injury from a discussion of CPR on a regular basis. As soon as the condition which precluded the discussion is alleviated, the physician must consult the patient.

The Task Force recognizes that creation of the exception opens the door to potential abuse. The Task Force believes, however, that the procedures it has proposed for reliance on the exception are sufficient to ensure its use only in those rare circumstances when the discussion itself may be life-threatening and, hence, should not be mandated.

The Patient without Capacity

Resuscitation decisions are most appropriately made by the patient. However, at the critical time the decision must be made, the patient may lack the capacity to choose the course of his treatment. Decision making on behalf of the patient is then very difficult: who makes the decision, on what grounds, and what procedure is used to ensure that the decision is based upon and realizes the patient's interests?

Generally, patients who lack capacity fall into three categories: (i) patients who have previously expressed their wishes about resuscitation; (ii) patients who have not expressed any prior wishes but for whom a family member, close friend or designee is available to act on their behalf; and (iii) patients who have not expressed prior wishes and who are alone and without familial or other support. Each circumstance gives rise to different concerns and requires an approach which recognizes the values and interests at stake in the resuscitation decision.

The determination of capacity

Standard for decisional capacity. The proposed legislation provides that every adult is presumed to have the capacity to make a decision about CPR unless determined otherwise in accordance with the procedures set forth in the legislation or by court order. The Task Force proposed "decisional capacity" rather than the traditional notion of "competence" as the yardstick for determining the ability to make a decision about CPR. The definition of capacity is included in the legislation:

> Capacity means the ability to understand and appreciate the nature and consequences of an order not to resuscitate, including the benefits and disadvantages of such an order.

The Task Force rejected the concept of competence for several reasons. First, the term often refers to a judicial determination and therefore invites confusion. Second, the traditional notion of competence generally describes a status – the ability to make all or, conversely, no decisions for oneself. In contrast, decisional capacity is a much more limited and specific concept; it refers to a person's ability to make a particular decision. It recognizes that people may be able to make some decisions and not others, and it relates the determination about capacity directly to the decision which must be made.

The Task Force also rejected an "outcome approach" which bases the determination of the patient's decision making ability on the content of the patient's decision. Under this approach, patients who possess capacity but make unconventional treatment decisions may effectively be denied the right to make the decision. Where physician and patient disagree, the physician may simply determine that the patient lacks capacity and substitute his own judgment for that of the patient.

As proposed in the legislation, capacity involves the ability both to understand *and* to appreciate the nature of the decision about resuscitation. Including both understanding and appreciation recognizes the importance of cognitive and conceptual skills as well as emotional development. Further, by requiring an understanding of the benefits and disadvantages of the order, the proposed standard establishes that the patient must be able to consider the nature and consequences of the decision, to evaluate the alternatives, and to reach an informed decision.

The proposed legislation limits the determination of capacity specifically to the ability to make a decision about CPR. If a patient is found to lack capacity to decide about CPR, the determination will have no relevance to the patient's capacity to make other decisions.

Surrogate decision making

When a patient lacks decisional capacity and has not previously expressed his wishes about resuscitation, a substitute or surrogate decision maker must be identified. Traditionally, family members have served that role. In some cases, they seek court appointment as the patient's guardian; the appointment grants the family member legal authority to act on the patient's behalf under court supervision. Yet, even in the absence of such appointment, family members, in consultation with physicians, routinely make health care decisions for incapacitated patients, including decisions about life-sustaining treatment. Ordinarily, it is only when the physician and family members disagree about the treatment, as in the *Quinlan* case, that families seek legal authorization.

The proposed legislation establishes a procedure for the selection of a substitute or "surrogate" decision maker for a patient without capacity, and empowers the surrogate to make a decision about CPR for the patient in accordance with the standards and limitations set forth in the legislation. Thus, the legislation recognizes the authority which, by long-standing custom, has often been vested in family members. The legislation also extends that authority to others outside the family circle where appropriate, and establishes substantive and procedural guidelines to prevent potential abuses and to ensure that the resuscitation decision promotes the patient's values and interests.

The legislation obviates the requirement under existing law for judicial appointment of a substitute decision maker. While court appointment of a guardian provides additional safeguards, including judicial assessment of the surrogate's character and good faith, the judicial process is often ill-suited for urgent medical decisions: it is too slow, too cumbersome and too costly.

The proposed legislation provides a system for selecting the surrogate to replace existing informal practices. That system is the establishment of a priority list of persons from which the surrogate must be chosen. Since the physician must obtain a surrogate's consent and rely on that consent, he will play an important role in identifying the surrogate, even when a surrogate is selected according to a priority list. The legislation, however, limits that role. While the physician's advice and guidance to the surrogate are critical, the surrogate must act as an independent decision maker. The independence of the surrogate and physician provides greater protection for the patient.

Limitations on surrogate authority

The most significant safeguard of the patient's interest in continued treatment is the restriction placed on the surrogate's authority to consent to a DNR order. Under the proposed legislation, the surrogate is granted the authority to consent to a DNR order only if one of three medical conditions exists: the patient is terminally ill; the patient is irreversibly comatose; or a medical judgment is made that resuscitation would probably be unsuccessful and would only prolong the dying process. The Task Force concluded that these limitations on surrogate authority strike the appropriate balance between a patient's competing interests in efforts to prolong life and the refusal of intrusive and often futile treatment.

Standards relating to a terminal illness or condition are often criticized as either too vague to provide meaningful guidance or so specific that they are unworkable given the uncertainties of medical prognosis. The proposed legislation defines terminal illness as "an illness or injury from which there is no recovery and which can reasonably be expected to cause death within one year." The Task Force concluded that the guidance provided by the one year time period was preferable to the confusion engendered by reliance on phrases such as "imminent" or "short time period."

The Task Force recognizes that the uncertainty of prognoses about the time of death makes the application of rigid standards impractical ([46], pp. 24–26). For this reason, the standard the Task Force proposes includes the phrase "reasonably can be expected" to cause death. This phrase is designed to clarify that the one year time period is only a guide-post and does not require a degree of certainty not afforded by medical prognosis. The third medical condition required, whether "resuscitation would probably be unsuccessful and would only prolong the dying process," is also flexible to accommodate the uncertainties of medical prognosis.

A physician must affirm, in writing, that one of the three medical predicates exists. The judgment must be made to a reasonable degree of medical certainty, a standard of proof for medical determinations which serves as the basis for decisions under a clear and convincing evidence standard.

The specified medical conditions present the clearest situations when surrogate consent to a DNR order would be appropriate. Obviously, they do not cover all circumstances under which a surrogate might make a compassionate and responsible decision to refuse resuscitation. For this reason, the legislation preserves the right of persons close to the patient to seek judicial approval of a DNR order on a patient's behalf. Although reluctant to channel decisions about resuscitation to the courts, the Task Force concluded that there is simply no other approach which adequately protects the patient in cases where the specified medical conditions are not present.

Standards for surrogate decision making

In cases involving health care decisions on behalf of persons without capacity, the courts have applied two standards: best interests and substituted judgment. The first standard, best interests, has long been established as the primary standard for decisions about minors. The second standard, substituted judgment, has been developed and routinely applied by the courts in cases involving the withdrawal of life-sustaining treatment for adults without capacity who had previously expressed their preferences.

The proposed legislation requires a surrogate to act in accordance with a substituted judgment standard where prior evidence about the person's wishes is available. The substituted judgment standard is inherently subjective; it directs the surrogate to rely on the patient's values and preferences and thus promotes the patient's right to self-determination. Those preferences may have been expressed several ways. First, prior writings too vague or ambiguous to constitute consent often state general preferences. Second, prior oral statements by the person to the surrogate and others are an important source of information. Finally, the person's wishes may be inferred from general information: religious or moral beliefs, attitudes and feelings about health care and personal goals or plans.

The expression of a person's prior wishes must be considered in light of the patient's medical condition, the prognosis for recovery and the expected benefits of resuscitation. Thus, the surrogate who relies on a substituted judgment standard has a clear obligation to ascertain both the patient's wishes and the medical facts. The proposed legislation grants the surrogate the right to obtain all medical information necessary to make an informed decision.

The substituted judgment standard has little meaning for persons who never indicated their wishes or who never had the capacity to do so. The Task Force therefore proposes that the best interests standard should be applied in those cases. This standard requires an independent assessment of the person's interests and an objective determination of how those interests are most appropriately served.

The best interests standard is often explained by reference to what a reasonable person under the circumstances would decide for himself. In the context of the resuscitation decision, the best interests standard requires the surrogate to make an objective assessment of the burdens and benefits of resuscitation. The diagnosis of the patient's condition and prognosis for recovery as well as the medical assessment of the outcome following resuscitation will be critical to that assessment.

The Task Force recognizes that there is no bright line between the substituted judgment and best interests standards. Substituted judgment is not a license to choose unwisely, even if the choice is consistent with the values and wishes of the patient; self-determination is afforded greater deference when it is exercised by the person directly. Moreover, the process of discerning the patient's wishes and giving them meaning in an unprecedented context will inevitably introduce the values of the surrogate.

Similarly, a determination under the best interests standard is likely to include some consideration of the patient's preferences and concerns. Nevertheless, adoption of the standards serves two important purposes. On the level of principle, it promotes the value of self-determination where that value can be meaningfully applied. As a practical matter the standards provide a clear frame of reference which shapes the surrogate's inquiry and, thus, the decision.

Decision making for patients without surrogates

Many people lack capacity to make health care decisions and have no family members or friends to act as surrogate. These individuals are vulnerable with respect to all health care decisions; they cannot assert their own wishes nor are others always available to ensure that health care institutions and professionals respond to their needs. Where the decision involves life-saving treatment, concern about their vulnerability is heightened.

The proposed legislation addresses this concern by limiting the issuance of DNR orders for such patients to two circumstances: (i) a judgment by two physicians that resuscitation would be medically futile; or (ii) a judicial finding that a DNR order would be consistent with the patient's known wishes or, in the absence of information regarding those wishes, with the patient's best interests.

The standard of medical futility is a different and higher standard than the three medical conditions which limit surrogate decision making. The standard requires a finding that resuscitation would be unsuccessful in restoring cardiac and respiratory function. Such judgments can often be made to a reasonable degree of certainty based on statistical experience with CPR.

The Task Force recognizes that imposition of the standard of medical futility or the requirement of judicial intervention addresses only the risk of improper issuance of the DNR order. It does not resolve the dilemma of resuscitation which yields greater pain or discomfort than benefit; in fact, it may exacerbate the problem. This policy reflects a presumption for resuscitation where the decision making process cannot adequately safeguard against the risk of a decision which does not serve the patient's interests in continued treatment. Where that risk is too great, the presumption in favor of resuscitation is appropriate.

Interinstitutional Transfers

When a patient for whom a DNR order is issued is transferred to another facility, the order is generally disregarded. In fact, receiving institutions are not always informed of the existence of the order by the transferring facility. While acute care hospitals often note the DNR order in the discharge planning report, nursing homes generally do not include DNR orders in a transfer summary. Upon admission to a new facility, patients are evaluated and the appropriateness of a DNR order is reconsidered.

The lack of guidelines regarding DNR orders for the transferred patient may present special problems. If the patient has lost decisional capacity since issuance of the order, reissuance of the order will be more difficult at the new facility. When a patient is transferred on an emergency basis, there is no time to undertake a reevaluation to implement a new DNR order. In either of these cases, it is likely that the receiving hospital will resuscitate the patient in violation of the decision expressed in the outstanding DNR order.

The proposed legislation allows, but does not require, the attending physician at the receiving facility to assume that the prior order was validly issued and to reissue the order. The physician therefore may issue a DNR order without making the determination about the patient's capacity and medical condition or obtaining the consent that would otherwise be required. However, if the attending physician concludes that the order is not medically appropriate, or if he is unwilling to rely on the procedures and medical evaluation of the transferring facility, he is not required to reissue the order.

Immunity

To promote good medical practice in the provision and withholding of CPR, it is essential to establish clear guidelines and to provide legal immunity to those who strive, in good faith, to act in accordance with those guidelines. Physicians and other health care professionals who adhere to prescribed procedures must be able to implement decisions about resuscitation without fear of criminal penalties, civil liability or professional sanctions. Moreover, surrogates, parents and legal guardians must be able to exercise their best judgment on behalf of patients, where empowered to do so, without fear of liability.

The proposed legislation confers legal immunity upon health care professionals who carry out decisions by or on behalf of patients pursuant to the legislation. The proposed legislation also grants protection from liability to health care professionals who resuscitate a patient despite the issuance of a DNR order if: (i) the professional was reasonably and in good faith unaware of the issuance of the order; or (ii) the professional reasonably and in good faith believed that the order had been revoked.

Immunity for failure to resuscitate a patient only extends to implementation of the resuscitation decision in accordance with the provisions of the legislation. Thus, a physician is not granted immunity if he fails to meet applicable standards of skill and care in making the medical diagnoses required by the legislation.

Surrogates, parents and legal guardians who carry out the responsibilities conferred by the legislation in good faith are also protected. The proposed legislation grants immunity to those who, in good faith, consent or decline to consent to a DNR order.

VII. CONCLUSION

The Task Force deliberated about issues concerning the provision and withholding of cardiopulmonary resuscitation for a period spanning close to one year. The rich variety of backgrounds and viewpoints represented in the Task Force's membership ensured the comprehensive nature of the deliberations. Despite the great diversity of its membership, the Task Force achieved a nearly unanimous consensus in support of the policies articulated in the legislative proposal and in this Report.

The Task Force believes that the legislation it proposes strikes the appropriate balance between the rights of patients, the concerns of health care providers and the interests of society in decisions about the provision and withholding of resuscitation. Resolution of these issues is long overdue. The Task Force urges immediate consideration of its recommendations and enactment of its legislative proposal.

* * *

RICHARD J. CONCANNON AND CHARLES J. TOBIN, JR.

Minority Report

This Minority Report focuses solely on the issue of the therapeutic exception to the requirement for obtaining the consent of a patient with capacity prior to entry of a DNR order. Everyone agrees that a therapeutic exception should only be applied in appropriate cases, but in those cases, its use has long been recognized in law and medicine and as matter of common sense. Present §2805-d.4(d) of the New York Public Health law provides for the exception and this Minority Report is submitted to urge that the same standards be applied in the proposed DNR legislation.

The simple fact of the matter is that the proposed legislation is so stringent that the therapeutic exception is virtually eliminated, which would be tragic for those few individuals who might have to endure needlessly and perhaps repeatedly, either the cruelty of a senseless discussion about their impending death or the infliction of full-scale cardiopulmonary resuscitative efforts for no sensible reason.

The proposed DNR legislation departs dramatically from the therapeutic exception presently embodied in Public Health law §2805-d.4(d), which provides that a physician need not obtain informed consent to treatment when that physician,

> [a]fter considering all of the attendant facts and circumstances, used reasonable discretion as to the manner and extent to which such alternatives or risks were disclosed to the patient because he reasonably

> believed that the manner and extent of such disclosure could reasonably be expected to adversely and substantially affect the patient's condition ([41] §2805-d.4(d) (McKinney's Supp. 1986)).

Thus, the existing statutory therapeutic exception requires a determimination that an attempt to obtain consent will have a substantial adverse effect on the patient's condition. The language of the proposed DNR legislation, requiring determination that the discussion will cause "immediate and severe injury," stands in stark contrast. Under statutory construction rules, such a difference in language would be presumed to be intentional, and would be so interpreted by the courts. Thus, the legislation will be interpreted as requiring that unless a physician can predict that a discussion of DNR will itself probably bring about a patient's death, he must discuss the DNR decision and obtain the patient's consent, even in cases where he reasonably believes that such a discussion will have a substantial and adverse effect on the patient's condition.

The physician, who has taken an oath "to do no harm," is forced to choose between two harms – *i.e.*, the harm of the substantial adverse effect on the patient that the physician reasonably believes will result from a discussion of DNR, or the harm resulting from the extremely invasive and traumatic CPR procedure itself. (Given that the DNR question arises only when the physician has determined that CPR is medically inappropriate and will serve merely to prolong the dying process, it is clear in such cases that to inflict CPR is to inflict harm.) Faced with such a choice, it is hardly difficult to understand why most physicians will be discouraged from issuing DNR orders in those cases and simply risk having CPR administered.

The therapeutic exception in the proposed DNR legislation is really no exception at all. And while its supporters feel that it enhances patient autonomy and inhibits mischievous, faint-hearted or unscrupulous physicians from issuing DNR orders without patient consent, the far more likely result will be an increase in the number of cases where CPR is inflicted on elderly, seriously infirm people who, while feeble and close to death, nonetheless possess "capacity"; a discussion might not kill them, as the proposed legislation requires as the risk before invoking the exception, but to do so could be the height of cruelty. Clearly, this result would be extremely unfortunate. Indeed, it raises the specter of the repeated infliction of a very traumatic procedure on terminally ill and elderly patients for whom such "treatment" presents a positive violation of the right to die with dignity and with as little pain as possible.

With respect to DNR orders, it is not difficult to imagine situations in which the discussion itself will be so traumatic to the patient that it would in fact have a substantial adverse impact on his or her condition. As the President's Commission recognized:

> Some patients in the final stages of a terminal illness would experience needless harm in a detailed discussion of resuscitation procedures and consequences. In such cases, the physician might discuss the situation in more general terms, seeking to elicit the individual's general preferences concerning "vigorous" or "extraordinary" efforts and inviting any further questions he or she may have ([46], at 241).

It is our concern that in cases where the physician has reasonably determined that a discussion of DNR will substantially and adversely affect the patient's health, the therapeutic exception provision of the proposed DNR legislation, as presently worded, will operate to place physician and patients between the Scylla and Charybdis of, on the one hand, the kind of discussion that the President's Commission and various commentators have recognized as cruel and unnecessary, and, on the other hand, the infliction of the highly invasive and traumatic procedures involved in CPR. It is also our concern that in an attempt to resolve this unfortunate dilemma, physicians will simply decide to resuscitate in every case. To avoid this result, it is recommended that the therapeutic exception provision of the DNR legislation be patterned on the therapeutic exception language of Public Health Law §2805-d.4(d). Specifically, the following language is proposed as a substitute for the language contained in the first sentence of §5.3(a) of the proposed legislation:

> In the event the attending physician, after considering all the attendant facts and circumstances, reasonably believes that such discussion would adversely and substantially affect the patient's condition, the attending physician may issue an order not to resuscitate without obtaining the patient's consent only after:
>
> (i) consulting with and obtaining the concurrence of another physician, selected by the hospital, concerning the assessment of the risk of substantial and adverse affect on the patient's condition from a discussion of cardiopulmonary resuscitation; and

(ii) ascertaining the wishes of the patient to the extent possible without subjecting the patient to the risk of substantially and adversely affecting the patient's condition; and

Subdivisions (iii) and (iv) of § 5.3(a), and the review provisions of § 5.3(b), would remain the same. Thus, the requirement of concurrence of another physician, ascertainment of the patient's wishes to the extent possible, involvement of a surrogate, recording in the patient's chart, and review, will remain intact and should provide more than ample protection against the concerns raised in the Majority Report.

MEDICAL SOCIETY OF THE STATE OF NEW YORK, NEW YORK STATE DEPARTMENT OF HEALTH, HOSPITAL ASSOCIATION OF NEW YORK STATE

DO-NOT-RESUSCITATE ORDERS: QUESTIONS AND ANSWERS FOR HEALTH CARE PROFESSIONALS

Introduction

This pamphlet states and answers questions posed by health care professionals since the do not resuscitate (DNR) law and implementing Department of Health regulations took effect in 1988. The DNR law is Article 29-B of the Public Health Law. The regulations can be found at Section 405.43 of Title 10 of the Codes, Rules and Regulations of the State of New York.

The Department of Health has prepared a pamphlet entitled, "*A Guide for Patients and Families*" to educate patients and their family members or others close to them about the law. All medical facilities are required to have copies of the brochure available....

The following procedures apply to decisions about CPR in hospitals, nursing homes and certain mental health facilities.

PATIENTS WITH CAPACITY

To enter a DNR order for an adult patient who has decision-making capacity:

1. **Discuss the order with patient** and inform patient about his/her condition, risks/benefits of CPR, and consequences of DNR order.
2. **Obtain the patient's oral or written consent.**
   - An oral consent must be witnessed by two adults, one of whom must be a doctor affiliated with the hospital.
   - A written consent must be signed by two adult witnesses.
3. **Record the decision in the patient's chart.**
4. **Enter the DNR order.**

R. Baker & M.A. Strosberg (eds.), Legislating Medical Ethics: A Study of the New York Do-Not-Resuscitate Law, 415–438.

DETERMINING INCAPACITY

To determine that a patient lacks capacity to decide about resuscitation:

All adults are presumed to have capacity unless determined otherwise by the procedure set forth in the law or by a court order.

1. **Attending physician** must find "to a reasonable degree of medical certainty" that the patient lacks capacity and make chart entry describing nature, cause and probable duration of incapacity.
2. **Second physician**, authorized by hospital, must concur and make chart entry. For patients who lack capacity due to a mental illness or developmental disability, second physician must have special qualifications.
3. **Inform the patient of determination of incapacity,** if patient can understand the information, and inform surrogate decision-maker.

PATIENTS WHO LACK CAPACITY: SURROGATE DECISION-MAKING

To enter a DNR order for an adult patient who lacks capacity and has not appointed a health care agent:

1. **Determine that the patient lacks capacity** as described above.
2. **Medical findings.**
   - Attending physician must find that *one* of the following conditions exists and make chart entry:
     - patient has a *terminal condition*; or
     - patient is *permanently unconscious*; or
     - resuscitation would be *medically futile*; or
     - resuscitation would impose an *extraordinary burden* on the patient in light of the patient's medical condition and the expected outcome of resuscitation for the patient.
   - Second physician, authorized by hospital, must concur and make chart entry.
3. **Obtain surrogate decision-maker's consent.**
   - Identify surrogate.
   - Inform surrogate about patient's condition, risks and benefits of CPR, and consequences of DNR order.
   - Obtain written consent, signed by surrogate before two witnesses.
4. **Inform patient,** if patient is capable of understanding information.
5. **Enter DNR order in chart.**

PATIENTS WHO HAVE APPOINTED A HEALTH CARE AGENT

To enter a DNR order for an adult patient without capacity who has appointed a health care agent by written proxy:

1. **Determine that the patient lacks capacity** as described above.
2. **Obtain health care agent's consent.**
   - Inform agent about patient's condition, risks and benefits of DNR, and consequences of DNR order.
   - Obtain consent of agent in writing or document oral consent in patient chart.
3. **Enter DNR order in chart.**

PATIENTS WHO LACK CAPACITY AND FOR WHOM NO SURROGATE IS AVAILABLE

To enter a DNR order for an adult patient who lacks capacity when there is no surrogate and no prior consent by the patient:

1. **Determine that the patient lacks capacity** as described above.
2. **Attending physician** must find that resuscitation would be *medically futile* and make chart entry.
3. **Second physician,** authorized by hospital, must concur and make chart entry.
4. **Inform patient,** if patient is capable of understanding information.
5. **Enter DNR order in chart.**

MINOR PATIENTS

To enter a DNR order for a minor patient:

Minors are *not* presumed capable of deciding about CPR.

1. **In consultation with parents, attending physician may find that minor has capacity.**
2. **Medical findings.**
   - Attending physician must find that one of the following conditions is satisfied and make chart entry:
     - patient has a *terminal condition*; or
     - patient is *permanently unconscious*; or
     - resuscitation would be *medically futile*; or

  - resuscitation would impose an*extraordinary burden* on the patient in light of the patient's medical condition and the expected outcome of resuscitation for the patient.
- Second physician, authorized by hospital, must concur and make chart entry.

3. **Obtain parent's consent.**
   - Inform parent about patient's condition, risks and benefits of CPR, consequences of DNR order.
   - Obtain written consent before two witnesses.
4. **Obtain minor's consent,** if minor has capacity.
5. **Attempt to notify other parent,** if other parent is not aware that DNR order will be entered.
6. **Enter DNR order in chart.**

I. GENERAL PRINCIPLES

Q: Where does the law apply?
The law applies to decisions about CPR (cardiopulmonary resuscitation) in:

- Hospitals;
- Nursing homes;
- Mental hygiene facilities operated or licensed by the Office of Mental Health; and
- Specific residential developmental centers operated by the Office of Mental Retardation and Developmental Disabilities.

  The law does not address DNR orders in other health care settings, such as at-home hospice programs and home care. This does *not* mean that DNR orders are unlawful in such settings, just that their use is not governed by the DNR law.

Q: What do DNR order and CPR mean?
Under the law, a DNR order is "an order not to attempt CPR in the event a patient suffers cardiac or respiratory arrest." CPR means measures to restore cardiac function or to support ventilation in the event of a cardiac or respiratory arrest. Examples listed in Health Department regulations include: mouth-to-mouth rescue breathing, direct cardiac injection, intravenous medications, electrical defibrillation, and open chest cardiac massage.

The definition of CPR *excludes* "measures to improve ventilation and cardiac functions in the absence of an arrest." Thus, a patient who is experiencing an arrhythmia or respiratory distress can be given cardiac or respiratory support, even if there is a DNR order.

Q: Does the DNR law require health care professionals to perform CPR on every patient who arrests and who does not have a DNR order?

No. Although there is a presumption that every patient who does not have a DNR order consents to CPR, that consent does *not* create any new duty to provide CPR. The obligation to perform CPR is defined by evolving standards of care, professional guidelines and, when applicable, Health Department regulations.

Thus, in an emergency, when the DNR law's requirements cannot be fully satisfied and the physician justifiably concludes that resuscitation would be futile, resuscitation may be withheld.

Under the law, futility means that "CPR will be unsuccessful in restoring cardiac and respiratory function or that the patient will experience repeated arrest in a short time period before death occurs." Decisions made on this basis cannot become a policy of unwritten DNR orders. Physicians must obtain advance consent from the patient or surrogate whenever it is possible to obtain consent.

Q: Does consent to a DNR order affect other care and treatment?

No. Consent to a DNR order by or for a patient is *not* consent to forgo other treatments; it is strictly a decision about CPR. However, nothing in the DNR law *prohibits* decisions to withhold or withdraw other life-sustaining treatments. Indeed, it's often advantageous to discuss CPR with patients or family members as part of a comprehensive discussion about the course of treatment.

Q: Does a DNR order in long-term care mean that a resident should not be transferred to receive CPR?

Yes. Under Health Department regulations, CPR is defined to include "the transfer of a patient to another facility if solely for the purpose of providing cardiopulmonary resuscitation." Hence, long-term care residents who have a DNR order should not be transferred to receive CPR. However, the DNR order does *not* affect decisions to transfer residents to receive other treatments.

Q: Must a DNR order be in writing?
Yes. A DNR order must be in writing in the patient's chart, although the writing may be an entry indicating that a telephone order was issued by the attending physician.

Q: Does the law require health care professionals to fill out particular forms?
No. The law requires physicians to write certain information in the patient's chart. Many facilities have developed forms to facilitate compliance with the law, but forms are not required by the law.

Q: What is an attending physician under the law?
The *attending physician* is the physician "selected by or assigned to a patient in a hospital, who has primary responsibility for the treatment and care of the patient." When more than one physician shares this responsibility, any such physician can be considered the attending physician.

Q: Can a physician write a partial DNR order, such as an order not to intubate the patient in the event of arrest?
Yes, with consent.

Q: Can a physician write a DNR order that does not apply in certain settings, such as the operating room?
Yes, if the patient or surrogate consents. The patient or surrogate can agree to suspend a DNR order as part of a consent to an operation.

Q: Can a physician write a DNR order that remains in effect over a series of discharges and readmissions to the hospital?
Yes, if the patient or surrogate gives informed consent to such an order which states specifically that it will remain in effect for a series of readmissions. The attending physician must review the chart of such patients on the day of each readmission and at least every three days of hospitalization thereafter to determine if the order is still appropriate in light of the patient's condition. This review does not require the physician to reobtain a patient's or surrogate's consent.

Q: Can the attending physician direct the entry of a DNR order by telephone?
Yes, if the order is followed by written confirmation.

Q: Do advanced age and infirmity alone justify a DNR order?
No.

II. PATIENTS WITH CAPACITY

Q: How is a decision made and recorded at a health care facility?
An adult patient in a health care facility can consent to a DNR order orally or in writing. The law does not require any particular form for recording the patient's consent although many health care facilities have prepared forms. A patient's decision should not be delayed for lack of forms.

Oral consent must be witnessed by two adults, one of whom must be a physician affiliated with the facility. An "affiliated" physician includes any doctor who is permitted to treat patients in the facility.

Written consent must be signed by the patient and witnessed by two adults – neither witness must be a physician. The oral or written decision must be included in the patient's medical chart.

Q: How is a decision made and recorded prior to admission to a health care facility?
An adult may consent to forgo resuscitation prior to admission to a health care facility. The consent must be in writing, signed by the adult, and witnessed by two adults. A living will can provide this consent if it is clear from the document that the adult wishes to forgo CPR.

Q: May an adult set conditions for consent to a DNR order?
Yes. Before or during admission to a health care facility, an adult may consent to a DNR order *conditionally*. For example, a patient may conclude that, if and when she becomes terminally ill and unable to make decisions directly, she wants a DNR order entered. Before entering a DNR order in these circumstances, the attending physician must conclude, to a reasonable degree of medical certainty, that these conditions are satisfied. That conclusion must be stated in the patient's chart.

Q: What are the attending physician's obligations when a patient consents to a DNR order?
When a patient consents to a DNR order, the attending physician must

record the decision in the patient's chart. The physician then must either:

- Issue the order (or issue the order when any conditions specified in the decision are met); or
- Promptly inform the patient of any objection to the order, and then make all reasonable efforts to arrange to transfer the patient to another physician, if necessary; or
- Promptly inform the patient of any objection to the order and refer the matter to the facility's dispute mediation system.

Q: What is a therapeutic exception?

If the attending physician determines that a patient capable of making decisions would suffer "severe and immediate injury" from a discussion about CPR, the physician need not obtain the patient's consent, but must then follow an alternative procedure for entering the DNR order. "Severe and immediate injury" is a strict standard. For example, the standard is met if the patient would suffer a heart attack or become suicidal as a result of the discussion.

The alternative procedure involves several steps. The attending physician must:

- Consult with and obtain the written concurrence of another physician that the patient would suffer severe and immediate injury. The second physician must be a physician designated by the facility, and must personally examine the patient;
- Ascertain the wishes of the patient to the extent possible without subjecting the patient to the risk of severe injury;
- Set forth the reasons for not consulting the patient in the patient's chart; and
- Obtain the consent of a surrogate, unless the order is entered based on the patient's previous consent.

Q: Must a physician make specific medical findings before entering a DNR order for a capable patient?

No. The patient's informed consent is sufficient. In contrast, medical findings are required when a surrogate consents, unless the person deciding has been appointed as agent under the health care proxy law.

Q: Must a living will or other written statement specifically refer to CPR or a DNR order in order to provide consent?

No. For example, a wish to forgo "heroic measures" or "extraordinary life-saving measures" may be sufficient. If health care professionals are uncertain about the patient's intent, they should ask the patient's surrogate. The surrogate must consider the living will or other written statement when deciding about CPR for the patient.

Q: What if the patient says "Doctor, you decide"?
The statement, if witnessed and recorded in the patient's chart, can be regarded as either consent to a DNR order or the appointment of the doctor as the surrogate.

Q: What if a patient consents to a DNR order, loses capacity, and then the patient's family opposes the order?
The physician's obligation is to honor the patient's decision. However, a dispute about the validity of the patient's decision may be addressed by the facility's dispute mediation system.

Q: Does the patient have to sign a form to consent to a DNR order?
No. The patient can consent orally if two adult witnesses sign the patient's medical chart or a consent form attached to the chart.

III. DETERMINING INCAPACITY

Q: What is "capacity" to make decisions?
The DNR law defines capacity as the ability to understand and appreciate the nature and consequences of a DNR order, including the benefits and disadvantages of the order, and to reach an informed decision. A patient may lack capacity due to a variety of conditions, such as unconsciousness, dementia or severe depression. A patient's disagreement with the physician's recommendation is not, by itself, proof of incapacity (nor is agreement with a physician proof of capacity).

Q: How is incapacity determined?
All adults are presumed to have capacity unless determined otherwise by the procedure described below, or by a court order. The DNR law does not require any determination or documentation that a patient *has* capacity.

The attending physician must determine that the patient lacks capacity "to a reasonable degree of medical certainty." A finding of incapacity for purposes of the DNR law does *not* establish the patient's lack of capacity for any other purpose.

The law requires a concurring opinion by a second physician, selected by a person with authority from the facility to make the selection. The second physician must examine the patient.

For hospital patients who lack capacity because of a mental illness or developmental disability, the second physician must possess special qualifications.

Q: How is the determination of incapacity recorded?

The attending physician and the concurring physician must write their findings about incapacity in the patient's medical chart. The entry must state the physicians' opinion about the cause and nature of the patient's incapacity as well as its probable duration. The entry can be made in the chart directly, or physicians can use a form.

Q: Who must be informed that the patient lacks capacity?

The patient must be informed of the determination unless it is clear that he or she cannot understand the information. These patients must also be given a copy of a statement, prepared by the Health Department, that describes the DNR law.

The person highest on the surrogate priority list must be told about the determination of incapacity. This will ordinarily happen as a matter of course, since the same person must be contacted to decide about CPR for the patient. Only one person on the surrogate list must be informed, unless the patient is from a mental health facility. More than one person may be informed.

Q: Are specific medical tests and procedures required for determining a patient's lack of capacity?

No. The persons who make the determination should follow generally accepted practices in ascertaining whether the patient meets the standard for capacity in the DNR law.

Q: What if the patient alternates between periods of capacity and incapacity?

Some patients, especially in long-term care facilities may be lucid and able to decide about treatment during one part of the day and confused at other times. In such cases, health care professionals should try to obtain the patient's decision about CPR when the patient is capable of deciding.

IV. PATIENTS WHO HAVE APPOINTED A HEALTH CARE AGENT

Q: What is a health care agent?
Under the health care proxy law, adults have a right to appoint someone they trust – a health care agent – to make decisions for them once they can no longer decide for themselves. An agent can make all health care decisions a competent adult can make, including decisions to discontinue life-sustaining treatment such as CPR.

Q: What is the difference between a health care agent and a surrogate appointed under the DNR law?
A health care agent can generally decide about all treatment. A surrogate appointed under the DNR law can only decide about CPR. The requirements of the proxy law, not the DNR law, apply when a health care agent decides about CPR.

Q: When does the agent's decision-making authority begin?
An agent's authority to make health care decisions begins when a physician determines that a patient has lost the capacity to decide for him/herself. Two physicians must determine that the patient has lost capacity for decisions about life-sustaining treatment, including CPR.

Q: If a patient has appointed a health care agent, must the proxy form contain the patient's wishes about CPR in order for the agent to decide?
No.

Q: Who has priority to decide about CPR, an agent appointed under the proxy law, or a person appointed under the DNR law?
A health care agent, unless the patient's written proxy or surrogate appointment states otherwise.

Q: Is surrogate consent to a DNR order required if a health care agent is available?
No. The agent's consent is sufficient, even if a surrogate is available. The agent's decision takes priority over any other surrogate decision-maker.

Q: If a patient has appointed an agent, should the patient still be involved in decisions about CPR?
Yes. Whenever possible and appropriate, the physician should speak to

the patient to seek consent for a DNR order, even if the patient has appointed a health care agent.

V. PATIENTS WHO LACK CAPACITY: SURROGATE DECISION-MAKING

Q: When is surrogate consent required?
The attending physician must obtain the consent of a surrogate decision-maker, if one is available, before issuing a DNR order for a patient who lacks capacity.

Q: What if the patient has appointed a health care agent under the health care proxy law?
Special rules apply. See previous section of this pamphlet.

Q: Who is the surrogate?
The surrogate – the person who has legal authority to give consent to a DNR order for a patient who lacks capacity – is the person in the highest category on the following list who is reasonably available, willing and competent to decide about CPR.

1. **A person previously designated by the patient to be the surrogate.** An adult may designate a surrogate to decide about CPR either:
   - in writing, dated, and signed in the presence of two witnesses 18 years of age or older; or
   - during the time the adult is a patient, orally in the presence of two witnesses 18 years of age or older.
2. **A committee of the person or an Article 17-A guardian.** This is a person appointed by a court to manage the personal affairs of an adult who is incompetent, developmentally disabled or mentally retarded. The DNR law and regulations do not require the appointment of any such committee or guardian.
3. **The spouse.**
4. **A son or daughter 18 years of age or older.**
5. **A parent.**
6. **A brother or sister 18 years of age or older.**
7. **A close friend.** A "close friend" is any person who presents an affidavit to an attending physician stating: (i) that he or she is a close friend of the patient and that he or she has maintained such regular

contact with the patient as to be familiar with the patient's activities, health, and religious or moral beliefs; and (ii) the facts and circumstances that demonstrate such familiarity.

Thus, a close friend might include a relative of the patient who is not on the priority list, such as a grandparent, a patient's unmarried partner, or a health care professional who has a close personal relationship with the patient.

A person on the surrogate list is "reasonably available" if he or she can be contacted with diligent efforts by an attending physician or another person acting on behalf of the attending physician or the hospital. The name of the surrogate must be entered in the patient's medical chart.

Q: Under what circumstances may a surrogate consent to a DNR order?
A surrogate can consent to a DNR order *only if two physicians determine that one* of the following conditions exists:

- **the patient has a terminal condition.** A "terminal condition," for this purpose, is an illness or injury for which there is no hope of recovery, and which reasonably can be expected to cause death within one year; or
- **the patient is permanently unconscious;** or
- **resuscitation would impose an extraordinary burden on the patient in light of the patient's medical condition and the expected outcome of resuscitation for the patient.** This encompasses cases in which the patient is so frail, debilitated or ill that CPR would cause more harm than benefit; or
- **resuscitation would be medically futile.** "Medically futile" means that CPR will be unsuccessful in restoring cardiac and respiratory function or that the patient will experience repeated arrest in a short time period before death occurs.

The attending physician and another physician selected by the hospital must determine, to a reasonable degree of medical certainty, that the patient meets one of these conditions. Both determinations must be based on personal examination of the patient and must be included in the patient's medical chart.

Q: How does a surrogate make a decision about CPR?
The surrogate must decide about CPR based on the patient's wishes, including consideration of the patient's religious and moral beliefs; or, if the patient's wishes are unknown and cannot be ascertained, based on an

evaluation of the benefits versus the burdens of CPR.

If a physician or family member is convinced that the surrogate has not applied these standards in making the decision, he or she may start the facility's dispute mediation system.

Q: What access does a surrogate have to medical information?
The surrogate has the same right as the patient to receive medical information and medical records. Health care professionals should ensure that the surrogate has information about CPR, the patient's diagnosis and the prognosis following CPR.

Q: What form does a decision by a surrogate take?
The surrogate must consent to a DNR order in writing. The decision must be dated and signed in the presence of two witnesses 18 years of age or older, who must also sign. Any health care professional or adult family member may act as a witness.

Q: What is an attending physician's obligation to respect a surrogate decision?
When a surrogate requests or consents to a DNR order, and one of the four medical conditions is met, the physician then has the same options that he or she would have if the patient consented to the order. The physician must either:

- Issue the order; or
- Promptly inform the surrogate of any objection to the order and make all reasonable efforts to transfer the patient to another physician, if necessary; or
- Start the dispute mediation process.

If the attending physician knows that any person on the surrogate list opposes the DNR order authorized by any other person on the list, the physician must submit the matter to dispute mediation. While dispute mediation is occurring, the physician cannot issue the order and any existing order must be revoked.

Q: Must the patient be informed of a surrogate's consent to a DNR order?
If a surrogate consents to a DNR order, the patient must be informed about the decision only if the patient can understand the information. However, the patient should not be informed if the discussion would cause severe and immediate injury to the patient.

Q: Is a surrogate's consent to a DNR order required if the patient, before losing capacity, consented to an order?

No. If the patient made his or her wishes known, a surrogate's decision is not necessary and should *not* be sought. For example, if a patient signs a document stating, "in the event I become terminally ill I do not want CPR" and later becomes terminally ill, the physician may enter a DNR order based on the patient's prior consent.

Q: What "diligent efforts" are required to locate a person on the surrogate list before moving to persons in the next level?

The efforts required depend on the circumstances. For example, in an urgent situation, the inability to contact a person on top of the list by telephone can justify seeking a decision from the next person on the list. The diligence requirement does not mandate unreasonable attempts to locate a patient's long-lost relatives.

Q: What if there is more than one person in the priority category who is available, willing and competent to make a DNR decision? Who decides?

Any of those persons – for example, any of the patient's adult children or siblings – can be the surrogate. There is no obligation to seek consent from all persons in the priority category.

Q: Must a surrogate be at the hospital to consent to a DNR order?

No. The law requires the surrogate's written consent but does not require the surrogate's physical presence. A physician can enter a DNR order based on a surrogate's written consent that was mailed to the hospital. In an urgent situation, the physician may rely on a surrogate's oral consent, by telephone, if the person agrees to send a written consent.

Q: May a physician be a surrogate?

Yes, as long as the physician is not one of the two physicians who confirm that the patient meets medical requirements for entering the order.

VI. PATIENTS WHO LACK CAPACITY AND FOR WHOM NO SURROGATE IS AVAILABLE

Q: When can physicians enter a DNR order for a patient who lacks capacity and has no person available to act as surrogate?
A DNR order may be issued if the attending physician determines, in writing, that, to a reasonable degree of medical certainty, CPR would be medically futile. Under the law, "medically futile" means that CPR will be unsuccessful in restoring cardiac and respiratory function or that the patient will experience repeated arrest in a short time period before death occurs.

A second physician selected by the hospital after personal examination of the patient must review and concur with the determination of medical futility, and write that determination in the patient's chart.

Q: Must a physician inform the patient that a DNR order has been issued on grounds of futility?
When a DNR order is issued by a physician on the ground of medical futility, the patient must be informed about the order if the patient can understand the information. It is not necessary to inform the patient if that discussion would cause severe and immediate injury to the patient. If the patient objects, the DNR order cannot be issued without court approval.

Q: What if the patient has no surrogate but, prior to losing capacity, left instructions to withhold CPR under certain circumstances?
If the patient consented to a DNR order, the order may be entered when the attending physician finds that the circumstances identified by the patient, such as the onset of terminal illness, have occurred.

Q: What if the resuscitation is not medically futile but physicians believe that a DNR order is appropriate?
The hospital must seek judicial approval for the order.

VII. MINOR PATIENTS

Q: Who is a minor?
A "minor" is a person less than 18 years old, who is neither married nor the parent of a child. A "parent" means a parent who has custody of the child.

Q: Is parental consent required before a DNR order is entered for a minor?
Yes. The attending physician must obtain the consent of a minor's parent or legal guardian before issuing a DNR order for a minor patient. The consent must be in writing, signed and witnessed by two adults. It must be entered in the patient's chart.

Q: Should minors be consulted about CPR?
In contrast to adults, minors are not presumed to have the capacity to decide about CPR. However, if the attending physician determines that the minor patient has capacity to decide about CPR, he or she must obtain the minor's consent – as well as the parent's consent – to the DNR order. The attending physician must make the determination about the minor's capacity in consultation with the minor's parent or legal guardian. There is no requirement of a concurring opinion.

The law does not specify any writing or witnessing requirement to evidence the minor's consent. There should, however, be a chart entry.

Q: Must the physician notify the other parent?
If the attending physician has reason to believe that there is another parent, including a non-custodial parent, who has not been informed of a decision to issue a DNR order for the minor, the attending physician must make diligent efforts to inform that person of the DNR order prior to issuing the order.

Q: What are the standards for parental decision-making?
A parent, like other surrogates, may consent to a DNR order only if the order is based on: (1) specified medical findings; and (2) a judgment about the minor's wishes and interests.

Q: Does the attending physician have to determine and document a minor patient's lack of capacity?
No. For minors, the physician only needs to document a determination that a patient *has* capacity.

Q: What if a parent consents to a DNR order but the physician knows that another parent opposes the order?
The physician must submit the matter to dispute mediation. While mediation is occurring, the physician cannot issue the order and any existing order must be revoked.

Q: What if neither parent changes his or her mind through mediation?

As long as one parent consents, the physician may enter a DNR order based on that consent, but is not obligated to do so.

VIII. MANAGING THE DNR ORDER

Q: How is consent to a DNR order revoked?

By the patient

A patient may revoke consent to a DNR order at any time by either:

- an oral or written statement to a physician or nurse; or
- any other act that shows an intention to revoke consent.

By surrogate or parent

A surrogate, parent, or legal guardian may revoke his or her consent to a DNR order by either:

- a written statement to a physician or nurse at the hospital; or
- an oral statement to a physician at the hospital, in the presence of one adult witness.

Obligation to cancel order

Any physician who is informed about the revocation of a DNR order should immediately:

- include the revocation in the patient's chart;
- cancel the DNR order;
- inform the staff responsible for the patient's care of the cancellation.

If a member of the nursing staff is first informed of or provided with the revocation, she or he should immediately tell a physician.

Q: When must a physician review a DNR order?

The attending physician must review the chart of patients who have DNR orders at least every three days for hospital patients and at each visit but not less often than every 60 days for nursing home patients to determine if the order is still appropriate in light of the patient's condition. This review does *not* require the physician to reobtain a patient's or surrogate's consent.

A physician's failure to review the order on time does not make the order ineffective; the patient's or surrogate's consent to the DNR order should not be disregarded in those circumstances. The order – and the immunity of staff for following it – remain valid.

Q: Does the three day or 60 day review apply to a patient in a swing bed or on alternative level of care (ALC) status?
The three day requirement applies to all ALC patients and to swing bed patients when the bed is considered a hospital bed.

Q: What happens if the patient's condition improves?
If the attending physician determines that a DNR order is no longer appropriate because the patient's medical condition has improved, he or she must immediately inform the person who consented to the order (i.e., the patient or the surrogate). In general, if that person refuses to revoke consent to the order, the physician must either:

- leave the order in place; or
- make reasonable efforts to arrange for the transfer of the patient to another physician; or
- submit the matter to the facility's dispute mediation process.

Q: What happens if the patient regains capacity?
If a DNR order was entered upon the consent of a surrogate and the patient at any time gains or regains capacity, the attending physician should obtain consent from the patient. If consent is obtained immediately, the previously entered DNR order may be continued without interruption.

If it is not obtained from the patient, the physician must promptly:

- cancel the order;
- inform the person who consented to the order; and
- inform all hospital staff directly responsible for the patient's care of the cancellation

IX. TRANSFERRING THE PATIENT: STATUS OF THE DNR ORDER

Q: What are the obligations of facilities and ambulance personnel when patients are transferred from one facility to another?
The transferring facility
When the transferring facility sends a patient who has a DNR order to another facility, it must inform both the ambulance personnel and the receiving hospital of the DNR order. The transferring facility should tell the ambulance personnel and receiving facility about the order, and include a photocopy of the DNR order or written statement of the order with any records that travel with the patient.

The receiving facility

When a patient who has a DNR order is transferred from one facility to another, the order is effective at the receiving facility, and remains effective until one of the following occurs:

- a physician at the facility cancels the order; or
- 24 hours elapse from the time of the patient's admission to the facility.

Unless the order is *canceled* by a physician at the receiving facility, an attending physician at that facility, upon receipt of a copy of or written notice of the order, may presume that the order was validly issued and may issue a DNR order continuing the prior order at any time. If the order is canceled, or if the attending physician decides not to continue the order, he or she must promptly inform the person who consented to the order.

The Ambulance

A DNR order is binding on emergency service personnel during transfer of a patient from one facility to another. If a patient who has a DNR order experiences cardiac or respiratory arrest during a transfer from one facility to another, he or she should not he resuscitated.

Emergency personnel are not required to honor DNR orders for patients who are picked up at home. Emergency service personnel may honor DNR orders presented to them in a hospice patient's home when the order is written on hospice stationery *or* when there is telephone confirmation from the patient's physician or a physician at the receiving hospital. Emergency personnel are not encouraged to honor DNR orders in other situations.

Q: If a patient who has a DNR order is transferred to another facility and the order expires after 24 hours, can the attending physician at the receiving facility still reissue the order?

Yes. The physician can reissue the expired order without obtaining the patient's or surrogate's consent. However, if the prior order was canceled by a physician at the receiving institution, it cannot be reissued without a patient's or surrogate's consent.

Q: If the attending physician at the receiving facility cancels a DNR order, what are his or her obligations if the patient or surrogate opposes that decision?

Just as in other disputes, the attending physician must either make all reasonable efforts to transfer the patient to another physician or refer the matter to dispute mediation.

X. DISPUTE MEDIATION

Q: What is the dispute mediation process?
Each facility must establish a process to mediate disputes about the issuance of DNR orders. Facilities have broad flexibility in creating a process. However, the process must meet special requirements when disputes involve patients who have a mental illness or developmental disability.

Q: What is the role of the dispute mediation process?
Depending on facility policy, the dispute mediation process can mediate all disputes about DNR orders. The process must mediate specific disputes, including disputes in which:

- A physician or hospital opposes a patient's or surrogate's consent to a DNR order;
- A parent opposes a minor patient's consent to a DNR order;
- Any person on the surrogate list opposes a surrogate's consent to or refusal of a DNR order.

The dispute mediation process can mediate, not decide, disputes. That is, it can advise, recommend, convey information, and take other steps to facilitate agreement. While the mediation process should help identify the decision that is most consistent with the patient's wishes and interests, mediators cannot issue or impose a decision about CPR.

Q: What is the required mediation procedure?
The DNR law does not include particular procedures for dispute mediation. The process should, at least, include a recognized means to initiate mediation (i.e., a person or office to contact) and an opportunity for those involved to present their views.

Q: What is the effect of mediation on the DNR order?
Once a matter has been submitted to dispute mediation, a DNR order cannot be issued – or if already issued, must be suspended – until

- The dispute has been resolved, or
- The process has concluded its efforts to resolve the dispute, or

- 72 hours have elapsed from the time of the submission of the dispute.

Q: What if dispute mediation fails to resolve the following sorts of disputes:

- *A patient insists upon a DNR order but the attending physician believes one should not be entered?*

The attending physician must either enter the DNR order, promptly transfer the patient to another physician or hospital willing to honor the patient's wishes, or seek a court order overriding the patient's decision.

- *A patient or surrogate opposes a DNR order but the attending physician believes one should be entered?*

The physician can transfer the patient to another physician or facility willing to provide CPR to the patient. If the physician determines that CPR would be futile, as defined by the law, the physician should inform the patient/surrogate and has no obligation to provide CPR when the patient arrests.

- *A surrogate insists upon a DNR order and an attending physician opposes it?*

If the patient lacks capacity and one of the four medical conditions that allow a surrogate to decide for the patient exists, the attending physician must either enter the order, transfer the patient, or challenge the surrogate's decision in court.

- *A surrogate insists upon a DNR order and a person lower on the priority list opposes it?*

The order should be entered unless the objecting person lower on the list goes to court to contest the surrogate's decision.

- *A surrogate opposes a DNR order and a person lower on the priority list or the physician believes the order should be entered?*

The physician can transfer care of the patient to another physician or the physician, facility or a person on the surrogate list can seek a court order to override the decision.

- *Two or more persons who are in the highest category on the surrogate list – for instance, the son and daughter of an elderly patient – disagree about the resuscitation decision?*

The attending physician may follow the instructions of either person, and should base the decision on an assessment of what the patient would have chosen, or if that is not known, on a judgment about the patient's best interests.

XI. MENTAL ILLNESS, DEVELOPMENTAL DISABILITIES AND MENTAL HEALTH FACILITIES

Q: How is mental illness defined?

For the purposes of the DNR law, the term "mental illness" covers conditions such as schizophrenia and psychosis. It does not cover dementias, such as those resulting from Alzheimer's Disease.

Q: How is a determination of incapacity made for a patient who has a mental illness?

If the attending physician of a patient in a general hospital determines that a patient lacks capacity because of mental illness, the concurring determination must be provided by a physician certified or eligible to be certified by the American Board of Psychiatry and Neurology. This requirement only applies to general hospitals – not to mental hygiene facilities or nursing homes.

Q: How are developmental disabilities determined and how does that determination affect the determination of capacity?

If the attending physician, in any facility, determines that a patient lacks capacity because of a developmental disability, the concurring determination of incapacity must be provided by a physician or psychologist who:

- is employed by one of the state-operated developmental centers listed in section 13.17 of the Mental Hygiene Law; or
- has been employed for a minimum of two years by a facility operated or licensed by the Office of Mental Retardation and Developmental Disabilities; or
- has been approved by the Office of Mental Retardation and Developmental Disabilities. OMRDD regulations will require that the concurring physician or psychologist possess specialized training or three years' experience in treating developmental disabilities.

Q: What is the role of the facility director?

When a patient is in or transferred from a mental health facility, the facility director must be informed of the following events:

- A determination that the patient lacks capacity;
- Consent by the patient or a surrogate to the DNR order, or entry

of an order for an adult patient who lacks capacity and has no surrogate.

Notice of the decision to enter a DNR order must be given to the director prior to the issuance of the order. However, the attending physician need not wait for a response from the director before entering the order.

A facility director may commence dispute mediation to challenge consent to the issuance of a DNR order, or commence a special proceeding in court upon the conclusion of dispute mediation.

ROBERT BAKER AND MARTIN A. STROSBERG

LETTER TO NEW YORK STATE ASSEMBLY MINORITY COUNSEL LARRY DIGIULIO

Mr. Larry Digiulio
Assembly Minority Counsel's Office
525 Capital Building
Albany, N.Y. 12248

April 23, 1991

Dear Mr. Digiulio,

Thank you for inviting us to comment on the amendments to the New York Do-Not-Resuscitate (DNR) Law (Public Health Law Article 29-B) proposed by the New York Department of Health.

Our comments reflect the results of a three-year study of the impact of the 1988 DNR reforms by an interdisciplinary research team from Union College and the Albany Medical Center. The primary researchers are: Robert Baker, Professor and Chair of Philosophy (Union College, NY), and a specialist in medical ethics; Martin Strosberg, Associate Professor and Director of the Health Administration Program of the Graduate Management Institute (GMI); I. Alan Fein, Associate Professor of Surgery and Director of Surgical Intensive Care for the Albany Medical College; Virginia Dersch, Visiting Assistant Professor of Sociology and a specialist in the sociology of medicine; and Joseph Schmee, Professor at GMI and a specialist in health statistics.

Our primary assessment instrument was survey responses from 223 New York ICU medical and nursing directors (representing 49% of New York hospitals with ICUs) and 172 New York board-certified hematologist-oncologists (27% of the New York population). They were surveyed approximately eighteen months after the DNR law became effective. Both samples are geographically representative (e.g., 46% of New York hospitals with ICUs are in the New York City-Downstate area and 77% of New York's hematologist-oncologists are in the same area; the figures for our respondents are 41% and 76% respectively). We also conducted a detailed study of the implementation of the DNR law at two

R. Baker & M.A. Strosberg (eds.), Legislating Medical Ethics: A Study of the New York Do-Not-Resuscitate Law, 439–444.

Upstate hospitals: one, a large teaching hospital, the other a small community hospital.

Coincident with the New York reforms was a revision of hospital accreditation standards relevant to DNR by the Joint Commission on the Accreditation of Healthcare Organizations (JCAHO). (New York was effectively denied this route by the refractory rulings of its courts, and so was forced to reform DNR decision making by means of a statute.) Nineteen eighty-eight, therefore, was the year of an intriguing "natural experiment" in which New York sought to reform DNR practices by means of a legal statute, while outside of New York there was an attempt to implement similar reforms through the professional self-regulatory process.

To assess the outcomes of this "natural experiment," we first determined that the 98 responses from New York critical care medical directors were the most representative; we then constructed a sample of 81 Non-New York critical care physicians (similar in age, experience, etc. to the New York sample) from 39 states who responded to a modified version of the questionnaire sent to the New Yorkers.

The questionnaire responses indicate that both the New York State and the JCAHO DNR reforms effectively eliminated undocumented, unconsented DNR orders and slow/show coding, while significantly increasing physician-patient/family discussion of and consent to DNR orders. We also found that, prior to the 1988 DNR reforms, non-compliance with bioethical ideals of discussion, consent, etc. were significantly lower in New York than outside of New York (quite possibly because of the uncertain legal status of a DNR order in New York, prior to the 1988 law). Yet, to reiterate, within eighteen months of the DNR law's enactment, New York clinicians at institutions which previously eschewed consent-based DNR were having discussions, seeking consent, and documenting DNR orders at the same levels as in the rest of the nation.

The success of the NY DNR reforms, however, is marred by a series of problems which appear to be artifacts of features unique to the NY DNR statute. Thus unlike their Non-New York peers, New York physicians report that the legal requirements significantly delay and inhibit DNR orders, *increasing* "futile" CPR, leading New York physicians (but not New York nurses) to be ambivalent or hostile to DNR reform. In contrast, no significant increase in delayed or futile DNR was reported by Non-New Yorkers, who (unlike their New York peers) believe DNR reform had *decreased* the bureaucratic delay of DNR orders while increasing the likelihood of patients receiving humane DNR.

On analysis, it became clear to us that the root cause of most problems was the substitution of legal for medical standards of documentation and concurrence. As one nursing director wrote:

> The emphasis is placed on obtaining signatures on multiple forms rather than the physical and emotional needs of the dying patient and his family.... In order to meet the letter of the law we address the need to get consent forms signed. The programs that I have attended address the consent process, not the dying process. I feel that the signing of consent forms has put new meaning into the cliche 'signing your life away.' The guilt feelings for some must be overwhelming.

Consent forms were universally identified as the major culprit in the "bureaucratization of the dying process" effected by the NY DNR law. Except for major interventions (e.g., surgery), it is normal clinical practice simply to document consent in the patient's medical record, which is precisely the practice mandated by the JCAHO for DNR consent, and the norm for DNR orders outside of New York. The New York law (§2965.6(a)), in contrast, substitutes legal norms, requiring surrogates to sign witnessed consent forms. The symbolism of the act of signing these "death warrants" not only traumatized many families, inhibiting them from giving legally effective voice to their desire for DNR, it required hospitals to turn to lawyers to draft new instruments, "DNR consent forms." Taking their cue from the legalistic documentation requirements in the law, hospitals lawyers tended to draft extremely defensive consent forms (some even required notarization of surrogate signatures). As one medical director commented to us:

> Our institution's implementation has been created to demonstrate to a review-type body that the patient had due process – not humane consideration.

Moreover, clinicians, who found the language of the statute difficult to fathom, tended to read it in terms of these consent forms – as interpreted by those of their peers deemed to have expertise. The result, as we were able to document, is pervasive over-interpretation of the law. For example, over half of all critical care directors and over forty percent of hematologist-oncologists, extrapolate the requirements for surrogate consent to the non-surrogate situation: they believe that competent patients must sign consent to DNR forms – even though the law explicitly permits patients to "express a decision consenting to an order not to resuscitate *orally*" (§ 2964.2). Ironically, these same nurses and physicians bitterly complain about the inhumanity of forcing patients to "sign their life away."

Yet another problem arising from the departure from standard clinical practice involves the use of extensive second physician concurrence whenever surrogate consent is involved (§ 2965). These requirements are especially problematic in smaller community hospitals because of the difficulty of finding a second physician. Clinicians from smaller hospitals told a number of "horror stories" about futile CPR being administered, despite a family's objections, because of the unavailability of a second physician. It is important to appreciate that second physician concurrence is virtually unique to New York. Fewer than 8% of the Non-New York physicians report that such concurrence is required for surrogate DNR.

The third problem attendant upon the New York DNR law involves "futile CPR." The problem of is not unique to New York, but is clearly exacerbated by the DNR law, since DNR reform lead to an *increase* in reports of futile DNR in New York, whereas elsewhere in the country DNR reform resulted in a *decrease* in reports of futile CPR. The problem is that, as NY physicians understand the law, CPR is required unless a valid DNR consent form has been signed. We recognize that both the Executive Director of the Task Force, Tracy Miller, and the former Counsel, Robert Swidler, have argued that this is a misinterpretation. Given the interpretive environment in NY, however, this unfortunate misinterpretation will continue to wreck havoc on the lives, or rather the deaths, of NY patients, unless there is a clear and explicit statement about futile CPR within the statute itself.

On the basis of our study we believe that the problems blemishing the outstanding achievements of the New York DNR law are best resolved by bringing New York's standards of documentation and concurrence into line with those used outside of New York. Our evidence indicates that the more stringent New York standards are more likely to impede to patient-family decision making and to promote futile and inhumane CPR than they are to serve as safeguards to patient rights. More specifically, we recommend:

Medical conventions of documentation in the patient's medical record.

Oral consent for both surrogates and patients.
Eliminating second physician concurrence requirements in cases of surrogate consent.
Permitting hospitals to set review requirements for DNR orders (which are generally misunderstood and seldom actually complied with).

On the issue of futile CPR, the simplest solution is to insert into the statute a statement that: "No physician is required by this statute to administer CPR which to a reasonable degree of medical certainty is medically futile." The Executive Director of the Task Force, Tracy Miller, has argued that such an exception might well "swallow the rule" opening an "escape hatch" for non-compliant physicians. A more cautious formulation, designed to eliminate futile CPR in contexts where patients/surrogates have not yet formally expressed their views about DNR/CPR is:

> Physicians have no obligation to administer CPR which to a reasonable degree of medical certainty is medically futile for patients:
> (i) who are new admissions, especially in the emergency room:
> (ii) Or, if the patient or surrogate has been informed that:
> (a) in the view of the physician, to a reasonable degree of medical certainty, CPR is medically futile and,
> (b) the physician has requested the patient/surrogate to make a decision for CPR or DNR, but
> (c) has yet to be informed of the patient/surrogate's decision.

The amendment we recommend seeks to eliminate futile CPR by default. The American Medical Association's recent "Guidelines for the appropriate use of Do-Not-Resuscitate orders" (*JAMA* 265, 1868-1871) go one step further permitting physicians who believe CPR to be futile to write a DNR order, provided that the patient is informed both of the order and of the right to seek alternative medical advice. We believe the new AMA guidelines may jeopardize the advances in DNR discussion and consent achieved in the 1988 DNR reforms. Our data indicate that New York physicians do *not* seek this degree of latitude with respect to DNR. They are willing to administer CPR they consider to be futile, provided that it is expressly desired by the patient or a surrogate. What they actually object to as inhumane and utterly unreasonable is administering futile CPR – an invasive, highly traumatic and often painful procedure – by default, merely because the patient or surrogate is ambivalent, or worse yet, because one of the various concurrence requirements of the DNR law has not been satisfied.

The various amendments we propose are designed to eliminate the most frequently cited conditions which lead to futile CPR under the present DNR law, without undercutting the law's impressive achievements in securing physician compliance with the bioethical ideal of informed patients deciding the management of their care in open discussions with their physicians.

Turning now to the DOH reform recommendations, we believe that while they are a thoughtful improvement on the present law, they stop short of addressing two fundamental problems: second physician concurrence requirements; and futile CPR, especially CPR by default. Unless these two issues are dealt with forthrightly, anyone dying in NY without an explicit DNR order will be at risk of assault from physicians administering futile CPR under the impression that this peculiarly technological rite of battering the dying is required of them by laws of the State of NY.

Finally, we regret that we cannot share with you at the present time the data from our study. We would, however, be willing to discuss the data, or our recommendations in further detail, or to give testimony should you hold hearings on amendments to the DNR law.

Sincerely yours,
Robert Baker, Ph. D.
Martin A. Strosberg, Ph. D.

NEW YORK STATE LEGISLATURE

AMENDMENTS TO THE NEW YORK PUBLIC HEALTH LAW 29-B (1991)

EXPLANATION – Matter underlined is new; matter in brackets [] is old law to be deleted.

An act to amend the public health law, in relation to improving procedural requirements for issuance of orders not to resuscitate, to govern issuance of nonhospital orders not to resuscitate, and to repeal certain provisions of such laws relating thereto

Approved July 15, 1991, effective as provided in section 20.

The People of the State of New York, represented in Senate and Assembly, do enact as follows:

Section 1. Subdivisions 7 through 19 of section 2961 of the public health law are renumbered subdivisions 9, 11, 12, 13, 14, 15, 17, 18, 19, 20, 21, 22 and 23; subdivisions 2, 14, 19 and 22 are added by chapter 818 of the laws of 1987 and subdivisions 14, 19 and 22 as renumbered are amended and four new subdivisions 7, 8, 10 and 16 are added to read as follows:

2. "Attending physician" means the physician selected by or assigned to a patient in a hospital or, for the purpose of provisions herein governing nonhospital orders not to resuscitate, a patient not in a hospital, who has primary responsibility for the treatment and care of the patient. Where more than one physician shares such responsibility, any such physician may act as the attending physician pursuant to this article.

7. "Emergency medical services personnel" means the personnel of a service engaged in providing initial emergency medical assistance, including but not limited to first responders, emergency medical technicians, and advanced emergency medical technicians.

8. "Health care agent" means a health care agent of the patient designated pursuant to article twenty-nine-C of this chapter.

10. "Hospital emergency service personnel" means the personnel of the emergency service of a general hospital, as defined in subdivision ten of section twenty-eight hundred one of this chapter, including but not limited

R. Baker & M.A. Strosberg (eds.), Legislating Medical Ethics: A Study of the New York Do-Not-Resuscitate Law, 445–454.

to emergency services attending physicians, emergency services registered professional nurses, and registered professional nurses, nursing staff and registered physicians' assistants assigned to the general hospital's emergency service.

14. "Mental illness" means a mental illness as defined in subdivision twenty of section 1.03 of the mental hygiene law, provided, however, that mental illness shall not include dementia, such as Alzheimer's disease or other disorders relating to dementia.

16. "Nonhospital order not to resuscitate" means an order, issued in accordance with section twenty-nine hundred seventy-seven of this article, that directs emergency medical services personnel and hospital emergency service personnel not to attempt cardiopulmonary resuscitation in the event a patient suffers cardiac or respiratory arrest.

19. "Patient" mens a person admitted to a hospital or, for the purpose of provisions herein governing nonhospital orders not to resuscitate, a person who has or may be issued a nonhospital order not to resuscitate.

22. "Surrogate list" means the list set forth in subdivision [four] two of section twenty-nine hundred sixty-five of this article.

Section 2. Section 2962 of the public health law is amended by adding a new subdivision 5 to read as follows:

5. (a) The provisions of article twenty-nine-C of this chapter, governing health care proxies and agents, take precedence over conflicting provisions of this article.

(b) When a patient who has a health care agent lacks capacity, the agent shall have the rights and authority that a patient with capacity would have under this article, subject to the terms of the health care proxy and article twenty-nine-C of this chapter.

Section 3. Subparagraph (iv) of paragraph (a) of subdivision 3 of section 2964 of the public health law, as added by chapter 818 of the laws of 1987, is amended to read as follows:

(iv) obtaining the consent of a health care agent who is available and would be authorized to make a decision regarding cardiopulmonary resuscitation if the patient lacked capacity or, if there is no such agent, a surrogate pursuant to section twenty-nine hundred sixty-five of this article, provided, however, that the consent of [a] an agent or surrogate shall not be required if the patient has previously consented to an order not to resuscitate pursuant to subdivision two of this section.

Section 4. Subdivision 1 of section 2965 of the public health law, as added by chapter 818 of the laws of 1987, is amended to read as follows:

1. (a) The consent of a surrogate or health care agent acting on behalf of an adult patient who lacks capacity or on behalf of an adult patient for whom consent by a surrogate or health care agent is authorized by subdivision three of section twenty-nine hundred sixty-four of this article must be obtained prior to issuing an order not to resuscitate the patient, except as provided in paragraph (b) of this subdivision or section twenty-nine hundred sixty-six of this article.

(b) The consent of a surrogate or health care agent shall not be required where the adult had, prior to losing capacity, consented to an order not to resuscitate pursuant to subdivision two of section twenty-nine hundred sixty-four of this article.

(c) A decision regarding cardiopulmonary resuscitation by a health care agent on a principal's behalf is governed by article twenty-nine-C of this chapter and shall have priority over decisions by any other person, except the patient or as otherwise provided in the health care proxy.

Section 5. Subdivisions 2 and 3 of section 2965 of the public health law are REPEALED and subdivisions 4 through 7 are renumbered subdivisions 2 through 5.

Section 6. Subparagraph (i) of paragraph (a) of subdivision 2 of section 2965 of the public health law, such subdivisions as renumbered by section five of this act, is REPEALED and subparagraphs (ii) through (vii) are renumbered subparagraphs (i) through (vi).

Section 7. Paragraph (d) of subdivision 3 of section 2965 of the public health law, such subdivisions as renumbered by section five of this act, is REPEALED.

Section 8. Paragraph (a) of subdivision 4 of section 2965 of the public health law, as added by chapter 818 of the laws of 1987 and such subdivisions as renumbered by section five of this act, is amended to read as follows:

(a) A surrogate shall express a decision consenting to an order not to resuscitate either (i) in writing, dated, and signed in the presence of one witness eighteen years of age or older who shall sign the decision, or (ii) orally, to two persons eighteen years of age or older, one of who is a physician affiliated with the hospital in which the patient is being treated. Any such decision shall be recorded in the patient's medical chart.

Section 9. Paragraph (b) of subdivision 2 of section 2967 of the public health law, as added by chapter 818 of the laws of 1987, is amended to read as follows:

(b) Where the attending physician has reason to believe that there is another parent or a non-custodial parent who has not been informed of a decision to issue an order not to resuscitate the minor, the attending physician, or someone acting on behalf of the attending physician, shall make reasonable efforts to determine if the uninformed parent or non-custodial parent has maintained substantial and continuous contact with the minor and, if so, shall make diligent efforts to notify that parent or non-custodial parent of the decision prior to issuing the order.

Section 10. Subdivision 3 of section 2967 of the public health law, as added by chapter 818 of the laws of 1987, is amended to read as follows:

3. A parent or legal guardian may consent to an order not to resuscitate on behalf of a minor only if there has been a written determination by the attending physician, with the written concurrence of another physician selected by a person authorized by the hospital to make such selections given after personal examination of the patient, that, to a reasonable degree of medical certainty, the minor suffers from one of the medical conditions set forth in paragraph (c) of subdivision [five] three of section twenty-nine hundred sixty-five of this article. Each determination shall be included in the patient's medical chart.

Section 11. Paragraphs (a) and (b) of subdivision 4 of section 2967 of the public health law, as added by chapter 818 of the laws of 1987, are amended to read as follows:

(a) A parent or legal guardian of a minor, in making a decision regarding cardiopulmonary resuscitation, shall consider the minor patient's wishes, including a consideration of the minor patient's religious and moral beliefs, and shall express a decision consenting to issuance of an order not to resuscitate either (i) in writing, dated and signed in the presence of one witness eighteen years of age or older who shall sign the decision, or (ii) orally, to two persons eighteen years of age or older, one of whom is a physician affiliated with the hospital in which the patient is being treated. Any such decision shall be recorded in the patient's medical chart.

b) The attending physician who is provided with the decision of a minor's parent or legal guardian, expressed pursuant to this subdivision, and of the minor if the minor has capacity, shall include such decision or decisions in the minor's medical chart and shall comply with the provisions of paragraph (b) of subdivision [six] four of section twenty-nine hundred sixty-five of this article.

Section 12. Subdivision 2 of section 2969 of the public health law, as added by chapter 818 of the laws of 1987, is amended to read as follows:

2. Any surrogate, parent, or legal guardian may at any time revoke his or her consent to an order not to resuscitate a patient by (a) notifying a physician or member of the nursing staff of the revocation of consent in writing, dated and signed, or (b) orally notifying the attending physician[,] in the presence of a witness eighteen years of age or older.

Section 13. Subdivision 1 of section 2970 of the public health law, as added by chapter 818 of the laws of 1987, is amended to read as follows:

1. For each patient for whom an order not to resuscitate has been issued, the attending physician shall review the patient's chart to determine if the order is still appropriate in light of the patient's condition and shall indicate on the patient's chart that the order has been reviewed:

(a) for [the] a patient excluding outpatients described in paragraph (b) of this subdivision and alternate level of care patients, in a hosptial, other than a residential health care facility, at least every [three] seven days;

(b) for an outpatient whose order not to resuscitate is effective while the patient receives care in a hospital, each time the attending physician examines the patient, whether in the hospital or elsewhere, provided that the review need not occur more than once every seven days; and

(c) for a patient in a residential health care facility or an alternate level of care patient in a hospital, each time the patient is required to be seen by a physician [in no case less often than] at least every sixty days.

Failure to comply with this subdivision shall not render an order not to resuscitate ineffective.

Section 14. Paragraph (b) of subdivision 2 of section 2970 of the public health law, as added by chapter 818 of the laws of 1987, is amended to read as follows:

(b) if the order not to resuscitate was entered upon the consent of a surrogate, parent, or legal guardian and the attending physician who issued the order, or, if unavailable, another attending physician at any time determines that the patient does not suffer from one of the medical conditions set forth in paragraph (c) of subdivision [five] three of section twenty-nine hundred sixty-five of this article, the attending physician shall immediately include such determination in the patient's chart, cancel the order, and notify the person who consented to the order and all hospital staff responsible for the patient's care of the cancellation.

Section 15. Section 2971 of the public health law, as added by chapter 818 of the laws of 1987, is amended to read as follows:

Section 2971. Interinstitutional transfers. If a patient for whom an order not to resuscitate has been issued is transferred from a hospital to a different hospital the order shall [be effective upon receipt] remain effective, unless revoked pursuant to this article, until[:

1. a physician at the transferee hospital cancels the order; or

2. twenty-four hours have elapsed from the time of the patient's admission to the transferee hospital, whichever shall occur first, except that if the order has not been cancelled by a physician at the transferee hospital an attending physician at the transferee hospital, upon receipt of a copy of or written notice of the order, may presume that the order was validly issued and may issue an order not to resuscitate continuing the prior order] the attending physician first examines the transferred patient, whereupon the attending physician must either:

1. Issue an order continuing the prior order not to resuscitate. Such order may be issued without obtaining further consent from the patient, surrogate or parent pursuant to this article; or

2. Cancel the order not to resuscitate, provided the attending physician immediately notifies the person who consented to the order and the hospital staff directly responsible for the patient's care of the cancellation. Such cancellation does not preclude the issuance of a new order pursuant to this article.

Section 16. Paragraph (b) of subdivision 1 and subdivision 2 of section 2972 of the public health law, as added by chapter 818 of the laws of 1987, are amended to read as follows:

(b) The dispute mediation system shall be described in writing and adopted by the hospital's governing authority. It may utilize existing hospital resources, such as a patient advocate's office or hospital chaplain's office, or it may utilize a body created specifically for this purpose, but, in the event a dispute includes a patient deemed to lack capacity pursuant to (i) paragraph (b) of subdivision three of section twenty-nine hundred sixty-three of this article, the system must include a physician [or psychologist] eligible to provide a concurring determination pursuant to such subdivision, or a family member or guardian of the person of a person with a mental illness of the same or similar nature, or (ii) paragraph (c) of subdivision three of section twenty-nine hundred sixty-three of this article, the system must include a physician [or psychologist] eligible to provide a concurring determination pursuant to such subdivision, or a family member or guardian of the person of a person with a developmental disability of the same or similar nature.

2. The dispute mediation system shall be authorized to mediate [(a)] any dispute [challenging consent to the issuance of an order not to resuscitate], including disputes regarding the determination of the patient's capacity, arising under this article between the patient and an attending physician or the hospital that is caring for the patient and, if the patient is a minor, the patient's parent, or among an attending physician, a parent, non-custodial parent, or legal guardian of a minor patient, any person on the surrogate list, the hospital that is caring for the patient and, where the dispute involves a patient who is in or is transferred from a mental hygeine facility, the facility director[, and (b) any dispute submitted by a person on the surrogate list, challenging a decision by a surrogate not to consent to issuance of an order not to resuscitate].

Section 17. Sections 2977 and 2978 of the public health law are renumbered sections 2978 and 2979 and a new section 2977 is added to read as follows:

Section 2977. Nonhospital orders not to resuscitate. 1. Emergency medical services personnel and hospital emergency service personnel shall honor nonhospital orders not to resuscitate, except as provided in subdivision ten of this section.

2. (a) A nonhospital order not to resuscitate shall be governed as an order not to resuscitate pursuant to this article, except as otherwise specifically provided in this section.

(b) The requirements for dispute mediation established in this article shall only apply with respect to patients during hospitalization.

3. A nonhospital order not to resuscitate may be issued during hospitalization to take effect after hospitalization, or may be issued for a person who is not a patient in, or a resident of, a hospital.

4. Consent to a nonhospital order not to resuscitate shall be governed by sections twenty-nine hundred sixty-four through twenty-nine hundred sixty-seven of this article, provided, however, that (a) an adult with capacity, whether or not hospitalized or a health care agent, may also consent to a nonhospital order not to resuscitate orally to the attending physician, and (b) a nonhospital order not to resuscitate based on the consent of a surrogate pursuant to section twenty-nine hundred sixty-five of this article, or the determination of the attending physician pursuant to section twenty-nine hundred sixty-seven of this article, shall only be issued during hospitalization to take effect after hospitalization.

5. The attending physician shall record the issuance of a nonhospital order not to resuscitate in the patient's medical chart.

6. A nonhospital order not to resuscitate shall be issued upon a standard form prescribed by the commissioner. The commissioner shall also develop a standard bracelet that may be worn by a patient with a nonhospital order not to resuscitate to identify that status; provided, however, that no person may require a patient to wear such a bracelet and that no person may require a patient to wear such a bracelet as a condition for honoring a nonhospital order not to resuscitate or providing health care services.

7. An attending physician who has issued a nonhospital order not to resuscitate, and who transfers care of the patient to another physician, shall inform the physician of the order.

8. For each patient for whom a nonhospital order not to resuscitate has been issued, the attending physician shall review whether the order is still appropriate in light of the patient's condition each time he or she examines the patient, whether in the hospital or elsewhere, but at least every ninety days, provided that the review need not occur more than once every seven days. The attending physician shall record the review in the patient's medical chart record provided, however, that a registered nurse who provides direct care to the patient may record the review in the chart record at the direction of the physician. In such case, the attending physician shall include a confirmation of the review in the patient's medical chart within fourteen days of such review. Failure to comply with this subdivision shall not render a nonhospital order not to resuscitate ineffective.

9. A person who has consented to a nonhospital order not to resuscitate may at any time revoke his or her consent to the order by any act evidencing a specific intent to revoke such consent. Any health care

professional informed of a revocation of consent to a nonhospital order not to resuscitate shall notify the attending physician of the revocation. An attending physician who is informed that a nonhospital order not to resuscitate has been revoked shall record the revocation in the patient's medical chart, cancel the order and make diligent efforts to retrieve the form issuing the order, and the standard bracelet, if any.

10. Emergency medical services personnel or hospital emergency service personnel who are provided with a nonhospital order not to resuscitate, or who identify the standard bracelet on the patient's body, shall comply with the terms of such order; provided, however, that:

(a) emergency medical services personnel or hospital emergency service personnel may disregard the order if:

(i) they believe in good faith that consent to the order has been revoked, or that the order has been cancelled; or

(ii) family members or others on the scene, excluding such personnel, object to the order and physical confrontation appears likely; or

(b) hospital emergency service physicians may direct that the order be disregarded if other significant and exceptional medical circumstances warrant disregarding the order.

11. If a patient with a nonhospital order not to resuscitate is admitted to a hospital, the order shall be treated as an order not to resuscitate for a patient tranferred from another hospital, and shall be governed by section twenty-nine hundred seventy-one of this article.

12. No person shall be subjected to criminal prosecution or civil liability, or be deemed to have engaged in unprofessional conduct, for honoring reasonably and in good faith pursuant to this section a nonhospital order not to resuscitate, for disregarding a nonhospital order pursuant to subdivision ten of this section, or for other actions taken reasonably and in good faith pursuant to this section.

Section 18. Subdivision 4 of section 2982 of the public health law, as added by chapter 752 of the laws of 1990, is amended to read as follows:

4. Priority over other surrogates. Health care decisions by an agent on a principal's behalf pursuant to this article shall have priority over decisions by any other person, [including decisions by a surrogate pursuant to section two thousand nine hundred sixty-five of this chapter,] except as otherwise provided in the health care proxy or in subdivision five of section two thousand nine hundred eighty-three of this article.

Section 19. Subdivision 4 of section 2977 of the public health law, as added by section seventeen of this act, is amended to read as follows:

4. Consent to a nonhospital order not to resuscitate shall be governed by sections twenty-nine hundred sixty-four through twenty-nine hundred sixty-seven of this article, provided, however, that [(a)] an adult with capacity, whether or not hospitalized or a health care agent, may also consent to a nonhospital order not to resuscitate orally to the attending physician[, and (b) a nonhospital order not to resuscitate based on the consent of a surrogate pursuant to section twenty-nine hundred sixty-five of this article, or the determination of the attending physician pursuant to section twenty-nine hundred sixty-seven of this article, shall only be issued during hospitalization to take effect after hospitalization].

Section 20. This act shall take effect immediately, provided, however, that (a) any person designated as a surrogate by an adult pursuant to subdivision 3 of section 2965 of the public health law, as added by chapter 818 of the laws of 1987 and repealed by section five of this act, shall continue to have the authority and responsibilities accorded by chapter 818 of the laws of 1987, if the designation occurred prior to January 1, 1992; (b) section 2977 of this act shall take effect January 1, 1992; (c) section nineteen of this act shall take effect September 1, 1992.

NOTES ON EDITORS AND CONTRIBUTORS

Editors

Robert Baker, Ph.D., is Professor and Chair, Department of Philosophy, Union College, Schenectady, New York

Martin A. Strosberg, Ph.D., is Associate Professor and Director, Graduate Management Institute, Union College, Schenectady, New York

Jonathan D.T. Bynum, was a Research Fellow in the Department of Philosophy, Union College, and is now a graduate student in Philosophy at Rutgers University

Contributors

Judith C. Ahronheim, M.D., is Professor, in the Gerald and May Ritter Department of Geriatrics and Adult Medicine, Mount Sinai School of Medicine, New York

George J. Annas, J.D., M.P.H., is Utley Professor and Chair, Health Law Department, Boston University Schools of Medicine and Public Health

Carolyn Shearer Antonelli, J.D., is General Counsel, Albany Medical Center

David Axelrod, M.D., is Former Commissioner of Health, State of New York, Former Chairman, New York State Task Force on Life and Law

Nancy M. Bennett, M.D., M.S., Department of Medicine, University of Rochester School of Medicine and Dentistry and The Genesee Hospital

R. Baker & M.A. Strosberg (eds.), Legislating Medical Ethics: A Study of the New York Do-Not-Resuscitate Law, 455–457.

Carol Clay, R.N., M.S., is Vice President Patient Services, Ellis Hospital, Schenectady, New York

Virginia Jonas Dersch, Ph.D., is on the faculty of the Gerontology Program, Southern Vermont College, Bennington, Vermont

Lawrence R. Faulkner, J.D., is Deputy General Counsel, New York State Office of Mental Retardation and Developmental Disabilities, and Co-Chair, Committee on Mental and Physical Disabilities New York State Bar Association

I. Alan Fein, M.D., is Intensivist, Critical Care Center, Baptist Hospital, Miami, Florida

David Finley, M.D., is Former Director, Critical Care Units, St. Luke's/ Roosvelt Hospital Center, New York City

Jane Greenlaw, R.N., J.D., is Associate Professor, Humanities in Medicine (Law), University of Rochester School of Medicine, Rochester, New York

James Horwitz, J.D., is Vice President, Legal Affairs, General Counsel to Glens Falls Hospital, Glens Falls, New York

Russell S. Kamer, M.D., Division of Clinical Ethics and, the Section of General Internal Medicine, Department of Medicine, New York Medical College, Valhalla, New York

Sathya Maheswaran, M.D., Assistant Professor of Medicine, New York University Medical Center, New York City

John A. McClung, M.D., Division of Clinical Ethics and the Section of General Internal Medicine, Department of Medicine, New York Medical College, Valhalla, New York

Tracy E. Miller, J.D., is Executive Director, New York State Task Force on Life and the Law

Phillip B. Oates, MSME, MBA., President, SYNETICS, Schenectady, New York

Deborah Damm O'Brien, Private Citizen, New York State

Timothy E. Quill, M.D., is Primary Care Internist, Associate Chief of Medicine, The Genesee Hospital, Professor of Medicine and Psychiatry, University of Rochester School of Medicine and Dentistry, Rochester, New York

Carl Rosenberg, Ph.D.

Josef Schmee, Ph.D., is Kenneth B. Sharpe Professor of Management, Graduate Management Institute, Union College, Schenectady, New York

Norton Spritz, M.D., J.D., F.A.C.P., is Chief, Medical Services, Department of Veterans Affairs Medical Center, Professor of Medicine, New York University School of Medicine, New York City

Robert Zussman, Ph.D., is Associate Professor, Department of Sociology, State University of New York at Stony Brook

INDEX

accreditation requirements (*see also* Joint Commission on the Accreditiation of Healthcare Organizations) i, 83–89, 263, 280–289, 305, 331, 342
acts/actions
  and inactions 35–37, 48–51
  and omissions 47–50, 373
ACP (*see* American College of Physicians)
Adler, W. 101
advance directives (*see* also Do-Not-Resuscitate, Orders; *Matter of Eichner*; *Matter of Storar*) 108, 422–423
  Annas on 145
Ahronheim, Judith xv, xvii, 78, 117, 130, **235–240**, 259–260, 326, 332, 333–335, 339, 341–344, 346, 455
Alesandro, Rev. Msgr. John A. 6
Alzheimer's disease 146, 446
AHA (*see* American Hospital Association)
AMA (*see* American Medical Association)
American College of Physicians xv, xvii, 60–62, 68, 138, 251–262, 334, 335, 346
American Heart Association
  Standards for cardiopulmonary resuscitation 38
American Hospital Association
  Patient's Bill of Rights 18, 33
American Medical Association xvi, 27, 34, 38, 46, 48, 59, 91–98, 114, 136, 143, 332, 259, 443
  Council on Ethical and Judicial Affairs 29, 260
Annas, George xvii, 53, 60, 98, 109, 122, **141–156**, 158, 159, 455
anti-Paternalism (*see also* paternalism) 57–59, 80–82, 98, 297–298
Ang, B. 250
Antonelli, Carolyn xvii, **163–168**, 455
Applebaum, G.E. 239
Aries, N. 321
Aries, Phillippe 223, 324
Association of the Bar of the City of New York (*see* New York City)
Atwood, Deborah xi, 300
authoritarian/latitudinarian (*see* bioethical reform; morality, legislation of)
autonomy (*see also* patient autonomy, self-determination) 12, 33, 57–60, 93, 111–114, 139–140, 216, 252, 305, 328, 372, 387–390, 396
Axelrod, Commissioner David xi, xii, xvii, 6, 10, 16, 26, 41, 54, 69, **137–140**, 141, 143, 153, 157–159, 300, 455

Badami, Rita xii
Baeza, Mario L. Esq. 6
Baker, Robert (*see also* Union College, Do-Not-Resuscitate Law Study) **xi–xii, xv–xviii**, 21, 23, 24, 27, **33–104**, 105 106, 114, 121, 124, 129–131, 158, 163, **263–301**, 321, 325–332, **333–346**, **439–444**, 455
Ball, Rev. David 6
Bayer, A.J. 250
Beauchamp, Tom 48, 57–59, 98
Becker, H. 304, 321
Bedell, Susanna 39, 84, 98–99, 130, 155, 224, 239, 300, 332
beneficence 57–59, 96
Bennett, Alan 157

Bennett, Nancy 30, 111, 117, 131, **235–240**, 326, 332, 333–334, 339–340, 343, 346, 455
Bhan, G. 250
bioethics 9–10, 33, 47, 59, 82–89, 206, 263, 297–300, 343, 345
  consensus 33–34, 42–45, 59
  reform xvi, xvii, 33–34, 82–88, 96, 293–294, 297–300, 345
    authoritarian vs latitudinarian (*see also* morality, legislation of) 85–89, 123–124
  revolution 33–34, 96
Bizzarro, Dominick xi
Blackhall, L. 130, 300
Bleich, Rabbi J. David 5, 6, 396
Bloom, S. 321
Bosk, Charles 224
brain death (*see* death)
Brennan, United States Supreme Court Justice 151
Brennan, T. 260
Brett, A. 99
Brody, Baruch 84, 99, 301
Brody, Howard 68, 89–91, 94–98, 101, 132, 140
Browne, C. 101
Bynum, Jonathan xi, **263–302**, **349–455**, 456

Calkins, Evan 6
Callahan, Daniel 6
Cain, K. 132
Campion, E. 99, 301
cardiac arrest (*see* cardiopulmonary arrest, code)
cardiopulmonary arrest 3, 35–37, 107, 133, 159, 170, 175, 183–185, 215, 220, 243, 350, 383–384, 418–41, 446
cardiopulmonary resuscitation (*see also* code) xv–xvii, **3–4**, 18, 20–23, 26–27, 35–40, 42–55, 57–61, 63–66, 68–69, 71, 73–80, 82, 83, 85–86, 88–98, 106–111, 114–122, 124–129, 134, 147–151, 155–156, 157–159, 164, 166–167, 170, 181, 184, 206, 208–209, 211, 215, 219–222, 227–233, 235–240, 241–250, 251–260, 265, 269–271, 275–276, 280–283, 288, 294–300, 309, 325–332, 334, 341–345, **350**, 378, 381, 383–384, 386, 388–391, 395–404, 407, 409, 411–412, 415–419, 421–431, 435–436, 440, 442–443
  automatic 35–37
  as entitlement 22, 73–74 151, 158–159, 390, 443, 444, 686–687
  as legal right 139, 159, 329
  by default 119–123, 248, 281–284, 344, 443–444
  civil disobedience to (*see also* code: no-; show-; slow-) 37–39, 64, 69–71
    collaborative 37–39
  "CPR exceptionalism" 46, 90–91
  definition **3**, **350**, 378–380, 383, 418–419
  decision matrix (President's Commission) 58–59
  futile (*see also* futility) xvi, 20–21, 26–27, 37, 44, 47–54, 59–77, 80, 88–98, 116–118, 129, 209, 255–256, 281–284, 287–288, 294–298, 327–330, 351, 407, 440, 442–443
  "horror stories" 442
  open-chest/closed chest 35
  presumption favoring 3, 20, 42–45, 121–122, 138, 345, 349, **351–352**, 378, 382, 390–391
  right to 157, 329
Cardozo, B. 391
Cassel, C. 132
Catholic (*see* New York State religious groups)
Childress, James 57–58, 98
Clay, Carol xvii, 72, **181–186**, 456
clear and convincing evidence standard 5, 11–12, 39–41, 146, 149, 191–192, 280, 336, 356–357, 364, 393, 427–428
closed chest cardiac massage (*see* cardiopulmonary resuscitation)

code (*see also* cardiopulmonary resuscitation) xv–xvii, 12, 25, 35–39, 44, 62, 76, 148, 181, 228, 243, 269–272, 281, 326, 334–335, 339, 345, 385–386, 440
as civil disobedience 37–39, 135
collaborative 37
blue 35, 135
calling/calling off 22, 35–39, 79–81, 181
chemical 38
no-code (*see also* do-not-resuscitate order) xv–xvi, 12, 35–39, 44, 76–77, 88, 148, 228, 269–272, 281, 334–336, 339, 345, 385–386
NTBR (Not to be Resuscitated/No temperature by rectum) 228
OBP (On the banana peel) 38
purple dots 12, 38, 41, 107, 229, 345, 385–386
show-code xv, 36, 38–39, 44, 78, 107, 148, 269–270, 326, 334, 386, 440
slow-code xv, 3–39, 44, 107, 148, 269–271, 326, 334, 335, 386, 440
team 78–81, 238
Cole, Elizabeth xi, 300
Concannon, Richard J. 5, 6, 10, 13, 29, 44, 50, **410–413**
Conovitz, Myron W. 6
consent (*see* patient, consent of)
Cook, E. 224
CPR (*see* cardiopulmonary resuscitation)
Crane, Diana 60, 92, 99, 294, 298, 300
Cranford, R. 233
"Crime of Compassion" 41
critical care
directors 24, 62, 67, 69, 70–71, 78, 83, 86–88, 93, 99, 123, 263–264, 267, 269–286, 289–296, 305–321, 328, 334, 337–338, 342, 439
medical 67, 70–71, 78, 86–88, 93, 99, 123–124, 264, 267, 269–286, 289–296, 305–321, 328, 334, 337–338, 342, 439
"paper" vs "working" 124, 306, 320
nursing 62, 69, 70–71, 78, 83, 86–88, 93, 99, 123, 263–264, 267, 269–286, **289**, **306–281**, 289–296, 305–321, 328, 334, 439
units xv, 86, 222, 225, 264, 267, 439
Croog, S. 321
Cruzan v. Director, Missouri Department of Health 12, 29, 39, 99, 142, 146–149, 151, 155
Cruzan, Nancy 146–151
Cuomo, Governor Mario xv, 10, 41, 107, 128, 151, 229, 381–382

Dana Foundation 300
Danaus, daughters of 60
Davis, F. 321
Dean A. 250
death 33, 36, 125–126, 142–143, 158, 161, 176, 205, 216, 223, 236, 242–249, 251, 313–314, 340, 349, 351, 382, 383–384, 386–387, 441
Aries, Phillippe on 223
brain death criteria 10, 142–143, 158
brain death statute 10
death warrant 70, 441
decisions about life and death 33
definition of 10, 142–143, 158
Harvard brain death criteria 10, 142–143
"Death out of the Closet" 13
decerebrate state 36, 61
decisional capacity (*see also* patient, capacity) 9, 12, 221, 226, 587, 598, 602, 609–611, 619
defibrillation (*see* cardiopulmonary resuscitation)
Delbanco, T. 30, 98, 130, 155, 224, 300
Department of Health (*see* New York, State of)
Dersch, Virginia J. (*see also* Union College, Do-Not-Resuscitate study) 113, 123, 130, **263–302**, **303–325**, 329, 332, 338, 346, 456
developmentally disabled (*see* New York State, Office of Mental Retardation and Developmental Disability)
Dieck, E. 29, 130, 301, 332, 346

Dinnerstein (*see Matter of Dinnerstein*)
DNR (*see* do-not-resuscitate)
Do-Not-Resuscitate Law (*see* New York, State of)
DNR orders (*see* do-not-resuscitate, orders)
do-no-harm principle 400, 411
do-not-resuscitate orders
  as death warrant 70, 441
  definition of 3–4, 35–39, **351**, 384, 418–419
  documented/undocumented (*see also* no-code; patient consent, oral/written) 3–4, 17–20, 26, 38–39, 62, 67–71, 79–81, 83–89, 105, 117, 135, 163–165, 176–179, 181–182, 192, 209, 238, 241–243, 248, 259, 264, 269–272, 280–281, 287–290, 292–294, 298, 334–336, 339–334, 342, 384, 441–443
  futility-based 22–24, 38–39, 44–55, 59–63, 73–80, 89–94, 110, 116–118, 124–127, 131, 158–159, 255–256, 281–284, 287, 294–300, 329–330, 440–443
    bioethical delegitimation of 42–55
  in advance of an arrest/at the time of an arrest 38, 74–80
    Hastings *Guidelines* on 52–54
  inverted nature of 35–36, 46–47, 80
  symbolic nature of 215–225
  telephoned 14, 25, 81, 174, 182, 185, 287, 370, 420, 429
Dunlop, G. 301

Eichner (*see Matter of Eichner*)
EMS (*see* Emergency Medical Service/Technicians)
EMT (*see* Emergency Medical Service/Technicians)
Elam, J.O. 233
Emergency Medical Service/Technicians 72, 169–179, 445, 451, 453
Emerson, J. 301
ethicist 65–66, 184, 237
ethics committee 167–168, 181, 184–185
Evans, Andrew 84, 99

Faber-Langendoen, 258, 260
Fader, R. 117, 130
family (*see* patients, family of)
Farber, Saul J. 6, 29, 130, 138, 140
Faulkner, Lawrence xvii, 72, **185–215**, 456
Fein, I. Alan xv, 1, 5, 138, **263–302**, 346, 456
Finley, David xvii, **205–214**, 456
Finucane, T. 130
Fisher, L. 239
Fitter, J. 131
Fleischman, Alan R. 6
Freidson, Eliot 304, 321
Fried, C. 233
Frier, J. 29
futility (*see also* cardiopulmonary resuscitation, futile; do-not-Resuscitate orders, futility-based)
  conception of 15, 59–61, 149, 255–256, 294–297
  definition of 27, 117–118, 126
  deprofessionalization of 15

Georgopoulos, B. 321
Gillerman, G. 100, 234
"Give the Dying Their Voice" 13, 30
Gossin, L. 101
Greenlaw, Jane xvii, 53, 109, **133–136**, 456
Grenvik, A. 99
Guidelines (*see* New York State DNR Law; Hastings Center)
Gulati, R. 250

Hackler J. 258, 260–261
Hades 60
Hamburg, Beatrix A. 6
Hartman, Thomas 73
Hastings Center xvi, 6, 40, 99, 250, 300, 346
  Guidelines on the Termination of Treatment and Care of the Dying 42–46, 51–54, 57–60, 72, 74, 76–77, 89, 92, 300

HAYNS (*see* New York State, Hospital Association of)
Health Care Proxy Law (*see* New York State)
Heimlich maneuver 231
Hemlock Society 146
Hershey, C. 239
High, D. 130
Hiller, F. 260
Hingson, R. 321
Hippocratic Oath 400, 411
Horan, M. 250
Hornbeck, Sean 300
Horwitz, James 78, 158–159, 456
Hospital Association of New York State (*see* New York State, Hospital Association)
"Hospital Is Investigated on Life-Support Policy" 41, 99
"Hospitals Seek Rules on Withholding Support" 41, 101
Hosseini, H. 301
Hotchkiss, E.J. 234, 250
Huttman, B. 99

ICU (*see* critical care units)
immunity, legal (*see* New York State Do-Not-Resuscitate Law, immunity for physicians)
In re (*see* Matter of, e.g., *Matter of Eichner*)
inaction (*see* action/inaction)
informed consent (*see* patient, consent of)
intensive care medicine/units (*see* critical care, units)

JCAHO (*see* Joint Commission on the Accreditation of Health Care Organizations)
Jecker, N. 100, 131, 301
Jews (*see* New York State religious groups)
Joint Commission on the Accreditation of Health Care Organizations 12, 29, 34, 39, 46, 83–89, 99, 123–124, 130, 263, 280–284, 287–289, 293, 297–298, 331, 338, 342, 440–441
Jonsen, A. 100, 131, 301
Jonsson, P. 99, 301
Jude, J. 99, 233

Kamer, Russell xvii, 29, 45, 78, 99, 111, 116, 130, 217, 224, **227–234**, 239, 250, 259–260, 301, 326, 332, 333, 335, 339–341, 344, 346, 456
Kapp, M. 99, 292, 301
Kaplan, Helene 6
Katz, J. 99
Kennedy, L. 321
Kevorkian, Jack 146
Kingdon, John 9, 29
Knaus, W. 31, 263, 273, 301
Knickerbocker, C. 99
Kouwenhoven, W. 35, 99, 233
Kramer, R. 99, 233, 250, 260
Krause, C.R. 100, 136, 234, 250
Kubler-Ross, E. 224

Lantos, J. 99, 130, 260, 301
latitudinarian vs authoritarian (*see* bioethics, reform)
lawyers, hospital 17, 163–168, 158–159, 292–294
legal guardian (*see also* patient's surrogate) 5, 109, 355–359, 404–407, 416–418, 425–431, 444–449, 454
legislating morality (*see* morality, legislation of)
Levkoff, S. 132
life-sustaining interventions termination of (*see* do-not-resuscitate orders)
Linn, B. 250
Linton, R. 321
living will (*see* advance directives)
Lo, B. 99, 131, 292, 301
Longo, D. 99, 301
Longo, E. 86, 93, 131
Luchi, R. 240, 250

Maheswaran, Sathya 117, 130, **235–240**, 259, 326, 332–335, 346, 456
Mann, F. 321
Mansell, Reverend Msg. 6
Mantel-Haenszel test 243

Margolis, D. 99
Marks, E. 31
Matter of Dinnerstein 233, 393
Matter of Eichner 108–109, 392
Matter of Harvey U. 202
Matter of O'Connor 11–12, 29, 99, 191–192, 202, 209, 233, 239
Matter of Quinlan 11, 34, 82, 96, 99, 228, 245, 391–392
Matter of Storar 11–12, 29–30, 99, 108–109, 191–192, 202, 209, 233, 391, 393, 395
Matter of Weberlist 202
Matter of Westchester County Medical Center 239
Mauksch, H. 321
McClung, John xvii, 29, 45, 78, 99, 130, 217, 224, **227–234**, 239, 250, 260, 301, 326, 332, 335, 339–341, 346, 456
McCullough, Laurence 99
McKinney, Rev. Donald, 6
McLeod, G. 99, 131, 301
McMurray, Georgia L. 6
McNamee, M. 99, 301
medical
  futility (*see* cardiopulmonary resuscitation; do-not-resuscitate orders; futility)
  directors (*see* critical care)
  records, nature of (*see also* New York State Do-Not-Resuscitate Law, documentation requirement; patient, medical records of) 38, 166, 217–224, 325–326, 333–336
  Society of the State Of New York (*see* New York State)
Mental Hygiene Law (*see* New York State)
Miles, S. 233
Mill, John Stuart 56
Mill's principle 56–59
Miller, Tracy xvii, xviii, 7, 26, 30, 41, 54, 75, 77, 82, 89–90, 100, **105–132**, 163, 258, 260, 300, **325–332**, 333–342, 346, 442, 456
Millock, Peter xi, 30, 177
Mintzberg, Henry 304–306, 321
morality
  legislation of 54–57, 63–69, 88, 330–331, 390
Moses, L. 301
Murphy, D. 131, 250, 258, 260, 261
Murray, John Courtney 390

National Academy of Sciences 38
  National Research Council of 227, 233
National Conference Steering Committee on Cardiopulmonary Resuscitation 233
National Institutes of Health 47, 59
New York, City of
  Association of the Bar 122
New York, State of
  Assembly 13–14, 30, 105, 110, 128–129, 132
  Court of Appeals (State's highest court) 11–12, 40–41, 108–109, 190–192, 391–394
  Department of Health xi, 9, 13–16, 21–22, 25–28, 30, 66, 72–75, 78–82, 101, 119, 121–122, 131, 153, 158, 166–167, 175–179, 183, 186, 187, 189, 191, 198, 200–201, 203, 239, 292–194, 329–330, 367, 382, **415–438**, 439, 444
  Do Not Resuscitate Law
    as consumer protection 13, 28, 345
    assessment conference (*see* Union College, Conference)
    capacity/competence (*see also* patient capacity/competence)
      determination of 350, 352–353
      distinction 403
    documentation (*see* patient, consent forms; consent oral/written)
    dispute mediation system 5, 167–168, 193–195, 201–202, 349, 362–364, 397, 435–437
      for OMRDD patients 193–195, 201–202
    immunity for physicians 5, 152–153, 159, 252, 349, 362–366, 401, 409

presumed consent clause (*see also* patient, presumed consent) 3, 20–22, 31, 42–45, 50–54, 75–76, 78–80, 121–122, 138, 150–151, 157, 295–297, 349, 351–352, 419
review of a DNR order (three-day/sixty-day) 16, 26, 71, 81, 361, 433
therapeutic exception 4–5, 10, 13, 43–44, 50–51, 53, 74, 110, 121–126, 253–255, 258, 349, 354–355, 400–402, 410–413, 422
Health Care Proxy Law 11, 29, 30, 81–82, 345, 425–426, 446
Hospital Association 25, 30, 110, 122, 131, 186, 239, **414–438**
Medical Society xvi, 13, 30, 45, 100, 346
Ad Hoc Committee on DNR 13
Do-Not-Resuscitate Guidelines
(1982) **369–370**
(1990) 25, 30, 110, 122, 131, 186, 239, **415–438**
Mental Hygiene Law 203
Nurses Association 13–14
Office of Mental Retardation and Developmental Disabilities (OMRDD) xvii, 14, 18, 19, 72, **181–187**, **187–204**, 282, 285, 350–351, 358–359, 367, 437–438, 456, 522
religious groups (pluralism) 9–10, 20, 137, 157, 390
Catholic Conference 10
Orthodox Jewish 10
Senate 13–15, 105, 110, 128–129
committees of 13–14
Health 13–14, 30, 142
hearings of 13–14, 30, 110
Surrogate's Court Procedure Act 203
Task Force on Life and the Law 30, 101 ,131, 136, 239, 260, 332, 346
Chairman of (*see* Axelrod, Commissioner David)
Counsel for (*see* Swidler, Robert)
Do Not Resuscitate Orders: The Proposed Legislation and Report xvi, **3–7**, 11, 30, 41–45, 50–52, 72, 134, 136, **381–414**
Executive Summary of xvi, **3–7**
Minority Report of **410–413**
Executive Director of (*see* Miller, Tracy)
members/staff of 6–7, 41
NIH (*see* National Institutes of Health)
no-code (*see* code; do-not-resuscitate order)
Nolan, K. 225
nonmaleficence (*see also* beneficence) 57
Nursing Directors (*see* Critical Care)

O'Brien, Deborah xvii, 72, 81, **169–172**, 173, 457
O'Connor (*see Matter of O'Connor*)
Oates, Philip **263–302**, 457
OMRDD (*see* New York State Office of Mental Retardation and Developmental Disabilities)
omission (*see* action-omission)
On Liberty 56–57
open-chest cardiac massage (*see* cardiopulmonary resuscitation)
Ouslander, J. 131

parens patriae 191–192
paternalism 55–59, 66, 80–82, 138–139, 297–298, 327, 330–331
strong versus weak 57–59, 327
Pathy, M. 250
patient
autonomy of (*see also* autonomy) 26–27, 57, 90–93, 98, 111–114, 139–140, 230–231, 233, 258, 328–329, 388–390
best interests of 4, 11, 97, 120, 144–145, 366, 406–407
chart of (*see* medical records of)
consent 4, 12–13, 17, 47, 49, 50–51, 53–55, 58, 70–71, 81, 90–94, 96–97, 125–126, 246–250, 253–255, 257, 269–281, 344–345, 390, 415

capacity/competence to consent 3–4, 17, 20–22, 190–192, 289–210, **352–355**, 396–397, 349–350, 352–353, 369, 396–403
determination of **350**, **352–353**, 402–404, 416, 423–424, 433
competent/incompetent (*see also* incapacitated) 4, 374–378, 392–394
New York Taskforce rejects distinction 403
contemporaneous 4
forms (*see also* oral/written) 20, 80–83, 120, 292–293, 441–442
oral/written 25–26, 80–82, 120, 287, 290–293, 441–443
presumed (*see* also New York State DNR law, presumed consent clause) 3, 20–22, 31, 42–47, 50–54, 75–77, 78–80, 121–122, 129, 138, 150–151, 157, 295–297, 343, 349, 351–352, 419
family of 5, 23, **170–171**, 246–250, 269–284, 350–351, 356, 359–360, 365–366, 389, 390, 418, 430–432
ambivalence of 23, 114–116, 119–120, 281–284
incapacitated/lacking capacity 62, 139, 190–192, **352–355**, 402–404, 416–418, 426, 430–432, 437–438
proxy for (*see also* New York Health Proxy Law) 11, 81–82, 345, 417, 425–426, 446
responsiblities 63
rights (*see also* Patient's Bill of Rights, self-determination) 13, 60, 65, 84–85, 90, 107, 110, 121, 139, 381
to cardiopulmonary resuscitation 157, 329
to consent to treatment 153
to refuse treatment (*see*, autonomy of, *Cruzan v Director*, *Matter of Dinnerstein*, *Matter of Eichner*, *Matter of O'Connor*, *Matter of Quinlan*, *Matter of Storar*) 91, 107, 153
self-determination of (*see also* autonomy; patient, autonomy of; patient self-determination act) 33, 37
surrogate for (*see also*, *Cruzan v Director*, *Matter of Dinnerstein*, *Matter of Eichner*, *Matter of O'Connor*, *Matter of Quinlan*, *Matter of Storar*) 4, 11–12, 33, 39–41, 47, 59, 62–63, 65, 81–82, 92–93, 108–110, 114–116, 118–119, 127–130, 138–139, 165, 231, 233, 288, **351**, **355–358**, 365, 374, 392–393, 404–407, 425–430, 436
Patient's Bill of Rights 18, 33, 54, 161
Patient Self-Determination Act, Federal (1991) 29, 261
Pearlman, R. 132, 258, 261
Pelle, D. 130
Peppe, Elizabeth 7
Piegas, L. 240
Plowe, C. 30, 100, 131
Ponemon, Lawrence xv, 300
Praeger, K. 30, 100, 131, 234, 260
President's Commission for the Study of Ethical Problems in Medicine and Biomedical and Behavioral Research xvi, 33–34, 42–49, 51, 53–54, 57–59, 72, 83–85, 89–91, 95, 100, 225, 346, **371–380**, 412
Principles of Bioethics 57–58
professional
self-regulation (*see also* bioethics, reform; Joint Commission on the Accreditation of Health Care Organizations) 83–86
Prohibition 55–57, 331
proxy (*see* New York State Health Care Proxy Law; patient, proxy for)
public policy
agenda-setting 9–11, 27, 41
clarification of 20–22, 122
evaluation of 22–24, 29, 120
formulation and adoption of 13–15, 27, 108–110, 128, 129

implementation of 15–20, 28, 163–168
publicity condition (Rawls) 64–65
purple dots (*see* code)

Queens County grand jury 12, 38–39, 41, 100, 107, 228–229, 265–271, 345, 385–386
Quill, Timothy xvii, 30, 72, 81, 100, 111, 117, 131, 133, 135, 136, **173–180**, 234, **241–250**, 298, 326, 331, 332–334, 339–340, 346, 456

Rabkin, M. 100, 234
Rachels, James 48–49, 100
Rahbar, B. 131
Rawls, John 64–65, 100
Regan, John 7
Reily, Charles 300
Rest, James 264, 301, 337, 346
religious groups (*see* New York State Religious Groups)
respiratory arrest (*see* cardiopulmory arrest)
respiratory function (*see* cardiopulmonary function)
resuscitation (*see* cardiopulmonary resuscitation)
Rettig, R. 31
Rice, N. 100, 234
Rivers v Katz 203
Roberts, J. 301
Rogers, Charles B. 13, 30, 31
Rosenberg, Carl xv, 130, **235–240**, 259–260, 332, 346, 457
Rosenthal, E. 100
Rosner, F. 131, 234, 250
Rosoff, Adrienne 260
Rudin, Rabbi James A. 7

Saika, G. 99, 301
Sanakaitis, J. 100, 234, 250
Sanctity of Social Life, The 294
Schiess, Rev. Betty Bone 7
Schloendorff v Society of New York Hospital 203, 391
Schmee, Josef **263–302**, 332, 346, 457
Schneiderman, L. 100, 131, 301
Schneier, Leslie E. 7
Schonwether, R. 131
Schultz, A. 233
Schumway, J. 130
"Sensible Answers to Death and Deceit" 13, 30
Sharpe, S. 31, 301
Sheehan, Rhonda xi, 300
Shmerling, R. 131
Singer, P. 130, 301
show-code (*see* code)
slow-code (*see* code)
Smith, Rev. Robert S. 7
Snowden, Marianne xi, xii, 300
Solzhenitsyn, Alexander 154
Sousa, J.E. 240
Spanguolo, Eugene xi, 300
Spritz, Norton 105, 112, 131, **241–250**, 333–335, 337, 339–340, 344, 346, 457
Stack, Elizabeth 7
Stankaitis, J.A. 136
Steinberg, A. 131
Storar (*see Matter of Storar*)
Strosberg, Martin (*see also* Union College, Do-Not-Resuscitate Law Study) xii, xvi, **9–30**, 41, 72, 114, 130, 163, **263–302**, 321, 330, 332, 346, 455
suicide, physician assisted 146
Sullivan, R. 101, 234
surrogate (*see* patient, surrogate for)
Sweeny, Raymond 73
Swendler, P. 101, 131, 261
Swidler, Robert xv, xviii, 20–21, 24, 31, 41, 75–77, 79, 80, 88, 95, 100, 101, 121–122, 131, 166, 234, 239, 250, 261, 289, 295–297, 300, 301, 329, 442
Symmers, W.St.C., Sr. 101

Taffet, G. 240, 250
Tagge, G. 101
Taskforce on Life and the Law (*see* New York State Taskforce on Life and the Law)
Teasdale, T. 240, 250

Tesdale, T. 131
terminal illness/patients (*see also* futility) 4, 236–237, 255–256, 269, 272, 278–279, 282–287, **351**, 357, 396, 405, 416, 427
therapeutic exception (*see* New York State Do-Not-Resuscitate Law)
Timerman, A. 240
Tobin, Charles J. 5, 7, 10, 13, 29, 44, 50, **410–413**
Tomlinson, Tom 68, 89–91, 94–98, 101, 132, 140
Toynbee, Arnold 137
Tresch, D. 240
Tymchuk, A. 131

Uhlmann, R. 132, 258, 261
Underwood, James xi
Union College xii, xvi
  Do-Not-Resuscitate Law Assessment Conference xi, xvi, 59, 65, 78, 127, **156–159**
  Do-Not-Resuscitate Law Study xv, xvii, 23–24, 59–63, 65–71, 75, 78, 80, 86–89, 93, 105–106, 111–114, 116–119, 123–124, **263–302**, **303–321**, 325–332, 333–346, 439–444

VerSteeg, D. 321

Walker, R. 301
Wanzar, S. 261
Warren, M. 301
Weiner, Terry xi
Weir, R. 101
Wetle, T. 132
When Others Must Choose 329
White, P. 346
Wilcoxon Signed-Rank test 267, 338
Wilcoxon, F. 301
Wilson, R. 321

Youngner, S. 101, 132, 234, 301
Yurt, R. 250

Zimmerman, J. 31, 263, 273, 301
Zoll, Paul 35, 101
Zugar, A. 261
Zussman, Robert **215–226**, 321, 335–336, 457
Zweibel, N. 13

Philosophy and Medicine

1. H. Tristram Engelhardt, Jr. and S.F. Spicker (eds.): *Evaluation and Explanation in the Biomedical Sciences.* 1975 ISBN 90-277-0553-4
2. S.F. Spicker and H. Tristram Engelhardt, Jr. (eds.): *Philosophical Dimensions of the Neuro-Medical Sciences.* 1976 ISBN 90-277-0672-7
3. S.F. Spicker and H. Tristram Engelhardt, Jr. (eds.): *Philosophical Medical Ethics: Its Nature and Significance.* 1977 ISBN 90-277-0772-3
4. H. Tristram Engelhardt, Jr. and S.F. Spicker (eds.): *Mental Health: Philosophical Perspectives.* 1978 ISBN 90-277-0828-2
5. B.A. Brody and H. Tristram Engelhardt, Jr. (eds.): *Mental Illness.* Law and Public Policy. 1980 ISBN 90-277-1057-0
6. H. Tristram Engelhardt, Jr., S.F. Spicker and B. Towers (eds.): *Clinical Judgment: A Critical Appraisal.* 1979 ISBN 90-277-0952-1
7. S.F. Spicker (ed.): *Organism, Medicine, and Metaphysics.* Essays in Honor of Hans Jonas on His 75th Birthday. 1978 ISBN 90-277-0823-1
8. E.E. Shelp (ed.): *Justice and Health Care.* 1981 ISBN 90-277-1207-7; Pb 90-277-1251-4
9. S.F. Spicker, J.M. Healey, Jr. and H. Tristram Engelhardt, Jr. (eds.): *The Law-Medicine Relation: A Philosophical Exploration.* 1981 ISBN 90-277-1217-4
10. W.B. Bondeson, H. Tristram Engelhardt, Jr., S.F. Spicker and J.M. White, Jr. (eds.): *New Knowledge in the Biomedical Sciences.* Some Moral Implications of Its Acquisition, Possession, and Use. 1982 ISBN 90-277-1319-7
11. E.E. Shelp (ed.): *Beneficence and Health Care.* 1982 ISBN 90-277-1377-4
12. G.J. Agich (ed.): *Responsibility in Health Care.* 1982 ISBN 90-277-1417-7
13. W.B. Bondeson, H. Tristram Engelhardt, Jr., S.F. Spicker and D.H. Winship: *Abortion and the Status of the Fetus.* 2nd printing, 1984 ISBN 90-277-1493-2
14. E.E. Shelp (ed.): *The Clinical Encounter.* The Moral Fabric of the Patient-Physician Relationship. 1983 ISBN 90-277-1593-9
15. L. Kopelman and J.C. Moskop (eds.): *Ethics and Mental Retardation.* 1984 ISBN 90-277-1630-7
16. L. Nordenfelt and B.I.B. Lindahl (eds.): *Health, Disease, and Causal Explanations in Medicine.* 1984 ISBN 90-277-1660-9
17. E.E. Shelp (ed.): *Virtue and Medicine.* Explorations in the Character of Medicine. 1985 ISBN 90-277-1808-3
18. P. Carrick: *Medical Ethics in Antiquity.* Philosophical Perspectives on Abortion and Euthanasia. 1985 ISBN 90-277-1825-3; Pb 90-277-1915-2
19. J.C. Moskop and L. Kopelman (eds.): *Ethics and Critical Care Medicine.* 1985 ISBN 90-277-1820-2
20. E.E. Shelp (ed.): *Theology and Bioethics.* Exploring the Foundations and Frontiers. 1985 ISBN 90-277-1857-1
21. G.J. Agich and C.E. Begley (eds.): *The Price of Health.* 1986 ISBN 90-277-2285-4
22. E.E. Shelp (ed.): *Sexuality and Medicine.*
    Vol. I: Conceptual Roots. 1987 ISBN 90-277-2290-0; Pb 90-277-2386-9

23. E.E. Shelp (ed.): *Sexuality and Medicine.* Vol. II: Ethical Viewpoints in Transition. 1987 ISBN 1-55608-013-1; Pb 1-55608-016-6
24. R.C. McMillan, H. Tristram Engelhardt, Jr., and S.F. Spicker (eds.): *Euthanasia and the Newborn.* Conflicts Regarding Saving Lives. 1987 ISBN 90-277-2299-4; Pb 1-55608-039-5
25. S.F. Spicker, S.R. Ingman and I.R. Lawson (eds.): *Ethical Dimensions of Geriatric Care.* Value Conflicts for the 21th Century. 1987 ISBN 1-55608-027-1
26. L. Nordenfelt: *On the Nature of Health.* An Action- Theoretic Approach. 1987 ISBN 1-55608-032-8
27. S.F. Spicker, W.B. Bondeson and H. Tristram Engelhardt, Jr. (eds.): *The Contraceptive Ethos.* Reproductive Rights and Responsibilities. 1987 ISBN 1-55608-035-2
28. S.F. Spicker, I. Alon, A. de Vries and H. Tristram Engelhardt, Jr. (eds.): *The Use of Human Beings in Research.* With Special Reference to Clinical Trials. 1988 ISBN 1-55608-043-3
29. N.M.P. King, L.R. Churchill and A.W. Cross (eds.): *The Physician as Captain of the Ship.* A Critical Reappraisal. 1988 ISBN 1-55608-044-1
30. H.-M. Sass and R.U. Massey (eds.): *Health Care Systems.* Moral Conflicts in European and American Public Policy. 1988 ISBN 1-55608-045-X
31. R.M. Zaner (ed.): *Death: Beyond Whole-Brain Criteria.* 1988 ISBN 1-55608-053-0
32. B.A. Brody (ed.): *Moral Theory and Moral Judgments in Medical Ethics.* 1988 ISBN 1-55608-060-3
33. L.M. Kopelman and J.C. Moskop (eds.): *Children and Health Care.* Moral and Social Issues. 1989 ISBN 1-55608-078-6
34. E.D. Pellegrino, J.P. Langan and J. Collins Harvey (eds.): *Catholic Perspectives on Medical Morals.* Foundational Issues. 1989 ISBN 1-55608-083-2
35. B.A. Brody (ed.): *Suicide and Euthanasia.* Historical and Contemporary Themes. 1989 ISBN 0-7923-0106-4
36. H.A.M.J. ten Have, G.K. Kimsma and S.F. Spicker (eds.): *The Growth of Medical Knowledge.* 1990 ISBN 0-7923-0736-4
37. I. Löwy (ed.): *The Polish School of Philosophy of Medicine.* From Tytus Chałubiński (1820–1889) to Ludwik Fleck (1896–1961). 1990 ISBN 0-7923-0958-8
38. T.J. Bole III and W.B. Bondeson: *Rights to Health Care.* 1991 ISBN 0-7923-1137-X
39. M.A.G. Cutter and E.E. Shelp (eds.): *Competency.* A Study of Informal Competency Determinations in Primary Care. 1991 ISBN 0-7923-1304-6
40. J.L. Peset and D. Gracia (eds.): *The Ethics of Diagnosis.* 1992 ISBN 0-7923-1544-8

41. K.W. Wildes, S.J., F. Abel, S.J. and J.C. Harvey (eds.): *Birth, Suffering, and Death.* Catholic Perspectives at the Edges of Life. 1992 ISBN 0-7923-1547-2; Pb 0-7923-2545-1
42. S.K. Toombs: *The Meaning of Illness.* A Phenomenological Account of the Different Perspectives of Physician and Patient. 1992 ISBN 0-7923-1570-7; Pb 0-7923-2443-9
43. D. Leder (ed.): *The Body in Medical Thought and Practice.* 1992 ISBN 0-7923-1657-6
44. C. Delkeskamp-Hayes and M.A.G. Cutter (eds.): *Science, Technology, and the Art of Medicine.* European-American Dialogues. 1993 ISBN 0-7923-1869-2
45. R. Baker, D. Porter and R. Porter (eds.): *The Codification of Medical Morality.* Historical and Philosophical Studies of the Formalization of Western Medical Morality in the Eighteenth and Nineteenth Centuries, Volume One: Medical Ethics and Etiquette in the Eighteenth Century. 1993 ISBN 0-7923-1921-4
46. K. Bayertz (ed.): *The Concept of Moral Consensus.* The Case of Technological Interventions in Human Reproduction. 1994 ISBN 0-7923-2615-6
47. L. Nordenfelt (ed.): *Concepts and Measurement of Quality of Life in Health Care.* 1994 ISBN 0-7923-2824-8
48. R. Baker and M.A. Strosberg (eds.) with the assistance of J. Bynum: *Legislating Medical Ethics.* A Study of the New York State Do-Not-Resuscitate Law. 1995 ISBN 0-7923-2995-3

KLUWER ACADEMIC PUBLISHERS – DORDRECHT / BOSTON / LONDON